WEST VIRGINIA UNIVERSITY

WEST VIRGINIA
UNIVERSITY
Founded by the Legislature
on February 7. 1867 as the
Agricultural College of West
Virginia under terms of the
Federal Land-Grant Act of
1862. On December 4. 1868,
the name was changed to
West Virginia University.

Learn more about the modern history of West Virginia University in
Aspiring to Greatness: West Virginia University Since World War II
by Ronald L. Lewis.

WEST VIRGINIA UNIVERSITY

SYMBOL
of
UNITY
in a
SECTIONALIZED
STATE

WILLIAM T. DOHERTY, JR.
FESTUS P. SUMMERS

FOREWORD BY CHARLES C. WISE

MORGANTOWN 2013

West Virginia University Press 26506
Copyright 2013 by West Virginia University Press
All rights reserved
Originally published in 1982 by West Virginia University Press

Printed in Canada

20 19 18 17 16 15 14 13   1 2 3 4 5 6 7 8

Cloth   978-1-938228-37-7
EPUB   978-1-938228-38-4
PDF   978-1-938228-39-1

Original ISBN (1982 edition): 0-937058-16-5
Original Library of Congress Catalog Card Number: 82-62028

Cover design by Galbreath Design
Art direction by Than Saffel
Front cover image: WVU Campus from Westover, courtesy of WVU News and Information Services. Back cover image: Entrance to Stewart Hall Library, West Virginia University, ca. 1910. Courtesy of West Virginia and Regional History Collection (WVRHC image no. 019475).

Contents

Foreword

WHEN DANIEL WEBSTER TOLD the U.S. Supreme Court that Dartmouth was but a small college "and yet, there are those who love it," his eloquence enshrined forever the traditional bond between a school and its alumni and friends. One's ties with his alma mater are cemented more firmly by complete knowledge of the institution he holds dear. Our University's struggle for maturity is a fascinating story of its almost insurmountable problems, dedicated support, the play of political forces, and occasional sentimental excess. Certainly, the University was never a coddled hot house plant. Indeed, throughout its 115 years, West Virginia University has constantly tested the principle of "sweet are the uses of adversity." Historian Doherty in his rich and full biography of WVU demonstrates that the heroic labors of many have flowered into a worthy institution in which all can take just pride. The readers, whether alumni, friends or the public at large, will be rewarded by this lucid, interesting and faithful account of the remarkable birth, growing pains, and the prime of this University.

CHARLES C. WISE, JR.
Past President,
West Virginia University
Board of Governors,
and Past President,
West Virginia University
Advisory Board

Preface

IN ITS ORIGINS, the history of West Virginia University properly should be viewed as a combination offering of the Department of History and the College of Arts and Sciences. For it owes much to the former dean of the College of Arts and Sciences, William E. Collins, who accomplished the necessary and time-consuming arrangements for its production. In the belief that the traditions and customs of the institution were worthy of preservation, Collins encouraged and liberally supported a WVU history in the late 1970s and early 1980s with the same energy and dedication he simultaneously bequeathed and displayed to his college in the physical restoration of Woodburn Hall, the historic center of the University.

The WVU saga also owes much in spirit to three former chairmen of the Department of History, James Morton Callahan, Charles Henry Ambler, and Festus Paul Summers, whose manuscripts and writings provided not only a framework of ideas and events, but also served as contemporary accounts of the University's early progress. I am indebted particularly to Festus Summers who first suggested that he and I collaborate to produce a centennial history, and to his wife, Helen Summers, who insisted following the death of her husband in 1971 that his materials be made available to his successor as University historian.

Not only am I pleased to extend recognition to my predecessors in the office of chairman of the Department of History with very special and affectionate reference to Summers, but I also am pleased to acknowledge assistance from my successor in that office, Jack L. Hammersmith, who helped provide a released schedule necessary to accomplish the work and who subtracted from his own heavy schedule much of his personal time in invaluable editorial assistance. Thus, the insistence that the University history be thought of as a departmental and college project is not without foundation in fact, and in many ways symbolically represents a collaboration of five departmental chairmen's efforts. To complete the story of a research effort viewed as a service function and being somewhat in the category of a public history project by an arts and sciences department, Edward Steel, John A. Williams, and Dennis O'Brien, departmental colleagues, made professional contributions, and Malcolm Maxon, Tom Howard, and Charles Knighton, graduate assistants in history, performed innumerable chores in behalf of its production.

However, others of the University family freely contributed their time and efforts to the publication and made the project institution-wide in scope. To those familiar with the WVU story, their names, along with positions of responsibility at the University, total years of magnificent dedication and devotion to the various tasks they have successfully assumed both in active service and retirement: Jay Barton, Maurice Brooks, Earl Core, Carl M. Frasure, Sr., Harry B. Heflin, Louise Keener, Mary McDaniel, Robert Munn, and Charles Wise. Extremely supportive has been Charles Wise, former chairman of the WVU Board of Governors and former chairman of the WVU Advisory Board, who in his undergraduate days at WVU happily decided to be a history major and who sustained his disciplinary interest, which was later buttressed by his professional training in law, with more than a half-century of service to his alma mater.

Others who have aided and abetted the publication of this book include former President Gene Budig; the curator of the West Virginia Collection, George Parkinson, and his several associates; the presidential archival staff supervised by Mary McDaniel; and the Office of Publications, including John Luchok and Harry Ernst, who edited it, and Paul Stevenson, who designed it. Representing WVU alumnae has been Mrs. Charles S. Armistead of Morgantown and representing WVU alumni has been Dr. J. William Hess, archivist of the Rockefeller Foundation of New York. Fred Armstrong of the State Department of Archives and History, Charleston, West Virginia, proved an able research assistant. Clerical services have been provided by Rita George, office assistant, and Sarah Michael, Amy Neal, and Terry Esko, secretaries with the Department of History, and Pam Krumpach of the word processing unit, College of Arts and Sciences. An outside reviewer has been Joseph E. Fortenberry of the Policy and Planning Division of the Department of Justice, Washington, D.C., and a distant critic has been Dr. Gary Stuart DeKrey of the Department of History, Colgate University.

University enrollment, University budget, and current alumni climbed to their highest numbers in the period following World War II and bear little comparison with the earlier era. Much of the administrative reorganization making WVU a university in fact as well as in name did first occur by present-day consensus in the post-World War II period as a direct result of the actions and policy decisions, as well as the favorable circumstances, of the Irvin Stewart administration.

This is not to suggest that the first eighty years were not truly formative ones, and that the University, from its earliest beginnings, was not called upon to overcome as best it could an intense sectionalism hampering the progress of the state. The more recent debates over reorganizing higher education in West Virginia may be seen as a modern version of ancient political quarrels. Recent proposals to develop other major centers of undergraduate and graduate education and research also may compare to the designs of earlier sectional advocates to locate WVU's major campuses somewhere other than Morgantown. The past does indeed become prologue to the present.

Yet the major theme throughout University history, valid in the beginning and still authentic today, is that WVU has stolidly remained the one institution serving as the land-grant university of the state, the only one with both national and state mandates to bring about educational progress throughout West Virginia, and the only public institution with large-scale federal funding to accomplish this assignment.

The original manuscript with its several hundreds of sometimes detailed footnote references is on file in the West Virginia University Library. It is intended to be useful rather than to serve as proof of scholarly diligence. As neither printed nor manuscript materials relating to the University itself have been systematically collected or located (but are just beginning to be), it is to be noted as well that there has existed no complete guide to University archival material. So in a particular sense, the original manuscript with its voluminous citations might aid as well as hasten the research of others at the most basic and elementary levels of primary materials. However, in its printed form, this publication omits most of the references in an effort to reduce the size of the history for the general reader.

There are other restraints which in time may be remedied by other renditions. Keeping the history from being complete (and impossibly bulky) is an absence of much anecdotal material, many human interest stories, references to all student organizations and to many prominent alumni, and complete lists of faculty and staff and their individual accomplishments over the years.

Those working inside the University also might have assumed that a University history might detail the power struggles and highlight the jealousies, antagonisms, and personal animosities inherent in any organization. These in-house quarrels have not been overlooked or avoided, but rather than maximized as ends in themselves, they have been fitted into the continuing theme of identifying educational objectives and academic goals. As for example, there were those who pushed for a more liberal arts orientation versus those who sought a more vocational, technical program, or those who saw the primary function of WVU as undergraduate education versus those anxious to emphasize graduate and professional training.

Because of their joint survival, joint development, joint achievement, and joint durability, the relationship between West Virginia University and the state of West Virginia resembles something akin to a marriage both of convenience and opportunism. Together they combined in overcoming separatist tendencies toward both sectionalism and isolation of its people. To document such concerns, much of the research which exploits the theme of WVU as a unification symbol of necessity has depended on many newspapers throughout the irregularly shaped and mountainous state. Because the University was historically destined to play an integrationist rather than a segregationist role, the inhabitants thereof also were committed to respond affirmatively or negatively to its unification performance, and to judge severely its efforts from their own particular vantage points. It is in these broader-based, journalistic research materials that perhaps this history diverges most from earlier research efforts which have depended in large part on the in-house materials of minutes, rules, regulations, catalog copy, formal reports of the schools and colleges, official reports, and other similar institutional paperwork.

It is hoped that this account will bring to its readers a comprehension of the diverse and complex elements which shaped a state university, an approbation of the University's myriad contributions to the economic, social, and cultural development of West Virginia and its geographical region of Appalachia, and an understanding of the limitations and restrictions, physical, intellectual, and emotional, that the state itself has defined as the academic parameters of the University's efforts. As others who have written university histories have noted, state institutions have been affected less by particular educational philosophies than by the mass culture of the people they serve.

This, finally, is another of the underlying themes of this

history. The interplay between the virtues and the vices of the state upon the state university, and vice versa, provide the institution with an unique history; in turn, its acceptance of the role as a land-grant institution with the federal government as a partner provides WVU with its primary leadership and unification role in the state's educational system.

For a variety of reasons, including affection, admiration, inspiration, and deep indebtedness, the author wishes to dedicate the first part of the University history to his wife, Dorothy Huff Doherty, and to the late Helen Summers. He wishes to dedicate the second part to Florence and Irvin Stewart who so served at a particular moment of change in University history that a president of the Ford Foundation remarked that more progress then was being made at West Virginia University than at any other land-grant institution in the nation.

WILLIAM T. DOHERTY
University Historian

Acknowledgment

The publication of this volume was made possible by a gift from Mr. Carl Delsignore and the support of the West Virginia University Foundation, Incorporated.

Illustrations

Part 1

The Morgantown School
1867–1945

Chapter 1

1862–1867

"Add to Your Faith Virtue, and to Virtue Knowledge"

Alexander Martin
April 3, 1867–August 12, 1875

AFTER TWO DECADES of regional agitation and experimentation in behalf of vocational or polytechnic education by farmers, industrial workers, and professional educators, Congress passed during the Civil War years the Morrill Land-Grant College Act. Although approved by Republicans in 1862 as a party measure, the educational statute was, in spirit, a reflection of the earlier Jacksonian Democracy because of its emphasis upon the common man. The legislation created, in the words of educational historians, "Democracy's Colleges," institutions of higher learning in each state for those capable of learning, and not for only those who could afford either the tuition charges or the classical curriculum of the private schools.

States received an endowment either in land or in land scrip of 30,000 acres for each of their senators and representatives. Congress, in carefully limited language, specified in its first comprehensive education act that the subsidy would support and maintain "at least one college where the leading object shall be, without excluding other scientific or classical studies, to teach such branches of learning as are related to agriculture and the

3

mechanic arts, in such manner as the legislatures, of the States and Territories may respectively prescribe, in order to promote the liberal and practical education of the industrial classes in the several pursuits and professions of life."

Abraham Lincoln showed neither objection nor enthusiasm toward the Morrill Act, although he did approve it. Later in the same year, he granted permission for the admission of West Virginia as a state into the war-torn Union. Although he characterized its creation from an old Confederate dominion as a "certain and irrevocable encroachment upon the cause of rebellion," he also could have explained the Morrill Act as a comparable expediency.

The 1862 educational legislation consolidated the interests of agriculture and labor helpful to the new Republican Party; it devised a political strategy particularly effective in the older West and throughout the agricultural regions of the East. It also highlighted a policy that had been looked upon with misgivings by the Confederate South, which viewed the act as an extension of centralized government, and the new West, which pictured the legislation as reserving some of its best lands for the benefit of the older states.

Toward both novel and unconventional measures, the Morrill Act and the admission of West Virginia, Lincoln could have explained his executive approval with greater political precision if such acts had not been questioned as to their legitimacy. But Lincoln then was enmeshed in creating a national "free" state rather than confirming the existence of a federal "slave" government, and both measures, constitutional or unconstitutional, obviously promoted the interests of "free soil" nationalism.

With the Chief Executive's signature, the Congressional Land-Grant Act became law on July 2, 1862. With its first Governor, Arthur I. Boreman, expounding upon the unredressed grievances against its mother state, West Virginia became a state on June 20, 1863. On October 3, 1863, West Virginia made known its acceptance of the terms of the Morrill Act. To make certain of its own eligibility for an act that became law when it was not then in the Union, the Legislature petitioned Congress to confirm or grant West Virginia the necessary retroactive rights and benefits. Responding to the request on April 9, 1864, Congress specifically extended the provisions and terms of the Morrill statute to West Virginia and authorized a two-year period of grace for the acceptance by other newly created state sovereignties.

Once assured that it fell under the terms of the Morrill Act, West Virginia petitioned Congress for more educational benefits. Finding itself near bankruptcy from the start, an unhesitant West Virginia asked Congress in a joint resolution of January 24, 1867, for an additional grant of 60,000 acres for each West Virginia senator and representative, a grand total of 300,000 more acres. To this plea, Congress proved unresponsive. If West Virginia wanted a college, it would have to extract sufficient funds from its citizens who were paying nominal taxes and from concerns like the Baltimore and Ohio Railroad Company, which was then totally tax-exempt.

With two senators and three representatives, West Virginia thus acquired a grant of land scrip entitling it to the proceeds of the sale of 150,000 acres of public lands, nominally worth $1.25 an acre, but then selling across the nation at about fifty cents an acre. As West Virginia itself had no government lands for public entry, its educational subsidy was located in Iowa and Minnesota. In his annual message to the Legislature in January, 1865, Governor Boreman asked for instructions regarding such an educational endowment; by the end of the year he had acted, in the absence of legislative advice, by selling the land for a total of $79,000, which the state invested in U.S. bonds, happily then below par.

Thus, the new state, with only a little educational money in its treasury, proceeded to invent its land-grant institution. The next, but hardly the last, political question concerning the establishment was where legislators should locate it. The answer to the query, which resulted in a sectional compromise, was only the beginning of West Virginia's political replies to matters affecting its land-grant university. From 1867 on, the state's responses to its educational creation often were framed in the interest of geographic balance in an oddly shaped state.

Because an agricultural college was contemplated, essentially small agrarian villages applied. Bethany in Brooke County, Frankford in Greenbrier, Greenwood in Doddridge, Harrisville in Ritchie, Morgantown in Monongalia, Philippi in Barbour, Point Pleasant in Mason, Ravenswood in Jackson, and Spencer in Roane entered the contest. Larger towns such as Charleston, Clarksburg, Parkersburg, and Wheeling did not formally apply. They stepped aside for they would do nothing at the moment to lessen their chances to obtain the state capital, whose final location was also to be decided.

Others that might have been favored were diverted from the contest by other interests. Moundsville in Marshall County, where the Legislature tentatively had established the state penitentiary, and Weston in Lewis County, where the state of Virginia had earlier located an insane asylum, deferred to others because, as the story goes, their promoters weighed the uncertainties of college enrollments against the patronage of prisons and asylums and lost all interest in the contest for an unpredictable agricultural college. Martinsburg in Berkeley County became an improbable location when Virginia sued West Virginia for the recovery of that county and the adjoining one, Jefferson. Then, too, it was unthinkable politically that Radical Republicans would locate the university in a part of the state long known for its Confederate sympathies.

Morgantown seemed the likely winner when, on January 19, 1866, Senator William Price of Monongalia County introduced a bill which offered the properties of the Monongalia Academy and the Woodburn Seminary to the state on condition that the Legislature locate the institution at or near Morgantown. Such an inducement of property valued at $51,000 simply made West Virginia conform to the patterns across the nation where: "In a number of cases the existence of some sort of educational enterprise on the chosen site, usually quiescent or moribund, with equipment ill-adapted to the new special purpose and with wholly unharmonious traditions exercised an inordinate influence."[1] Although the Senate supported its Monongalia County member and sent his bill to the House of Delegates a month later, the lower chamber balloted, not in accordance with the wishes of the upper chamber, but upon Charleston, West Liberty, Point Pleasant, and Flemington as well as Morgantown. In further defiance of the Senate, the House of Delegates named Charleston as the site on the second ballot.

Although a joint conference committee of the two houses chose Morgantown, the southern-dominated House of Delegates again rejected the decision. The next year, 1867, with Charleston definitely bowing out of the contest, southern interests centered on Frankford, which offered 400 acres of prime farmland and a promise of 600 additional acres in the fertile limestone region of the Greenbrier Valley. Senator Samuel Young of Pocahontas County, supporting the claims of Frankford, avowed that if Morgantown were chosen, the university would be nothing more than a Pennsylvania school; or if any site in the Northern Panhandle were selected, such a location would serve the convenience of Pennsylvania and Ohio more than that of West Virginia. Thus, a legislator from southern West Virginia pictured Morgantown as an unfit site for the state university — an image that persisted for the next century in University history and biography.

The frail decision in favor of Morgantown, however, reflected a political accommodation to both Morgantown and Charleston interests as delegates from Kanawha and Monongalia counties reciprocated with their ballots to locate the land-grant college on the Monongahela at Morgantown in 1867 and two years later to locate the capitol on the Kanawha at Charleston. On January 31, 1867, when the Senate voted 17-5 and the House 32-21 to place the university at Morgantown, the West Virginia Legislature satisfied Radical Republican requirements that prize state agencies were to be located in loyal Union territory. With the passage of a few more years and the transition to Democratic rule, it became possible for the West Virginia Legislature to locate the capitol in what had been friendly Confederate territory.

As early University catalogs described it, West Virginia University was located in Morgantown where the sites of the Woodburn Seminary build-

Monongalia Academy, which occupied this building at the northeast corner of Spruce and Walnut Streets in 1831, was one of the leading educational institutions in western Virginia. Established in 1814 to educate boys, it opened a companion school for girls in 1839, Morgantown Female Collegiate Institute, which later was merged with Woodburn Female Seminary. WVU's first classes were held in this building, which was sold for $13,500 to the Morgantown Independent School District in 1867. The funds were used to help build Martin Hall.

ing, situated "at the extreme point of the convex of a graceful bend in the beautiful Monongahela," and the Monongalia Academy, which overlooked Decker's Creek from its location on the corner of Walnut and Spruce Streets, offered unparalleled vistas to faculty and students alike. The Morgantown of 1867 also was described by one distinguished historian as "sitting there on its industrial hands . . . and waiting for the locomotive and the heavy draft steamer" to turn a "remote, unspoiled village of seven hundred, a totally undistinguished location except for the fact that it was located midway between Fairmont, West Virginia, on the Baltimore and Ohio Railroad and New Geneva, Pennsylvania, on the Monongahela River,"[2] into a college town. In its determination to receive small benefits proffered by an isolated village of 700 inhabitants, West Virginia fell into a national pattern where: "Contrary to the sensible advice of the *American Agriculturist* that the colleges should be established in well-settled regions as the students had experienced enough of pioneering on their home farms, most of the new institutions, from necessity or choice, were located on forest clearings, abandoned homesteads, or the open prairie."[3]

In an act of February 7, 1867, which established the Agricultural College of West Virginia at Morgantown, the Legislature accepted the gift of the grounds, buildings and personal property from the trustees of the Monongalia Academy which also encompassed the Woodburn Female Seminary. In addition, it accepted a sum of $10,000 in cash, bonds, bank stock, and bills receivable, representing the complete assets of the two schools.

By other terms of the act, the Legislature vested control of the new institution in a Board of Visitors, composed of one member from each of the eleven state senatorial districts. The governing agency first met in the Woodburn Seminary building on April 3, 1867. After electing its officers, it created an executive committee of Morgantown residents to act on its behalf between meetings. Thus, there was some validity to the initial charge, to be repeated over the years, that the University was in reality "only a Morgantown school." Exercising the powers later associated with twentieth-century WVU presidents, the executive committee was expected to save board members scattered across the state from making too many arduous journeys to Morgantown. Therefore, it was charged with the care of buildings and grounds, the choice of faculty, and supervision of the daily operations of the institution during the long intervals between sessions of the board. It also served as a court of appeals for students and a court of original jurisdiction in faculty cases.

The legislators in 1867 directed the Board of Visitors to establish and implement "such departments in literature, science, art, and agriculture, as they may deem expedient, and as the funds under their control may warrant, and purchase such materials, implements and apparatus as may be requisite to proper instruction in all said branches of learning, so as to carry out the spirit of the act of Congress."

The spirit of the congressional act also was acknowledged when the West Virginia Legislature provided for appointment by the Board of Visitors of "not fewer than one nor more than two" young men between the ages of sixteen and twenty-five from each of the eleven state senatorial districts, who in return for remission of fees and tuition and the perquisites of free textbooks and stationery, would be obligated to serve as members of the uniformed public guard, better known as the Cadet Corps. Enabling the college to claim for its own most of the students at the Monongalia Academy, the lawmakers authorized the board to establish a Preparatory Department.

But the spirit of the act was perhaps defied as frequently as it was followed. One instance was in the institution's financing. In its first year of

WVU opened in Woodburn Seminary in 1867 when Morgantown's population was 700. Monongalia Academy and Woodburn Female Seminary were donated to West Virginia to help begin WVU. When Confederate troops invaded Morgantown in 1863 to search for horses, they occupied the Seminary grounds. Mrs. Elizabeth Moore, Principal of the Seminary, invited them for bread, butter, and coffee and her hospitality is credited with preventing the soldiers from burning the Seminary. This photograph was taken in 1865.

operation, it received nothing from the Legislature. The University's land-grant endowment, however, was kept intact. Instead of using the permissible 10 percent for experimental farms, the Legislature authorized the expenditure of up to five thousand dollars of the funds received from the trustees of Monongalia Academy with the stipulation that the board acquire land contiguous to the Woodburn Seminary grounds.[4]

The spirit of the act perhaps also was defied when the Board, by unanimous vote, elected the Reverend Alexander Martin president of the faculty. Here again, early decisions affecting WVU fit into the larger national pattern of selecting ministers as presidents of the new land-grant colleges, and underscored, in the words of one critic, the fact that "whatever the experience in the sectarian realm, a clerical leader of a polytechnic would be the height of absurdity."[5]

Born at Nairn in northern Scotland on January 24, 1822, Martin had come to Jefferson County, Ohio, in 1836. In 1847, he was graduated at the head of his class at Allegheny College in Meadville, Pennsylvania. After graduation, he had held Methodist pulpits at Charleston, Moundsville, Wheeling, and Parkersburg. But fortunately, in addition to his sectarian experiences, he also had served as principal of an academy at Kingwood and another at Clarksburg. Something of an itinerant scholar in both West Virginia and Pennsylvania, he had occupied the chair of Greek at his alma mater during the Civil War.

As consultant to the committee on education at the West Virginia Constitutional Convention, Martin had helped draft provisions for establishing the new state's free school system. In this effort, he had not only envisioned a comprehensive system of general education, crowned with a first-class college or university, for the state, he also had foreseen Morgantown as its site.

At his formal inauguration as President of the West Virginia Agricultural College on June 27, 1867, Martin indicated a most liberal interpretation of the Morrill Act when he declared that the true concern of the new college in the young state would be "to educate men, as men, and not as machines." Asking whether the federal grant was for the exclusive purpose of training farmers and soldiers, and whether the college was to be strictly a manual labor school or one comprising every essential department of learning, Martin said the latter was the proper direction. As he saw it, "Man should be educated not because he must study, or work, but because he is a man, allied to God, and destined for immortality."

There were special reasons, Martin believed, why West Virginia must follow such a path. Striking at Virginia for failing to provide public schools within her former boundaries, Martin emphasized the need of 60,000 illiterates in West Virginia for a general education. It was "enough to make one weep," he said, to see ". . . hundreds and thousands and tens of thousands of our fellow-citizens in such brutish and besotted ignorance as to be absolutely unable either to write their names or read God's word—confined, so far as mental culture is concerned, to the very childhood of existence." To Martin, it would be folly to restrict instruction in a state college to the cultivation of the earth or the profession of arms. As he saw it, both congressional and state legislation contemplated more than those narrow purposes. Since he visualized the West Virginia Agricultural College as agricultural in name only, he looked forward to the day when the institution might play a leading role in the life of the state, and to a period of time

when the pressure of present burdens is somewhat removed, civil order at length restored, the ravages of war repaired, population rendered more homogeneous, public buildings provided, and the whole organism of the State perfected and in smooth working order . . . her College shall be to her what Yale is to Connecticut, Harvard to Massachusetts, Charlottesville to her parent state, Ann Arbor to Michigan, or Oxford to old England — her brightest ornament and crowning glory.

In continued support of his inaugural theme, he wrote Governor Boreman on January 24, 1868, "If the State not only adopts but, in part, endows the school it might with entire propriety be called the 'West Virginia College.'" He wished to leave out, he told the chief executive, "the misleading and somewhat inconvenient word 'Agricultural' which makes some think it is only a Farmers School." The Governor agreed, and in a special message to the Legislature, recommended that "as the College is in a great measure a State institution, subject to the legislative authority of the State, and dependent on it for a liberal, comprehensive and permanent establishment, and affords all the facilities for a thorough education . . . it should have a more general title."

But in June, 1868, the Legislature adopted the name West Virginia College for another institution, a private, coeducational institution to be located at Flemington, Taylor County. Martin was not upset by the legislative move, for he could now argue that the Flemington school had "an unfair advantage over us" because of the similarity of names and two such named schools would produce confusion in the mails and in advertising. To correct its mistake, the Legislature on December 4, 1868, passed an act which renamed the Morgantown institution, West Virginia University.

Joseph T. Hoke, speaking for the Board of Visitors, tried his hand at familiarizing the citizenry with the new name. In a report to Governor William E. Stevenson on June 17, 1869, he called attention to the fact that nowhere in the United States was there yet a "very distinct line of demarcation between 'the terms College and University,'" and as he explained the work on the Morgantown campus, the nature of its activity was already to a large extent proper to a university. From the perspective of time, the institution prematurely had adopted the new name "like an attitudinarian putting on the dog."[6]

In keeping with the new law, which provided a new title, the Board of Visitors became the Board of Regents, and as befitting its new status, the new University acquired both a motto and a seal to symbolize its aims and to authenticate its papers. According to the board's minutes of June 15, 1869, the seal was to be of a design that its center had

as its device a perspective of the College grounds and buildings or as much of the same as may be conveniently embraced in a seal serving as an indication of the design of the Institution. Its stability to be indicated by the hills appearing in the rear of the buildings. Its prosperity to be indicated by a rising sun above the hills and beyond the buildings. The Motto, in Greek, being in the inner circle, and next to the device as follows: 'add to your faith virtue, and to virtue knowledge.' The outer circle to contain, in Latin, inscribed in full, or contracted, the following words and letters namely, 'Seal of the West Virginia University. Established 7 February, 1867.'

Such symbols and such rituals, as explained by Board Visitor Joseph T. Hoke at Martin's inauguration, were "calculated to cause the meditative individuals to cast about and, if possible, to peer over the vista of time."

Before the first school term opened in 1867, both the board and the faculty had numerous policies to establish. The Board of Visitors at its first meeting decided upon three instructional departments: (1) collegiate, (2) scientific, and (3) agricultural. It also acknowledged the need for training in military tactics and the continuation of the Preparatory School as a feeder of students to the University.

At its second meeting on June 26, 1867, the board named Alexander Martin professor of mental and moral science; John W. Scott, professor of ancient languages; F. S. Lyon, professor of English literature; Colonel J. R. Weaver, professor of mathematics and military tactics (succeeded by Captain H. H. Pierce in 1868); and Samuel G. Stevens, professor of philosophy and natural science. For those who possessed administrative as well as teaching talents, there were enough duties to go around, for Martin served as president; Scott as vice-president; Lyon as principal of the Preparatory School; Stevens as secretary of the faculty; and the professor of mathematics and military tactics also undertook the position of librarian.

Weaver was a Methodist minister as was Martin; Stevens and Scott were Presbyterians; Lyon, the nephew of Mary Lyon, founder of Mount Holyoke Female Seminary, was a Baptist: all met the tests of Protestant and Republican orthodoxy. All had been loyal to the United States in the recent Civil War; all could be considered for that day and age to be qualified academically. But Weaver, as commandant of cadets, and George Hagans, who served as superintendent of grounds as well as head of the Morgantown Executive Committee, were most important to the new president. Such a triumvirate, Republican as well as Methodist, underscored the politics and religion of practically all of the founding fathers of West Virginia who served in the state's early administrations.

By 1870, Martin had lost most of the original faculty. In his report to the board in 1871, he noted his difficulty in persuading others to join the institution because he had stiffened his requirements for candidates. For he did not want those "who would subvert well settled and approved methods of instruction"; he bypassed "those who seek to rise by trying to injure nobler men"; and he would not hire those who displayed an "infirmity of temper, ignorance of the science of education, overweening conceit of themselves or of their departments."

The first board worked hard at laying out the governing procedures prior to the opening of the college; the faculty in its original meetings labored even

The WVU Seal.

more diligently to set the course for the first students. With keen attention, it prepared the curriculum and drafted and adopted the "Code of Laws and Regulations."

Loving detail, the faculty considered subjects ranging from the choice of textbooks to an order denying boys not registered in the institution the privilege of playing on the college grounds; adopted the use of the Spencerian system in penmanship classes, and the continental system of pronunciation in Latin and Greek classes. It even showed an early interest in possible coeducation by delegating the president to confer with the principal of the Morgantown Female Collegiate Institute concerning the normal (teacher training) class Martin planned for the spring semester.

In the closing minutes of his inaugural, Martin had defined colleges as "nurseries of sound learning and of earnest, elevated piety," and elaborated on what he conceived to be the duty of the faculty *in loco parentis:*

Tell the friends and parents of youth that we know the solicitude and anxiety with which they follow their children and wards when removed from the vigilant guardianship of home to the comparative freedom of College life, and that while seeking with sacred fidelity to be true to all other interests, our paramount duty will be to supply such compensating watchfulness over their members and morals as will in some measure stand in place of a father's counsel and a mother's love; that it will be our constant effort, by all proper exercise of discipline and influence to foster and encourage that nobility of soul, elevation of character and purity of Christian morals, without which increasing knowledge is a curse . . .

However, the rules adopted were a far cry from the "father's counsel" and "mother's love" that had been promised. There were sweeping injunctions against "indecent and profane language, rude and boisterous conduct, tippling, frequenting taverns, inns, beer-houses, places of mere idle amusement and resort to bad company." Students were forbidden "gambling, betting, games of chance, smoking tobacco within the college enclosures, carrying concealed firearms or other deadly weapons and every species of immoral conduct." Students and faculty alike were required to attend chapel exercises daily on the campus and the church of their choice on Sunday; and "no member of the faculty shall connect himself or continue connected with any secret college fraternity." In fact, professors were required to "exert their influence for the suppression of all such secret associations." Students were denied free assembly, and though not compelled to testify against themselves, were expected to answer against their fellow students. Thus, the code equated righteousness with scholarship, and promoted a program of behavior designed better to quicken than suppress disorder of irrepressible teen-agers and seasoned veterans of the Civil War.

When the first class of 124 assembled in September, 1867 (only six were college-level students and 118 were in the Preparatory Department), the Radical Republican, Methodist, pro-Northern University had gone on record as favoring coeducation, a Preparatory Department, rigid discipline, and a prescribed curriculum, and had set the stage whereby pro-Southern, Democratic successors could go on record against each and every item. Such became the attitude of the *Wheeling Intelligencer,* when at the end of the Martin presidency, it challenged the authority of the Legislature to appropriate for the University since it had failed to make a grant to Bethany College, a denominational institution in the state catering to the needs of the Disciples of Christ (Christian Church). Because of the role played by prominent churchmen in its founding and the presence for years on the board and faculty of a majority of the Methodist persuasion, WVU had become a church-related institution in the eyes of the *Wheeling Intelligencer.*

As long as Martin was president, the University continued to support the principles he acknowledged on the opening day. As the rift between pro-Northerners and pro-Southerners deepened, it was well that the students who found themselves in the middle had been given one advantage: a cheap education. In 1867, tuition per term of 13 weeks was $8.00 for the college class; $5.00 for the preparatory class; $3.00 for the primary classes. Board and room could be had for $3.50 per week. If one went for three terms, the full year, the total student cost was estimated between $187.50 and $249.00. The sum was, without doubt, a bargain, especially given the faculty-student ratio of the collegiate group: in 1867 it was six to six, the best in its recorded history. What is more, according to West Virginia University's first annual report of 1868, students the first year could reside in College Hall which "enabled Parents to place their sons under the immediate personal supervision of President and Faculty, and so relieve themselves from the apprehension of detriment to the moral character while away from parental influence."

The only ingredient that was missing was public relations, and it was thought best to handle that through advertising in the state's newspapers. But University officials, hard-pressed for funds with which to meet contractual obligations, felt the wrath of at least one paper. Turning upon the "W. Va. College Bosses," the editor of the *Clarksburg Conservative* declared on July 26, 1869:

We have never before in our dealings with men supposed to be D. D.'s and honest men generally had as much devilish annoyance in collecting our dues as we have had with your college. The first six months was payable almost six months ago. We have wasted all our profits in buying stamps to send bills to the concern, and now the fall year is nearly completed, and we bill it for the full amount, $10. We need the money and we *want it*. If you are not going to pay, tell us so at once, and we will continue an adv. for your school with much pleasure, and to our own satisfaction, if not to yours.

Thus it was, as the biographer of its first graduate, Marmaduke Dent, put it, that West Virginia University had its beginnings as "a primitive institution with as many enemies as friends,"[7] even among those expected to propagandize in its behalf.

Chapter 2

1867–1885

Yankee Centralization to Confederate Decentralization

John Rhey Thompson
March 28, 1877–March 12, 1881

William Lyne Wilson
September 6, 1882–June 11, 1883

WITH THE FACULTY and student body embarked upon creating a university in the fall of 1867, President Alexander Martin began his behind-the-scene task of convincing the West Virginia Legislature that the University should receive a "pittance so fairly deserved and really required." The exact sum he left the lawmakers to determine as best they could, "Whether this should be by a stated contribution, or by such an appropriation as will, when funded, annually supply the means for this end."

Working originally in a political atmosphere affected by the reconstruction plans of Presidents Lincoln and Johnson and of the Radical Republican Congress, the first WVU president not only found himself contending with other state agencies for badly needed monetary assistance but also witnessing from his northern college site the legislative struggle over disfranchisement and enfranchisement in central, southern, and eastern West Virginia.

Such battles in the Mountain State were between whites and whites; whereas in the Confederate South the conflicts were emotionally projected as political contests between whites and blacks. This was despite the fact that although abolitionist-created West Virginia had not committed political suicide during the Civil War as had its secessionist mother, Virginia, and was not reduced to the status of conquered federal territory administered by military authorities from 1867 to 1870, its native Confederate sympathizers nonetheless were made to suffer the pains of reconstruction. In such an immediate post-Civil War atmosphere, the University had no choice but to project itself as a Yankee, Republican, Methodist seat of learning.

On March 3, 1868, the Radical Republican Legislature responded with its very first contribution to the University from its own limited resources: $10,000 for the endowment and $6,000 for current expenses. In his annual report Martin applauded the "wise and liberal policy" which had secured such an appropriation, expressed the hope that no one would "grudge the continuance for a few years" of that small benefaction until the college attained full stature, and counted one other special University blessing in 1868 by noting: "The health of the students and of the Faculty has been remarkably good. It is said to be now about one year since any death occurred in Morgantown, a circumstance rarely equalled in a village of this size, and which is demonstrative of its general healthfulness."

But in matters of overall appropriations during his seven-year stint as president, Martin went from bad to worse as the state passed from Republican to Democratic control. In June, 1869, the Board of Regents adopted a resolution requesting the Legislature "to perfect the endowment fund" by an annual appropriation "of ten thousand dollars, for the term of ten years." It was refused, and when the board renewed the request in 1870, it was denied again. As a consequence, the Regents borrowed from the permanent endowment the $10,000 appropriated in 1868 to complete University Hall, repair College Hall, and meet faculty payrolls. In turn, the executive committee came to the rescue by making themselves responsible for $5,950 of the sum loaned the construction fund, and the Legislature rewarded the benefactors by refusing to legalize their actions.

In the 1871 session of the overwhelmingly Democratic Legislature, the lawmakers surprisingly appropriated $10,000 for the endowment; but even with this unexpected windfall, the board found it necessary to sell $3,100 of Virginia state bonds, "a part of the assets from the Monongalia Academy donation," at the highest market price in the East (about forty-four cents on the dollar) to clear the contingent fund of a deficit of $1,500.

In 1872, Martin and the board persuaded the Legislature to grant $10,000 to replace the sum borrowed from the endowment fund by the executive committee to complete University Hall and thus raise the permanent endowment to a peak total of $110,000. Receipts from tuition, boarding hall, and endowment together were providing an income of $8,680 yearly.

Concerning a permanent endowment, Governor John J. Jacob gave the University no comfort when he denied the institution an emancipation from politics and an assurance of a steady income by stating in 1872:

Even if our resources were ample, I conceive it would not be good policy to grant the request of the Board an additional appropriation for permanent endowment. This is nothing more than the imposition of an extraordinary burden upon the present generation, in order to relieve our successors for all time to come. The University is a public institution and there can be no good reason given why its future wants should now be provided for, that would not apply to the Hospital for the Insane, or the Deaf, Dumb, and Blind School. The legitimate effect of this policy would be to build up a corporation independent of the control of the Legislature — an end not to be desired.

Martin's woes were best seen with respect to his building program, and constant loss of Republican, Methodist faculty who were replaced with Confederate sympathizers. Like future presidents, Martin wanted to be remembered in University history as a builder. When local school commissioners announced plans to construct a public school next door to Monongalia Academy at Spruce and Walnut streets and would not shift ground in deference to the University, the President convinced the Board of Visitors to sell the Academy properties and use the proceeds to construct a new building on the Woodburn Seminary grounds.

This produced $15,000 which permitted the laying of the foundation for University Hall at the second annual commencement in June, 1868. Opened at the commencement exercises in June, 1870, when the University's first and only member of the class of 1870, Marmaduke Herbert Dent, was graduated, University Hall (later called Martin Hall for its first president) was considered a true beginning for the land-grant school on the former campus of the female seminary.

When the War Department in 1871 proffered the use of ordnance, small arms, and ammunition for the Cadet Corps without cost to the University, the Legislature in its 1872 session appropriated $2,500 for the erection of an armory building which was to be constructed in accordance with a plan furnished by the War Department. The Armory, which became the Agricultural Experiment Station Building and later the site for the mast of the U.S.S. West Virginia following World War II, opened in 1873. It was then considered by the Legislature a structure "ample for all future wants of the Military Department of the University."

On January 25, 1873, natural causes came to the rescue of President Martin's stalled building program. College Hall, or Old Woodburn, the University's first dormitory housing 30 students, went down in flames caused either by an ember from an open grate in a student's room or the sparks from a student lamp. In an act passed April 7, 1873, which levied five cents on

Martin Hall, WVU's oldest building completed in 1870 at a cost of $159,810, stands beside Woodburn Seminary (left), which means this rare photograph was taken between 1870 and 1873 when the Seminary burned. The name Woodburn was selected by the Reverend John R. Moore, Principal of Monongalia Academy and later Superintendent of Woodburn Female Seminary, who was Elizabeth's husband. Woodburn, meaning "a streamlet in a shady glen," described the grove of beech trees and the Falling Run stream which used to border Woodburn Circle.

each one hundred dollars of taxable property, the Legislature came to the rescue of the University by permitting its executive committee to contract in October, 1873, with Klives, Kraft and Company of Wheeling for the erection of a new building, costing $37,386. Its cornerstone was laid on June 18, 1874; it was to have been ready for occupancy December 1, 1874. But not until 1878 was New Hall, for want of a name which later became Woodburn, available.

When political power passed in West Virginia from the Radical Republicans to the Bourbon Democrats, the latter chose to wait until after the departure of the first president to appropriate funds to finish the interior walls and provide the central section with furniture.

President Martin had practical ideas on curriculum. Because of an 1868 grant of $500 from the Peabody Education Fund which awarded "in sums of twenty dollars each, to twenty-five of the most advanced, promising and yet needy pupils" on condition that the recipients pledge themselves to teach at least two years, normal (teacher training) classes became a fixture of the Yankee curriculum until 1875. A faculty committee also debated, according to its minutes of April 2, 1869, "the lawfulness and expediency" of coeducation, considered another Yankee notion. Concluding that it could find no way to permit the faculty to construe the law "as to allow females the privileges of the University," the committee also questioned the practical wisdom of admitting them as students to any class connected with the University.

In making a pretense at agricultural study, Martin supported the Volunteer Labor Corps, organized in the spring of 1868, by George M. Hagans, superintendent of grounds and buildings. As an alumnus described the ploy, "After we had become settled and accustomed to the name college, the conscientious faculty one morning at Chapel . . . announced with a flourish, that it was necessary, in order to keep faith with a generous Congress, that something purely agricultural must be done."[1]

Sixteen students responded to the call to learn about practical agriculture and were assigned strips within Woodburn Seminary grounds of about one-sixth of an acre each "for agricultural operations." For their services and commitment to the Morrill Act, the University furnished free implements and allowed the students to retain the profits of their labors on condition that each file a report at the close of the season showing average depth of soil, effects produced by fertilizers, time of planting and harvesting, average amount of work done monthly, total hours for the season, and the market price of the crop. According to the official University report, besides providing healthful exercise and jobs for needy students, the "system of Volunteer Labor, together with the accuracy required in the reports," promised to impress upon students "the importance of attention to details of farming and induce habits of close observation without deterring any from attending through fear of being compelled to engage in manual labor."

At least one student remembered the experiment less favorably. After that portion of the college grounds was broken by plow and divided into plots fifteen by twenty feet, he recalled:

We went to work in earnest while the faculty and delinquents watched us with sympathetic eyes. Some contented themselves with planting potatoes and corn alone as easy and productive crops requiring the simplest kind of farming, while others elaborately laid off their plots in all manner of artistic shapes, and planted all garden vegetables including onions, lettuce, beans, radishes, and tomatoes. Some planted the seeds so deep that if they sprouted they could not reach the surface during the season, others so shallow that they might sunburn. After we had finished planting we had an inviting-looking garden and retired from our labors in happy, hungry triumph, as the table which we shortly surrounded could well bear testimony. In the night the storm came, the winds blew great gusts and the rain fell in torrents. It was

Original Woodburn Hall was completed in 1876 at a cost of $41,500 on the site where Woodburn Seminary stood. It was called New Hall, then University Hall in 1878, becoming Woodburn Hall in 1902. North wing was added in 1900, south wing in 1911, and the entire building was renovated in 1979.

a regular gully washer. The early morning light revealed a scene of havoc. All our beautiful beds were in common ruin. Great seams made by the waters traversed them in all directions and the seeds, except the deep planted, were either washed away or lay scattered over the surface. We however were not to be daunted but soon renewed our labors. Although our plots were not so handsomely decorated they were more carefully protected from the wash of the hillside. In a few days before the plants appeared the weeds began to arrive in squadrons. No spot was barren of them . . . We kept our plots well hoed and the vegetables in good trim until our June vacation, and having no Summer quarter to cause us to linger, we departed for our homes. When we returned two months later a dreary waste of weeds ripening in the September sun hid from the view the few surviving and decaying vegetables. As we looked upon our departed hopes we could not help but think that this is the seeming result of all man's labor.[2]

With the agricultural experiment failing, and the ranks of the labor corps diminishing to nine the following spring, the University substituted "a system of remunerated labor." The next year the corps mustered 54, but only 18 volunteered during 1871-72. Despite the going wage rate of 15 cents per hour and the well-known resistance of students to manual labor, the corps increased to 22 in 1872-73 and 30 in 1873-74. But with the advent of the Bourbon Democrats to power in West Virginia in 1872, the dismissal in June, 1873, of George M. Hagans, the depression of 1873, and the demands of the State Grange for a comprehensive program in agriculture, Martin's agricultural program was seen as an unsuccessful and farcical response to the demands of the Morrill Act.

It also seemed as if the University were responding in similar manner to the Morrill Act's demands for military instruction. Colonel James Riley Weaver seldom appeared in uniform but instead came upon his charges dressed to the hilt in silk hat and frock coat. When he took over the training of students who lacked both uniforms and a sense of drill field discipline, the Cadet Corps presented "a rather motley appearance, some being in blue uniform with tailless coat, . . . others with 'store clothes,' and still others . . . in 'homespun,' which together with the peculiar military dress of the Commandant . . . presented a spectacle that would have made a regular army officer throw all kinds of 'fits.'"[3]

But when H. H. Pierce replaced Weaver, the corps quickly changed from a joke to an activity desired for reasons other than free tuition and textbooks. Requiring uniforms and introducing order on the drill ground where he had found disorder, Pierce moulded the cadets into an elite corps by persuading the faculty to adopt a code for cadets which required the highest academic averages.

Other academic changes during Martin's presidency included the abolition of the professorship of natural science in favor of a chair of astronomy and physics and a chair of chemistry and natural history, the latter to in-

As a land-grant institution, WVU has an obligation to train military officers — a tradi-tion as old as the University. In 1876, the Cadet Corps stood for inspection beside the $4,000 Armory built in 1873. University Avenue hadn't been built yet so a white picket fence delineates Woodburn Circle. Martin Hall includes an entrance porch with a balcony.

dicate that the University had not lost sight of agriculture, even though its occupant, Professor John J. Stevenson, dedicated it to the study of geology, both theoretical and practical. Emphasizing the need for scholarship, Professor Stevenson insisted that the Preparatory Department had no place in a university and that he would have no part of lower-level instruction. Rejecting an additional assignment in beginning algebra, in addition to his regular work in chemistry and natural history, Stevenson began a fight, not won for many a year, that a professor was not required to take care of public school subjects or any other extra-curricular activity not included in his professorship.

Faced with strong-minded faculty, Martin also had to contend with what later would be considered Confederate faculty stances: the segregation and/or abolition of the Preparatory Department and the diminution of *in loco parentis* responsibilities of a professor. Contending in reports to the Board of Regents in 1873 and 1874 that someday the University might dispense with secondary studies, Martin believed that in the last half of the nineteenth century the paucity of academies and high schools in the state, "to say nothing of our legal obligations," showed the time was not ripe. Holding such a department indispensable "both as a large source of supply for our higher classes, and as a means of maintaining an elevated grade of preliminary scholarship on the part of those so admitted," he wanted his faculty engaged in the Preparatory Department for "we should, if possible, have the best talent connected with that department where the mind is first taught . . ."

Other academic contributions of the Martin years included the president's organization of the West Virginia Historical Society, which sponsored a life of Philip Doddridge written by Waitman T. Willey in 1875; the establishment of a museum; and the ready acceptance of "noble gratuities" from citizens, institutions, and government. A constant academic worry to Martin as he attempted to expand the curriculum and improve the campus was holding on to a faculty. According to his reports to the Regents, departures were "with the kindest feelings of good will, and only from necessity arising from inadequate compensation." His observation was echoed by the president of the Board of Regents, Dr. T. H. Logan, who lamented to the Governor in an 1870 report, "While discharging duties requiring rare scholarship, peculiar mental endowment, and much experience, [professors] were receiving salaries only equal to, or even less than, the lowest grades of government clerks, whose duties are only mechanical or routine." By the end of his reign, Martin nevertheless had doubled the faculty's original size.

Whatever the ups and downs of the building program, the curriculum, and problems of faculty retention due to the parsimonious Legislature, Martin doggedly tried to present the University in the best light. The first president, in periodic bursts of public relations, claimed the University was offering by way of a Bachelor of Arts degree "a comprehensive and thorough course of general study equal to that of our best American colleges"; that the school had perfected a course leading to the Bachelor of Science which, although omitting the classic languages, required two years each of French and German; and that for students interested in law, medicine, and engineering, programs were available in their junior and senior years devoted exclusively to professional studies. Martin always was careful not to deprecate any course of study; all work was in harmony, he suggested; and in answer to the Confederates' desire for an elective system as practiced at the University of Virginia, Martin contended in an 1871 report that a liberal margin of choice was allowed at West Virginia University — "without running after the chimeras of the age."

With the Democrats returning to power, Martin might well have not bothered with apologies for himself or the school he headed. When the West Virginia Constitution was rewritten in 1872, the Legislature was charged with providing "a thorough and efficient system of free schools," but state and local governments were denied the power to contract indebtedness. When Martin tried to make himself more amenable to the Confederate point of view by requesting additional acreage so that practical experiments in horticulture, agriculture, and related subjects could be carried on, Democratic Governor John J. Jacob in his address to the Legislature in 1872 found "The present grounds are not well improved, and until this is done, there is little propriety in adding to them . . ." Instead, the Governor suggested that the Legislature might, in addition to increasing the number of cadets, "meet deficiencies in salaries, provide for contingencies, chemical apparatus, armory, insurance, and expenses of regents."

Rapid political changes were threatening to end Martin's presidency. On April 12, 1873, the Legislature abolished the incumbent Board of Regents, created a new nine-member governing body with a Democratic majority, and authorized each new Regent to appoint "not more than four cadets," which amounted to increasing the Cadet Corps from 22 to 36. Thus were all former Republicans purged from the regency and patronage broadened for Democrats by permitting growth in the University's Cadet Corps.

The new board did not hesitate to act in the interests of political change. On June 19, 1873, it ordered that the Preparatory Department "shall be constituted a separate Department of the University"; on July 31, 1873, it next relieved the President from all teaching duties and charged him "with the executive business of the University, including traveling in the interests of the Institution and in general with promoting the prosperity and success of the same . . ." On June 17, 1874, it assigned the President such studies "as will as far as possible equalize the labors of the Professors, and at the same time not interfere with the executive duties, and the plan for traveling in the interest of the University," even though such classes were not compatible with Martin's academic training.

At a special meeting in Martinsburg on August 11, 1875, the Board of Regents repealed that section of the University code which required the board to give sixty days notice before discharging a professor, declared all University positions vacant, and proceeded to fill the vacancies with those faculty sympathetic to the new political forces. It disposed of Martin by directing its secretary to advertise in national newspapers for the unfilled position of "Astronomy and Physics (Executive Chair)." However, it was mere coincidence, said one of the Regents, that all professors reelected were Democrats and those invited to retire were all Republicans. Politics, it was said, had nothing to do with the board's actions; it simply had agreed that "a change would be for the interest of the University."

When Martin received the news, he invited more recrimination by publishing an open letter to the board on August 21, 1875, which read in part:

The snarling of a few low curs, whose mendacity is only exceeded by their malignity, at the heels of the University, has had very little effect . . . It is their nature to oppose everything in the way of progress and improvement, and especially tends to elevate the common life of humanity above the slums in which they themselves delight to wallow . . . Under God a good work has been well inaugurated and considerably advanced . . . The lukewarm or inimical, if such there be, I pity and forgive.

All West Virginia pretended to be more aghast by Martin's letter than by the board's action. Wrote one observer: "I am of the opinion that the diligence which he or some one for him circulated it among the Methodist families of the State has done the U. lasting injury. The Institution ought to have been spared this blow from his hand even though he felt he had been personally wronged."[4]

The *Weston Democrat* editorialized on September 18, 1875, that

a minister of the Gospel, who aspires not only to stand as a watchman upon the walls of Zion, but to occupy the first place in the State as a preceptor of youth—such a man, who will so far forget the dignity of his position as to blackguard and vilify public officials whose action happens to be contrary to his own personal interests, is not a fit person to preside at a State university.

However, Marmaduke H. Dent, the University's first alumnus, was one of the few who rebuked "those who have been covertly seeking his downfall in hope of self-advancement," and the *West Virginia Journal* at Charleston, one of the few periodicals to support Martin, suggested that all inhabitants of the state "hang crepe on the College doors, and drape it in mourning from belfry to the ground."

But the man who had taken the first steps toward the creation of West Virginia University was not one to remain on the sidelines dressed in mourning. He accepted the presidency of Asbury College at New Castle, Indiana, which, under his leadership, became DePauw University in 1882 and which he was to serve as president until 1889. As for the WVU presidency that he involuntarily left behind, the *Wheeling Register* of June 30, 1877, noted,

Political jobbers took an interest in it, but it was the interest which the passenger takes in the railroad car. Sectarian churches took an interest in it, but it was the interest which the artist takes in the implements of his craft. Localities took interest in it, but was not an unselfish one. Under the attention of these numerous friends, the disgusting strifes of rival creeds, and the devigorating warfare of ambitious men for a share in the University influence, it must be submitted that it seemed for a time that the next legislative appropriation in order was the fund for the expenses of a funeral, including the erection of a monument.

The board, while scanning applications for the presidency which fell "thick as leaves in Vallombrosa," appointed Vice-President J. W. Scott acting president. It was a short and somewhat futile assignment. Scott, in an effort to reverse an enrollment trend that dipped to 93 in 1877, prescribed unusual remedies: enactment of legislation to authorize the admission of both sexes upon terms of equality; creation of departments of medicine and teacher training instruction; and abolition of all tuition fees. Also showing striking independence, Scott and his faculty in their minutes of February 5, 1877, responded when the Board of Regents again ordered separation of preparatory and collegiate departments: "A literal execution of said order would require an immediate and entire division of the Military and Music Department, leaving four or five cadets in the Preparatory Department and three students in the Preparatory Music class — not enough to drill in the one case nor to sing all the parts of a piece of music in the other."

Obviously, the board needed a new president, and preferably one who was Methodist and Republican to pull Democratic chestnuts from the fire. Methodist students were boycotting the school and the West Virginia Conference of the Methodist Episcopal Church in April, 1876, was suggesting that students attend schools outside the state "and especially" Alexander Martin's Asbury College. In response, the Regents offered the eminent Waitman T. Willey, who met the religious and political qualifications, the title of chancellor. But he declined, saying he could not tolerate the August 12, 1875, order of the Regents which required the annual election of officers and professors. Willey refused, in short, to subject himself "to such a miserable dependency."[6]

But if Morgantown's best-known resident passed up the honor, another townsman accepted: the Reverend John Rhey Thompson, pastor of the Morgantown Methodist Church and a Republican (but a liberal Republican who had supported Horace Greeley whom the Democrats had also endorsed for the presidency in 1872). Twenty-five years of age, Thompson was expected to bring vigor to the University. And to give expression to his youth, he traveled eight weeks through most West Virginia counties. But the effort seemed not worth it when he informed the Regents in his 1877 report that he was "surprised and startled that such ignorance and apathy, and suspicion, and distrust, and downright opposition should prevail among the citizens of West Virginia concerning their own university."

Thompson was also to find that with the rise of the Grange in West Virginia and the failure of the University to maintain agricultural courses on a par with classical and scientific subjects, the situation was conducive to the establishment of an institution that would be agricultural both in name and in fact. Such an institution might not only be a beneficiary of future federal grants but also a competitor for students and legislative appropriations. This was especially true after 1875 when the West Virginia Legislature incorporated the Jefferson County Agricultural College at Leetown "for the purpose of establishing a college for the education of youths and for teaching all branches of useful information usually taught in colleges, and especially those sciences desirable to fit a person for agricultural pursuits."

The effort at creating a second agricultural institution was the handiwork of Daniel B. Lucas of Jefferson County, a politician who was incorporating Grange objectives into principles of Democratic Party faith. But Lucas perhaps was taken care of when Governor Henry M. Mathews tendered the eastern Jefferson County leader an appointment to the University Board of Regents. In turn, the board offered Lucas the chair of law and equity which it created along with a chair of medicine in 1878.

Lucas declined the faculty appointment but recommended instead the election of his brother-in-law, Henry St. George Tucker Brooke, and sweetened the suggestion by offering to contribute $500 toward the cost of the chair during the first year.[7] When the Board, by executive committee action on September 2, 1878, agreed to the choice of Brooke as a professor of law and equity, as well as to the appointment of Dr. Hugh W. Brock of Morgantown to the chair of anatomy, physiology and hygiene, the president and Board again were able to relegate agriculture and agricultural education to the background of West Virginia University interests and simultaneously promote the professional interests of law and medicine.

With a rival institution disposed of, Thompson turned his attention to public relations. A first priority was to revive Methodist belief in the institution. In this, he was most successful when on October 4, 1877, the influential Methodist Church endorsed the institution in glowing terms. The result was an increase in enrollment from a low of 93 in 1876-77 to 132 at the end of 1880-81.

In the interests of students, Thompson also perfected an arrangement with the Methodist Church that provided books to students at cost, encouraged student boarding clubs, and secured free tuition for ministerial students. To the rapidly increasing number of students, he appeared a savior from the harsh discipline of the first administration. Substituting "the element of personal moral influence" in the governance of students, Thompson declared in a presidential report of June 25, 1877: "The attempt to govern young men in attendance upon a State University by laws conceived in the same spirit as those which obtain in the conduct of reform schools and inebriate asylums is foredoomed to miserable failure."

So Thompson rode with students, boated with students, entertained them in his home, and upset townspeople by his effort to protect his charges from the sins of Morgantown. Where Martin had only the theatre and billiard halls to contend with, Thompson had six or more licensed bars (four in hotels), each said to be fitted with two entrances, "one for the old drinkers and a private one for the young ones."[8] With liquor now available at the very edge of the campus, the city fathers empaneled grand juries, which had a field day bringing in indictments "faster than the busy prosecuting attorney, George C. Sturgiss, could prepare the bills." Generating conflict between town and gown, such episodes produced personal confrontation between non-students and the University president. Thompson, according to a report in the *Wheeling Register,* was accosted on the street by a crowd led by a certain Fitch with club in hand, but the young and unarmed executive rid himself of his armed foe without a blow by saying, "You do not need that club and you do not need this crowd — you can crush me to earth with your fist, but you cannot terrorize me. As long as I am president of the University I shall continue to denounce you and your nefarious business and to do all I can to annihilate it."9

Skillful at publicizing himself as the friend of students, the young Thompson founded the *West Virginia Journal of Education* as a weekly to promote with parents and other interested persons his version, as well as vision, of education at all levels of the state. To those who contended that compulsory attendance would work hardship on those too poor to buy shoes and books for their children, he answered that after two years of careful observation of the habits and homes of West Virginians it was his "deliberate opinion that the dogs of the State — the cur dogs, the bull dogs, the terrier dogs, the pointer dogs, the setter dogs and the hound dogs — cost more money annually than would be required to provide all the necessitous [sic] children with such shoes and books as would enable them to attend school."

Using language easily understood by those outside academe, Thompson stressed in 1879 the need for decent salaries for teachers, better school buildings, longer terms, state aid, and free tuition for University students. Knowing the value of advertising, he saw to it that a special edition of the *Journal* featuring the University was sent to each member of the Legislature during its sessions. But editors of the *Morgantown Weekly Post* were upset when Thompson awarded the printing to their competitor, Julian E. Fleming, editor of the recently established Democratic weekly *New Dominion.* The governing board also hinted that "a successful discharge of the duties" of the presidency required "the entire time and energy of one man." So Thompson gave up the editorship on December 10, 1879, assigning his interests in the paper to the *New England Journal of Education.*

Thompson's major problem had been selling himself and his institution to the West Virginia Democrats who had made many demands on his University administration. In 1879, the board had ordered no repairs on buildings, and no traveling expenses had been allowed the president of the faculty or any member of the executive committee or faculty. In turn, the Legislature had insisted on an itemized University budget and had specified that "no money appropriated for a particular purpose shall be used for another and different purpose." The lawmakers also assigned the duties of the secretary and treasurer of the Board of Regents and the superintendent of grounds and buildings to members of the faculty without pay. Although their action had saved the state about $1,000 annually, their professed objective had been to remove the University from local politics.

The Republican *Wheeling Intelligencer* on August 9, 1875, in approval of Democratic fiscal concepts, had supported a curtailment of appropriations, "since the inauguration of the free school system in this State, the taxpayers have paid a mint of money for the erection of school houses and support of instruction." To the *Intelligencer,* University salaries were too high and the school served only the aristocratic element of the state because in fourteen years it had graduated only four students with agricultural training. The paper therefore recommended that the University "with its buildings, apparatus, cabinets, museum, grounds and endowment" be sold to the highest bidder. On December 25, 1880, the *Hinton Herald* had a stronger suggestion: the abolition of the institution root and branch and the conversion of its "buildings into a colored insane asylum." During a period of newspaper attack, Delegate N. M. Lowry of Summers County had introduced on January 28, 1881, a resolution into the House of Delegates to inquire into the expediency of abolishing the University and establishing in its stead "a Reform School for all idle and uncared for youths of both sexes in the State and the school buildings now at Morgantown to be used for such school." In Thompson's own backyard, "a small clique of restless intriguers in Morgantown," as identified by the *Morgantown Weekly Post* on December 11, 1880, had demanded that the president and all remaining Republican members of the faculty be removed and that professors' salaries be reduced.

Thompson's mounting difficulties had been aggravated by internal faculty problems. As Radical Republican strength had ebbed, the cry had become louder for reforms modeled after the University of Virginia: abolition of the Preparatory Department; abolition of the presidency; introduction of an honor system; substitution of the Virginia system of elective schools for the single curriculum; and a relaxed set of standards. As to the latter, when it became known that final examination papers disclosed deficiencies in the spelling of common English words, the faculty in its minutes of December 10, 1880, directed the preparation of a list of one hundred words and ordered "that each student in the four college classes be required to write out these words, from dictation, correctly spelled, and that all who shall fail to spell correctly ninety-five of them shall be required to report in the Preparatory Spelling Class until such time as the teacher of that class shall be satisfied that they have removed their deficiency."

Partisans of the Virginia system had found their issue; they opposed the resolution. The students had found their issue; the spelling requirement was *ex post facto* legislation. On January 24, 1881, the Board wisely ordered students to submit to the requirement until it could consider the matter more fully at its June meeting, after all had departed the campus for the year. The Board also had a message for the faculty when it ordered "all discussions and proceedings of the Faculty shall be secret and confidential, and no member of the Faculty shall disclose the vote or opinion of any member or members of the Faculty unless required to give evidence before a court of Justice in due course of law."

On the question of standards, the Board on June 8, 1881, upheld the faculty, but not before Thompson had resigned the presidency on January 1, 1881, effective March 12, 1881. Most newspapers expressed no surprise at his decision. Soliciting the Republican National Committee for speakers and funds and appearing with candidates on platforms, the University president had appeared either too political or too much on the side of the losing political party. The Board undoubtedly was grateful he resigned rather than force the issue as the first University president of Republican persuasion had done.

What West Virginia Democrats were looking for was a liberal who espoused Jeffersonian and Jacksonian Democracy, and they could not accept Acting President Daniel Boardman Purinton as their president even though he was an alumnus of the class of 1873, a former teacher in the Preparatory Department, son-in-law of Professor Lyon, and since 1878 a member of the University faculty as professor of mathematics. Purinton was also a devout Baptist. What troubled some Regents was Purinton's Republicanism and his identification with Morgantown. One official was certain all Radical Republican elements needed weeding out of the University administration and another wrote the Governor that the Morgantown influence was pernicious for he had found that "the University was being utalized [sic] as a sort of Assylum [sic] for the Community in which it is, the salaries for a certain proportion of the faculty were so low as to preclude any but 'home folks' from accepting the professorships, men wholly unknown to fame in educational matters, that parents having children ready to enter college were in doubt as to the capacity of the faculty to properly and thoroughly educate them."[10]

If West Virginia could not find the right man, its temptation was strong to abolish the presidency and assign executive duties to a chairman of the faculty as at the University of Virginia. The Legislature considered such a measure, which caused the campus newspaper to respond on June 6, 1881: "A young school in a young and undeveloped State must have a president — interest must be aroused and kept alive, correspondence must be conducted, friends must be stimulated, enemies conciliated, prejudices allayed, untoward influences abated, patronage secured, and discipline enforced."

Such sentiment had little influence upon a Democrat swept into office by a landslide vote. In his first message to the Legislature on January 11, 1882, Governor Jacob B. Jackson took exception to student opinion by recommending abolishment of the offices of University president and vice-president and the election by the faculty of one of its number as presiding officer. Said the economically minded executive: "The presiding officer thus appointed could discharge all the duties heretofore performed by the President, for the compensation given him as a professor, and the additional expense heretofore incurred saved."

Despite the temptation, the Legislature was not yet ready to follow the suggestion of the chief executive. Taking its cue from recent election returns, the board hastened to elect William L. Wilson, an ex-Confederate, a Democrat, a former professor of Latin at Columbian College (now George Washington University), and a lawyer and politician from Jefferson County, who, as a Rebel soldier during the Civil War, had entered Morgantown and pronounced it "the meanest Union hole we've yet been in."[11]

The saga of Wilson as president was short and not so sweet. Elected on June 8, 1882, he assumed his duties with the opening of the fall term on September 6, 1882. Unable to find suitable housing for his family, he lived by himself at the Wallace Hotel. On September 20, 1882, he was named Democratic candidate for Congress in the Second West Virginia District only three weeks after arriving in Morgantown. With another three weeks for campaigning, Wilson won the election on October 10, 1882, with a plurality of ten votes. He submitted his resignation as president effective March 1, 1883, but the board refused to accept it. Agreeing to serve until the end of the academic year, he refused salary while campaigning and effected an understanding that, beyond unavoidable expenses, his services to WVU were to be without compensation.

When those who rejoiced at his nomination learned of Wilson's forsaking them, they were disturbed about their fate and that of the University. In his diary Wilson reported their perplexity: "Poor fellows, they have had such a hard time under the former rule of the University, and had been so ostracised and goaded because of their being Democrats and Southern men that they were startled at the idea of being remitted to their former condition."

Wilson may have been correct in describing their dejection, but he was wrong if he thought they would passively accept their situation as a permanent condition. Instead, they used his term to prepare for the complete establishment of the Virginia idea.

Such an idea had been set in motion at the board meeting when Wilson had been selected. Determined that the Preparatory Department should be separated from University administration, the board also was determined that rules for student conduct should be relaxed. According to its minutes of June 7-8, 1882, compulsory chapel attendance was eased, and the word "gamble" was substituted for playing "at cards or any game of chance," yet both faculty and teachers were to show "an exemplary diligence in study and in the communications of knowledge and performance of every moral religious duty."

The University reorganized its studies according to the Virginia plan and simultaneously raised standards. Related subjects were organized horizontally into separate departments and introduced as a modified elective system. As Wilson pointed out to the faculty, to the board, and to state newspapers in 1882, the graduate would enjoy the intellectual and moral advantage of knowing one thing or several things well, instead of having a superficial and dangerous knowledge of many things; and the faculty member within his own department could practice thoroughness through specialization and enjoy that independence which his highly individualistic nature craved.

Students were at first pleased and reveled "in their new found liberty," until they took final tests and received their embarrassing scores under the elevated standards. The casualties were so great that twenty or more out of 140 students enrolled "left for other colleges, several others subsequently withdrew, and some efforts were made to produce a general exodus by filling the University with catalogues of other colleges."[12]

The Republican Party took advantage of the situation, with the *Wheeling Intelligencer* of January 27, 1883, defining the University as reduced to "ten teachers instructing seventy young men in false doctrine," and fanning a report that when a student asked if a recent biography of Charles Sumner was in the library, the librarian replied, "You could hardly expect to find such a book in a Southern institution."

Four days later Wilson struck back in an open letter to the editor of the Wheeling paper, saying the stories were false and in effect calling for the end of the Civil War within the University. As he saw it, "West Virginia is neither a Northern nor a Southern state, and students from every section should be welcomed with equal hospitality, and meet no influences which are not catholic and patriotic, and I am sure that the University never was as free from the spirit of sect, party, or section as it is today."

But when the assaults did not stop against "the introduction of 'Old Virginny ideas'," Wilson confided to his diary on June 13, 1883, that it was not so much Confederate and Yankee antagonisms causing trouble as it was sectarian strife: "I have long ago settled in my mind that the chief source of the assaults is the Methodist influence, and that it works right here in Morgantown."

But even Wilson could not stop what he had started with the implementation of the Virginia educational concept: attacks upon the presidency itself, honorary degrees, and antagonism toward coeducation. He attempted to stop the abolition of the presidency, and he tried to prevent the conferring of three honorary degrees by the board without faculty recommendation and over his own protest. But he failed in both matters. The board abolished the office and named Professor Robert C. Berkeley as chairman of the faculty. And it gave one of Wilson's benefactors, Daniel B. Lucas, an honorary doctorate.

With Berkeley's ascension, the Virginia experiment seemed almost culminated in the chairman's own person. Born in 1837 in Hanover County, Virginia, of parents descended from the Carters, Lees, and Spotswoods, and educated in the traditions of a gentleman at the University of Virginia, Berkeley had joined the Confederate Army in 1862. Before joining the WVU faculty in 1873, Berkeley had conducted a private school at his home in Amherst County and served as principal of Washington College at Chestertown, Maryland. Despite this background, however, he was to those of Yankee persuasion "devoid of magnetism, utterly destitute of executive ability, and about as full of enthusiasm as an alligator," according to the *Parkersburg State Journal* of July 12, 1883.

Berkeley's appointment produced vehement criticism of the Virginia plan, with the *Parkersburg State Journal* featuring a series of articles in June and July, 1883, written by A. L. Purinton, superintendent of the Parkersburg schools and a brother of Professor Purinton of the University faculty. To Purinton, Berkeley knew nothing but the stagnant ideas of the University of Virginia. It was senseless, he charged, to ape the method and provisions of such a school for "such pompous pretensions were mere educational quackery." Besides, he argued, West Virginia had no use whatever for a university, but "it did need, and could use a good college."

The Confederate Berkeley was not the only target, but he was a good one. Perhaps because he was not only a Southerner, but also a devout Episcopalian, the Methodist Episcopal Conference in its October, 1883, meeting at Wheeling again removed the University from its list of approved institutions. Certain Republican newspapers refused to carry University advertising, and in July, 1883, the *Fairmont West Virginian* demanded "a cleaning out — a thorough cleaning — and purifying of the Augean stables."

The Board of Regents appointed a Committee on Scurrilous Publications which released its report in August, 1884. It defended the use of the elective system and the separation of the Preparatory Department from the collegiate departments. It reported that collegiate enrollment had increased steadily since 1876, doubling by 1882, and tripling under the Wilson presidency.

But Berkeley and enrollment statistics were not the only convenient targets; other Confederate faculty members played into the hands of the Republicans. On June 10, 1884, George B. Foster, Thomas E. Hodges, and George C. Baker, recent graduates of the University, charged Professor

Robert C. Berkeley

Woodville C. Latham of the chemistry department with drunkenness, profanity, neglect of duty, conduct prejudicial to order and discipline, and an irascibility of temper that made him both morally and temperamentally unfit for the classroom. Two days later twenty students sent a letter to the board urging his removal.

At a hearing on July 25, 1884, Latham denied the main charges against him except that of absenteeism from chapel. This he excused on the ground of necessity as "I did not have time to attend. The janitor neglects my rooms and I haven't time to attend to them and go to Chapel too. Danser seldom cleans them up." As to witnesses who had testified to his drunkness, "I say unqualifiedly that all who have sworn that I was drunk, etc., have committed perjury," Latham said.

Four days after the testimony, the Regents found that while Professor Latham was thoroughly qualified for the duties of his chair, he was "occasionally rigorous in his disciplinary methods, sometimes irascible and imprudent in his administration thereof"; that he was "temperate in the use of spirituous liquors, but that his use thereof, as disclosed by the testimony, has caused scandal or been the occasion for it, especially in the estimation of strictly temperate persons, or those unfriendly to him or to the University, or those uninformed, and perhaps, others."

Unable to unseat Professor Latham, a member of the 1885 Legislature offered a resolution in the House of Delegates to abolish the chairs of law and medicine, occupied by Professors Brooke and Allen of the Virginia persuasion. Regent Daniel B. Lucas countered with what most construed to be an attack upon Professor Franklin S. Lyon, alleged leader of the Northern faction. In a letter of February 20, 1885, to Professor Willey, professor of equity, jurisprudence, and history, a fellow Regent, and secretary of the faculty, Lucas called attention to the fact that Foster, who had preferred charges against Latham, was now the son-in-law of Lyon. He wrote that it "would be well to intimate that if any more assaults are made on the professors, there will be several vacancies created in the Faculty before we adjourn."

Willey himself, because he absented himself from the campus at the end of the winter quarter, was threatened by the executive committee with the withholding of part of his salary. In April, 1885, he explained he had been absent to help one of the Regents secure appropriations for the University, had neglected none of his classes, nor had his students suffered loss by his absence. "But," said Willey, "I submit that it is not your business if they had," and added:

I do not understand that your committee has been appointed censor over the work of the professors at the University. Each professor has been put in charge of a particular School for the term of one year. He is not employed by the day or the month. He is not required to meet his classes more frequently than his own judgement dictates. If he meets them but once a week, or once a month, or once a term, that is a matter between him and the Board of Regents — it is not your business.

At the contrivance of Professor William P. Willey and considered as a personal affront to Confederate sympathizers, daughters of Professor Lyon, who had been admitted informally to classes as a courtesy to their father, were joined in a history course by other Morgantown women at the opening of the 1883 fall term. Because of agitation by a group of students, the board again considered the matter of coeducation at its June, 1884, meeting. It agreed "to take the matter under advisement" and appointed a committee to confer with Mrs. J. R. Moore, principal and chief owner of the Morgantown Female Seminary, to ascertain the availability of the building for dormitory purposes and to obtain from her the conditions and terms of sale. Although Mrs. Moore expressed her readiness to cooperate, the board at a special meeting in July, 1884, postponed consideration of the question until June, 1885.

In 1885, Nathan B. Scott of Ohio County sponsored successful legislation in the State Senate for admission of women to the University. But when a similar bill was reported in the House of Delegates, Daniel B. Lucas, University Regent, led the fight against it. An amendment declared that the leading purpose of the Morrill Land-Grant Act of 1862 was to give a practical education in agriculture and the mechanic arts. Because the House bill specifically exempted women from military training, a subject strictly required by law, the House of Delegates tabled the bill by a margin of 33 to 30.

But all was not lost. In June, 1885, the board accepted the resignation of the controversial Professor Latham and terminated the contract of Professor Lyon, the latter without apology or explanation. These changes, the *New Dominion* suggested on June 20, 1885, had to be made "for harmony inside the University." According to the newspaper, the axe had fallen "a little

West Virginia University faculty in 1885. Seated (from left): Saint George Tucker Brooke, Daniel Boardman Purinton, President Eli Marsh Turner, B. W. Allen, Adams Wilson Lorentz, and James S. Stewart; standing (from left): John I. Harvey, Robert C. Berkeley, Lieutenant James L. Wilson, Powell Benton Reynolds, Alexander R. Whitehall, Israel Charles White, and William P. Willey.

hard on one of the Professors displaced. Nobody expected it. He was one of the oldest, most experienced and able instructors in the Faculty." His removal was not to be taken as a reflection "on his character or as a man or a Professor" but for the good of the cause.

And for the good of the cause, which signalled the end of elective studies and decentralized administration, the Regents restored the office of president and elected Eli Marsh Turner of Harrison County as fourth president of West Virginia University, effective July 1, 1885. Two of the first three presidents had not survived because of their politics, and the other had found political life on the Potomac more satisfying than academic life on the Monongahela.

When the faculty secured one of their own to lead the University away from arbitrary academic centralization to a states-rights haven, they obtained the following results: a loss in enrollment, a violation of academic freedom, a campus of antagonized students, and a limitation on campus improvements to a single physical accomplishment — a clock added to Martin Hall, chiming away the class hours in empty, unfinished buildings.

Decentralization to Centralization

Eli Marsh Turner
June 11, 1885–July 21, 1893

James Lincoln Goodknight
June 13, 1895–August 6, 1897

ELI MARSH TURNER WAS a native West Virginian who had graduated from Monongalia Academy in 1864 and became, in turn, valedictorian of his Princeton University class of 1868, a tutor, an instructor in Greek, and an assistant librarian at Princeton. In 1873, however, he had forsaken teaching for law and politics. Becoming first a Clarksburg lawyer and in time a member of the West Virginia Senate, Turner assumed both the glories and splendid miseries of becoming the fourth president of West Virginia University on July 1, 1885.

The last of the WVU presidents to arrive in Morgantown by stage, he was the first to witness a train — the Fairmont, Morgantown, and Uniontown Railroad — entering the University city on February 14, 1886. So rapidly did new lines multiply in the next few years that Morgantown seemed a bustling city by comparison with its past, and the University appeared accessible to students from most counties of the state.

Symbolic of a quickening tempo in higher education, the clock atop University Hall (now Martin Hall) which ran twenty minutes behind B&O time was synchronized with the train's clock, enabling the new Turner administration, implied a local editor, to run the machine on railroad time, like all enterprising people. What was more important, the iron horse plus a change in reckoning tuition enabled the University to cease being the Morgantown school as documented by its enrollment statistics. In 1883-84, enrollment had fallen to 96, but it increased to 107 in 1884-85. By 1892-93, the Turner administration recorded an enrollment of 228.

Because Turner was both a low-tariff Cleveland Democrat and a farmer in a rural state, he had been chosen as the properly educated and practical man of affairs to right the wrongs of an institution chaotically administered by a faculty of Confederate sympathizers. Until July 21, 1893, the approximate time when West Virginia began to shift from Democratic to Republican control, he remained president. It was an eight-year stint during which he experienced victory at first and then defeat. His objectives: first, to impose centralized control upon an independent-minded faculty that considered themselves co-equals of the president; second, to dispose of the Virginia elective system, as well as the Preparatory Department; third, to rid the institution of what he believed were grandiose notions of becoming a university without having first been a respectable college; and fourth, to establish high schools across the state as feeders to the University.

Even before he became president he had warned interested West Virginians that the Regents had undertaken a questionable policy in establishing a full-fledged university without funds for strong professional schools. For examples of expensive legal and medical education, Turner suggested in the *Wheeling Register* of December 30, 1884, West Virginians should go elsewhere to see "how futile is the attempt to establish a university which will afford such facilities in all departments as Harvard, Yale, Princeton, Columbia, Cornell and other similar institutions which count their endowments by millions of dollars."

Turner's remarks had displeased many, including a *Wheeling Register* correspondent who one week later scornfully admonished prospective Mountaineers: "Go to your State University and get an academic education, and then emigrate to Germany or England, or some New England State and get your University education." The journalist pointed out that West Virginia's neighbor, Ohio, was supporting forty-odd colleges. Why, he argued, could not West Virginia support one all-embracing institution?

On Turner's final day in office, after failing to realize most of his elitist undergraduate principles, janitor William (Doc) Danser, having been given instructions by a fast-disappearing Board of Regents on July 21, 1893, to serve termination notices upon Turner and the entire faculty, met the president on the steps leading to his office with the guillotine notice in hand. As tradition has it, the janitor, who had been openly defiant and at times impudent

First issue of the student newspaper, The Athenaeum, *was published on November 3, 1887, featuring an engraving of the campus on its cover. It was a biweekly publication of the Columbian and Parthenon Literary Societies, which set this goal in the first issue: "It will be the aim of* The Athenaeum *to be courteous to all, to foster the interests of the Societies, to discuss subjects of weight and usefulness, to do whatever it can to ameliorate the condition of mankind." The first issue noted that WVU was prospering with an enrollment of 164 students, and called for men of wealth to create a University endowment fund.*

to Turner, delivered his one and only heart-felt speech certain to be recorded in all University histories: "Mr. President, it is my pleasure to present to you your walkin' papers and may the Lord have mercy on your soul."

The *Clarksburg News,* one month after the Regents' action, with reference to a day when the highest University official had been unduly humiliated by the lowest, passed the following judgment on the employer of both:

A majority of the Board of Regents of the West Virginia University have demonstrated the fact that their appointment to that very responsible position was a mistake. In fact, the entire proceedings of the Board have nearly more resembled the proceedings of a political convention than of a Board having high and important duties to discharge.

Of all observers and participants in this latest of the University's dramatic productions, Turner, perhaps as a Presbyterian schooled in the pre-destination doctrine, was the least surprised at the turn of events. While a member of the West Virginia State Senate in 1879, he profoundly observed to one of his colleagues: "I desire to say to the gentleman, that Education and Politics, like oil and water, will not mix and that certain defeat awaits the man or party that attempts to mix them."[1]

Before Turner, with his own mismatched mixture of elitist educational principles and West Virginia frontier politics of leveling democracy, went down to his several defeats, he managed to procure more victories in building and in general appropriations (including federal ones) than any other president between Martin and Trotter and between Trotter and Stewart. Like all presidential builders of West Virginia University with strong edifice complexes, Turner probably would not have been successful had he rested his case and restricted his pleas to West Virginia. For during his presidency the state would not even reimburse faculty members who had dug into their own pockets to pay additional instructors deemed necessary in the ever-growing Preparatory Department, the University's feeder unit, whose embarrassing-

Vol. 1.   W. Va. University, November 3, 1887.   No. 1.

The Athenaeum.

ISSUED BI-WEEKLY BY THE

Parthenon and Columbian Literary Societies.

OF THE

West Virginia University.

Entered at the Postoffice at Morgantown, West Virginia, as second class mail matter.

EDITORIAL STAFF.

CHIEF.

U. S. GRANT PITZER, COLUMBIAN.

LITERARY.

D. L. JAMISON, PARTHENON.
FRANK SNIDER, COLUMBIAN.

ALUMNI.

STUART F. REED, PARTHENON,

EXCHANGE.

J. E. BROWN, PARTHENON,

LOCAL.

H. H. RYLAND, COLUMBIAN.

BUSINESS MANAGER.

PHIL A. SCHAEFFER, COLUMBIAN.
(Office over Postoffice.)

Terms of Subscription.

One copy per College Year $1.00
One copy per College Term .... .35
Single copy .... .10

ADVERTISING RATES ON APPLICATION.

Correspondence solicited from the Alumni, under-graduates and friends of the University. Address
THE ATHENAEUM,
Morgantown, West Va.

To Our Readers

"Our doubts are traitors,
And make us lose the good we oft might win,
By fearing to attempt."
—*Shakespeare.*

To-day another bark puts out upon the tempestuous sea of journalism. Shall it drift with the tide, or pursue a voyage of its own selection? On every billow may be seen the drifting remnants of other crafts that sailed to sea with "white wings" fluttering in the morning breeze and brazen beaks kissed into gold by the dazzling sun. These foretell breakers and dangers ahead. But with a strong determination to succeed, we face the promising future, and prepare to wield the editorial tripod. Should this paper reach the high standard of excellence desired by those in charge, it is certain that its patrons will be satisfied. It will be the aim of the ATHENAEUM to be courteous to all, to foster the interests of the Societies; to discuss subjects of weight and usefulness; to do whatever it can to ameliorate the condition of mankind. It is intended to make this paper pre-eminently of the West Virginia University, therefore, short, pithy contributions upon living questions are earnestly solicited from members of the faculty and the students. By giving a helping hand, each will share in the good work, and reap the fruits of discipline and pleasure.

We bespeak a prosperous year for the ATHENAEUM and trust that our patrons shall find therein food for the soul and intellect, as well as things pleasing to the æsthetic nature.

ly enlarged size was a direct result of the failure of Morgantown to provide adequate local public educational facilities.

During Turner's administration, 1885 to 1893, the federal government twice rescued the president from a stalled building program by providing him with surplus federal funds. These funds in truth may have led Turner down steep mountain paths he did not intend to go. In its own mixture of education and politics, Washington offered the Hatch Act of 1887 and the second Morrill Act of 1890, both of which increased the probability of further specialization and professional development and spelled doom for the classics.

The Hatch Act granted $15,000 a year to each of the states to establish an agricultural experiment station "under the direction of the college or colleges or agricultural department of colleges in each State or Territory" that owed their being to the 1862 Land-Grant College Act. Purpose of the station, stated the president in his 1888 report, would be to gather and diffuse "useful and practical information on subjects connected with agriculture."

Such federal action forced Turner into urging the appointment of a station director, the purchase of a station farm, and the erection of a building suitable for laboratory work, although he told the Regents with some reservation that "we must not allow ourselves to be persuaded into doing what may, in the end, result in great friction among professors, because it may seem desirable in itself."

The Board of Regents responded on June 11, 1888, with the skeletal organization of the West Virginia Agricultural Experiment Station. Next the Board proposed a multi-purpose building large enough for an armory, a drill hall, a gymnasium, and a commencement hall; and employed John A. Myers, agricultural chemist at Mississippi State University, as the first director. Myers promptly directed attention to testing seed and milk and supplying farmers with plans for building and equipping creameries and silos. For the moment the Board failed to interest the Legislature in purchasing a farm.

But the station, like the rest of the University, was not immune to political attack, despite its many services of practical application of theoretical knowledge. Republicans questioned the wisdom of the Democratic Regents in overspending for libraries, fruit trees, and professors of the wrong political persuasion, such as Dr. A. D. Hopkins, an entomologist. When Hopkins traveled to Europe to study German methods for combating insects then ravaging the pine and spruce forests of West Virginia, State Senator Alexander R. Campbell dismissed the sharing of international science by telling one audience that at the agricultural station, "They also have an entomologist . . . [which] . . . means a man learned in bugs . . . [who] . . . is now in Germany studying the habit of German bugs for your benefit, and when he returns he will issue a learned bulletin on bugs and tell you in Ger-

many the potato bugs have one more stripe on their backs than in America
. . . you are paying the bill."[2]

The second Morrill Act, passed by Congress on August 30, 1890, forced
Turner and the Board into more recommendations to the Legislature than
they had made when the Hatch Act became law. Not only did Congress appropriate to each state $15,000 for the year ending June 30, 1890, to endow
the land-grant colleges, it also specifically provided that such a fund "be
applied only to instruction in Agriculture, the Mechanic Arts, the English
language, and the various branches of Mathematical, Physical, natural and
economic science, with special reference to their applications to the industries
of life, and to the facilities for such instruction."

With the second Morrill Act in hand, Turner and the Board were able
to pressure the Legislature into appropriating money for an engineering
building, first called Machinery Hall, completed in 1894 on the river bank,
and Science Hall, opened in 1893 within Woodburn Circle. Before the passage
of the Morrill Act in 1890, Turner had asked the Legislature to provide an
addition to University Hall to accommodate classes in physics, chemistry,
biology, and engineering. He even had disclosed the smelly fact that the professor of modern languages had been compelled during the winter term to
vacate his room for several weeks due to the stench from cadavers in the
medical professor's dissecting room next door. Said Turner, with an eye
toward expansion, in his 1889-90 biennial report to the Board of Regents:
"There is nothing so offensive as the odor of a dead body, and practice of
dissection ought either to be abolished or a proper place should be provided
for it, where it will not offend those who must frequent the University rooms."
Because of the second Morrill Act, he could count four buildings to his credit
plus small tracts of land between the Circle and the Morgantown business
district which would provide for expansion south of the original Woodburn
Seminary buildings. He also could claim credit for equipping buildings later
known as Martin and Woodburn halls with steam-heating to replace hot-air
systems. In 1894, the total value of all University buildings did not exceed
$250,000.

Whereas federal legislation had forced Turner to expand the academic
curriculum which he had hoped to contract, an act of nature provided him
with the possibility of broadening the enrollment, which had eroded during
the faculty's two-year experimental administration of the institution.

At mid-morning on April 23, 1889, the Morgantown Female Seminary,
a three-story brick building located at High and Foundry streets, burned to
the ground. On June 11, the Board of Regents adopted a resolution providing for the admission of women to all University departments after
September 1. It was timely action. During 1889-90, ten women attended
WVU, with President Turner reporting to the Board that they had "demon-

Chitwood Hall, the last building to be constructed in Woodburn Circle, was completed in 1893 and named Science Hall. In 1972, it was renamed in honor of Oliver P. Chitwood, long-time professor of history. The interior of the building was renovated in 1978 to house the Department of Foreign Languages.

strated their ability to do as thorough work as the young men," and that their influence had been wholesome on the male students. In particular, one female student outshone all other students. During 1890, Miss Harriet E. Lyon was the only student to achieve perfect marks in all her classes; as a member of the Parthenon Society she won the Regents' literary prize for essay writing; and she was not only the first of her sex to receive a degree from West Virginia University but she also ranked first academically in her graduating class of 1891.

Both before and even after Miss Lyon's graduation, the battle against the admission of women to West Virginia University frequently was heated. Democratic floor leader Daniel B. Lucas had persuaded his party colleagues to defeat the proposal to admit women in the House of Delegates in February, 1885. To offset Lucas and the Legislature, students and faculty members such as Robert A. Armstrong through the Parthenon Society, Professor Samuel B. Brown before teachers' institutes, and Professor William P. Willey in speeches across the state argued for "co-education in West Virginia." By June, 1888, Daniel D. Johnson, president of the Board of Regents, presented a motion for the admission of female students to all University departments, only to see the motion fail for want of a quorum.

In 1889, both houses of the Legislature considered the question, but action was delayed by those lawmakers who believed that before admitting women the Legislature would have to provide special housing and the University would need to adjust its curriculum by adding more offerings in music and other fine arts. In the words of one legislator, it would not do "to send the girls to Morgantown and turn them loose." According to another representative, "The girls who adorn our homes need the most watchful care. You will not get in the University the class of young girls you would like to see there," he insisted, if they have to reside in town boarding houses, "but only those whose parents do not care especially to watch over them."[3]

Others saw the University's acceptance of coeducation as contrary to its founding principles and its very reasons for being. As one said, "We need much more a school of technology, where our young men may be equipped for the development of the wondrous natural resources of this State. It is time we have been working up our own raw material." This one argument seemingly worked, for the Senate resolution failed to pass by a vote of 13-11 on February 12, 1889, leaving the matter to the Board of Regents. It was assumed that the Board also possessed the power to change University policy, power delegated by its own charter.

When the Regents acted favorably upon coeducation, Regent James F. Brown resolved that he would "bring up the subject at every meeting [of the Board] until it is done away with." And so he did, according to the Regents' minutes of June 10, 1897, offering a motion to repeal the order and supporting the motion with the argument that women were not able to take care of themselves "from a moral standpoint" in "a place like Morgantown." By the time Brown gave up his efforts, coeducation had gained the necessary political momentum as seen by the increase in women attending WVU from 10 in 1889-90 to 112 in 1897-98. The sudden increase in 1897-98 enrollment from 38 women the previous year was aided by Professor William P. Willey, who urged the Board of Regents to authorize the admission of women to the Law School and by admission procedures in 1897 which permitted women to enter the Preparatory Department as well as all departments and schools of the University, except the military.

Had Turner surrendered his presidency in 1889, he would have had nothing but victories to recount: a successful building program, increased enrollment, coeducation, and the establishment of new schools of biology and engineering, the extension of courses in geology and law, and calling the attention of West Virginians to the need for library improvements as well as for better high schools in the state.

In 1889, however, Turner, determined to end the flexible Virginia elective system at WVU favored by the faculty, pushed forward on several fronts. One attempt was to ask the Board for a definition of the duties of the presidency; another was to seek an end to political control of the University through legislation. The first effort was only superficially successful, for the Regents, according to their minutes of June 12, 1889, while content to designate the president "as the head of the University . . . responsible to the Board of Regents for its general policy and management," also required the president "to superintend all its interests in every department and see that the ordinances of the Board of Regents and of the Faculty are faithfully observed." He could "propose to the faculty such changes and modifications in the work of the University as may seem necessary to secure greater efficiency and promote its interests," but he could not dispose of such matters. In short, he could only report his recommendations to the Board. The faculty, however, was expected to cooperate with the president "in maintaining discipline and in securing proper conduct," whatever that effort was worth to an executive championing his own prerogatives.

No doubt recognizing his lack of authority, Turner was responsible for the introduction of House Bill No. 204 which provided for reduction of the Regents from 13 to 5; abolition of the select Cadet Corps and its replacement by the requirement that all male students over fifteen years of age serve in the Cadet Corps for three years; granting of free tuition for all state residents except for students in law and engineering and any other professional schools to be established; and authorization for the Board to accept any monetary gift for University use with whatever conditions the donors might prescribe.

The House bill was challenged immediately and changed, especially those sections establishing compulsory military training and restoration of the Cadet Corps. But even alterations did not stop the charge that, "It is an open secret that the main object of this bill is to put more power in the hands of the President, and enable him to effect what he has long wanted, namely, to get rid of certain members of the Faculty whom he could not persuade the present Board to remove . . . These Professors . . . that have opinions of their own, and are not willing to sit down quietly and allow the President to run rough shod over them, and carry out arbitrary measures."[4]

It was the beginning of the end for Turner. In accordance with its minutes of June 10, 1891, and June 9, 1892, the Board added Thomas C. Atkeson and Howard N. Ogden to the faculty without the consent of the president; it also gave the president a voice in the employment and supervision of janitors but denied him the power to discharge them.

Still, the president refused to drop his fight. Turner told the Board in his June 5, 1891, report that the faculty had in fact destroyed his modified single curriculum "owing to the unwillingness of professors to give up any part of the time now required of students in the various subjects." To resolve the impasse, Turner asked for a standing committee of Board members, called the Committee on Instruction, to work with the faculty and another committee of the Board "to take into consideration the State of the University and to examine, investigate and inquire as to the organization and working of the Faculty and as to the state of harmony or lack thereof, alleged to exist therein."

Five days later, the latter committee promptly investigated and blamed the faculty for all the troubles. "It will become the duty of this Board, which it will promptly discharge, to remove such discord, contention and want of harmony by a resort to more vigorous measures," the committee added.

The faculty may have been knocked down, but it was not yet to be counted out. It urged its friends on the Board to make further inquiries. In a letter of June 25, 1892 to Governor Fleming, E. A. Bennett, a Board member, articulated numerous objections to Turner as expressed by members of the faculty and student body:

His temper is irascible and wholly ungoverned. His manner is imperious and repelling. To his associates in the Faculty he is haughty and exasperatively overbearing, resulting in outbursts of passion over ordinary affairs, with exhibitions of ill temper and rage that greatly impair his power as a disciplinarian and utterly destroying all considerations of personal and official respect for him. Chiefly for this cause the Faculty stands as a unit against their chief as the only means of making their situation tolerable. Students complain that at their first interview with him they are sent away with harsh words and with their determination unalterably fixed to approach him no more if possible . . .

Internal conditions at the University worsened so appreciably that Professor I. C. White left his alma mater to devote full time to consulting work in geology. Flatly refusing to accept the title of professor emeritus, he wrote to the Board of Regents on December 6, 1892: "I do not desire to become even nominally connected with a school whose official head is personally unfriendly to me, and who has long regarded my connection with the school as detrimental to its interest."

But still Turner could not soften his policies or turn his back upon the creation of a dictatorial University presidency. Moving from generalized charges in his June 5, 1891, report to the Board that some of the professors indulged in "wholesale excuses and other delinquencies," Turner zeroed in on more specific indictments, declaring that "if a few professors are to insist that all work in their departments is to be required of every candidate for a degree, some of our teachers will have very little work to do because the students will have no time to do it." Displaying his animus toward Howard N. Ogden, Henry G. Davenport, and Thomas C. Atkeson, Turner informed the Board that its "policy of making a professor out of every teacher who has served a year or two needs to be radically changed." Wholesale promotion was an unnecessary expense and not practiced in the better universities, Turner declared. "Its only result," he continued in a June 4, 1892 report to the Board, "is to down the standard and dignity of your professorships, and thus make them the object of a disreputable scramble on the part of incompetent men, whenever a vacancy occurs, or a new chair is to be filled."

Preparing to prove that there were men on the faculty absolutely unfit to be employed, Turner lodged charges of insubordination against Professors Brooke, Willey, Davenport, and Ogden on June 12, 1893. After hearing within three days the charges, the rebuttals, and the call for additional witnesses, the Board avoided actual trials, public or private. On July 21, 1893, it adopted a resolution by Regent J. H. Stewart which recognized the unhappy feeling existing among the faculty and observed that "whereas it appears that there is a greater number of chairs than the patronage of the University requires; now, therefore, for the purpose of harmonizing all said differences, and for the further purpose of the reorganization of the various chairs, the immediate resignation of each Professor, tutor, and the President is hereby requested."

After turning thumbs down on President Turner, the Board permitted the outgoing president a slight victory by refusing to reinstate six members of the faculty — Atkeson, Davenport, Ogden; the veteran Robert C. Berkeley (because of age); James S. Stewart (for alleged reasons of economy); and A. W. Lorentz (who had resigned to prove to the world of academe he could be a successful man of business). It named as Acting President a professor of metaphysics, Powell B. Reynolds.

Reynolds may have seemed an imperfect symbol around which to rally a reorganized faculty of scientific bent, for he was a former Confederate, a Democrat, and a Baptist. But, surprisingly, he was actually more than that. He was the perfect compromiser, somewhat in the mold of Henry Clay whom he idolized. Uninterested in day-to-day administration, Reynolds was the perfect man to make the presidential chair more attractive and more workable, not only for himself, but for subsequent occupants. What is more, Reynolds' occupation of the chair of metaphysics and his position as vice-president and acting president did not deprive him of power or ideas to transform the institution from an old-fashioned into a modern university.

In his first recommendation to the Board in June, 1894, he called for the appointment of a business manager and other officials who could be considered proper adjuncts to the presidency. He recommended appointment of new professors on a trial basis, the introduction of the semester system, the printing of all diplomas in English, the abolition of money prizes to students, the revision and abridgment of the disciplinary code into general terms, and a review of the whole tuition and fee system with a view toward lowering the cost of attendance to students of college grade and raising it as a bar against students in the Preparatory Department.

As to the Preparatory Department, its days seemed numbered when in 1895 the Legislature established the Preparatory Branch of West Virginia University at Montgomery in Fayette County. To the northern press, the action appeared variously as "a useless piece of jobbery" intended to move an important part of the University to the great Kanawha Valley; an "adroit play" executed by Republican leadership to win the approbation of the miners and laboring men of the Kanawha Valley; a preposterous mistake which located an integral part of the University in a town and region inhabited by "degraded foreigners rampant with anarchism" in "a place where wickedness and lawlessness abound to an alarming extent." But, in a larger sense, it was simply another action by the Reynolds administration intended to broaden the base of University support in the absence of high schools and to relieve it of a load the faculty carried with resentment and poor grace.

Reynolds, on the basis of past experience, favored dealing by committees with such matters as curriculum, admission requirements, and schedules of recitations and examinations rather than by meetings of the entire faculty. He recognized the need of having all departments no longer under the control of the general faculty but subject to the supervision and approval of the president of the University or the committee of instruction. He urged the completion of all buildings on campus, the unification of the state school system from kindergarten to the University, and an active program of public relations.

Like his predecessor, Reynolds urged in his June 9, 1894, report to the board that duties of the executive be defined "so he may avoid inefficiency by attempting less than his duty and collision by attempting more." He was aided in this when the Legislature the following year ordered the reduction of the unwieldy governing Board from thirteen to nine members, and prescribed that at no time could it number more than five members of the same political party. Overnight, the Legislature converted the Board from a strictly political to a bipartisan agency; and the Board, in turn, responded by making the office of the president more attractive.

The Regents found a secretary for the president; created the post of registrar; abolished the Easter vacation; and appointed a committee to codify the rules. More importantly, it authorized the president on June 13, 1895, to suspend any faculty member, subject to final action of the Board; and it empowered the president to remove other employees of the University subject to review by the executive committee. West Virginia University at last had the makings of a modern executive.

But the Board's principal task was to find a president. After several candidates and sponsors had been heard, State Senator D. S. Walton of Waynesburg, Pennsylvania, an uninvited participant, appeared on behalf of his pastor, the Reverend Dr. J. L. Goodknight. Born in Kentucky, educated in a log-cabin school, at Cumberland University, and the Union Theological Seminary, Goodknight had served as a pastor of several Presbyterian churches. He also had traveled abroad, studied at Edinburgh and Jena, and in 1891 accepted the Waynesburg pastorate. He looked good to the Board, perhaps because he was a Republican, perhaps because he convinced the Board that he would devote considerable time to organizing and managing University affairs.

Determined "that the reorganization of the University should be brought about as an evolution and not as a revolution," Goodknight first organized a cabinet of the heads of academic units to advise him on questions "pertaining to discipline and administration which are unprovided for by law or precedent." Delegating all matters pertaining to the work and discipline of the Preparatory Department to its faculty, he swept his desk clear of petty administrative matters by dividing the remainder of the University into four colleges and four schools. Goodknight admired his plan, not only because it put the University into a state of "advanced formative growth," but because it provided reorganization room for the "indefinite future expansion of Colleges, Schools and Departments" and because there would never be any need or cause for a future reorganization. As he saw it: "The present organization can be expanded so that a hundred or five hundred teachers could be employed without any conflict of work or interest."

And the central administration, he contended, by having placed individual responsibility upon specific individuals such as deans, directors, and department heads, would be "able at once to put their fingers upon the spot where there is weakness. It will enable them to detect at once any cause of friction by locating the person with whom the friction arises. This will eliminate the spreading of dissatisfaction throughout the University faculty, because it will demand each individual connected with the University to answer primarily to the one above him in authority."

Having brought the faculty under control, Goodknight's next step was to do the same with students. For this purpose, the fifth president advocated a system of faculty advisers for students, a new system that would provide not only governance but also guidance for the University's youthful clientele. It would be wrong to think that under such a system the advisers would be spies upon students, said the *West Virginia School Journal* in June, 1896.

According to the publication, the faculty would be "their friends and advisors in all things, helping them into desirable companionship, directing them into good habits, helping them out of difficulties, advising them in their studies."

At the same time, however, the official University catalogue of 1895-96 saw the faculty in roles other than friends: "Each student will consult his adviser as to the course of study best suited to the student. No student will be permitted to change his course of study without the permission of his adviser. The conduct of the student while at the University will be under the immediate supervision of his adviser."

Among Goodknight's reorganization efforts were projections and recommendations for more adequate compensation for faculty members. Suggesting in his 1896 report that each professor receive "an extra $100 for each five years of service, until a salary of $2,000 per annum shall be paid to all," Goodknight was able to convince the Board to endorse such an increase. But the plan never received the necessary funding because, in Goodknight's words, "it was thought best not to place the plan before the Legislature." However, in matters of budget making, the Board did authorize Goodknight to work for enactment of a mill tax plan for University support comparable to the laws then in force or in process of passage in states such as Ohio, Nebraska, Michigan, and Wisconsin.[5] The enthusiastic president advocated an assessment of one half a mill on each dollar of taxable property for the use of the University, but this scheme failed to pass the Legislature. The same was true for Goodknight's efforts to establish one or more high schools in each county of the state with a uniform high school curriculum. Yet the president earned credit for the enactment of a compulsory attendance law for students in the public schools and for the establishment of the West Virginia Economic and Geological Survey as an appendage of the University itself.

Goodknight sought vast expansion and change in the University. In his 1897 report, he urged better facilities for graduate study, the establishment of colleges of commerce, pharmacy, medicine, fine arts, and new developments along departmental lines such as the division of the department of chemistry and physics into two departments; creation of a department of political science, economics, and history; establishment of a department of pedagogy whose services would depart radically from those offered by the state normal (teacher training) schools; and creation of a department concerned with physical training. Although failing in most of these objectives except departmental reorganization, Goodknight was responsible for the establishment of a dispensary which provided medical service to students.

With regard to the College of Agriculture, he asked for and obtained separation of the Agricultural Experiment Station from the College of Agriculture. He also obtained the Swisher farm for the bargain price of $3,900.00. This farm of about 81 acres was situated on the Cheat River Road about one mile from the University. Goodknight also attempted a nation-wide campaign for the establishment at land-grant colleges and universities of federally and state-funded engineering experiment stations in imitation of federal funding projects for agriculture.

With respect to military instruction, another necessary ingredient of the Morrill Act, the Goodknight administration also was responsible for seeing that Cadet Corps members were furnished uniforms in addition to tuition and textbooks free of charge and, in accordance with acts passed by the 1897 Legislature, that the Corps of Cadets was made a part of the West Virginia National Guard, "subject to such duty as the commander-in-chief may order." In 1897, he saw additional funds appropriated for equipping the Agricultural Experiment Station farm, placing seats in the Commencement Hall gallery, re-cataloguing the library, constructing a wing to University (Woodburn) Hall, and purchasing the Old Cemetery land.

Successful in administrative and academic reorganization, Goodknight was singularly unsuccessful in handling matters of student conduct. Above all other criteria, he saw himself as a strict disciplinarian. He believed he should ferret out misbehavior before it became widespread across the campus. After getting wind of an epidemic of poker playing, Goodknight rushed into a student's room and received the necessary confirmation. As the *Morgantown Weekly Post* reported the president's intrusion into the private quarters of the students: "The boys were too amazed to make an attempt to conceal their stacks of blues, but one of them was polite enough to offer the doctor a chair, which he gracefully but coldly declined."

The president had his way with the card sharks. The faculty on January 11 and 14, 1896, tried the offenders, suspended two of them indefinitely, and two more for a year, and decided a fifth should be given probation for a like period. The statewide press was jubilant that a first step in disciplining students finally had been taken and the *Wheeling Intelligencer* editorialized on January 25:

The West Virginia University Faculty had done a good thing to discipline the students who have been giving up their rights to playing poker. We take it for granted that faculty would be sustained in this policy if the result should be to empty the university. The state does not maintain the university as a school for gamblers; and parents do not send their sons to the university to have them instructed in gambling arts.

Before Goodknight became president, the Board of Regents in 1894 had directed the faculty, as well as students, to attend chapel exercises. In 1895, a second order made chapel attendance by faculty and students compulsory, unless excused for good reason by the president. In behalf of the Board's ultimatum, the student roll was to be called every morning, and the unexcused absences of each professor reported to the Board. One newspaper editor had observed that the Board made "our chapel rules a little less like unto those necessary for a kindergarten . . ." and later said, "The President has acquired bronchitis in excusing chapel absences and in trying to command order during the holding of that entertaining exercise."[6] But the WVU catalogues of 1895 and 1896 spelled out the requirement in no uncertain terms:

Punctuality and regularity in attendance upon all required exercises; . . . Students who can not, or will not, comply with these requirements will not be allowed to remain in the University. Offenders will be warned, and will be given reasonable time to correct their conduct; if they do not amend, they will be dismissed.

The faculty minutes of March 5, 1896, interpreted reasonable time as no more than three unexcused absences in one year. When students took it upon themselves to show their displeasure by stamping during chapel exercises, the faculty added another warning on March 17 that "any student who is found guilty of creating disorder in chapel shall be dismissed from the West Virginia University."

On legal grounds, the students observed that compulsory chapel attendance was contrary to the principles of separation of church and state, principles upon which the institutions of West Virginia and the United States were founded. Great universities, the students added, never had required such attendance.

On April 11, 1896, the Board recognized Article 3, Section 15, of the West Virginia Constitution and the First Amendment of the Constitution of the United States by amending the chapel rules. Setting aside all previous regulations on chapel attendance, the Board required students to assemble at 10:15 a.m. for roll call and to hear necessary announcements. After this University business was attended to, any student was permitted to withdraw quietly and orderly after which simple devotional exercises would be held with regular class work resuming at 10:30.

The state press was aghast when it received reports of the Board's directive. Two weeks later, the *Parkersburg State Journal* lamented that "a state cannot teach religion nor direct public money derived by taxation to promulgating Christian culture, Christian doctrine and religious training."

One week after the directive, the *Morgantown Weekly Post* was of the opinion the fight had been "against compulsory attendance and the severe penalty inflicted for absence," and not against devotional exercises. A few newspapers wondered whether the Regents had been intimidated by organized students. If so, the press was certain they had made a grave mistake:

Boys or young men are not understood to be sent to college or to the State University to make rules, but to learn to obey them; and if they are to be encouraged by the authorities in the spirit of insubordination to law, better by far they be kept at home and the college closed. It is the besetting sin of the age and needs no assistance from the State for its encouragement; on the contrary, if the facts are as stated, the next Legislature should investigate the regents.[7]

There really was no doubt that the students had won the chapel battle, and they next sought to win student supervision over athletic operations. During one of his many reorganizations, Goodknight assigned control over athletics to a triumvirate comprised of the president, the commandant of cadets and the instructor in the School of Physical Training. But neither the president nor his athletic creation seemed strong enough when pitted against the students.

In his attitude toward athletics, Goodknight was bucking the development of an overemphasis on football. As he explained to the Board on June 6, 1896: "The athletic sports are likely to materially interfere with the work of this School. This should not be, because athletics do not give the physical improvement that the weak need. Athletics are in a large measure constituted for those who need little or no physical development by physical culture." But the president's philosophy on physical development for all students did not interest the students, nor did they consider his opinions binding. In this matter, students were guided by William J. Bruner, president of the senior class, athletic editor on the *Daily Athenaeum* staff, and guard on the football team in 1895 and 1896. According to Bruner, in his remarks to the student newspaper on October 13, 1896:

Students, especially the older and more experienced ones, being in close touch with their own student body and everything connected with the school have a better and more intimate knowledge of its needs. While students are often impetuous and self-willed, yet older persons must concede that generation after generation comes with *new* needs. The sober-minded students of a school know its needs better than any other persons can.

What Bruner wanted was the power for students to appoint the football coach and to dismiss Dr. J. W. Hartigan, director of the School of Physical Training, from control over University athletics. When the faculty suspended J. M. (Pat) Orr, a senior, for the remainder of the term on a charge of hissing at Dr. Hartigan when the latter passed a crowd of students, Bruner had found his issue. With his encouragement, the students bolted chapel. These events the faculty dutifully recorded in their minutes of October 28, October 30, and November 20, 1896.

Bruner, with Orr, could now be charged as a leader of the movement which had publicly arraigned the athletic faculty council. But the general faculty was conscious of the growing influence of students, if the presidential council was not, and the vice-president reminded his colleagues "that Mr. Bruner's sentiments and opinions are the same as those of about 300 other students . . . if his punishment was of such a nature as to give an offense to the student body, then we would have 300 students on our hands."

With extreme caution the faculty restricted its censure of Bruner to read that certain language used by him was considered a breach of discipline, that the faculty disapproved of such language, and if such an offense was committed by him or any other student in the future, the penalty would be more severe. Bruner was not found guilty of any other charge. The Board was angry, saying on February 9, 1897, it disapproved of the faculty's action in the Bruner trial, both as to the finding in the case and the punishment inflicted. In response to the Board's expression of disappointment, Vice-President Reynolds, who had led the fight for leniency, resigned his position as vice-president and dean of the College of Arts and Sciences.

Undeterred by Reynolds' actions, the Board rescinded all authority the faculty had exercised as a body in the field of student discipline and ordered that all matters regarding discipline be placed in the hands of a special triumvirate: the president of the University, the commandant of cadets, and the dean of the College of Agriculture.

Encouraged by the Board's actions, Goodknight next imposed censorship on the *Daily Athenaeum*, which had begun to lampoon the disciplinary council. The student newspaper also had derided the overseas travels and study of the president as well as calling attention to his peculiarities and personal eccentricities and those of the "Hayseed Dean." For such offenses, the editor, Howard L. Swisher, was hauled before the new Committee on Discipline. But after invoking the right of free speech and free press, and with appropriate apologies, Swisher was allowed to continue as editor on condition that he would obey the rules of censorship. The net result was that critics went underground and anonymously contributed the following literature on Hartigan, Myers, and the "red-nosed" Goodknight:

Oh cast your gaze on Prexy, triumphant standing there
His hot Kentucky ruby is red beyond compare
He has the hated faculty all in a horrid hole
By telling to the Regents a tale both weird and bold.

A tale of baffled justice, of punishment gone astray
Of efforts at discipline that have turned his whiskers gray.
Of a noble fight defeated, made by a martyr band
Of smart and brainey Profs, who by their Prexy stand.

Oh would the Board of Regents were smart instead of chumps
Then would the frauds triumphant right quickly get their bumps.
Facts only would be taken, base lies would hardly count
Brains, truth and common-sense with right be paramount.

Oh that the day may hasten on which the frauds are fired
With the thousand tales of villainy the student body's tired,
Unutterably we yearn and sigh with eagerness to see
The headless trunks of John A. Myers, Doc, Prex and his pedigree.[8]

Not only did the undercover publications continue, but they increasingly lampooned Goodknight, printing a biography of the president which claimed that he never had gotten much beyond his log school education, that he had graduated from Cumberland University only because school officials were tired of having him around and did not wish to injure the institution, and that all he had received from Union Theological Seminary was a red nose and a semi-sanctimonious twang to his voice. It suggested that his trips to Europe were spent talking with janitors and not the scholars of the institutions he claimed to have visited, that his research was limited to making a careful study of the menus of cheap hotels where he stopped, trying to discover the tendency of microbes to inhabit partly decayed food.[9]

With such indelicate flyers inundating the campus and the town, the *Morgantown Weekly Post* of March 6, 1897, urged a policy of "catch, kill and destroy" in dealing with students who were "so maliciously and slanderously making trouble." *The Wheeling Register* of April 1, 1897, recommended unlimited powers for a president who had been too long preempted by "a board that visits the institution occasionally and knows practically nothing of its practical needs."

By way of response to the stories of student misconduct and to the fact that Republicans were extending their political control to the executive department, the Legislature sent a joint committee on February 3, 1897, to investigate conditions at the University, and considered Senate Bill No. 167, providing for reorganization of the Board of Regents. The outgoing Democratic governor vetoed the reorganization bill by declaring:

I submit that it is wrong that any question of partisanship should obtain in any way, shape or form in the management of this institution; that those who are interested in this should not be dependent upon the mere whim of public political opinion, but should be dependent purely and entirely upon their qualifications to perform the important duties which under the law are set before them. The faculty should not be taught that they are dependent upon public opinion except in the manner of their work. Whenever, in my opinion, the faculty of a great teaching institution has thus learned that it is dependent not upon its ability to teach the youth, but rather upon its ability to trim with the political current, then, I say, we shall no longer have proficiency in educational matters; but rather we should look to teachers for proficiency in political trimming.[10]

The old Board was out and the new Board was in, and a majority of its members were Republican. The new Board refused to rehire either the president or the agricultural dean, and Goodknight and Myers thus became sacrificial lambs to the new industrial age. When both men, who had kept their faith with the evangelical orthodoxy, refused to quit their places, the Board suspended them from their offices and directed them to surrender and vacate their rooms and the premises. This request, the Board said on

The first Mountaineer football team runs through offensive drills with elliptical-shaped football in 1891. Building in rear is the Agricultural Experiment Station that includes the old Armory.

August 6, 1897, was not "intended to reflect upon any member of the late Board nor to justify insubordination on the part of students or members of the faculty."

But students had matters other than administrative turnovers resulting from political changes with which to concern themselves. In 1891, because of the enthusiasm of two WVU students, Melville Davisson Post and Billy Meyer, WVU had created its first football team, called in its early years the "Snakers." The two students raised $160, bought a football, uniforms, and a rule book, recruited players, practiced under Professor F. L. Emory who had been assigned the coaching duties by the University president, and met Washington and Jefferson College. Proceeds came from "Richard III," an amateur theatrical directed by Post. The inexperienced WVU team was defeated 72 to 0.

In 1893, with John C. Rane of Princeton serving as coach without pay, WVU lost to Washington and Jefferson, 58 to 0, but won over Mount Pleasant Institute 12 to 0, and the Uniontown Independents, 12 to 2; in 1894, with the same coach, it won two (Mount Pleasant and Bethany) and lost two (the Connellsville, Pa. Independents and Marietta College).

In 1895, WVU students produced their first outstanding team. Led by Fielding (Hurry Up) Yost as left tackle, coached by Harry McCrory, and captained by W. J. Bruner, the team won five of six games, losing only to Washington and Jefferson. The series with Pitt, then known as the Western University of Pennsylvania, began that season with a WVU victory, 8-0.

In 1896, WVU finally hired a full-time coach, Thomas G. (Doggy) Trenchard, Princeton All-American in 1893, who compiled a record of three wins, seven losses, and two ties. In 1897, George R. Krebs, who served as captain, took over the coaching job, producing a 5-4-1 record; in 1898, WVU, coached by Harry Anderson, had a 6-1 record. In addition, WVU was billed as "the champion of the South" because it beat Virginia 6-0 at a game in Charleston.

In 1899, coached by one of its players, Louis Yeager, WVU fell to a record of two wins, three losses; it recouped under Dr. John E. Hill (Yale) in 1900 and 1901 by fashioning 4-3 and 3-2 seasons. Schedules between 1899 and 1901 were shortened to a total of seventeen games, with WVU winning nine. In 1901, Ed Kenna produced one of the most notable performances in this early era in WVU football by dropkicking three field goals in the 37 to 0 victory over Grove City. Although football was not yet entrenched as a major WVU sport, it was on its way.

Chapter **4**

1897–1901

The Inner Wickedness
of Sociology

Jerome Hall Raymond
August 10, 1897–March 20, 1901

WHEN THE BOARD OF REGENTS announced on August 6, 1897, the selection of twenty-eight-year-old Jerome Hall Raymond, Ph.D., University of Chicago (1895), as president of West Virginia University and professor of sociology, the national press had a field day in broadcasting the choice of so young a man to such an eminent position. Journalistic interest was news in itself because earlier a local newspaper had observed that election of a WVU president was "attracting about as much attention as did the appointment of the Collector of Internal Revenue a few weeks ago."[1] Crucial to the selection, the press was certain, would be a healthy amount of logrolling. The candidate best able to keep up appearances and preserve the status quo doubtlessly would win. When national magazines and newspapers reacted to the Regents' surprising decision, it was hard to say who profited most from the news releases, the youthful president or the adolescent University. Certainly Raymond was different from the past ministerial-type presidents.

A newsboy, telegraph messenger, and office boy in his early youth, a stenographer at thirteen, and an employee of the Pullman

Palace Car Company at sixteen, Raymond had become private secretary to its president, George M. Pullman. He also had served as secretary to Miss Frances E. Willard, president of the Women's Christian Temperance Union. "For three years he was my stenographer," Miss Willard wrote of the Northwestern University student, "and in the quiet den where I worked with joyful continuity . . . he helped me as perhaps hardly any other has ever done, for his work was at once so rapid and so accurate that I did not have to look it over, and I was able to put several days' effort into one . . ."[2] To Miss Willard, Raymond, the student working his way through college, had become the embodiment of the perfect man, for during a fatherless youth "he learned none of the evil ways of the street, never wasted a penny on tobacco, liquor, or any other evil indulgence, and brought home all that he earned to the mother and sister who formed his world."

Raymond also had served as assistant to the president of Northwestern, and, after receiving his bachelor's and master's degrees there, was principal of the University's academy. He also pursued post-graduate studies at Northwestern, the University of Chicago, and Johns Hopkins University of Baltimore. Traveling abroad in the summer of 1890 with Bishop James M. Thoburn of the Methodist Episcopal Church as the prelate's private secretary, Raymond visited the leading universities in Europe and studied Sanskrit in Asia. When he returned from this world-wide tour, he lectured at the Chautauqua School and next occupied the chair of history and political science at Lawrence University in Wisconsin. While completing his Ph.D. in sociology, he served as an assistant in the department of sociology at the University of Chicago, and, when called to West Virginia University, the young and successful academician held the dual posts of professor of sociology and secretary of extension at the University of Wisconsin.

Associations with Bishop Thoburn, George Pullman, and Frances Willard, while perhaps endearing Raymond to churchmen, corporate interests, and the "drys," did not prevent him from receiving the support of the liberal side of academe. Endorsed by President Charles W. Eliot of Harvard University and by President William Rainey Harper of the University of Chicago, he also was supported by faculty members at Princeton, Yale, Wisconsin, Chicago, and institutions such as the Smithsonian. Professor Richard T. Ely wrote to Raymond from Madison, Wisconsin, on November 6, 1897: "You have evidently roused a great deal of enthusiasm, and it is manifest that your administration has opened a new epoch in the history of the University of West Virginia. The institution was scarcely heard of before you went there."

Charles Zueblin, sociologist with the University of Chicago, prophesied on October 13, 1897, that Raymond would ". . . do for Morgantown what *Pabst has done for Milwaukee.* You'll have 'a hot time in the old town tonight' tomorrow and tomorrow night and many more nights we hope and believe." Dr. Lester F. Ward, geologist and sociologist with the Smithsonian Institution, penned the following congratulatory note to the new president on December 12, 1897: "Your name and picture must be as familiar throughout the land as McKinley's . . . It seems as though every newspaper and periodical I pick up has you in it. When people marvel at what you have accomplished I tell them that what you have done is 'small potatoes' to what you will do and to keep their eyes on you and watch the sparks fly."

Amidst the congratulatory messages and favorable coverage by the media, Regent William E. Powell cautioned Raymond that his task ahead would be difficult. In prophetic language he advised the sixth president of West Virginia University on January 15, 1898:

Be as patient as possible with the slowness and stupidity of our people. While it takes time to build a University, it also takes time to develope [sic] a people who have never had a chance to be what they should be . . . You have made not only a good but a brilliant beginning and it would be most unfortunate for you personally if any thing should seem to make it necessary for you to leave Morgantown . . . You are young, but be as wise, as discreet and careful as possible so there shall be no real room for complaint such as is likely to arise when dealing with such people as you find in W. Va.

Raymond, however, steamed ahead, seemingly unmindful of Powell's concern that he might kill himself by overwork. One of Raymond's immediate objectives was increasing WVU's enrollment and he tackled the problem head-on by using old techniques presented as new ones and by fundamental curriculum changes aimed at being more appealing to the twentieth-century student. By augmenting WVU's head-count, he judged himself successful. Before he completed his four-year tenure, all departments, schools, and colleges had been enlarged, strengthened, and better equipped with laboratories, apparatus, and facilities; and professors, instructors and assistants had increased from about thirty to sixty-five while attendance doubled from 465 to 882.

Instituting correspondence work, which he presented as innovative, Raymond failed to deceive perceptive observers who saw simply a new form of extension service. Without funds to employ a separate staff for such activity, Raymond leaned heavily upon professors who volunteered, some willingly, others grudgingly. Professor St. George Tucker Brooke, one of the latter, wrote the president indignantly, on May 20, 1898: "If you receive any more letters from parties desiring instruction in Blackstone, please return the money to them, or turn it over to some one else — I shall not receive it."

But faculty dissatisfaction with correspondence work was minimal, the program was advertised nationally, and Raymond's effort paid off with inquiries and enrollment from many states. Although qualifications for admission to the program were purposefully vague, 160 students enrolled in correspondence courses during the first year of operation.

Another of Raymond's cosmetic changes was renaming the student adviser system the class officer system, whereby such officers adopted a new-fangled "card system" of registration. But more fundamental to the problem of sustaining enrollment, if not necessarily increasing it, were changes in the requirements for degrees. For example, the philosophical course leading to the degree of Bachelor of Philosophy required one classical language "but not both"; the modern literature course leading to the Bachelor of Letters required neither classical language but an equivalent amount of French or German; a two-year course leading to the Bachelor of Agriculture degree could be obtained without any foreign language requirement at all.

Raymond not only watered down the curriculum, but also reshaped it to fit a new system of four quarters, one of which was a summer session. Thus, he provided for one long continuous session of twelve months in a given University academic year. The summer session, new to the University and to West Virginia, was also new to most of the country at that time. Because of the novelty of summer school, the president advertised it widely, and to make it popular to students of all ages, he recruited a platoon of lecturers known to be capable of stimulating their audiences anywhere.

Attracting students of all ranks from thirty-one West Virginia counties and thirteen states, the very first summer quarter had an enrollment of 190, of which 100 were new students. The summer attendance not only boosted the resident enrollment in 1897-98 to 744, but also permitted Raymond to see significance in the fact that the number on the rolls during the twelve-week summer session exceeded the total in attendance in any single year of the University before 1889. Because of his success in stimulating the student census, the Legislature responded to his budgetary needs with an appropriation of $3,000 per year for the maintenance of the summer quarters for the 1899-1900 biennium. In 1899 and 1900, enrollments reached 250 for each of the two years of special appropriation. Again, Raymond was able to provide a splendid array of public lecturers for each of the sessions. On March 18, 1899, former WVU President William L. Wilson, then president of Washington and Lee University at Lexington, Virginia, wrote Raymond with envy about his innovative summer school: "You have the best and clearest field in the South, and it is encouraging that the State is rising to its duty in helping you to cultivate it with success."

Raymond borrowed the idea of correspondence work and visiting lecturers from Chicago and Wisconsin. The elective system, certain to be popular and, hopefully, conducive to increasing the WVU headcount, originated not at Virginia but at Harvard. In fact, in his report to the Board of Regents in 1900, Raymond was fond of quoting Harvard's President Eliot who had said: "A well instructed youth of eighteen can select for himself a better course of study than any college faculty, or any wise man who does not know him and his ancestors and his previous life can possibly select for him . . . The safest guide to a wise choice will be the taste, inclination and special capacity of each individual."

What was good enough for Harvard was therefore good enough for WVU. With Raymond's encouragement, the faculty adopted and the Board approved the new methods for the new century.

According to the 1899-1900 WVU catalog, the rules were amazingly simple. After a student working toward the A.B. degree had completed ten courses and a thesis in a major subject, the professor in charge of the student's major prescribed minor study or collateral work, not to exceed six courses, as he, the adviser, might consider needed. All remaining work, twenty-six courses, was elective with the student free to choose any subject taught in the University for which his studies had prepared him. Previously, of seventy hours of work, forty had been prescribed, with mathematics, English, physics, chemistry, Greek, and Latin dominating the requirements.

Not only did Raymond make academic work more palatable to increasing numbers of students, but he also recommended the abolition of chapel exercises which nineteenth-century students "had not meekly endured." Chapel was a bore to most students and enforcing attendance had become the most difficult problem in managing the University. Advising Raymond to rid the state institution of the religious obligation were four former presidents of the University, two former acting presidents, and countless others. Raymond, recognizing in an undated office memo that daily chapel exercises had been "the danger point in the administration of the University," observed that "the daily chapel audience, therefore, is much like a powder magazine, requiring only a single spark to ignite and explode the whole."

Converting chapel into an optional exercise by abolishing the roll call, the Board had provided on June 8, 1898, for devotionals each morning beginning promptly at eight o'clock and concluding at eight-thirty. Featured at these services were singing, prayer, Scripture reading, and a brief lecture. In addition, the faculty approved college credit for one third of a course (equivalent to one hour) for each quarter of attendance, provided the student submitted to the chaplain satisfactory notes of the lectures.

Because of the lack of feeder schools in the state, Raymond urged retention of the University's Preparatory Department. Since the department had bolstered enrollment in the past, it could do so in the future; and until the state possessed many more high schools than it then had, Raymond vehemently opposed its dismemberment. While not opposing the establishment of a preparatory school at Keyser, comparable to the one at Montgomery, the president found himself at odds with the legislative report that argued the

University's preparatory school might well "give way to the pressing necessity for room and opportunity for those seeking more advanced study."[3] To Raymond, the University Preparatory Department was economically justified because there was "no other place in the state where so good a school could be maintained at so small a cost." Besides, such a school offered advantages that the state could not provide other schools: the largest library in the state, museums, public lectures, a gymnasium, a military department, and a music department. Raymond was overruled, although he later won the battle in absentia several years after leaving Morgantown.

Before the question was settled, Raymond secured admission of women to the Preparatory Department as well as to the schools of music and fine arts. By such action, the Raymond administration heralded in its 1898 report to the Board the idea that "the co-education of the sexes was completely established in the University." It was another victory for Raymond, who always was interested in improving enrollment statistics. In 1895-96 and 1896-97, female students on campus numbered only 35 and 38; in 1897-98 and 1898-99, the figure jumped to 112, and by the 1899-1900 academic year, the number of women soared to 240. In their own interest, they organized the Women's League, a clearing house for social and intellectual activities on campus and in town.

Not only did women break the barriers of the Preparatory Department, the fine arts, and liberal arts, but also one of the professional schools, law. The first woman to receive the LL.B. from West Virginia University, the first to be admitted to the bar in Monongalia County, and the first woman lawyer in West Virginia was Agnes J. Morrison, who, with her husband, Charles J. Morrison, was graduated in the class of 1895. When Mrs. J. G. Frazier, another law student, arrived in Morgantown from Martinsburg on horseback in 1898 wearing a "divided skirt," riding "man fashion," and carrying "a brace of pistols," women gave evidence of further iconoclastic triumphs. Love of outdoor exercises prompted the novel ride, explained the *Morgantown Weekly Post* on March 17, 1898.

The advent of women in ever larger numbers led Raymond to make three requests of the Legislature in 1898, 1899, and 1900 for a dormitory for women, "where home comforts and home surroundings might be provided for the girls from out of town"; a dean of women who would be "a college woman, broad-minded, cultured, refined, sympathetic, for a woman understands women as no man could"; and a department of domestic science "for the purpose of teaching good cooking and scientific housekeeping." The election of Hannah Belle Clark, Ph.D., University of Chicago, as assistant professor of domestic science and dean of women on August 15, 1899, realized two of those goals. To allay suspicion that expenditures for such items were a waste of money, Raymond carefully explained that the department of domestic science was to be maintained from the Morrill fund and therefore did not cost the state a penny.[4]

Raymond's obvious interest in the number of students did not mean he was disinterested in the quality of faculty or other academic concerns. He gave the library, housed in a single room in Preparatory (later Martin) Hall, special attention. When he arrived at WVU, he found 14,000 books and 2,000 pamphlets uncatalogued and unclassified. This, he reported to the Board in June, 1898, made the library "a hopeless tangle" in that "the books were not arranged but simply placed upon the shelves anywhere where space allowed." An untrained librarian, Clara Hough, "found time to retire to the alcoves and devote herself to fancy work, while generally too busy to cut her books and magazines, or hunt up a book for some student." Raymond also discovered that library conditions were complicated by the existence of several departmental libraries where scarce money had "in many cases been invested in books for the professors' special use," some of which were duplicates of works in the main library.

In a program of sweeping reform, he hired a trained librarian, Eliza J. Skinner of the library school of the Armour Institute of Technology at Chicago, who classified the library material according to the Dewey Decimal System, merged the departmental libraries into the main library, and kept the library open on a regular, scheduled basis. Reading lists were posted, a charging system was initiated, and instruction in using the facility was given by Miss Skinner each summer quarter with special attention to methods of research. As a result, Raymond argued, the University now had a "model library."

In ridding his administration of the stigma of awarding honorary degrees, Raymond acted upon the advice of his mentor, President Harper of Chicago, who wrote him on March 7, 1898: "Your friends all over the country will look with reproach upon your administration if you begin giving honorary degrees . . . I sincerely hope that you will stand firm regardless of consequences. I would go so far as to make an issue on the question even if I lost my presidency." Regent William E. Powell concurred, although he wrote on March 29, 1898, that he had not known "of the desperate efforts being made for degrees." Still, Powell allowed, he was not surprised "because there are a lot of hungry ones." Not only did the Board refuse complimentary degrees in 1898 and 1899 but it authorized and instructed the University President on June 21, 1899, to insert in the next catalog the announcement: "No Honorary Degrees are Conferred."

In the matter of earned degrees, Raymond ordered each faculty member to submit all degrees for publication in the 1897-98 Catalog, with full descriptive matter showing source, year, and description of study (graduate and undergraduate). This was decreed without faculty approval, and resulted in some embarrassment to those who held only honorary degrees.

To strengthen the faculty, Raymond proposed in his inaugural address to establish a department of University extension lectures, similar to what he had been doing at the University of Wisconsin. His roster of lecturers was of high order, but there were those in Morgantown left aghast at some of the new ideas the lecturers cultivated. One of the more bothersome was Lester F. Ward, called by some the father of American sociology and by others the "architect of the modern welfare state." One unidentified "observer" in a letter to the *New Dominion* dated August 3, 1898, characterized Ward as teaching that marriage was more a convenience than a sacred institution, that a man should leave a woman he did not love and live with one he did love, that present marriage laws were responsible for the high divorce rate, and that of all the forms of marriage, monogamy was the most absurd and ridiculous.

Even University professors were incensed. On July 30, 1898, Professor Robert W. Douthat wrote to former Governor A. B. Fleming an indictment of Raymond's guest lecturers as well as a criticism of the discipline of sociology:

Knowing you to be a good man, a lover of all that is best for the individual, the State, and the Nation, and as particularly interested in the welfare of the University, let me beg you to come over to Morgantown for just one piece of a day and see with your own eyes and hear with your own ears. Nothing like it has ever been here before: it stirs the indignation of all good people, and yet the Professors are so hampered that they cannot utter themselves. Please come over 'on business' and I assure you the inner wickedness of Sociology will be understood as never before. 'Come over & help us!'

As an aid to faculty teaching, Raymond also proposed teaching assistants in 1898; the Legislature and the Board of Regents concurred. The appointment of "fellows" helped serve yet another Raymond purpose: the overhauling and broadening of graduate study. By order in the faculty minutes of September 14, 1897, a master's degree now consisted of "twelve hours work, or its equivalent," and a satisfactory thesis. A graduate committee formulated requirements for the Ph.D. comparable to those at Chicago, Wisconsin, and Johns Hopkins. The faculty adopted these changes without question.

Raymond also reorganized the academic programs. Schools and courses within Arts and Sciences, Engineering, and Agriculture became departments. The only schools remaining were the preparatory and the commercial, to which was added a school of music in 1897. After changing the military school into a military department, Raymond also added four departments: elocution and public speaking, drawing and painting (fine arts), correspondence, and physical training. Raymond took special interest in abolishing the school of pedagogy and relegating it to the College of Arts and Sciences as a department. Separate departments of history and political science were established, and Raymond announced courses in sociology and economics which he himself would teach with the aid of special lecturers.

Raymond was responsible for securing full rights for all members of the faculty; even assistant professors enjoyed the right to be heard and the right to vote. Raymond also encouraged the Board of Regents to provide a definition of the professional ranks, with the salary for each rank and the annual election of all officers of instruction below the rank of professor. Since he had been able to introduce the year-round quarter system, Raymond obtained an order from the Board on June 9, 1898, providing for payment of University salaries in twelve installments.

He encouraged one department above all others to aspire for greater status — the medical department. In 1899, the Board of Regents ordered that the medical course in the College of Arts and Sciences be extended to cover two years of work following completion of such general education requirements as the faculty deemed proper. The student who took the A.B. medical course, which prescribed scientific and medical studies during the junior and senior year, would be graduated with the A.B. degree and a certificate which hopefully would be credited according to the 1899-1900 Catalog, "everywhere as the equivalent of the first two years in a medical school."

New appointments also were made in the Department of Medicine, notably Alfred Edward Thayer, appointed professor of *materia medica* and pathology. It was Dr. Thayer who made lasting contributions to the medical program by insisting upon an anatomical law to legalize the procurement of cadavers for dissection, as well as seeking additional space for laboratories. and classes and University membership in the Association of American Medical Colleges.[5] This latter suggestion, however, was not realized as the Association recognized only a year of work done outside the jurisdiction of an accredited medical college and urged WVU to organize such a school. Responding to the recommendation on June 22, 1900, the Board of Regents created a College of Medicine to be operated "without additional expense for professors and instructors." Being unable to augment the instructional staff meant that the A.B. medical course had in fact little more than a new name. However, a course in pharmacy was offered for the first time at the beginning of the autumn quarter in 1900.

Along with his plans for academic reorganization, Raymond announced that the faculty would share in the conduct of University affairs. To fulfill his promise, the Board of Regents authorized on August 14, 1899, the appointment by the president of twenty-three standing committees, each with authority to act in its own jurisdiction. But in case the faculty became too heady with this power, the Board of Regents specified on April 5, 1900, that the president be ex-officio chairman of all committees. As further evidence of democracy, Raymond abolished the position of vice-president. This meant that Professor Robert Allen Armstrong, who had been in charge of the University during the interregnum before Raymond's appointment, was without his office of vice-president, which he had occupied without formal reappointment since the expiration of his one-year term in June, 1898.

To accompany the many academic changes, Raymond planned to improve and expand the physical plant valued at $396,000 in 1898. With an eye to beautification, maples and elms were planted, brick walks to all buildings were laid, and an iron fence was erected around most of the campus. "To provide room that [would] soon be indispensable, and to avoid being crowded by the town," the Board purchased in 1898 the Fife property of about eight acres adjoining the northeastern side of the campus and two lots adjoining the Methodist Cemetery that made the total in that area exceed three acres. It also hired a University night watchman in 1898 and a University gardener in 1899.

On March 4, 1899, the Mechanical Building, containing the wood and metal-working shops, the mechanical and electrical engineering laboratories and drawing rooms, and the electric light and power plant, went up in smoke. Consequently, the University had to construct a new mechanical hall, and this set the stage during 1899-1900 for the planning of two additional buildings.

Centered on the old Methodist cemetery site was a library building, a three-story structure built of native sandstone in the Richardson Romanesque style, begun during the autumn quarter of 1901. The new Armory was constructed as a result of the martial spirit generated by the war with Spain in 1898. Located at the east end of the Fife tract facing the drill ground, it was built of brick and faced with stone. At the same time the Armory was constructed, the Board of Regents recommended expanding the Cadet Corps, limited by law to 144 members. The 1903 Legislature responded by placing the ceiling at 225 members, and repealed that section of the existing law which made the Cadet Corps a component of the West Virginia National Guard.

By purchasing the 91-acre Gilmore farm in 1898, Raymond replaced the two-year-old University farm which was sold. This purchase was for dairy experimental purposes. In 1901, the north wing of University (Woodburn) Hall finally was completed.

At the time of his inauguration, Raymond had called for a central light, heat, and power plant; "church halls" at the University to resolve student housing problems; a woman's hall; a library building; and a music building. He also had asked alumni and other friends of the University to subscribe funds for the purchase of a pipe organ and had recommended construction of an infirmary building and hiring of a trained nurse. To some of his critical

First home exclusively for WVU engineering programs was Mechanical Hall, built in 1892 and destroyed by fire in 1899. It was located on Beechurst Avenue near what is now Stansbury Hall.

friends, he was moving too fast. As one said, "His idea about how to run a University seemed to be to pick it up and shake it to pieces and make it over some morning before breakfast."[6]

But Raymond was not one to count his victories or his defeats in terms of a projected building program. Neither was he one to overlook the need for physical improvements on behalf of showier projects. Water pipes were extended to the top floors of all buildings, landslides checked in the rear of Science Hall, athletic and drill grounds were graded, and the mayor of the town of Seneca (in which the campus was located from 1898 to 1901) was given the option of repairing the tottering bridge over Falling Run hollow or seeing the structure torn down. Even the naming of buildings originated in the Raymond administration. Regent James Brown recommended, and the Board adopted on April 19, 1899, the suggestion that the structure known as Preparatory Building be named Martin Hall, in honor of Alexander Martin, the first president of WVU.

Raymond's victories were such that some thought him enlightened in all matters pertaining to academe. As A. E. Winship, editor of the *Journal of Education* saw it on October 12, 1899, West Virginia University under Raymond's leadership had been "transformed from a quiety [sic], old-time country college into a thoroughly modern institution, equipping itself with the best talent, and dealing heroically with every problem." A greatly improved faculty, a building program, the picturesque surroundings, freedom-of-choice in admission standards, fellowships, correspondence courses, and an elective system all showed that the president had the vision to encourage his institution to enter new fields. "All praise to President Raymond, and to his ardent, social, scholastic, and professional companion, and to his assistant Waitman Barbe, who has familiarized the youth of the state with privileges awaiting them at the University," editorialized Winship.

But Winship was in error when he pictured Raymond as the total academician perceptive in all matters relating to students, faculty, and the state. To some, Raymond was impossibly puritanical. Regent W. E. Powell, whose social and moral views often duplicated those of the president, approvingly wrote Raymond on January 18, 1899:

I notice that you are sifting out some of the rubbish — the fellows who go to the University to smoke, drink, dance, and loiter and play, and do anything else but study. If a few inferior students believe more in the exersize [sic] of their toes than they do in the exersize [sic] of their branes [sic], that is their privilege, but it does not in any way, as I understand it, compel you or the Board of Regents to provide for such low and degrading exercise in connection with the closing days of the school year.

Raymond, whose opposition to dancing amounted to an obsession, persuaded the Board of Regents to restrict Saturday night dances in the gymnasium to once a month. Moreover, they were to begin at eight o'clock

North wing of Woodburn Hall was completed in 1900.

and end promptly at ten. He also ruled on November 5, 1897, that the mid-winter and Commencement balls were "understood to be in lieu of, and not in addition to the usual Saturday night ball in the month in which they are held." With the support of the student YMCA and YWCA, the Protestant clergy, and the newspapers, Raymond was able to persuade the Board to abolish the Commencement ball.

Raymond also ordered that "no member of the faculty shall at any time, under any circumstances, use tobacco." As a result, Raymond became the butt of practical jokes; students filled his desk with cigarettes; and the faculty openly defied the order. The story goes that the irrepressible Professor Brooke, who, if he ever had smoked, long since had abandoned tobacco, promptly "stocked up" with "Wheeling tobies" and smoked them on his front porch as the president passed by.[7] In like manner Raymond's injunction against singing "Dixie" at University programs "popularized that tune throughout the length and breadth of West Virginia" and further cost him popularity among students and members of the faculty.

Try as it might, the administration could not prevent battles between students and police. After defeating Washington and Jefferson College in a baseball game and winning an oratorical contest at Bethany College in May, 1900, students rallied around a bonfire contrary to the order of a patrolman. When the officer attempted to make arrests, the students threw him down, broke his helmet, stole his mace, and ripped the brass buttons from his coat for souvenirs. Because of this episode, Thomas R. Horner, a law student, was arrested for assaulting an officer. Though defended by Dean Okey Johnson of the College of Law, Horner was fined $25.00 and costs in Mayor S. A. Posten's court.[8]

The same Thomas R. Horner later was dismissed from the University by order of the Board of Regents for having "written and caused to be published certain articles reflecting upon and abusing the management of the University"; and for having "circulated . . . among the students of the University certain petitions asking for the removal of the President." When the Grand Lodge of the West Virginia Knights of Pythias held a meeting in Morgantown at Commencement Hall on October 10, 1900, the students got their revenge for Horner's dismissal. Hissing Mayor S. A. Posten, and crying "Dixie" whenever the Glee Club sang, the students kept the committee on student affairs busy disciplining those who had created the disorder by producing a "mighty noise — applauding, hissing, catcalls, and shouting of all kinds."[9] Meeting in October, the committee ordered H. G. Chapman, William G. Milligan, and Second Lieutenant Matthew Mansfield Neely suspended from the University until September 1, 1901. It further ordered Milligan and Neely dismissed from the Cadet Corps and Neely deprived of his commission. The severity of punishment imposed upon Neely, a future governor and U.S. senator from West Virginia, was thought necessary because "he took part in the hollowing; his voice seemed to be the signal for the beginning and end of the hollowing."[10]

On October 22, the committee ordered that two officers, Cadet Major James R. Moreland and Cadet Major Frank B. Corbin, be dropped from the Cadet Corps for their failure to prevent disorderly conduct. Four days later, Moreland and Corbin appealed to the State Adjutant General and to the Board of Regents. Neely, who had been arrested on a state warrant and bound over to a Monongalia County grand jury on the charge of disturbing a public meeting, decided on another course of action when a jury found the evidence insufficient for indictment. Neely sued for reinstatement as a student and as a cadet in the University. But the case of Matthew Mansfield Neely vs. the Regents of West Virginia was disposed of by action of the Board. On December 20, 1900, the Regents ruled that the penalty of suspension to date had been adequate punishment for Neely, that he be reinstated, that the order dropping Neely from the Cadet Corps be set aside, and that the president of the Board be instructed to make an amended return to said writ of mandamus.

On December 22, 1900, the Committee on Student Affairs not only restored Cadet officers Moreland and Corbin to their respective commands but ordered the reinstatement of Chapman and Milligan, with amnesty for others. If the Board of Regents closed the Neely action with notice that it did not recognize the right of petitioner Neely to sue and that it accepted no liability for the costs of the case, students were to have the last word in the 1901 yearbook: "The conflict is over, the din of battle has hushed, the smoke has cleared away, and Moreland, Corbin, and Neely are with us yet."

But Raymond's problems with students were nothing compared to his problems with the faculty. Perhaps this troublesome relationship was due to factors one aroused alumnus had written about in a description of WVU teachers: "Practically every man in the institution, when I left it in '93, had secured his position through some pull and held it in mortal terror. Most of them were unfit for their positions."[11] To the former student, there were members of the WVU faculty he respected as men but not as instructors, men he respected as instructors but not as men, and men he did not respect at all.

The last sentiment undoubtedly was held by President Raymond, particularly when he thought of James W. Hartigan who had vehemently opposed the establishment of a two-year medical school. Hartigan was to pay dearly for having accused the president and the Regents of padding the University Catalog and falsifying records in their effort to promote a medical college. As an expression of the president's displeasure (and the Board's), Raymond ordered on June 9, 1898, the abolishment of all medical and dispensary fees which Hartigan had collected from students on a semi-private basis since 1896. As evidence of further annoyance, Raymond also found it necessary to eliminate from the catalog Hartigan's claim of having a Doctor of Science degree from Wooster College when evidence appeared to indicate the credentials were doubtful.[12]

With Hartigan dispatched on a leave and Armstrong eliminated from the vice-presidency, the Raymond administration displayed a tendency to label most internal criticism as stemming from the partisanship of Democrats. But when State Superintendent of Free Schools James Russell Trotter, a Republican and a graduate of Harvard, voiced objections, the same could not be said.

Trotter charged that a change in entrance requirements had become a cheap way to increase enrollments, an effort to get quantity at the expense of quality in education. As he saw it, scholarship was "no longer the prerequisite for either student or instructor"; for the student it was graduation or attendance at the University of Chicago; for the instructor it was the grand total of students that counted.

Trotter also charged that University standards had been lowered through the admission of women, through the use of correspondence courses, through the elective system, and through the cheapened summer quarter with the result that degrees were easy to obtain. To the State Superintendent of Free Schools, the standard of scholarship had become lower and lower in the frantic scramble for students. Raymond, he added, had demonstrated no fitness for the position he held, for he was "faddish, impractical and extravagant."

Rushing to the president's defense, the *Athenaeum* claimed that coeducation had strengthened the University; that professors, though underpaid, did not object to helping earnest students through correspondence courses; that not one person in a thousand could escape taking basic courses in English and in mathematics; and that the summer quarter should have further trial. In opposition to Trotter's opinion, the *Wheeling Register* of October 26, 1899, was also quick to point out that scholarship was safe at WVU and "if there is any criticism along this line that might be thought justified, and which some have been disposed to make, it is that the standard of the University has been advancing too fast to suit the conditions of the population of the state."

Perhaps the few newspapers that challenged Trotter's remarks encouraged the president to further action. Certainly the defeat of Trotter as State Superintendent of Free Schools at the beginning of the new century must have seemed a favorable omen. In an obvious bid to discipline a recalcitrant faculty, Raymond requested (and the Board ordered on April 5, 1900) that all members of the faculty and staff be present at their posts on the opening of each quarter and that throughout the quarter, "up to and including the last day of the quarter," they "meet their classes unless excused by the President of the University." At first Raymond merely indicated that the measure was directed at the truancy of certain unnamed professors, but before long those individuals were identified. The recognition dramatically occurred when the president sought the dismissal of Professors James S. Stewart, Robert A. Armstrong, Robert W. Douthat, James W. Hartigan, and Samuel B. Brown, all on the grounds of insubordination and incompetence. He also requested that the Board reprimand Professors St. George Tucker Brooke, R. L. Morris, and Director James H. Stewart for behavior unbecoming men of their stations and deportment inconsistent with University policy and aims.

Following a hearing for each of the accused, the Board postponed action until its regular June meeting. The delay caused Raymond to offer his resignation, which read in part:

I am moved to do this, and thus to give up some of the most deeply cherished hopes of my life, because I see no prospect of final success in my work. It is impossible to build up a University save on the basis of sound morals and sound scholarship with the generous cooperation of those engaged in the work. I have asked the removal of certain men known to you and to me and to the community to be grossly deficient in one or all of these regards. This demand your honorable Board refused to grant for reasons which I cannot deem sufficient. I therefore ask you to relieve me of any responsibility for the conduct of the University, this act to be effective June 21, 1900.

Laying Raymond's communication on the table, the Board soon received another message from Raymond asking leave to "withdraw and modify his letter of resignation of April 6, 1900." The Board granted his request, and Raymond submitted a shorter communique: "I beg to tender my resignation as President of the University and Professor of Economics and Sociology, to take effect October 1, 1900."

By a 5-4 vote on June 22, 1900, the Regents declined the second resignation. Adopting resolutions condemning "disloyalty to properly constituted authority," they asserted their determination to bring an end to such activity by "prompt and summary dismissal of any person connected with the University, if such conduct is persisted in." Thus, by a 5-4 vote in special meetings on December 17-20, 1900, the Regents ordered the dismissal of Professors Armstrong and Hartigan.

Governor G. W. Atkinson encouraged Raymond to believe that he approved of Raymond's conduct of University affairs. In friendly vein, he wrote the president on December 24, 1900:

I have been on College Boards long enough to know that the President of a University or College must be absolutely sustained by the Board of Directors, or no success can be attained.

I have several times, in the past twenty years, as a member of two or three College Boards of Directors, voted to dismiss Professors, simply because they were hostile to the Presidents of the institutions.

The University has grown remarkably under your management. This is generally conceded; but because you possess aggressive qualities, and are determined to push things, a great many people are opposing you.

This is only to be expected. If you were simply a figurehead President you would have no opposition. The men in public places, who do something and amount to something, are the ones that are invariably abused.

I like a man with teeth and corners and edges. There are plenty of 'gummers' in the world, but they never accomplish anything. I mean with teeth, when he shuts his mouth, generally makes somebody squeal, because as John Allen, of Mississippi says, 'He has a piece of the other fellow's Y'ear in his mouth!'

But Atkinson was the outgoing governor, and A. B. White, the incoming governor, preferred to let the Legislature resolve the University crisis. True to form, the 1901 Legislature appointed an investigating committee which recommended removal of President Raymond, reorganization of the Board of Regents, abolition of fellowships at the University, termination of the Preparatory Department of Morgantown, and ending of the summer quarter. The president was found to be "too young and inexperienced to deal with men"; his views and policies were declared "unsuited to West Virginia conditions."

Agreeing with the recommendations, the Legislature required the governor to appoint a new board, and the Senate attached riders to the University appropriation bill freezing all funding until "the Board of Regents accepts the resignation of the present president of the University." In addition, the Legislature decreed that even after Raymond's departure, no funds could be used to maintain a summer quarter or a Department of Domestic Science. It was unquestionably a political rather than an educational decision because all state boards and agencies were reorganized in 1901 and Atkinson's Democratic appointees were removed by the Republican organization under the domination of Stephen B. Elkins, the emerging political force in West Virginia.

The new board met in special session on March 17, 1901; and on March 20 accepted the resignation of President Raymond, effective at the end of the spring term. It vested the powers and duties of the president in the former vice-president and acting president, P. B. Reynolds, who would serve from March 21, 1901, until August 1, 1901.

On May 14, 1901, the executive committee of the old board placed on record a summary of the "Work of the Last Four Years." It highlighted coeducation, abolition of honorary degrees, the four-quarter session, establishment of schools of music and medicine and the departments of pharmacy, fine arts, domestic sciences, rhetoric and elocution; correspondence instruction; voluntary chapel attendance; abolition of public balls and dances in University buildings and under University auspices; a "scientifically classified" library; and a department of physical training equipped with a gymnasium, swimming pool, and bath room.

But it remained for Professor Hartigan to put the final shabby touches on the affair in contrast to the outgoing board, which was attempting to put the best face possible on the incidents. Having been denied redress by a decision handed down by the State Supreme Court of Appeals in March, 1901, declaring that a professor was not a public officer, Hartigan brought a slander suit in Monongalia County Circuit Court against President Raymond. This suit, too, was dismissed. Hartigan's last effort was to attempt to attach Raymond's baggage at the railroad station. Again, the court denied his petition, contending that the outgoing president's trunks also contained the wearing apparel of his wife, and, therefore, were not liable to seizure in a civil suit.

In truth, both Hartigan and Raymond were losers. The old board provided the best defense for Raymond. The many innovations were attributable to Raymond who "in all these changes . . . has been the inspiring and moving spirit" and who had "the hearty support of the Board, in nearly every instance, and of a very large majority of the Board in each movement." However, as long-time executive committee member George Sturgiss concluded on May 14, 1901: "No matter what abilities, experience and high qualities the President of any University may possess, unless he has the loyal co-operation of his faculty, and the support and confidence of his Board, he cannot succeed."

The defense for Hartigan and the other dismissed faculty members came from Marmaduke Dent, the University's first graduate and a member of the State Supreme Court of Appeals. Because Dent's son-in-law was Professor Robert Allen Armstrong, other members of the court suggested that Dent excuse himself from the case. As one legal scholar has noted, "Not only was Dent emotionally committed to the old faculty and not only did his son-in-law stand to benefit if Hartigan won, but Dent's brother was arguing Hartigan's case."[13] Dent refused, however, and his colleagues therefore barred him from their determinations.

Thus, the Raymond years came to an end. A professor was out, denied due process. A Supreme Court justice, barred from the conference room because he had no business sitting in judgment on a matter so close to his own interests, was left shouting about his judicial ostracism to an amused West Virginia and a somewhat bemused outside world. A president was fired in a manner too reminiscent of the roguery practiced in the ousting of another president, Eli Marsh Turner, and every professor President Raymond had recommended for firing was restored except the one who sought redress through the courts.

A dean of women, more interested in teaching sociology than domestic science, resigned, causing the disappearance of a department of sociology from the University Catalog until the year 1919. The summer session was discredited, and the idea of faculty leaves of absence was deemed not justified. Discontinuance of fellowships was urged on the grounds that the selection of fellows had resulted "in a great deal of jealousy and bad feelings among students" and the advantage of these appointments was not "sufficient to justify the additional expense required." Termination of the Preparatory Department was recommended, and the Legislature was urged by the new board to take the necessary steps to develop and perfect the academic departments of the six normal schools. Disturbed at the discovery that the actual cost of buildings under construction exceeded "the cost fixed in the appropriation," the Legislature contemplated a standing policy that money be appropriated for only one building at a time.[14]

At the time of her husband's death in 1928, Mrs. Raymond wrote with some justification: "West Virginia University today is what it is because of the idealism and courage of my husband, who at twenty-eight was thrown into the midst of political turmoil and petty personal differences in Morgantown."[15]

She seemed to be saying that the Raymond regime had not been, in the words of one West Virginia historian, "a fruitless effort to Civilize, Christianize and Elevate West Virginia Haw-Eaters," but that it had succeeded by the end of the next generation through the deliberative workings of the young president's successors. The mission, however, took time, for the successors were not of Raymond's age and could not follow as athletically an injunction Governor G. W. Atkinson had given WVU's sixth president on November 7, 1898: "Verily 'the world do move' and the young men like yourself, are the pushers. Keep your back against the wagon and shove it forward."

Conservative Management versus "New Education"

Daniel Boardman Purinton
August 1, 1901–July 31, 1911

Thomas Edward Hodges
October 1, 1911–August 31, 1914

BY 1901 THE WEST VIRGINIA LEGISLATURE had established all institutions in the present system of public higher education with the exception of two community colleges created in 1971. It had not, however, ultimately determined its method of governance for these schools. As the twentieth century began, West Virginia University and its preparatory branches at Keyser and Montgomery each had an individual Board of Regents; the West Virginia Colored Institute and Bluefield Colored Institute each had a Board of Regents, while all other institutions of higher learning were controlled by the Normal School Board of Regents. As if establishing six separate Boards of Regents were not enough, the West Virginia Legislature in the first year of the twentieth century reorganized once again the University's Board of Regents, making it mandatory for the governor to appoint a new bipartisan board, only one of whose members might be from the same senatorial district or the same county.

The new Board convened on March 17, 1901, and three days later accepted President Raymond's resignation, effective at the end of the spring term. It vested the powers and duties of the office in a former vice-president and acting president, P. B. Reynolds, who would serve as acting president a second time, from March 21, 1901, to August 1, 1901. Thus the search began for new twentieth-century leadership. After the turmoil of President Raymond's administration, state officials considered it necessary to find as the head of WVU not necessarily a modern man but only one who was the opposite of the last president, who had been a liberal in education, a puritan in personal morals, and an outsider to West Virginia.

With the resignation of Raymond in hand, C. E. Haworth, editor of the *Huntington Herald*, wrote Governor A. B. White on May 27, 1901, that ". . . the general good feeling about the University is very noticeable and the Professors especially are feeling good as if in escape from long imprisonment." He added, however, that "the school, of course, recovering from a long illness, needs nursing."

A few weeks later the kind of nursing the school needed was spelled out in frugal terms by Regent J. B. Finley to W. M. O. Dawson, Secretary of State, in a letter of April 18, 1901:

It is my belief that the expense of the institution should be kept strictly within the appropriations made by the legislature. This State has a great future, but it is wrong to attempt to anticipate that future ten or fifteen years. The State cannot afford to spend the amount of money other states are spending on similar institutions, and it has no endowments by wealthy men. I for one am thankful that it has none, because I believe that an education derived from an institution supported by the taxes of all the people is better than one from an institution built merely for the glorification of some individual. I want to see the institution establish a reputation for good, solid, sound, sane education, and not go off spending money on every new theory, or making a struggle for mere bigness. I have had no opportunity to confer with any member of the new Board, and do not know what their views are, but I feel so strongly the need of a conservative management of the University that I trust the views I have expressed are also theirs. The tax payers of the State and those who have children to educate must be considered, and, while they will gladly support a proper institution, many will do what I know many are now doing; send their children out of the State to older and more conservative institutions, unless there is an inclination to keep the institution on a solid basis and well within the means the State can afford to spend on it.

No innovative ideas, economy in education, and retrenchment from what was considered the extravagance of the Raymond administration were the reinstituted policies of former years. A series of Regents' orders in June of 1901 signaled the retreat. One ultimatum stated the president was "authorized to use as much of the current and contingent fund as may be absolutely necessary for keeping the apparatus in the various Departments in repair, but it is distinctly understood that this order does not authorize the purchase of any additional apparatus."

The finance committees of the Board reported on June 18, 1901:

. . . that to continue the present full force of Professors and Assistants in all of the courses now conducted, regardless of the moneys available, would make another deficit at the end of the next fiscal year of nearly $90,000. Your committee would therefore strongly recommend that the Board abolish some departments, consolidate others, and otherwise reduce fixed expenses so as to come clearly within the funds appropriated by the Legislature, and funds otherwise available for the administration of the University.

The Board rescinded a June 22, 1900, order establishing a College of Medicine. It also ordered that a Department of Biology be formed from the Departments of Botany and Zoology, with the Department of Zoology abolished and the services of Professor E. B. Copeland, professor of botany, dispensed with.

To ride herd over these parsimonious objectives, Regent W. E. Powell had reported to his colleague on the Board, George C. Sturgiss, as early as May 7, 1900, that

I have kept my ears open since I was in Morgantown last, as to the next president of our university and have heard a great many of the Alumni express themselves, as to this matter, and so far every man has expressed a desire that Dr. Purinton be elected. I heartily concur in what you say as to the very great importance of prompt action in this matter and know of no other man who could come to the University at this time, with so much hope of meeting the demands and save us from a great avalanche of harmful criticism.

In deference to such growing sentiment, the Board unanimously elected D. B. Purinton, president of Denison University in Granville, Ohio, and a former vice-president and professor at West Virginia University, its new president on June 14, 1901, for he "possesses peculiar qualifications for the position." To close observers of the political scene, such an endorsement was translated to mean that Purinton was a Republican, a Baptist, more than twice the age of Raymond, and was a resurrected leader of earlier years.

Born in Preston County, Virginia (later West Virginia), on February 15, 1850, Purinton had been associated with WVU from 1869 to 1890 as student, professor, acting president, and vice-president. Receiving his A.B. from WVU in 1873, and his A.M. in 1876, he served in the Preparatory Department from 1873 to 1878. From 1878 to 1880, he occupied the chair of logic; from 1880 to 1884, the chair of mathematics; and from 1885 to 1889, the chair of metaphysics. He also had been an instructor in vocal music. He even had married into the institution, taking as his wife Florence D. Lyon, daughter of Professor Franklin Smith Lyon. He published *Christian Theism* in 1889. When elected WVU's seventh president, he was in his eleventh year of service as president of Denison, a Baptist institution.

As J. B. Finley had written to W. M. O. Dawson on April 18, 1901, in his definition of the Board's selection duties and with a backward glance at the Raymond administration:

The University will be relieved of the disfavor with which it is now undoubtedly regarded in many sections of the State and be put on a safe basis for the future by the selection of the right man for this high office, . . . The President of the University should be the President, but he should rule not by virtue of his position, but by virtue of the esteem and regard in which he is held by his associates, the students and the public generally. He should be young enough to have energy and enthusiasm, but old enough to have the balance and tact age and experience alone can give. He should be a man of broad sympathy as well as broad scholarship, but not so broad as in any way to do violence to any of the well fixed moral sentiments of a large part of our people.

Purinton, of course, was not one to violate fixed moral sentiments of the people. Rather did he prove to be one to bring church and state into a very close relationship. As earlier presidents had tied the fortunes of the University to the Methodist Church, Purinton aligned its interests with the Baptist Church. For Purinton, who was granted leaves of absence during his presidential tenure to attend the World's Sunday-School Convention in Jerusalem, was responsible for setting up the first School of Methods for Sunday School Workers held in connection with the regular WVU summer school. Thus as president of a secular state university, he dramatized the campaign to restore the Christian ethic both at home and abroad.

According to the University Catalog of 1904-05, methods in Sunday School instruction represented the first attempt by any state institution to give such training and with "over one hundred Sunday School teachers and officers in attendance, the enterprise was a distinct success in every way." According to the 1903-04 Catalog, the movement "has the cordial approval and support of all of the Leading Sunday School representatives in West Virginia, as well as the various religious organizations."

There were still other avenues open to the president to enhance the Christian spirit on a secular campus. From the Board of Regents, Purinton obtained an order to spend the sum of $200 for the benefit of the Young Men's Christian Association. He also saw to it that registration blanks for students contained queries as to their religious affiliations because, as he wrote to Richard C. Hughes of Madison, Wisconsin, "free access to those application blanks is given to the city pastors of Morgantown immediately after the opening of the University each year; and they are otherwise used to advance the religious and spiritual interests of the students."

On some occasions Purinton found it difficult to adhere steadfastly to fixed moral sentiments of the people because of the state's predilection to permit its politics to intrude upon its University. When an agent of the office of Governor A. B. White asked Purinton what the political affiliations of members of the faculty might be, the president properly stated that he did not and should not inquire into the politics of candidates before their selection in such way as to make his recommendation contingent upon such knowledge. But he did concede in his September 25, 1902, acknowledgment to Governor White that "if I know the politics, other things being equal, I should always favor the one belonging to the party whose administration is responsible for the conduct of the University." He added with caution: "Of course this is a thing that ought not to be announced publicly."

Because of repeated requests from the gubernatorial office about the faculty's political affiliations, Purinton did ascertain for Governor White the following facts: that there were twenty-seven Republicans, seventeen Democrats, two gold Democrats, and two Prohibitionists, which, he took pains to point out, made a clear majority of Republicans over all other parties.

As to two politically active professors, Professor Willey of Republican Party faith and Professor Armstrong, a Democrat, Purinton was happy to report to the governor that he had not heard of any offensive attitude of Professor Willey in matters political but, "If you know of anything which he has done during my administration which is objectionable, I shall be very glad, if you wish it, to speak to him frankly in regard to the matter." As to Professor Armstrong, Purinton made known to the governor that he had felt it wise to say to him in a personal interview before his restoration to active service that Armstrong should refrain from active partisan politics. He divulged that Armstrong agreed, that he had sold his partisan newspaper, and that he had retired entirely from such activities.

In a response of October 2, 1908, to General E. L. Boggs, private secretary in the Governor's Office, Purinton fended off a request that he submit the names of WVU employees and their home counties. Scholastic employees, he insisted, were not credited to any county. "In fact," he stated, "a majority of them were drawn from other states than West Virginia." As to custodial-type employees and their geographical origins, Purinton assessed that they were too few in number to be of any political consequence.

On one unhappy occasion Purinton was made aware that the Governor's Office was displeased with the awarding of certain printing contracts to others than the public printer at Charleston. When A. B. White learned that the University Catalog had been printed by the *Parkersburg News*, which White in a letter to Purinton on May 26, 1904, characterized as a "newspaper which is a sewer of constant vituperation and abuse, and which does not do the printing itself, but sub-lets it and 'farms it out,'" Purinton could only excuse his error in economic terms. Within two days of receiving the Governor's letter, he explained that the price paid for the job was "far and away below that which would have been paid had the State Printer done the work." But Purinton's justification for cutting expenses did not meet the political needs because all parties resolved the dispute in accordance with the Governor's wishes by a Regent's rule of June 16, 1904, that printing contracts, by law, must go to the public printer.

If Purinton could not keep politicians happy in all respects, he could make amends by satisfying them on husbandry. As he advertised his own success in the matter to Arnold C. Scheer of Charleston, on April 13, 1905: ". . . Of course you realize that when I started in, over three years ago, everything about the University was practically overdrawn and the aggregate of overdrafts reached $60,000. We have been pulling ourselves out of the hole, and I am sure that by the close of this fiscal year, we will be in fine shape."

Despite these retrenchment policies, Sydney Lloyd Wrightson, dean of the School of Music, believed he saw the way out of the dilemma, at least for his own school. Authorized in his novel actions by the University President and the Board of Regents, he simply called upon public spirited citizens of the state, through private donations, to help him adorn his school with the necessary equipment. One such appeal he addressed to Governor A. B. White on November 17, 1903, as well as other prominent men, asking for subscriptions anywhere from $250 to $1,000 apiece for the School of Music.

Wrightson's most spectacular endeavor, again supported by means of public subscription, was staging a two-day Richard Strauss festival in Morgantown attended by the University community, the governor, other state officials, and the mayor and city council. Thus the city (with about 15,000 residents) found itself a part of the larger musical world witnessing composer Richard Strauss joining with Victor Herbert in conducting the Pittsburgh Symphony Orchestra, and hearing Strauss's wife, the dramatic soprano Pauline de Ahna, sing.

As the *Morgantown Post* observed, Morgantown was a trifle hazy as to just what a tone poem was before Strauss led the orchestra through "Til Eulenspiegel's Merry Pranks." Even *High Fidelity* magazine, in a retrospective article entitled "A Case of Hard-Earned Bread" in June, 1964, was amazed, as was the national capital, by the extraordinary spectacle of a two-day Strauss festival in such a small town. In a review of Strauss's unpublished writings, it uncovered the fact that Strauss had more than earned his honorarium in his effort to surmount the unusual topography he encountered on his way to the University city. As the composer reminisced to a friend:

Believe me — it was hard-earned bread . . . We traveled fourteen hours to Wheeling — through rain, fog, soot, storms — a hillside landscape that resembled Elberfeld; the other afternoon a pleasant auto drive through charming suburbs surrounded by wooded hills — but after the concerts a two-hour-long tram car ride through Indian territory to Steubenville, from there twelve hours' train ride to New York — and again,

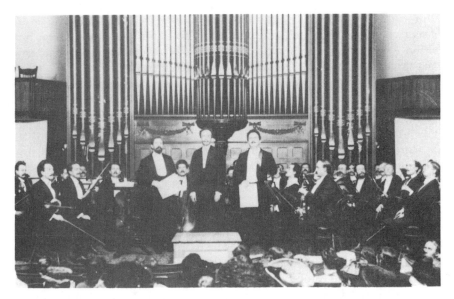

Two famous composers-conductors, Richard Strauss (standing, center) and Victor Herbert (standing, right), visited the WVU campus in 1904.

three hours after arrival, rehearsal for last night's chamber music concert. When it was over, I almost collapsed.

Having put his financial house in order, Purinton next moved to correct administrative disorder. Because of constant faculty uproar in the Raymond years, Purinton looked for safer means of University control than a legislating faculty. He found this device in a University Council, an organizational scheme lasting many years beyond his own term as president and retitled an Administrative Council. To this body of eleven members chosen by the president, Purinton gave authority to approve new courses, to determine requirements for entrance and degrees, and to care for discipline and all matters of athletics. The council also could ratify or modify actions of University committees but in all cases was restricted by the president's veto power.

Purinton's new council and new committees began to approve as well as disapprove actions taken in the Raymond years. Not only did his administration discontinue the awarding of honorary degrees, it withdrew from the catalog reference to the Ph.D. degree. It raised the standards in the Law College, whereby "bar law" and the "diploma of graduation" were abolished; it reduced the School of Commerce as well as the School of Elocution and

Oratory to departmental status within the College of Arts and Sciences. In disregard of legislative antagonism toward Raymond's summer quarter but with a view toward meeting the needs of the growing numbers of elementary and secondary school teachers in the state, Purinton considered one of his most successful accomplishments to be the establishment of a summer school. The Purinton summer session was financed by each instructor sharing the total of student fees collected in proportion to the number of students taught.

In contrast to the Raymond administration, the Purinton administration stiffened the University's entrance requirements, even for the preparatory school. In his quest for higher standards, Purinton had the satisfaction of realizing certain benefits that accrued from a superior student body by presiding over WVU's first four successful quests for Rhodes Scholarships. The recipients were Charles Frederick Tucker Brooke in 1904; Robert P. Strickler in 1907; Thomas Porter Hardman in 1910; and Van W. Gilson in 1911. Brooke, who took an academic first class at Oxford, set such a good pace for subsequent Rhodes Scholars that on July 25, 1911, George R. Parkin, a Rhodes official, wrote from Seymour House in London to President Purinton:

I think I ought to congratulate you on the fact that Mr. Hardman, one of your scholars, has just taken a first class in the school of jurisprudence in Oxford. This is the third time that a first class has been taken by your West Virginia students . . . I doubt a good deal whether there is any other state that has the same record, and it says much for the ability and earnestness of the young men you have sent to us. The wish to maintain so good a tradition ought to be a strong inspiration to your succeeding scholars.

In its building program, the Purinton administration supervised the completion of the north wing of Woodburn Building (formerly University Hall), the Library, and the Engineering and Armory buildings by 1902. In addition, it began and finished the construction of the president's house in 1904-05, a central heating plant in 1908, a third story on Science Hall in 1909, and the south wing of Woodburn Hall in 1909-11.

In 1902, when John N. Simpson became head of the Department of Anatomy and Physiology, Purinton recognized his reorganization of the first two years of a standard four-year course for WVU students. Purinton and Simpson also supported the affiliation of WVU with the College of Physicians and Surgeons at Baltimore, which in time became the Medical School of the University of Maryland. Through such affiliation, students could receive their last two years of clinical instruction. Thus Purinton and his new Board restored the College of Medicine as an administrative unit on March 3, 1903, and kept it alive until 1910. But before its revival once again as a

The first separate library building was in what is now called Stewart Hall in honor of Irvin Stewart, WVU President from 1946 to 1958. It was built in 1902. Architectural embellishments decorate both the exterior and interior of Stewart Hall, including several mice sculpted into the columns in the reception area.

college in 1912, the Board in 1910 diminished medicine to departmental status within the College of Arts and Sciences.

The raising of standards had no adverse effect on the recruitment of students. The Purinton administration almost doubled its initial enrollment of 755 to 1,500, with women's registration jumping from 249 to 586. This resulted in the appointment of Susan Moore as dean of women in 1903, the renting of Episcopal Hall in 1907 for a woman's hall, and the establishment of three national sorority chapters on campus.

Although economically minded Purinton had been chosen as a contrast to liberal spender Raymond, and therefore did little to encourage graduate study and research, he was responsible for obtaining a considerable number of new faculty, men of high scholarship, who easily could have directed a graduate program. Among them were such long-lasting and distinguished

Two buildings completed in 1902 were the second Mechanical Hall, which was located across from the Chemistry Research Laboratory, and the Armory on the site of the Parking Garage behind Mountainlair.

scholars as J. H. Cox, professor of English philology; J. M. Callahan and O. P. Chitwood, professors of history; J. A. Eiesland, professor of mathematics; and A. M. Reese, professor of zoology. Purinton also lost able men, notably Walter Fleming, professor of history, who after writing his monumental Reconstruction history at WVU, departed for glory at Louisiana State and Vanderbilt universities.

As economic pressures within WVU mounted, faculty discontent with Purinton's parsimonious ways of doing things grew, and new governing procedures for higher educational institutions in West Virginia were developed. Purinton offered his resignation from the presidency in June, 1910, to become effective July 31, 1911. The Board quickly agreed, and the presidential pronouncement was timed for Commencement proceedings, because the Board agreed that "it would be very much less embarrassing to him to make the announcement public himself rather than have the Board make it directly or indirectly by seeking his successor."[1]

WVU's eighth president, Thomas E. Hodges, who somehow missed the cue that Purinton's approach was no longer applicable in the bustling twentieth century, said to the public via the *Morgantown Post Chronicle* of September 27, 1910: "You may be sure that there will be no radical break in the continuity of the educational policies of the institution when the change in presidency becomes effective."

Hodges had predicted his own administration of WVU correctly, and thereby missed the major purposes for which some had sought governance changes in the West Virginia educational system and the accompanying administrative turnovers at the University. Governor M. O. Dawson's message, to the 1907 Legislature pertaining to the educational system had questioned the existence of "too many boards of administration in this state." Believing that there would be real savings if the public institutions were managed by fewer controlling units, Dawson looked forward to the day when "we may have a system of education in the state which would lead from the common schools to the University . . ." A year before Purinton announced his resignation, a legislative committee had agreed with the Governor by recommending the adoption of two boards: a Board of Control, which would administer the business and financial matters, including all buildings and grounds, of the educational institutions; and a Board of Regents, to administer the educational affairs of the University, the preparatory schools in Keyser and Montgomery, the state normal schools, and the two institutions for blacks. The 1909 Legislature quickly responded by adopting the committee's suggestion of two boards of three and five members, respectively, which, according to their count, replaced nine boards of regents and sixteen boards of directors with the two new boards and reduced the total number of board members from 148 to 8.

West Virginia politicians may have thought they had formulated a progressive as well as less expensive tool for educational control, but more experienced administrators doubted the accomplishment. Speaking before a national association of state universities in special reference to the WVU governing formula, President Charles Richard Van Hise of the University of Wisconsin found the thirty-fifth state's fundamental principle of educational control contrary to that obtained in all complex affairs of government; that is, higher education in West Virginia lacked "single authority and single responsibility."[2] To Hise, even if the several West Virginia boards cooperated, which he doubted, it still would seem a useless expenditure of energy to have two boards working at a task which one could accomplish better. Contending that a single, separate board for each state institution remained the best method of governing an educational institution, Van Hise also suggested a non-paid board of seven to twenty members.

The *Morgantown Post Chronicle* of January 12, 1912, agreed with the Wisconsin educator and called for a non-paid board of distinguished citizens (with liberal representation from the alumni) for WVU. It also suggested turning the educational management of the normal schools over to the State Department of Education. The *Chronicle's* advice, however, was not to be followed for several years. The Board of Control lasted until 1947, and the Board of Regents gave way in 1919 when the educational policies of all public institutions of higher learning were vested in the seven members of a new State Board of Education including the State Superintendent of Schools, *ex officio*. Not until 1927 did the Legislature remove the University from the State Board's jurisdiction and place it under its own Board of Governors.

Under the new educational mechanisms existing from 1909 to 1927, administrators explored expanded roles for normal schools, Marshall College supporters entertained ideas of their alma mater's becoming the state's second university, and West Virginia University administrators unsuccessfully resisted efforts by the normals to expand course offerings beyond those necessary for teacher training. At no other time in the history of the University, according to its early historians, were its supervisory boards so well under control of the new educators; that is, men who subscribed to the progressive professional educational philosophies of a Thorndike, a Dewey, or a Butler; who believed that teachers were not born, but made; who emphasized methods and professional training rather than aptitude and scholarship; and above all else, who stood for "progress." The leading educational personality of the era, West Virginia's most politically gifted new educator, was Morris Purdy Shawkey, State Superintendent of Schools from 1908 to 1921, who in *ex officio* capacity served as president of the Board of Regents and of the State Board of Education, and in 1919 as the president of the new State Board of Education.

First President's Home is now called Purinton House for the first president who lived in it, Daniel Boardman Purinton, in 1905. Construction of the house stirred a controversy because it was unauthorized by the West Virginia Legislature, it cost $42,611.94, and the price of the lot was considered excessive.

Particularly effective at the secondary and normal school levels, the new educators were responsible for increasing the number of fully accredited high schools in the state from twelve in 1910 to 233 in 1925. This increase, in turn, caused important jumps in college and university enrollments, so hard to come by in the nineteenth century and so readily available during most of the twentieth (except in times of wars and depressions). President Purinton proudly had recounted to the *New Dominion* on January 8, 1910, the growth of West Virginia University from 1889 with "14 members in its faculty and 113 students . . . to January, 1910, with 70 instructors, 1,338 students, and 500 courses . . . " He also had noted the legislative appropriation in 1889 was $29,000 as compared to $160,000 in 1910. Commented a local newspaper in approbation of Purinton's record, "Twenty years ago the institution was a good college but not a real university in any adequate sense of the term." However, in 1927, F. B. Trotter, whose administration most directly benefited from the growth of high schools, received from the outgoing Board of Education an expression of its appreciation for a record reflecting an increase in students to 3,385, a growth of the regular teaching faculty to 265, and an increase in appropriations to $1,220,000. It was said in the time of Trotter, as it had been inferred during Purinton's tenure, that WVU for the first time advanced to true University status.[3]

Hodges, like Purinton, was one of West Virginia University's own, having received his A.B. degree in 1881 and his A.M. degree in 1884. He was also one of Morgantown's own, for he had served as principal of the Morgantown public schools from 1881 to 1886, and as head of the WVU Department of Physics from 1896 to 1910. Although he also had served as principal of Marshall College from 1886 to 1896, it was during a period when the State Superintendent of Schools had adopted the policy of recruiting the normal school staffs from among University graduates. In addition, Hodges had been secretary and treasurer of the Morgantown Savings and Loan Society and the first president of the Bank of Morgantown. Although a Democrat in a Republican state, neither his politics nor his residence far from the state capital proved a liability, for his University administration coincided with that of Governor William E. Glasscock. Born on a farm in Monongalia County, Glasscock was also a WVU graduate, as well as a former Monongalia County superintendent of schools, and a Morgantown resident.

Because of Hodges' academic, administrative, business, and political connections, Glasscock appointed him in 1909 to the newly created State Board of Control, and he served as its first treasurer until 1911, but without salary after August, 1910 to meet the legal requirement of having received no pay from a board controlling the destiny of an institution for at least one year before accepting the presidency. The *Morgantown Post Chronicle* was jubilant over his selection and advertised on September 24, 1910, the five reasons the Regents had given for Hodges' selection: (1) his ability and personality; (2) his successful management of affairs in teaching, in private business, and as a member of the Board of Control; (3) the support given him by the alumni and "school men of the state"; (4) his sympathy with the Board of Regents' plans for bringing the University in closer touch with the state and its varied interests; and, (5) the fact that he was a true West Virginian, having been born near Buckhannon in 1858.

In anticipation of his new position, Hodges resigned from the Board of Control, and departed on a vacation in this country and in Europe to study the leading educational institutions of the world before assuming the WVU presidency, which he held from October 1, 1911, until July 18, 1914. During Hodges' absence, despite the recent selection of a Democrat to the WVU presidency by the Republican machine, and the belief that politics would no longer intrude upon University affairs,[4] the lame-duck Purinton administration was beset by political problems: continued efforts of some Republicans to declare Hodges ineligible for the presidency because of prior service on the Board of Control and the dismissal of two faculty members for assorted reasons, compromising whatever position the University might have held on academic freedom.

The dismissals were staged by members of the legislative finance committees who nominally objected to certain professors engaging in activities beyond their classroom duties. For these transgressions, the legislators threatened to veto the University appropriations. They named as their first victim Charles E. Hogg, dean of the College of Law, engaged as counsel for the state of West Virginia in its litigation with its mother state, Virginia, over a certain indebtedness West Virginia had agreed to assume when it became a new state in 1863. The law students rushed to Hogg's defense stating that the dean never had neglected his duties as professor or dean while serving as counsel for West Virginia in its litigation with Virginia. The students argued that Hogg's appearances before the U.S. Supreme Court reflected credit upon the WVU law school.

In his own defense before the joint committees, Hogg reminded the members that he was engaged by the state's attorney general as co-counsel in the West Virginia-Virginia litigation before being employed by WVU. When he had relinquished his practice to take charge of the WVU College of Law, he reminded the committees that it was with the understanding that he would continue his relations as attorney in the debt case and would engage in such other professional work as he felt inclined to do — so long as he did not neglect his University work or impair his usefulness and efficiency as head of the law school. At no time since assuming the duties of dean, declared Hogg to the *Morgantown Post Chronicle* of February 21, 1911, "have I omitted to do everything required of me as an instructor and the executive head of this department." When Hogg called for a full-scale investigation of his varied responsibilities, the committees curtailed their investigation.

While unable to force the dismissal of the WVU law dean, Republican legislators were successful in their opposition to Professor Henry S. Green of the Greek Department, and Professor R. B. Brinsmade of the Mining Engineering Department. In Green's case, the finance committee charged that in his capacity as editor of a local newspaper he was neglecting his University duties. When as editor Green heavily criticized the Republican members of the State Senate for fleeing to Cincinnati, Ohio, so that they would not have to organize the Senate, a measure taken to prevent the Democrats from electing both U.S. Senators in 1911, the professor offended the state's dominant politicians. Green, who resigned from WVU rather than having himself restricted in his political criticism, made political capital in his own newspaper, the *Morgantown Post Chronicle* of March 11, 1911, about the loss of free speech at the University.

The second victim, Professor Brinsmade, received notice from Board President Shawkey in the summer of 1910 that his services no longer were needed because in essence he was an advocate of Henry George's single tax concept. Through the *Morgantown Post Chronicle* of June 13, 1911, Shawkey explained the dismissal by maintaining that WVU was searching for a man "who had the magnetism and personal qualities, together with the ambition to build up the engineering department . . ." He contended to Brinsmade that his efforts to accomplish the mission had become "seriously discounted by your active interest in certain economic questions which you discuss to the exclusion of the legitimate work of your classes."

The *Morgantown Post Chronicle* tied the Green and Brinsmade cases together, citing them as examples of the "determination of the present administration to suppress anything that savors of 'advanced' thought, anything like freedom of speech, among members of the university faculty." Because of the cumulative effect of the Hogg, Brinsmade, and Green cases, the *Parkersburg State Journal* not only complained about the cost of the University but suggested on June 20, 1912, "that the people of the state are tired of the fact that this institution is 'one constant scene of turmoil.'" In exasperation, it concluded:

For thirty years it has been the seat of practically all the educational difficulties of the state. All of the other schools are carried on peacefully, affairs progress smoothly at them, but the university is one constant scene of turmoil. The public is certainly getting tired of all this and if there is not a change, the time is bound to come when there will be a general sentiment in favor of wiping out the institution — especially in view of its great cost.

A *Morgantown Post Chronicle* editor disagreed with his Parkersburg counterpart by editorializing that whatever turmoil had risen in connection with the institution in the past decade had had its origin in Charleston and was "chargeable to the petty politics of the regime of the machine and the boss." Its advice was not to abolish the University but the machine. To the local newspaper, the faculty member had to keep political and economic ideas "to himself on pain of losing his job," and this was reason enough for turmoil at the University.

In a report three years after the Brinsmade affair, the State Board of Regents attempted to identify its employment procedures. In its clarification, it frankly admitted its conservative bias. Before any applicant was considered seriously, the Board tried to determine whether the candidate was a person of good health, average physical appearance, well-balanced human interests, and approved habits. Then, said the Board, in its formal report for the year ending June 30, 1914:

His general attitude toward the well established moral tenets, commonly accepted rules and principles of society and government as interpreted by the American people is determined. Our attitude on the last mentioned points may be subjected to slight

The President of the United States, William Howard Taft, came to Morgantown for the inauguration of WVU's eighth president, Thomas E. Hodges, on November 3, 1911. Six University cadets guarded the presidential railroad coach all night on a siding above the Baltimore and Ohio Railroad Station. A White Steamer automobile was brought from Pittsburgh for President Taft to ride in during an eight-car parade on High Street. A reception was held for him in front of Martin Hall.

criticism, but we believe schools maintained at public expense should respond as nearly as possible to the public mind. Even if we grant to some of the largest institutions of our country the privilege of experimenting with 'cranks' and their opinions, we think the custom would be very pernicious in small institutions, such as ours, where eccentricities and strange doctrines stand out in exaggerated form.

Upon Hodges' return from his vacation abroad, all abstract notions such as academic freedom were ignored. Attention was directed to a three-day inauguration dominated by major Republican politicians of both the state and the nation. Never before or since had West Virginians seen a WVU presidential inauguration graced by the President of the United States. On the day preceding the formal installation of the WVU president, William Howard Taft toured the town, breakfasted with WVU's local benefactor, I. C. White, addressed 2,000 school children assembled on White's lawn, and used the porch of the WVU President's House as the occasion for an address entitled "World Wide Peace," an explanation of the arbitration treaties his national administration was then sponsoring.

Never, declared a local paper on November 3, 1911, had the city or state seen on an inauguration day "such a gathering of academicians and scholars as was present at Commencement Hall," with the cadet band leading the academic procession from Martin Hall, around the Woodburn Circle, and down Front Street (now University Avenue) to the inaugural site between lines formed by the Cadet Corps. The dignitaries who spoke were not only impressive personages but delivered addresses with impressive themes. Fletcher B. Dressler of the U.S. Bureau of Education detailed "The Duties and Opportunities of the Modern Scholar" and Edwin A. Alderman, president of the University of Virginia, discussed "The Influence of Universities upon the National Life." Flanked by Governor Glasscock, Board President Shawkey, and others, the eighth president of WVU accepted the office "not because I feel myself worthy, but rather because I am constrained to hope that with the help and sympathy so ungrudgingly pledged to me here today, I may be able to render some return to the institution which was my own Alma Mater I love, and which as the exponent of the State's interest in higher education should be of great service to her people."

Expressing his desire that the University expand its functions in the state, Hodges dedicated his administration to all who wanted to take advantage of higher education. He emphasized agriculture and extension work, asking for liberal appropriations. He also hinted at the need for a graduate school. His inaugural address was followed by talks by President H. P. Judson of the University of Chicago on "The University and the State," and President William O. Thompson of Oklahoma State University on "The University and the People."

Following the inauguration, a new Board of Regents and a new administration went quickly to work. The Preparatory School, ordered closed at the end of the 1910-11 academic year, became a relic of the past, although the University Council was given authority to arrange studies for those coming from high schools offering only three years of study. A School of Agriculture, including domestic science, was created to provide the necessary training to enable young men and women to make farming "more enjoyable and practical." Advertised as neither a University preparatory school nor a competitor of the high school, it had a school year of six months and was designed "to give interest in and sympathy with country life so as to educate students back to the farms and make them influential in developing the best life in their communities." Since it was for students who could come for only part of a year, it was officially dropped in 1914.

Modernization also was the order of the day with the adoption of a new summer session and the two-semester system. On November 18, 1911, the *Athenaeum*, a strong supporter of change, listed as reasons for approval of the latter: students could expect fewer examinations; a good student need not sacrifice his time and energy in keeping up with each day's work, "so necessary in the three-term system," and could use the released time to follow any line of work which he found particularly interesting; a student could transfer credits to other institutions more easily; a student would experience fewer interruptions in his year's work of study. The semester system, the student newspaper was convinced, would allow the student the time "to find his strong points and develop them."

On October 14, 1911, the *Morgantown Post Chronicle* also heralded "radical changes" imposed by legislation and the Regents in University administration: the creation of distinct colleges with deans; the elimination of the old University Council in favor of a legislating faculty; and a new Council of Administration. A committee on classification and grades and a committee on graduate work attended to internal rules and regulations for students. A social committee controlled fraternity and sorority life, and a University business office supplanted former financial officials. By the time of the semi-centennial celebration of the Morrill Act, the *Athenaeum*, in a special souvenir edition of June 14, 1913, proudly detailed many of the changes that had occurred at WVU.

The College of Arts and Sciences had been expanded to include work in twenty departments. After a first year of prescribed work, the student could choose his major area, but should continue to take "a liberal amount of work in languages, philosophy, and sciences." According to the College, because "the unusual development of high schools makes the training of teachers absolutely imperative and the increasing demands of the University for thoroughly prepared students from the high schools absolutely necessary," the major work of the College was the preparation of teachers for the secondary schools. The few changes in the College of Arts and Sciences during Hodges' presidency were the dropping of the Art Department to release money "to be used to better advantage in the furtherance of some other departments" and abolition of the chair of elocution and oratory in the Department of English so a Department of Public Speaking could be established.

The College of Law advertised in the *Athenaeum*'s souvenir edition that the degree of Bachelor of Laws could be obtained in three years of work, and a Master of Laws could be obtained within a time period decided upon by members of the College of Law and the College of Arts and Sciences. Teaching methods provided "well grounded knowledge of substantive law, with special pains taken with each student to enable him to acquire an efficient understanding of pleading, practice, and evidence . . ."

There were, however, critics who called for substantial changes in the law school. According to one law student, utilizing the *Morgantown Post Chronicle* of June 24, 1912, to voice his complaints:

In respect to the equipment, the law school is now in a sad condition. In the first place, the rooms occupied by it are about as unsightly and dismal as can be imagined. The walls are dingy, and even dirty. The chairs are in a dilapidated condition, and a student is lucky if he can find one without a broken leg or back, or one with a bottom that will not fall out when he sits down on it. In a corner of one room will be found a heap of broken chairs that reminds one of a store room or a garret. Around the walls of another room are empty book cases of rough wood that reminds one of pioneer days. The ventilation is bad, and the heat so uncertain that the classes are often dismissed because of the intense cold. The library facilities are entirely inadequate. The rooms are too small and the number of reference books is entirely insufficient to meet the demands of the courses outlined or of the number of students.

The student-critic asked that new rooms be opened, and that rooms already in use be completely renovated and refurnished; that the law library be given more space, more books, and additional attendants, and that it be open fourteen hours a day instead of eight; that the case system of instruction be adopted as extensively as practicable, and that at least one additional instructor be secured who could teach law by the case system.

Replying to "the author of the article who registered in this college only last fall, and is a neophyte in the pursuit of professional knowledge," the law school dean noted in the *New Dominion* of January 29, 1912, that his school required a minimum of 1,600 hours in class compared to 1,100 required by the Yale, Harvard, Michigan, Pennsylvania, and Virginia law schools. Indicating that the WVU school favored the Dwight system of instruction, he described its teaching methods as making use of the textbook, accompanied by short, explanatory lectures, quizzes, and illustrative cases selected by the instructor himself.

Believing the Dwight system among the many virtues of the WVU law school, the dean also thought the discipline and decorum observed was superior to that found in the great majority of law schools in the country. He did, however, admit the school needed physical improvement, that the rooms were poorly ventilated, and that the library was inadequate, but added that plans were under way for improvement. That such improvement had occurred was visible in the *Athenaeum's* semi-centennial edition, which permitted the law school to advertise four full professors, one assistant, four lecture rooms, a reading room and library with 5,200 books.

The College of Engineering informed *Athenaeum* readers that it had reorganized a four-year course for the Department of Mining Engineering, and had extended practical instruction to other WVU colleges, particularly to students in agriculture and home economics. The College of Engineering emphasized the establishment of summer courses in manual training, the establishment of a sanitary option in civil engineering courses, a special summer course of six weeks for practical mining, and a three-year practical course for those not attending high school. The college advertised physical improvements that resulted in enlarging the mining and electrical laboratories, establishing a laboratory for testing road materials, purchase of a complete rescue outfit and apparatuses for determining the heating value of fuels and the detection of mine gas.

Also undergoing change in Hodges' administration was the medical college. Its students, upset by the decision of the Regents in 1910 to diminish the school to departmental status in the College of Arts and Sciences, hired counsel to represent their interests in matters of both recognition and credit before the Board of Regents. Under pressure from students and medical accrediting agencies, the Board rescinded its earlier rule by converting the department back to the independent status of a school, with J. N. Simpson as dean. Within the next year, President Hodges was able to announce the recognition of the school by the Association of American Medical Colleges, which was allowing credit for work already completed and up to two years of credit transferable to a four-year school. According to the *Athenaeum's* souvenir edition, the University medical school offered "well equipped laboratories, small classes, and individual instruction" for students in medicine as well as cheaper educational expenses than most medical colleges afforded. It noted that, in WVU's previous connection with the College of Physicians and Surgeons in Baltimore, a WVU student never had failed to graduate or failed to pass state medical boards.

The *Athenaeum*, in the semi-centennial year, described the University Library as having grown from 275 books to 46,500 books, of which 5,000 were located in the Law Library and 5,500 in the Experiment Station Library. The Library advertised 55,000 catalogue cards in the main collection, and received 250 papers and periodicals annually. Open 14 hours a day on school days, the Library boasted that about 12,000 items were checked out in 1912.

The student newspaper described the College of Agriculture's work as being "along strictly practical lines," and offered in three phases: instruction by the College of Agriculture; investigation by the Experiment Station; and provision of state services through agricultural extension work. Greatly enlarged by students and strengthened through reorganization, the College employed 25 instructors; operated a modern dairy and creamery plant; and boasted that its agronomy and horticultural departments were well-equipped, and that its entomology department possessed a complete collection of insects. By introducing new methods, new crops, new ideas, and stimulating local communities in every section to greater agricultural efforts, the agricultural extension department had increased its sponsorship to 15 extension schools in agriculture, 5 in home economics, and 110 farmer institutes; and had enlisted 6,500 boys and girls in agricultural clubs. Its faculty had traveled 1,000 miles by special trains through West Virginia to display agricultural exhibits. In coordinating its many activities, the College consolidated its three phases into one; in particular, the often autonomous Experiment Station was merged with the College of Agriculture.

Among those pleased with the University's progress was Governor Glasscock, who suggested to the Legislature that WVU should have suitable buildings for the College of Agriculture and for the College of Law. Although conservative in labor relations, the Governor identified himself as a political progressive in educational matters when he reported to the *Morgantown Post Chronicle* on January 25, 1913:

President Hodges and his faculty, under the direction of the state board of regents, have done much to increase the efficiency of this school and it is now serving the people of this state as it has never done before. We sometimes hear complaints of the cost of maintaining this institution, but if you will take pains to compare its per capita cost with the per capita cost of similar institutions in other states you will find that we have not been as liberal with our university as we should have been . . . it is too much to expect the schools of our state to produce the results that they are capable of producing unless we furnish them with the means and equipment with which to do the work. I hope that you will be liberal in your appropriation of moneys to be used in agricultural extension work.

It was with the arrival of Henry Drury Hatfield as governor in 1913 that Hodges lost his special connections in the Governor's Office, and found himself more at the mercy of Superintendent Shawkey, with whom he differed on educational matters concerning the normal schools and the University. Because dissatisfaction and misunderstanding among state normal school students coming to WVU had developed over credits accepted for transfer, the Board of Regents had urged the heads of the normal schools to make their work more acceptable to WVU. Despite being satisfied with their efforts at the time, Hodges later expressed himself as unhappy. Because of WVU complaints about the normal schools, Shawkey became dissatisfied with Hodges as president, and Hodges showed increasing restlessness in his job. In view of Shawkey's political strength and Hodges' political weakness in an era of Republican control, it has been assumed that Governor Hatfield would have appointed Shawkey as WVU president if the State Superintendent of Schools had requested the position.[5]

As a matter of public record, Governor Hatfield in his first biennial message to the Legislature of 1915 indicated his dissatisfaction with the institutional situation in Morgantown as it had been administered by Hodges. Having personally inspected the institution, the Governor found the College of Agriculture handicapped for room with professors of agriculture and chemistry compelled to lecture upon the same subject three times because of the large number of students and inadequate classroom space. He also discovered that the classrooms of the Department of History and the College of Engineering were overcrowded. It was imperative, he believed, that dormitories be built at the University, especially for young women. He was distressed by the location of both the Medical School and the Domestic Science Department in the basement of Woodburn Hall.

Hodges' failure to launch a building and campus improvement program, to substitute his own authority for faculty authority, and to produce winning football teams, as well as broad hints of disapproval from both the Governor and the Superintendent, all contributed to his growing unhappiness. Cornered by events at the University, Hodges permitted himself on July 18, 1914, to be named by the Democrats as Congressman-at-large. According to Charles Brooks Smith, Washington correspondent for the *Parkersburg Dispatch News,* Hodges pressed for the nomination because of a promise of a gubernatorial bid in 1916 and because of the effort to oust him from the University presidency. In his congressional campaign, Hodges advanced himself as the "scholar in politics," conferred with President Woodrow Wilson who welcomed "another college man into political life," and thus secured the blessings of both the national and state Democratic Party. But whereas Wilson won in 1912 because of both Theodore Roosevelt's and William Howard Taft's efforts to secure Republican votes, Hodges failed in an off-year election in West Virginia which had earlier expressed approval of Theodore Roosevelt for President but had retained regular Republicans in state offices. In July, 1915, Hodges was appointed Morgantown postmaster, a position he held until his death on July 13, 1919.

Throughout the winter months of January, February, and March, 1914, both the *Morgantown Post Chronicle* and the *New Dominion* concentrated upon WVU students' craze for dancing, which offended some Morgantown residents.

One who was particularly bothered by the new dance steps was Grover C. Casto, an employee of the Second National Bank of Morgantown, who viewed at a Panhellenic gathering in the Armory a display of the tango, which he believed to be "morally wrong, whether in college or 'red-light' circles, and not one bit better when danced by a coed than when danced by an unfortunate of the underworld."

If student spirit had been lacking before, it manifested itself against Casto. Seizing him in the bank and carrying him to the Monongahela River for baptism, students were stopped by police intervention. On another occasion Casto was met by students when boarding a streetcar. The conductor and motorman warned the students either to stop molesting Casto or to get off the car. They did neither, and when Casto joined the motorman in his locked compartment, the students became so enraged that they attempted to break down the door.

The streetcar operators called for police assistance to escort Casto home, but when the police arrived, another delegation of students was waiting. Threatened with arrest, the students finally permitted Casto's entry into his own home. Thereafter, for several days, Casto was provided with a police escort. The prosecuting attorney warned that students who threatened Casto with personal violence and injury would be subject to prosecution. When the editor of the *Post Chronicle* was informed that students were taking him to the river for publishing the Casto letter, he welcomed their efforts. "A dip in the Monongahela," he thought, "might be a trifle chilly despite the spring-like weather, but the circumstances would make the incident right good 'copy' from a newspaper viewpoint."

University authorities, when questioned, were somewhat vague about the episode which enraged Casto. Professor Robert Armstrong, chairman of the social committee, took exception to an account which indicated that chaperones were absent during the concluding hours of the Panhellenic dance. Affirming their presence, Armstrong could not recall their names, but did remember that the committee had granted permission for the dance to last until 1:00 a.m. President Hodges characterized the criticism as "unjust" and "unkind," but observed that faculty members and students were taking steps to curb "objectionable features." In the future, students agreed to attend dances only in University buildings and under social committee supervision. The Second National Bank's board of directors voted to support the views of its employee as well as to deny the report that many students were removing their accounts.

One individual, O. O. Carman, suggested that the entire question of dancing be put to state voters as had the liquor question. With a definite viewpoint in mind, he recommended that the question be phrased in this manner: "Do the people of this state who maintain and support the university mean to say by their indifference that they have no higher ideals than to care whether or not their children, while in or out of school, whirl to a musical rhythm as did the people of the dark ages, or do they desire clean, wholesome amusement which leaves the indulger with a countenance free from the stain of evil."

If Presidents Purinton and Hodges showed themselves more liberal than President Raymond by allowing dancing once a week, their conservatism in matters other than dancing was reminiscent of Raymond's views. The editor of one of the local newspapers believed that the social life of young men and women at the University "has probably never been more sedulously guarded from untoward influences than it is today." The use of cigarettes was perhaps the greatest of the arrant influences. In response to a stringent state law banning the smoking of cigarettes on University property, male students at first acquiesced. This was because they had found a substitution for their vice in a Corn Cob Pipe Club. The *New Dominion* of March 8, 1912, reported that the by-laws required the membership to smoke "nothing but bona-fide legitimate smoking tobacco . . . the line being drawn on stronger brands and corn silk."

Occasionally, Halloween caused trouble between town and gown and indicated an undercurrent of class warfare. Posters signed by presidents of the freshman, sophomore, junior, and senior classes warned workmen of the Sabraton tin mill of bodily harm if any were caught out after 9:00 p.m. on October 31st. However, students disclaimed all knowledge of the posters, sent their expressions of good will to the mill men, and the workers responded with a resolution expressing no hostile feelings toward the students whom they wished well in their studies. The *New Dominion* in its Halloween edition of 1913 offered a $25 reward to find out who played the prank.

Another Halloween brought evidence of a substantial treat for those concerned with academic excellence in the founding of a Phi Beta Kappa chapter at WVU. To the editor of the *Athenaeum:*

Formerly there has been little reward for excellency in the classroom equal to that received for work on the athletic field. Membership in this honorary fraternity more than meets the need and the possession of its key means more to a graduate than a 'W.V.'[6]

But just in case an organization devoted to scholarship proved too heady for the University, law students organized the Alfa Chapter of Fi Batar Cappar, and the University extended it recognition in 1914. Fifty-seven years later in 1971, WVU permanently removed all recognition from Fi Batar Cappar after its members displayed an obscene banner at the Penn State football game.

Athletic disappointment was more apparent in the Hodges administration than in the Purinton era. From 1900 through 1911, the Purinton era, under coaches Dr. John E. Hill from Yale, Louis Yeager from West Virginia, H. E. Trout from Lafayette, Anthony Chez from Oberlin, Carl Forkum from Penn State, Clarence Russell from Chicago, and C. A. Leuder from Cornell, West Virginia won 63 football games, lost 36, and tied 3. From 1912 through 1915, the Hodges era, under coaches Dr. W. P. Edmunds of Michigan, E. R. Sweetland of Cornell, and Sol Metzger of Penn, West Virginia won 19, lost 13, and tied 3.

Under Purinton, there were many athletic firsts. The 1902 team became the first team to win seven games; the 1903 team scored WVU's first victory over Washington and Jefferson, 39-0. In 1904 West Virginia, though winning six games, suffered three trouncings: Pitt won 53-0; Penn State 34-0, and Michigan administered an unbelievable 130-0 beating. In a 1910 game with Bethany, Captain Rudolph Munk, halfback star, died of injuries received in the game, having provided his team with a touchdown and a field goal before receiving a blow on the head during the second half. He remained WVU's most advertised athletic fatality.

It was in the Hodges administration that WVU lost for the first time (in 1912) to Wesleyan 19-14 and also was defeated for the state championship. In 1913, when it lost again the state championship game with Wesleyan, 21-0, it was decided that only a nationally known football coach, Sol Metzger from Penn, could prevent further humiliation. But in his first year at WVU, Metzger witnessed a third straight Wesleyan defeat, 14-9, and a 48-0 trouncing from Washington and Jefferson. The situation was desperate. The alumni, capturing new talent, including Errett Rodgers, who would become WVU's first All-American, helped provide WVU with a winning season in 1915. A forfeit charged against WVU in the Washington and Lee game was balanced with a 92-6 win against Marshall, the largest number of points ever amassed by a WVU football team. In 1915, the record was sufficiently improved for the WVU team to become known as the Mountaineers.

Almost Heaven and
Almost a University

Frank Butler Trotter
July 1, 1916–June 30, 1928

WHEN, IN 1914, THE REGENTS named WVU's dean of Arts and Sciences and professor of Latin, Frank B. Trotter, to succeed Thomas E. Hodges as president, they managed, according to the *Morgantown Post Chronicle* of July 18, 1914, to stage "a complete surprise to all those in authority at the University." Indeed, so unexpected was the assignment of a classicist to head the state's land-grant institution in the new era of practical achievement that no one apparently took the nomination very seriously. In a spirit of *deja vu* many considered Trotter merely the latest in the growing number of figurehead leaders. Not the least of these astonished observers was Trotter himself, who was advised to hold on to his deanship while he occupied on an acting basis the president's chair.[1]

Far from an administrative novice, however, Trotter would last longer as president than any of his predecessors or successors while ostensibly helping the Regents locate "the ideal man" as his replacement. One of the academic deans of the period later captured the essence of the new president's staying power, as well as his pragmatism, when he reminisced that Trotter was "a West Virginian

105

by adoption, by adjustment and long residence, and by wide acquaintanceship."[2] Another colleague simply acknowledged that Trotter always had had friends and relatives who counted in the conduct and control of University policy. Two examples were a close associate, J. S. Lakin, president of the State Board of Control, and his own brother, James Russell Trotter, formerly State Superintendent of Schools and University Regent, who served until his death in 1925 as a professor in the WVU College of Law.[3]

Trotter knew academe was changing, and neither he nor his friends intended to resist twentieth-century notions of progress. In writing to one applicant who was seeking his former position in Latin, Trotter simply noted on June 23, 1915, that the recent dropping by the faculty of the ancient language requirement had so depleted the Latin work "that my assistants do it all and then have time to spare." To another, he admitted that "Latin is fast losing its hold with us here, there being few students in Latin and fewer still in Greek." He was certain, therefore, that in a few more years his successor would be compelled to do some work in English "as it looks now there will not be a full man's work in Latin." He seemed to be denying that he, as president, had either the authority or desire to turn back the clock in behalf of his own chosen discipline, and to be asserting that he at least was not resisting bringing the University more in line with the original vocational objectives of the Morrill Act.

But to those outside of academe, Trotter's ability to adjust to the twentieth century was untested and therefore unknown. After the University's recent experiences with Purinton and Hodges, the state press sought a different kind of leadership; and Trotter seemed on the surface too much in the pattern of his old-fashioned predecessors. Like them a product of Civil War days and since 1907 a participant in the highly factionalized affairs of the WVU faculty, Trotter had received administrative posts from both WVU's seventh and eighth presidents.

Calling for innovative changes rather than a continuation of past practices, the *State Journal* stated on July 25, 1914, that "It would pay West Virginia to get an educator of at least national, if not world-wide, reputation and prominence for president — even if he cost twenty thousand dollars a year." In rare agreement with the newspaper from the southern part of the state, the *Wheeling News* on the same date endorsed such liberality and furthermore urged the Regents not to restrict themselves to West Virginia natives in their search for a modern candidate, for "we ought to have a big man for president of the University. A very big man. We hope the board will find such a man."

The *Morgantown Post Chronicle* disagreed with its journalistic brethren, stating that as a simple proposition the University did not need a "very big man" because is was not a "big university." Because a big man needed the resources of a giant university, it explained, such a leader would be disappointed with WVU because "a great university presupposes, for one thing, a state full of crowded high schools, a state with a highly organized and generously maintained system of common schools. . . . The biggest kind of 'big man' could not create, off-hand, a great university in a state as lacking as was West Virginia of a decade or two ago in facilities for preparing students to enter college." Admitting West Virginia lagged in secondary education, it nevertheless optimistically added: "We are making rapid progress along these lines in West Virginia these days, but a very large proportion of our high schools are less than ten years old." But, shrewdly guessed the *Chronicle*, any educational advancement would necessarily have to await the State's decision to tax its natural resources to produce an adequate revenue for its schools.

An assured income for the state's educational institutions became a theme, but not a reality, of the Trotter period. E. G. Smith, president of the University Alumni Association, in a strong address before the State Board of Trade on November 7, 1914, found the answer in a mill tax he advocated for the University. Comparing West Virginia to Nebraska, states similar in population and assessed value of property, he showed by example that Nebraska, utilizing the mill tax, was able to provide its university with over a million dollars of assured income, four times as much as West Virginia which lacked such special funding devices.

To Smith, the mill-tax plan would produce maximum results and offered the perfect contrast with "the present hand-to-mouth system or want of system," which he described as "wasteful and inefficient." Surprisingly, in view of its commitment to Marshall College, the *Huntington Herald-Dispatch* agreed that a fixed plan was necessary for WVU which had not progressed as the people of the state desired. To the *Herald-Dispatch*, whose editorial was reprinted in the 1914 report of the State Board of Regents, the University

. . . has had its periods of progress and prosperity, but these have been too frequently broken in upon by periods of adversity. Its financial existence has been hazardous and uncertain. Its guardians have been unable to tell what a year might bring forth. Whether its needs shall be adequately supplied is left to the whims of a Legislature which meets biennially and whose members make the matter of providing for the University a brief divertisement, taking little heed of its actual needs, and frequently having as little sympathy with its purposes as they have knowledge of its financial requirements.

When the *Wheeling Intelligencer* learned on January 22, 1915, of the Board of Trade's preliminary endorsement of the mill-tax proposal, it pointedly questioned whether such a formula would not remove the control of the state's revenue from the hands of the Legislature. Admitting that the Univer-

sity needed liberal support and some fixed annual income might be bequeathed to the University, it nevertheless judged that "to grant complete independence of any state institution from the legislature is undesirable."

Others called attention to the state's economic advance in the first quarter
of the twentieth century as all indices of growth underscored material gain.
Economic progress seemed particularly apparent in the University's
hometown. From a population of 2,000 in 1900, Morgantown had grown
to more than 9,000 by 1910. By 1920, if one counted in its overall members
those who resided in the immediate adjoining towns, its population approximated 20,000. As the population increased, so did tax valuations and wages.
In 1887, its real and personal property was valued at only $569,852; in 1910
at $8,938,659; by 1925 it had almost quadrupled to $33,974,205. In the small
but increasingly industrial center of Morgantown, the annual payroll of the
glass factories approximated $1.5 million; the American Sheet and Tin Plate
Company at Sabraton $3 million; and the local miners were adding $6 million
in wages to the county's personal income. WVU students, faculty, and staff
were believed to be contributing $2 million annually to Morgantown's new-
found wealth.

In West Virginia, a record 146,088,121 tons of coal were produced by
1927, and only numerous mining accidents, which were sometimes of
disastrous proportions, kept West Virginia from being first in the nation as
a coal-producing state. Its standing as a natural location for industrial growth
also was blemished by the fact that West Virginia coal operators often
repudiated contracts with the miners' union, arbitrarily reduced wages,
employed armed guards at the mines, and made frequent use of injunctions
to restrain striking workers.

In the early days of the Trotter administration, however, more serious
to the University than the kinds of financial support it might obtain from
a Legislature heavily influenced by mine operators was whether it would continue to exist in its original location as determined in 1867. A resident of
Kanawha County, in a direct attack upon Morgantown, reported in the
Morgantown Post Chronicle on December 31, 1913, that "its citizens appear
to be banded into a league for the purpose of bleeding to the last cent any
student who goes there," and that University faculty were hardly ever elected
to local office. He for one could find no law requiring the keeping of the
University at Morgantown, "which is an out-of-the-way place anyway for
. . . the greater portion of our people."

The *Morgantown Post Chronicle* hurried to rebut those charges. It
reported that certain students, enjoying "cooperative association," were
boarded for $3.50 a week; that fraternity men generally paid $4 to $4.50
a week; and that no fraternity charged more than $5 to $5.50 a week. Comparing lodging in other towns, the reporter assessed Morgantown "moderate."

The *Chronicle* also noted University faculty members had served on City Council, and that the Morgantown school board always had included one or more University graduates or faculty members. It was suspected that the Kanawha citizen's complaint was part of a larger threat to remove WVU elsewhere. Therefore, the editor argued, the people of Morgantown should manifest a "conspicuous demonstration" to save the University — such as offering to build a city hospital which could be managed cooperatively with the College of Medicine.

The *Huntington Herald-Dispatch* did nothing to allay Morgantown's fears when it characterized on June 12, 1914, the "fine little city on the northern border" as inconvenient to most people in the state. If the decision were still to be made, it believed the University would be repositioned. "Although loyal to the University," it frankly reported that "Huntington and southern West Virginia are more directly interested in Marshall College, which is rapidly forging to the front as an educational institution of magnitude and stability."

When a resolution was introduced in the West Virginia Senate to appoint a committee of five legislative members to investigate and report upon the advisability of removing WVU from Morgantown to a more central site in the state, Morgantown residents knew they might have to relive events of 1867. The 1915 timing seemed particularly bad, for WVU was now "between presidents."

University supporters and the acting president girded for battle. The theme in behalf of the Morgantown location became, "Character is Greater than Geography," which it was hoped would relegate location to a minor issue. What was primary was that Morgantown had no saloons, had a long history of educational support, and therefore had long partaken of the classical atmosphere. The "relentless commercialism of a great city or the political chicanery of a state capital," unfavorable to the spirit and purpose of life for which universities should stand, became the inspired attacks upon Charleston in the *Morgantown Post Chronicle* of February 18, 1915. Such cities, Morgantown argued, from both ethical and social considerations, would injure immature students.

In what became styled as "the Charleston views," location was obviously more important than city character. The *Gazette* saw Morgantown on February 20, 1915, as "a splendid little city, but virtually a suburb of Pittsburgh," located in an inaccessible portion of the state and subject to out-of-state influences. Because the *Charleston Mail* at the same time saw the "Morgantown School" as not accessible to the Legislature, it recommended Charleston as the new site. As was often true in West Virginia history, certain other cities not necessarily friendly to Morgantown in all matters were not so certain they wanted Charleston, the possessor of the state capitol, to get a corner on the University. On February 22, 1915, the *Wheeling Intelligencer* thought the talk of removing the University from Morgantown was "absolutely silly"; the *Parkersburg Sentinel* dismissed the Morgantown accessibility argument as irrelevant in 1915 because of the existence of railroads and assumed that no matter where the University was located, "local interference," would be a problem; the *Huntington Herald-Dispatch* saw the removal as both impractical and harmful. In its mind, the University did not need relocation; it needed advertising, a consistent educational policy, an "accredited head," and if the acting president were satisfactory, his elevation to the presidency.

Nonetheless, Morgantown was worried, and although not disturbed that the entire campus would disappear overnight, was tormented by the possibility that segments such as agriculture, medicine, or law might be moved to other locales. Agriculture seemed particularly vulnerable to relocation because of lack of space in Morgantown for laboratory farm work. The college also seemed ripe for plucking because of its ability to generate federal funds. The Smith-Lever Act of 1914 and the Smith-Hughes Act of 1917 had provided federal funds for cooperative extension work and education in agriculture and home economics to be matched by state funds. With the federal payment the first year set at $10,000, it was expected that the colleges of agriculture with their experiment stations would receive much more each subsequent year. In addition, state universities across the land were expecting increases in women's enrollment because of the demand for domestic science courses.

Playing upon Morgantown's fears, Trotter tied the first phase of his building program to Monongalia County's ability to raise $75,000 for land purchases. The Legislature in turn agreed to the construction of an agricultural building and a girls' dormitory if Monongalia County delivered. In addition, the Legislature released money appropriated the year before for a medical building and an addition to Mechanical Hall. With the girls' dormitory erected on Observatory Hill on the site of the University tennis courts, the agricultural building in the rear of the Agricultural Experiment Station on the site occupied by the greenhouses, and the medical building located near Woodburn Hall but fronting on Beechurst Avenue, Trotter had gone far to anchor the University in Morgantown.

Agitation over naming the new buildings ensued; in particular, the women desired their dormitory be named "Elizabeth I. Moore Hall" in honor of the principal of Woodburn Female Seminary. After consultation with Governor John J. Cornwell, the Board of Control chose the name Woman's Hall, the state agency desiring that during Cornwell's administration no state buildings bear an individual's name. Nevertheless, when the Agricultural Building was completed in 1918, it was named Oglebay Hall in honor of a

Woman's Hall overlooking the old Athletic Field in 1919. The dormitory was renamed Stalnaker Hall in honor of Elizabeth M. Stalnaker, professor emeritus of psychology, in 1972. She bequeathed almost $500,000 to WVU for student loans. The site of Stalnaker Hall used to be called Observatory Hill because of the University Observatory on it, which apparently was burned by students in 1919 while celebrating a football victory over Princeton University.

member of the Board of Regents, E. W. Oglebay. If the naming was for purposes of receiving an Oglebay endowment, the design failed in its objective. What Oglebay had done for his alma mater, Bethany College, when he donated a farm, a building, and underwrote the department of agriculture, was not repeated at West Virginia University.

To no one's surprise or dismay, Trotter was elected president by the Board of Regents at the close of the 49th annual Commencement exercises on June 13, 1916. Again, Trotter gracefully accepted the position until a successor could be found. Not all credit went to Trotter, the man, however. Some attributed his promotion to the fact that he adhered to the Republican Party faith and the tenets of Morris P. Shawkey, proponent of the "new education." The *Charleston Mail* gave credit on October 4, 1916, to liberal Republican principles for producing a "new university" which previously had starved under Democratic leadership. The *Mail* believed that Republicans possessed

. . . a much broader view of what education — especially higher education, consists in. The aim has been to make it practical and useful as well as cultural and ornamental. The aim had been to afford development to the greatest degree possible in as many directions as possible so that the benefits of this higher learning should not be the exclusive privilege of those only who would follow the so-called learned professions or return home imagining they were above the ordinary and necessary tasks of life.

Noting the superior facilities the University now offered, it was still aware that WVU "can not yet compete with some of the larger and richer and older institutions in other states."

Because of the physical plant, the *Mail* concluded that the debate was now over regarding the removal of the University. Although it admitted "the means of ingress and egress by rail are meagre and the institution is almost cut off from access from the central, eastern, and southern parts of the state save by long, tedious, tortuous, and costly routes of travel," it listed certain commanding positions as more conclusive than geography. One advantage was that "Morgantown presents the typical appearance of the college town — clean and neat, quiet and composed as if the air of study had permeated the atmosphere of the place." Another was that the newspaper was not prepared to witness the unseemly scramble among other West Virginia cities and towns to acquire the University. It held the door open to relocation, however, by stating, "if we must move the University, let us do it right this time" by placing it on 1,000 acres of land some three miles from a convenient city, allowing for expansion and assuring clean air.

James S. Lakin, member of the State Board of Control, closed the door to other University sites by intimating that when Monongalia County offered $75,000 for seven hundred acres of land, the state contributed $200,000 ($100,000 each to the Agricultural Building and the women's dormitory), and a deal was a deal. In an effort to end the perennial question, he stated to the *Charleston Mail* on December 28, 1916: "The seat of the institution is now so well settled, there is little probability that the question of relocating it would be given any serious consideration."

Other events helped keep the University stationary. When a gift to WVU of 931.25 acres located on the Capon River in Hardy County was made by the Lawrence A. Reymann estate "to promote, develop and advance the science of agriculture in its most comprehensive scope, and, in addition, to give particular care and attention to the breeding and development of the herd of registered Ayrshire cattle which constitutes a part of the gift," the University's chance of providing a practical education to its students now seemed assured. The farm, a memorial to Anton Reymann and his son Paul O. Reymann, included not only seventy cows, three mature bulls, and assorted calves, but machinery and buildings, and a recently constructed cheese factory.

Initially, the outbreak of World War I in August, 1914, had a negative effect upon WVU. Seemingly, only the global conflict kept Trotter from continuing his campus improvements, making the University the sports center of the state through the appointment of Harry Stansbury as director of athletics, and nailing down for good his own presidency. On the eve of World War I, many wondered to what heights Stansbury would carry WVU in the world of big-time athletics. Loyal alumni remembered only that Stansbury was from the camp of the enemy, West Virginia Wesleyan College. His appointment had been fought by the alumni, the student body, and local supporters of University athletics because, according to the *Morgantown Post Chronicle* of December 23, 1916, "It seems those in power have completely disregarded all indication of the desires of those most interested in the school." But in behalf of a larger victory, the Allies over Germany and the Kaiser, sports events as well as sports disputes were shunted aside.

Following the enactment of the selective draft law in May, 1916, and the disappearance of many students through immediate enlistment, students remaining on the campus protested the taking of final examinations. Having learned that many universities were canceling exams in the months immediately following the United States' declaration of war on April 6, 1917, the WVU student body picketed the entrances to all University buildings in an effort to convince the faculty to rescind its customary testing. In a cry for help, they telegraphed Governor Cornwell, asking for his intercession with the faculty. From the Governor they received only modest encouragement. Indicating to the *Morgantown Post Chronicle* that he had asked the faculty to reconsider, the Governor noted on June 2, 1917, that he had not ordered them to surrender their prerogatives.

Accompanied by a drum and bugle corps, the students marched to the courthouse square for speeches. Local citizens, reported the paper two days later, advised the students to return to the campus and if the faculty ruled against them, "to take their medicine and say nothing." In an effort to end the conflict between themselves and the faculty, the student body accepted a motion for a secret ballot. If 90 percent of the students voted for the strike, the student body ruled, it would continue. However, 21 percent voted against the strike, and the demonstrations collapsed. Although a minority, unhappy with the results, set out to obtain 400 signatures to an agreement not to take exams, they could not muster half that number.

Because of World War I, University enrollment plummeted. From 2,788 students enrolled in 1916-17, attendance dropped in 1917-18 to 2,370; in 1918-19, to 1,613. Not until 1919-20 was a new enrollment record set when 2,800 students registered. At the beginning of the 1918-19 academic year, President Trotter wrote to young men from the ages of 18 to 21 in the state who might cancel their WVU registration. He urged them to enter school in the fall and remain until called for active service. It was the administration's expectation, according to the *Charleston Mail* of September 14, 1918, that men aged 20 would remain in school three months; those 19, about six months; and those 18, for a year; however, those in medicine, engineering, chemistry, and pre-medicine programs could expect to remain until their course work was completed.

To prospective WVU entrants, Trotter explained the collegiate program which had been developed largely by a native son, Secretary of War Newton D. Baker. Academic institutions had been directed to break down their programs into two parts, one for collegiate work and one for vocational training. Students who qualified for regular college entrance and registered with their draft boards could enter the collegiate branch, and receive $30 per month, plus housing, boarding, uniforms, and exemption from all fees. Those in the vocational section had to meet the qualifications of a grammar school education and be of draft age. They would receive instruction in woodworking, forging, pipefitting, sheetmetal working, auto repairing, telephone installation, telegraphy, radio, acetylene welding, and other comparable subjects. All such students would be considered in the Students' Army Training Corps (SATC). For such services, it was expected that the government would pay the University $1.74 per day per capita for board, lodging, and tuition.

In 1917-18 the College of Engineering, assisted primarily by the Department of Physics, gave training in war mechanics and science to its first 167 draftees. In the fall of 1918, the University virtually became a military camp when it enrolled 921 vocational students and 585 academic students in the SATC. In West Virginia, only WVU, Bethany, Davis and Elkins, and West Virginia Wesleyan colleges had SATC programs. The training program was coordinated by the Reserve Officers Training Corps (ROTC), which had been created out of the University's Cadet Corps under the National Defense Act of 1916. Whereas the College of Engineering, the College of Arts and Sciences, and the College of Medicine were kept unusually busy, the College of Agriculture and the College of Law ceased to function for brief periods. The Department of German was stopped cold because the state forbade any pupil from kindergarten through the University from "studying the language of our enemy."[4]

Many of the faculty aided the war effort outside the classroom. Professor T. P. Hardman was with the legal department of the American Red Cross; Professor A. L. Darby, foreign languages, served as interpreter for the YMCA in Italy; J. R. Trotter became the state food distributor for West Virginia; J. L. Coulter was with the Overseas Educational Commission; and H. C. Jones with the Director General of Civilian Relief. C. R. Titlow of the Agricultural Extension Department helped make the slogan "Help West Virginia Feed Herself" come true.

Educational programs on a wartime basis were no sooner instituted than the dread influenza struck the campus and the town. Turning the Delta Tau

Delta Fraternity house into an emergency hospital, University authorities saw to it that SATC patients were taken care of in the best possible manner. With a major relief agency, the Red Cross, providing sheets and blankets, city nurses volunteering services, and the townspeople supplying food to the students, the number of deaths was kept down. The likelihood of contagion became so bad, however, that the SATC commanding officer dismissed all men on furlough until October 14, and President Trotter suspended all work at the University pending further notice. At a joint meeting of city and county boards of health officials, the city fathers issued orders closing all theatres and churches and prohibiting public meetings until further notice, because there were known to be according to the *Morgantown Post* of November 9, 1918, 116 cases of flu among SATC men and more than 100 other cases in the city.

During World War I, it has been estimated that 2,697 West Virginia students saw active service; that forty-six gave their lives, eight of them in action; and that thirty-one died from either pneumonia or influenza.

With the armistice on November 11, 1918, the University quickly reverted to its normal mode of operation. But in consideration of the kinds of educational experiences the University had undergone during the war, Trotter announced changes in the WVU entrance rules, including recognition of work being done by the normal colleges. Because of new world conditions and a national progressive movement which had linked vocational work with institutions of higher learning, Trotter stressed the need to break with the classical prejudices of the past. On August 18, 1919, he proudly proclaimed to the *Charleston Gazette:* "No University in the country, of the standing of West Virginia University, has more liberal entrance requirements today than has this school. The broader entrance requirements will doubtless appeal to many students. The only required subject is now four units in English."

For fear the president might have overstated this educational emancipation from archaic studies, the Charleston paper hastened to explain that a total of fifteen units had to be presented to the University by a high school student, with English comprising four units. The newspaper also noted that a student needed to present "three units of any one subject, two on a second subject, two on a third subject, and four units made up of any miscellaneous subjects to go with the four units of English to give the 15 units."

After the low point of 1,613 students in 1918-19, enrollment jumped to its highest ever — 2,800 in 1919-20. President Trotter therefore planned more advising and counseling services for the ever-increasing number of students who now found it easier to meet entrance requirements. In 1916, he had provided for a new social committee, of both faculty and students, to oversee social activities of the student body and of the increasing fraternity and sorority life. But it was in the 1920s that the social organizations greatly increased.

Five fraternities had been organized in the 1890s and five from 1900 to 1910, but from 1910 to 1920 only one national joined the other ten. In the 1920s and early 1930s, a dozen new fraternities doubled the original group. As for sororities, three nationals came to WVU in the decade from 1900-1910, joined by one more in the next decade. In the 1920s and early 1930s, seven new sororities more than doubled the sorority population.

In June, 1922, President Trotter named H. E. Stone to be dean of men, and in 1923 appointed Martha T. Fulton as dean of women, following two decades of service in this position by Susan Maxwell Moore. At the same time, he appointed an alumni secretary and planned for providing denominational student pastors on campus.

Concerned for the physical as well as the spiritual well-being of students, Trotter recommended provisions for the regular physical training of all non-military students in 1922 and helped provide better health care. Toward the close of his administration, he also participated in the plans for the new men's fieldhouse and the women's physical education building, whose supporters accomplished its naming as Elizabeth Moore Hall. Because of such facilities, WVU authorities created in 1928-29 a division of physical education with its own director, and ended the practice of relying on part-time personnel for such services.

In addition to making life more comfortable for entering students, Trotter tried to make life more pleasant for faculty members. One successful effort was the organization of a faculty club. Anyone connected with the instructional staff was permitted to join at a cost of $10 a year that provided access to the club, with meals an additional expense. The club's only requirement was that all members revert to the title of "mister." One hundred faculty enrolled, and forty signed up for meals.

Even more important as a morale booster was higher pay, which Trotter was reasonably successful in obtaining. In 1917, 1918, and 1919, he obtained increases which averaged 5 percent a year. In February, 1920, he procured 10 percent salary increases for the year 1919-20 and increases of 20 percent to 30 percent after July 1, 1920. Thus, deans' salaries went from $4,000 to $5,200; professors from $3,600 to $4,200; associate professors from $2,700 to $3,300; assistant professors from $2,100 to $2,700; and instructors from $1,000 to $2,100. In 1921, he procured larger salaries only for the College of Law. By 1923, he had obtained maximum salaries for professors of $4,500, and by 1927 a top salary of $5,000 for a professor in the College of Arts and Sciences.

Nonetheless, during his administration the number of faculty fluctuated greatly. Beginning in 1914 with a general instructional faculty of 67 above the rank of instructor, 27 instructors, and 19 assistants, he ended his administration with a faculty of 79 professors, 29 associate professors, 20 assistant professors, 74 instructors, 52 assistants, and 27 student assistants. Intent upon upgrading the faculty as well as increasing it, Trotter saw faculty with doctorates rise from 21 in 1919-20 to 72 in 1927-28. On August 17, 1922, for example, the *Morgantown Post* proudly noted that every new instructor hired by the University for the new academic year had a Ph.D.

Increases in numbers of both students and faculty after World War I revived the University's efforts for campus expansion and additional buildings. Although talk of moving WVU to southern West Virginia persisted, Morgantown's approval in 1925 of Charleston's retention of the state capitol after its destruction by fire tended to ensure the positioning of the state's highest educational institution in northern Monongalia County. In an attempt at long-range planning which might encompass more than just new gymnasiums, Trotter and Shawkey, along with several members of the Board of Regents, met with business and professional men of Morgantown. At one of these meetings, Shawkey expressed the hope that the building and expansion programs as envisioned by these groups would meet the needs of the next fifty or seventy-five years. He recommended, therefore, an option on the Jamison and Hess farms, lying a few miles north of the site of the University in present Evansdale and Suncrest. He not only envisioned that the next University buildings be placed there, but also urged that the Board adopt a dormitory system so that eventually housing for 4,000 to 5,000 students might be located on the new campus.

Disagreeing, the University's local benefactor, I. C. White (who owned real estate south of the Downtown Campus) objected to Shawkey's projection that WVU move north. If University buildings were to be built on a farm up the river, he declared, the University might as well be removed to some other city in the state. Any additional buildings, he felt, should be in the direction of the state farm on or near the Cheat River Road, commonly referred to as the Mileground.

Trotter bypassed these suggestions by recommending certain steps Morgantown itself could take, such as a new hotel. All agreed that Morgantown should pave more streets in its encouragement of University expansion. There were even some who thought Morgantown itself could be bypassed in University expansion plans by building a bridge over the Monongahela River to Westover, where the University could easily accommodate a student body of 10,000 in a new location.

Shortly thereafter, the alumni declared themselves united in an all-out effort for the needed expansion of the University. They called for the purchase of additional land, and passed a resolution looking forward to an annual state tax to be fixed by the Legislature for support of the University. White encouraged expansionist sentiment and enhanced his own reputation as a benefactor when he made a donation of 1,900 acres of the Sewickley vein of coal in the Hare's Run section of Marion County, a gift whose value was estimated to be between $3 million to $4 million, with the University and the city equal beneficiaries (by 1981, it still was not economically feasible to mine the coal).

In the expectation of getting, the University gave all it had to offer. It awarded wholesale honorary degrees, which it had recently promised never to do again. In a second observance of the semi-centennial, it awarded all living ex-governors its highest diploma. In addition, the University awarded honorary doctorates to Judge James F. Brown of the 20th Judicial Circuit; Earl Oglebay, Wheeling industrialist; Mrs. Livia Poffenbarger who had headed the women's division in selling World War I Liberty bonds; I. C. White; Daniel Willard, president of the Baltimore and Ohio Railroad; Secretary of War Newton D. Baker; Ambassador John W. Davis; and Bishop Mathew Hughes.

Having secured approval from both local and state interests, and from students and alumni, Trotter launched a million dollar building program in which his first priority was the Law Building, commenced in 1921, and finished in 1923. At its dedication on January 20, 1922, Dean Roscoe Pound of the Harvard Law School delivered the chief address, and Dean J. W. Madden revealed the present status and future goals of the school. In Madden's view, the school's assets were a law building which in beauty and utility surpassed all others in the nation and the world; an enrollment larger in size and superior in preparation than in the past when many had lacked substantial undergraduate work; a minimum requirement of admission, beginning in 1924, of two years of college work; and a reasonable start toward a working library of 15,000 law books. It seemed appropriate that Governor E. F. Morgan, an alumnus of the College of Law, handed President Trotter the keys to the new building.

Another of Trotter's priorities was a chemistry building. Commenced in 1923 and completed in 1925, the Chemistry Building, of Georgian style, was "intended to surpass any present structure on the campus," according to the *Morgantown Post.* Consisting of four stories, a basement, and a serviceable attic, the brick-and-stone fireproof building contained one hundred rooms, a lecture hall with 300 seats, and was expected to accommodate more than 2,000 students. Its construction was urgently needed in view of the fact that chemistry enrollments were clearly on the rise.

A more modest request was a cafeteria, completed in 1924 at a cost of $30,000. Erected on a lot between the Library and Mechanical Hall, it was to accommodate all male students at the University. Meals were sold at "merely a break-even price," but the cafeteria was expected to pay its way. Moreover, it was expected to provide work for students who needed additional money to meet college expenses.

College of Law, WVU's oldest professional school established in 1878, moved into its own home in 1923. Sculptures of the West Virginia seal decorate both ends of the building and the names of eminent legal scholars are chiseled in relief on concrete across the front of the building. In 1972, it was named for Clyde L. Colson, who was dean of the College of Law and acting president of WVU. Colson Hall was renovated in 1979 to serve as an undergraduate library center and to house the West Virginia and Regional History Collection.

At the beginning of 1926, the University for the first time in its history inventoried its physical property. Its total valuation was $7,076,267.89, and consisted of the following items: agricultural implements, $5,333.50; scientific apparatus, $297,007.61; books, $180,491.29; furniture and fixtures, $155,126.11; livestock, $55,132.00; machinery, $110,455.63; office equipment, $16,444.74; tools, implements, appliances, $60,521.59; miscellaneous properties, $97,405.15; and University buildings and lands, $6,098,350.27.

Not on Trotter's list of needed University buildings was Mountaineer Field. The new 34,000-seat football stadium was supposed to be a gift from nearly 7,000 alumni and other citizens who subscribed $400,000 in 1923-24 to add to $300,000 borrowed money.[5] In behalf of this, newspapers after World War I had fanned interest in such a project across the length and breadth of the state. Editorials on the subject proclaimed that students should support the project as "a permanent memorial of their love for the institu-

Mules, horses, wagons, and a steam shovel helped build the first Mountaineer Field, which was dedicated in 1925.

tion," and alumni should support it for "its influence strikes out at unknown angles and unmeasured distances; it will unite and activate West Virginia alumni as will no other building placed on the campus."

Two misconceptions, both of major proportions, marred the performance of the Stadium Corporation, an organization of private citizens approved by the Board of Control and charged with the erection of the stadium "with the understanding that the structure as erected, from the footers to the coping, shall be and become the property of the state of West Virginia." One was the expectation that the stadium would cost only half a million dollars (it cost $1 million); the other was that its costs would be paid off in a very short period of time (the state eventually had to pay off the debts).

To ensure success, benefactors had been lined up in advance with I. C. White, treasurer, and A. B. Fleming, vice-president of Consolidation Coal Company, co-chairmen of the campaign. Direct solicitors, F. Roy Yoke, alumni secretary, and Harry Stansbury, director of athletics, were expected to make unnecessary the hiring of expensive outside fund-raisers. The expenses of the campaign were to be borne by profits from successful football seasons, and the keystone of the campaign was a plan to raise, according to the slogan, "Five hundred thousand dollars in fifteen minutes " during halftime of a regular football game. But despite the noteworthy preliminary efforts, only $100,000 of the $500,000 was proffered at the rainy Thanksgiving game of 1923 with Washington and Jefferson College — and some of it by football fans whose signatures on the soaked pledges were so illegible as to preclude later identification.

A second campaign had to be instituted through special appeals to towns and cities across the state. Morgantown itself raised $106,000 of its $150,000 quota. In an effort to arouse enthusiasm, the editor of the *Morgantown Post* reminded the city's readers on December 18, 1923, ". . . that the rest of the state will receive from the stadium only gratification in seeing the University football team well taken care of, but to Morgantown it means an addition to 'points of interest' in the city, and added dollars to the local merchants." Although he hated to see the campaign presented as a business proposition, the editor nevertheless admitted it had become necessary to make the appeal on that basis. He would have preferred, he said, to consider it "a test of city pride, of city appreciation, of city generosity," but such arguments had missed the mark with Morgantowners.

The arguments were far from convincing. A decade later with $245,000 in interest paid, with $30,000 in interest in arrears, and with athletic profits drained of nearly $100,000 in ten years, there existed a total of $497,000 in debts, of which $337,000 was in 6 percent bonds, $30,000 in interest, and $130,000 in current obligations.

What had gone wrong within the decade to transform the original call for private support to a request that the state assume the financial obligation of the stadium? One was a rapid drop of gate receipts during the Depression years; another was a decline in the coal industry as early as four years before the 1929 crash; and a third was that the Golden Age of WVU football was but a fleeting moment lasting less than half a dozen years. When the era ended, critics lamented the wrongheaded decisions that had made Stansbury director of athletics, with authority to run the athletic program virtually without supervision from faculty, students, or even, it seemed, the governing boards. But while it lasted, the Golden Age was glorious, and Stansbury was widely praised. According to the September 27, 1924, *Morgantown Post:* "Today there can be no questioning of the wisdom that brought Harry Stansbury to Morgantown . . . He, more than anyone, is responsible for what the University has done in athletics. He is also the man most responsible for the new stadium. . . . The stadium is the gift of loyal graduates and friends of West Virginia University, but without Harry Stansbury, its materialization would have long been delayed."

The Golden Age of WVU football had begun in 1916 when Trotter had become permanent president. In 1916, Mont M. McIntire began his four-year coaching stint in which his teams won 24 games, lost 11, and tied 4. Even more impressively, his teams outscored their opponents 854 to 248. During these years Ira Errett (Rat) Rodgers, considered by many to be the greatest football player in WVU history, played his four years of college football. "The smashing, bruising, runner and catapultic passer," with "amazing drive in his solid legs and a throwing arm as limber as Dizzy Dean's,"[6] was named All-America fullback in 1916, 1917 and 1919 and was joined in 1917 and 1919 by Russ Bailey, who made All-America as center. In 1918, due to the influenza epidemic, the University did not attempt to field a football team.

As many of its football stars returned from military service overseas, WVU began the slow climb to national recognition as a football power. In 1919 WVU easily captured the attention of sports writers with an 8-2 record, 7 shutouts, and a 326-47 point spread over its opponents. But in 1920 when the record fell to 5-4-1, including emotional losses to Pittsburgh and Washington and Jefferson, sports writers and fans clamored for a new coach.

In 1921 Dr. C. W. (Fats) Spears of Dartmouth, All-America guard in 1915, was brought to the coaching job, and with him "a new discipline and a 'shift' formation that eventually developed into a powerful offense." The new formation, by its nature, demanded speed. Spears looked for talent that was quick, regardless of size, and found it mostly in West Virginia and nearby states. In his first year, Spears repeated the disappointing record of the year before, 5-4-1, but his coaching magic laid the groundwork for the only undefeated record in Mountaineer history in 1922 (9 victories, 1 tie), followed by a post-season victory over Gonzaga on Christmas Day at San Diego, California. In that year WVU outscored its opponents by 267-31. Russ Meredith, a tackle, made the All-America team.

In 1922, WVU upset Pitt 9-6, the first over that rival since 1903. To combat Pitt's jinx over the Mountaineers, Spears had clothed his team in drab gray jerseys rather than the traditional gold and blue. Because the costuming seemingly worked to break the spell, the Mountaineers later resorted on frequent occasions to such special clothing whenever they faced their archenemy. Because of the unusual win, Trotter declared a holiday, and the student body snake-danced down High Street led by the cadet band. As part of the celebration, a dance was scheduled in the Armory, and in a most unusual relaxation of discipline, Coach Spears released his ban on dancing long enough for the football players to participate.

In 1923, the Mountaineers beat Pitt again, 13-7, but lost to Washington and Jefferson by 7-2, which may have put a damper on the campaign to raise stadium funds. The overall season showed 7 wins, 1 loss, and 1 tie. In 1924, 8 victories, and 1 defeat (to Pitt, 14-7) ushered in the new stadium. At least on subscription day WVU beat its long-time worthy opponent, Washington

WVU's only undefeated football team compiled a 10-0-1 record in 1922, winning a bowl game against Gonzaga University on Christmas Day in San Diego, California.

and Jefferson, by 40-0. And in 1924 Fred Graham, an end, became All-America.

When Spears accepted the head coaching job at Minnesota in 1924, he had compiled the best record in the history of the school: 30 victories, 6 losses, and 2 ties. But fans were not immediately worried by his departure, for his assistant, Ira Errett Rodgers, took over. The former WVU star, holding the head-coaching reins from 1925 through 1929, managed 28 victories, 14 defeats, 6 ties. In 1925 Walter "Red" Mahan, a guard, became All-America. To most fans, however, the Golden Age peaked in 1926-27. Only once, in 1928, was Pitt defeated; however, West Virginia always beat West Virginia Wesleyan in the Rodgers years, as well as Washington and Jefferson three of five times.

In the Trotter era, basketball, although eclipsed by football, was also on its way to becoming a major intercollegiate sport. Having begun in 1904-05 and having carried on hesitantly until 1908-09, the sport was then abandoned for lack of suitable playing facilities. But with the building of an improvised frame structure known as "The Ark," basketball was revived in 1915. Between 1915 and 1917 Director G. E. Pyle compiled 28 wins against 22 losses; in

1918 Harnus P. Mullenex of Davis and Elkins College gained only 4 wins against an undetermined number of losses, and in 1919 balanced 8 wins against 8 losses. It was then thought advisable to look outside the state for the next coach, and Francis H. Stadsvold, former University of Minnesota basketball star and a member of its advisory coaching staff, was selected to coach the WVU Varsity Five.

Stadsvold's tenure, lasting until 1933, peaked between 1920 and 1929. Overall, he produced 112 victories and 84 defeats and in seven seasons his teams won a majority of their games; his low point came between 1930 and 1933 when WVU's win-loss record was 37-48. His best years were 1924, in which he won 14 of 16 contests, and 1928, when he won 12 of 18. The 1924 team was particularly strong and included Pierre Hill, captain in 1924; Douglas Bowers, captain in 1923; Homer Martin, captain in 1921; Nathus Rhorbaugh, captain in 1926; and Roy M. Hawley, captain in 1925.

Because the Trotter administration had paved the way for big-time sports, those who were opposed struck quickly when they saw a decline in football success, failure in stadium giving, or trouble with accrediting agencies because of the nature and kinds of athletic subsidies. One critic was State Superintendent of Schools George M. Ford, an opponent of high salary increases for the WVU director of athletics, of extra money for athletic budgets, and of special autonomous status for the athletic director. Working through the State Board of Education, he intended that WVU head the state educational system but at the same time take direction from one governing board. Therefore, when the president of the West Virginia Athletic Conference, an organization of state and private colleges, requested the Board of Education in 1925 to make WVU a member, the opportunity existed to bring WVU back in line, yet, paradoxically, at the head of the state educational system. J. F. Marsh, secretary of the Board of Education, wrote Trotter that WVU should seize leadership of the state conference. Interested observers in the state sat back to await the results.

At first, Trotter handed the request to the University Athletic Board, consisting of two faculty members appointed by Trotter, two alumni elected by the Alumni Association, and two undergraduates elected by the student body. The Board voted unanimously against entering the conference, citing major objections. In brief, reported the *Morgantown Post* on February 4, 1926, the Athletic Board perceived few common interests with the smaller institutions whose programs were far more modest than those at WVU, and much potential trouble in political interference from Charleston.

With the response of the Athletic Board broadcast across the state, the *Morgantown Post* urged that everyone "sit tight," and that Trotter veto the Board of Education's request. Conceding that the Board had control over physical education policies, the newspaper stated on February 5, 1926, "it's doubtful the lawmakers of the state intended it should regiment University athletics on the same level with the secondary schools." To the *Post*, Superintendent Ford had "become a victim of the itch to centralize which seizes most people sent to Charleston to serve the 'whole' people."

To its regret, the *Post* learned that to "sit tight" and watch the matter disappear was faulty logic. Trotter, it seemed, had no discretion about making the University a member of the newly formed West Virginia Athletic Conference, and the State Board ordered the University to join the conference. Displeased with the recommendation of the Athletic Board, Ford suggested that Trotter appoint a new board and assume the authority to enter the conference. Ford's determination placed Trotter in a bind, and angered Stansbury. Ford, too, was annoyed. In response to a letter from Stansbury explaining the negative vote of the Athletic Board, Ford took the occasion to rebuke Stansbury. In laying down specific instructions to be "observed strictly," Ford indicated "the order relating to the University membership in the West Virginia Athletic Conference will be complied with without undue delay."

Stansbury charged that the University would lose prestige and position now held in national educational and athletic circles if placed educationally or athletically with prep schools, normal schools, and junior colleges via an association with institutions with less than a fourth the enrollment of the University. If it were not for obligations to 500 men in the state who had endorsed a $200,000 note for the stadium fund, Stansbury confessed to the *Post* on March 10, 1926:

I have been ready to leave the employment of the University for two or three years. I mention this point because it has to do with a conviction that has grown upon me . . . that there is a dead hand on all attempts to make this institution as great as the large and creditable state universities of Ohio, Illinois, Minnesota, Wisconsin and others . . . the reasons underlying this failure are widely known and widely discussed . . . my judgement is that a day of reckoning in matters of educational policy as they adversely affect the University and stifle its growth is near at hand.

The buck had now passed to Trotter. In February, 1926, he recommended joining the conference, and the University Council of Administration concurred the following month. Trotter later explained his recommendation by saying that the University had nothing to fear, that a state conference had no authority whatever over the University's schedule. Moreover, he suggested the day after Stansbury's threat, that a very good reason for joining the conference was that the University had "an unsavory reputation about athletics in other states," and a conference would help "rid that reputation." (The University faced expulsion from the North Central Association of Colleges and Secondary Schools following Stansbury's admission that athletics were subsidized by the alumni and athletic receipts, and expenditures were not audited.) Stansbury had a ready answer for President Trotter. If the

University were relieved of joining the conference, he would agree not to meet any school not in the conference; this, he contended, was what the Board of Education said it had in mind. However, the Board declined Stansbury's offer on April 1, 1926.

The action failed to reckon with student and alumni reaction. The student body called on WVU athletes not to participate in any contest with members of the West Virginia Athletic Conference, and an informal canvass of members of the Varsity Club showed wholehearted approval of the proposed boycott. For good measure, Stansbury said he knew of no way to compel team members to play.

Student activity energized the state presses the entire month following the Board's decision. The Romney weekly, the *Hampshire Review*, equated the Board's action to the New York Giants breaking up their National League schedule in order to play bush teams. "To us the ruling appears absurd, notwithstanding the board's approval and President Trotter's apologetic defense of it." Because of the first-rate teams the University had played, WVU had received great publicity; the team had become the state's ambassador; and the superintendent of schools should have kept out of the situation.

To *The Charleston Gazette*, as long as students paid their own way they should be permitted to run their own athletic program. To the *Huntington Herald Dispatch*, it was good for students to let off steam; it reminded the Board that if students refused to participate in athletic contests, the decree of the Board could hardly be carried out. To the *Parkersburg News*, it was astonishing that the University president would take a stand against the student body in matters concerning undergraduate affairs. The *Charleston Mail* simply asked that more light be shed on the subject.

The University Alumni Association asked the State Board of Education to withdraw WVU from the state athletic conference. Without a dissenting vote, alumni also asked for legislation to establish a separate constitution and a separate board of governors for the University, a millage tax for the support of all state higher educational institutions, a bond issue of $25 million to run for 30 years to complete at once the building programs for all state schools as well as the State Capitol, and to provide for a committee to raise a revolving fund for the aid of University students. The meeting was the best attended in years, and the alumni supported Alumni Secretary Yoke and Athletic Director Stansbury with their votes of confidence.

In September, the Council of Administration, reconsidering the matter, reversed its previous position by ruling that membership in the conference was undesirable and impossible; by October, West Virginia University had resigned from the state athletic conference.

In the midst of the athletic controversy, Trotter asked the Board to entertain his third request to resign, and this time the Board agreed to seek a replacement. The Board's first official offer went to J. W. Withers, dean of the College of Education of New York University. Withers, a native West Virginian born at Ben Lomond, Mason County, was interested, but cautious. By not immediately accepting a tendered salary of $15,000, Withers was reported by the *Morgantown Post* on August 20 and 22, 1926, to be holding out for $18,000 and a five-year contract, as he was then 59 years of age.

Withers' delay afforded the state educational leaders an opportunity to protest the decision. In an October, 1926, letter to State Superintendent Ford, a copy of which he sent to each member of the Board, Shawkey, now president of Marshall College, expressed grave reservations about paying Withers such a high salary to head WVU. "I do not believe a man who can only be persuaded to accept the service by the payment of an unusual salary has the right spirit for the work," declared Shawkey, who also asserted the reported salary hardly compared to the payments that he and other educators in the state received. The Shawkey letter, creating great newspaper interest by being published on November 13, 1926, perhaps influenced Withers to hesitate even more in accepting the position. Despite offers of alumni support and Governor Gore's personal endorsement, Withers firmly refused the presidency by the end of the year.

Failing to secure an executive for WVU and losing the battle to keep WVU in the state athletic conference, the State Board of Education made one last effort to placate WVU supporters. On January 8, 1927, the Board proclaimed that the normal schools would adhere to the purposes for which they were created—that of training teachers for the schools of the state—and not "advertise themselves as junior colleges or half-way universities of the state."

Despite the capitulation of the State Board of Education, supporters of the University had had enough of its kind of governance. On behalf of the University, they introduced in the 1927 Legislature a bill creating a separate board of governors for West Virginia University. Passed on April 14, 1927, the act became law without the signature of Governor Gore. Thus, the search for WVU's tenth president passed to a new governing body.

To *The Charleston Gazette*, on April 7, 1927, the University victory was easily explained: it was accomplished not because of a belief in the differentiation of educational missions by the several colleges of the state; it was accomplished as a result of the dispute over athletics. When the new Board of Governors selected John Roscoe Turner, dean of New York University's Arts College, colleague of Dean Withers and also a native West Virginian, the fact that he was a cousin of the WVU Athletic Director seemed to underscore the interpretation of the Charleston paper.

While faculty, alumni, and some students were intrigued in the 1920s by the controversies between WVU and the normal schools, most University students and some faculty were absorbed in their own campus lives. Breaking with the past, teachers and students in the 1920s began to search for their own identities and to test their own sources of power. They usually acted through organizations: a student council, a religious group, a social fraternity or sorority, or a class with which they identified. If women adopted bobbed hair, lipstick, short skirts, silk stockings, and both men and women smoked cigarettes and talked openly about sex, they were only doing what everyone else was doing and were possibly more regimented in their conduct than they cared to admit.

Such a search for new life styles often brought students into direct conflict with townspeople. Disturbed about the rise in prices of items considered essential to better campus living, such as Cokes, ice cream, milk, grape juice, and sundaes, students initiated on May 4, 1920, an indefinite thirst strike against local merchants until prices on their list were lowered. Subscribing $30 to a publicity fund, WVU propagandists utilized newspaper ads, handbills, and signs to present their side in the price war. When the two most influential proprietors of soda fountains in the city, the Comuntzis Brothers and the Sturgiss Pharmacy, accepted the students' fair price list on soda water products "virtually in its entirety," the protestors promptly removed their ban, but relentlessly continued it against other dealers. When all merchants capitulated, the students donated the $20 which remained in their publicity fund to the YWCA. On October 11, 1921, they successfully campaigned to force the reduction in the prices of haircuts and restaurant meals through the strategy of compiling and comparing prices in other cities to those in Morgantown.

In contrast to the students, faculty members in the prosperous twenties were less successful in their war against Morgantown prices, particularly as reflected in real estate costs. The head of the German Department, Allen W. Porterfield, expressed to the *Morgantown Post* on October 18, 1924, the belief that Morgantown real estate was so high that, unless lowered, the faculty would depart, bringing grave and permanent injury to the University. In turn, President Trotter did his best to picture the University as an economic asset to the town and to suggest in a *quid pro quo* manner that the town should not take advantage of either students or faculty. Stating to the *Post* on March 9, 1927, that University clientele should be treated as neighbors rather than as a source of an annual $3 million income, Trotter suggested neither housing nor food should be priced too high.

The faculty, unsuccessful in besting Morgantown real estate agents, were more successful when combating national figures like William Jennings Bryan, who contended that too many college professors were forgetting God in their teaching and were making evolution a cause rather than an agency in the world's development. Speaking in Commencement Hall, on March 11, 1922, to a packed audience on the subject of "The Bible and Its Enemies," Bryan charged: "The teaching of evolution and Darwinism by University professors is ruining the faith of the young people of America." Using figures from nine representative colleges, he showed to his satisfaction that the proportion of students who did not believe in the Deity increased two or threefold between their freshman and senior years. Characterizing evolution as "tommyrot," Bryan offered $100 to any person in the audience or elsewhere who would set down the teachings of evolution in such a manner to show that they coincided with the doctrines of the Bible.

After weeks of thought, Professor R. C. Spangler of the WVU Department of Biology decided to accept Bryan's challenge. Expressing in a letter to Bryan a belief in the supernatural, in the Old Testament, the virgin birth of Christ and His resurrection and immortality, Spangler insisted it was possible to reconcile faith with evolution. Bryan immediately replied to Spangler through the Reverend W. O. Baylor of the Morgantown Christian Church. Denying that Spangler's statement met the requirements, Bryan nonetheless enclosed his check saying "It is worth $100 to me to see a college professor guilty of cowardly evasion." Proclaiming that he had tied the tongue of one evolutionist and thus protected many students, Bryan insisted that Spangler answer the next important question, "From what ape did you descend?" Bryan, who recalled that he recently had met one man who preferred to be descended from a Jersey cow and another who preferred a setter dog, in effect asked Spangler what choice of animal he preferred as an ancestor.

Not knowing at first whether he would keep the check, Spangler ultimately decided to accept Bryan's money as a token of victory. In direct reply to Bryan's question of descent, Spangler traced his own ancestry from the protozoan period, up through ascending grades of animal life to the point where the ape-man, with a brain developed sufficiently to distinguish between right and wrong, became a human being. Reminding Bryan that the latter's ancestry was the same as his own, and that Bryan's relatives included not apes alone but "the skunk, the lizard, the turtle and venomous snakes," Spangler described the embryological development of man at one stage as being equipped with a tail longer than its legs. Taking a thrust at Bryan in *The New York Times* of June 13, 1922, he remarked: "Your ancestry was just the same as mine, and I assure you that your embryological development was the same, except for this one point — I cannot say, I do not know, whether your tail degenerated before birth or was amputated after birth."

On June 20, 1922, President Trotter wrote Professor Spangler, who was spending the summer at the Null Botany Laboratory at the University of

Chicago, that two members of the State Board of Control emphatically had disapproved any further controversy between the biology professor and Bryan. As Trotter explained to Spangler:

In their minds there is no lack of confidence in you. They are not afraid of the truth but so many people doubt the truth as expressed by yourself in the matter of evolution that it is destined to do the University quite a serious injury in our campaign for students and general recognition. Therefore, if you will write for the syndicate this coming summer, please do it entirely incognito as far as yourself and the University are concerned.

Confessing to Spangler that he was no doubt right in his writing, Trotter felt compelled to add:

. . . you cannot educate the state in one brief season and you know how touchy some people are and how matters may seem to conflict with their early beliefs. This is in no wise intended to limit the freedom of speech or limit academic freedom but to protect all our interests.

Spangler caught the point and replied the following day: "No more replies to Bryan will be given out for publication; so, that everything you and the Board wish will be strictly adhered to."

Before the affair was dropped, other faculty of scientific bent who were being attacked across the state for corrupting the morals of the young jumped to the defense of Spangler. One was E. P. Deatrick, WVU professor of agronomy, who warned in the *Athenaeum* of March 21, 1922, that William Jennings Bryan was no scientist and all must guard against the power of his words as an orator.

Another was Professor A. M. Reese of the Department of Zoology. Speaking at a convocation on May 12, 1922, he warned students of the propaganda being spread against the doctrine of evolution and against University professors accused of teaching atheism and agnosticism in particular. Believing that such attacks hurt not the professors but the University as an institution, Reese challenged those making the charges to produce the lists of "scores of students who have been made unbelievers in the Bible" in his classes.

When students were not protesting the actions of townspeople, they were frequently trying to reform themselves. For example, Methodist students in 1923 enumerated in the October 20, 1923, *Athenaeum* campus evils crying for rectification: dancing too late on Saturday night and being unable to attend church on Sunday; drinking; practicing dishonesty in school work; swearing; engaging in "petting parties"; and editing scandalous magazines such as *Moonshine*. In a somewhat resigned fashion, religious spokesmen determined that the only way to improve conditions was for every student to denounce those evils in an open and courageous manner.

In matters of smoking, however, University authorities decided it was best to take direct action against the offenders rather than await the volun-

Aerial view of the campus in the 1920s.

tary elimination of the habit. President Trotter confirmed reports in the February 3, 1925, *Athenaeum* that disciplinary action had been taken against a number of students accused of smoking, that at least one girl had been asked to withdraw from the University because of her bad habit, and that other girls might meet the same fate. But despite the president's stance, a newspaper reporter learned that smoking was very general among WVU students and that at least half the women smoked, saw nothing wrong in the practice, and reported they had received permission from home to smoke.

Other institutions often were cited as examples of how WVU students should behave. When it was discovered that fifty-two eastern colleges represented at the tenth annual conference of the Woman's Intercollegiate Association had stricter rules than the University, WVU representatives immediately brought back two reform suggestions: a rule forbidding un-chaperoned automobile rides after dark, and a lights-out rule after midnight for all dwellings housing women. Although no reason was deemed necessary for the first rule, according to the *Athenaeum* of December 6, 1923, justi-fications for the second included consideration for a roommate's health and welfare, the need to lessen social duties extending over many hours of the day, and the promotion of higher scholastic standing that would be brought about by the proper amount of sleep.

Although university class identification was strong in the 1920s, its enthusiasms had to be checked. In an editorial entitled "The Bold Brave Sophomores," the *Athenaeum* of September 23, 1924, censured the activities of the second-year students: "Roving the streets in gangs, armed with oaken paddles, they gather in the University freshmen and indulge in playful entertainment of giving them a welcoming blister that often goes beyond making freshmen realize their 'place.' "

At one fall-term convocation, President Trotter warned against attacks on freshmen because fights throughout the city between freshmen and sophomores could not be condoned as college custom. In a charge to the student government, he said on September 30, 1925: "Student officers will please see that further melees do not occur on city streets. Keep your foolishness off the streets. We have an athletic field here where you can club each other, but in the future keep student frays off the streets. This is not what the streets are for, nor what you are here for."

Via student mass meetings, class officers made efforts to settle the sophomore-freshman conflict by permitting "class warfare" under rules set by the student council and restricting the major freshman-sophomore confrontation to the class rush set at half time during an October football game. Through student council, both classes eventually pledged their assistance in effecting a truce, and the city breathed easier when the *Athenaeum* reported on October 1, 1925:

Everybody ought to be satisfied with the outcome of class clashes at the University. The students have demonstrated a capacity to manage their own affairs and that ought to reassure townspeople and parents all over the state. The melee of Monday night was noisy and earnest enough, but it never was as serious as most reports made it seem. It was entirely proper that it should be left for the students themselves to handle.

But the diminution of street fights did not mean the end of freshman disciplining. Simultaneously, the council ruled that all freshman women were required to wear class armbands every day including Sunday. For the several women who disobeyed these rules, the council warned that all social privileges would be restricted.

The importance of dress also differentiated the 1920 "rebels" from later students. When the University cadet band proudly displayed its new blue-and-gold uniforms, all approved of the change. Previously dressed in khaki, the University band had "never been able to cope with the richly dressed organizations of other schools." The commandant of the Cadet Corps expressed satisfaction that the band could now "step out with the best of them." The University also added a bugle and drum corps to the cadet band. In the words of the *Athenaeum* on September 18, 1926, "Many large universities have one" and "its formation should allow more students to be accepted in the military department."

The student body also went on record favoring strict observance of the Eighteenth Amendment four years after the measure had been approved by the Congress and the states. Such action was precipitated in an open meeting of the student body when a public speaking class presented the case for implementing prohibition. With speakers stressing that legal observance and not legal enforcement had been lacking in American practices, that prohibition had not failed in the United States, that foreign nations had no right to ridicule this country, and that the new measure must gain strength with age, the WVU student body sent its resolution directly to President Calvin Coolidge.

But somehow the sentiment on behalf of prohibition did not last. Three years later, President Trotter spoke of the "ever-present bootlegger," the dealer in illicit liquor in Morgantown. His remarks were carefully detailed in the March 9, 1927, *Morgantown Post*. Telling the local Kiwanis Club that any boy at the University could get liquor where "I couldn't get a drink if I was starving for it," Trotter insisted that the town government remedy the situation. Saying he approved of the police putting drunk students in jail, he added, "We must send away that class of students in order to keep the University clean."

Perhaps both town and gown authorities were relieved when prohibition came to an end with the advent of the Franklin Roosevelt administration. Jane Holt, WVU student, wrote to her brother, Rush Holt, of changes ahead:

You would be surprised at the excitement the opening of the bar at Point Marion tomorrow is causing. The bus company called all the fraternity houses and asked them if they didn't want to charter a bus to go over. All the boys are arranging ways to go. I'm afraid I'd rather stay in the house tomorrow cause there surely will be plenty of drunk people around. I've got a date but I've decided we're going to stay in all evening.[7]

The era of prosperity had concluded and with it the Trotter administration. Before Trotter could call it quits, he presided over one last controversy, an internal struggle of the faculty over the question of a new college of education and the propriety of the new school awarding degrees that were similar in name, if not in content, to those of other undergraduate bodies. In October, 1926, the Board ordered the establishment of the College of Education, with Professor J. N. Deahl as dean. On July 2, 1927, it authorized this new college, which had been carved out of the College of Arts and Sciences' Department of Education, the right to grant an A.B. Degree in Education and vested in it "full control in recommending to the State Department of Education for the certification of teachers, principals, supervisors, and superintendents." For good measure, the Board also brought under the wing of the new college the University Rural High School.

Many faculty members were dismayed. In special session, they passed resolutions approving requirements for admission into a College of Education for two years of work, but holding that no A.B. Degree in Education should be granted. They suggested that President Trotter appoint committees to confer with the State Board of Education about limiting the certification of high school teachers by the new college. To the faculty, high school teachers could be certified by colleges other than the College of Education, and if such teachers met the requirements of the State Board of Education, they did not need to enter the special teacher-training college to procure the necessary licensing. In addition, the faculty framed a petition to the Board asking reconsideration of its July 2, 1927, action "in order to preserve the integrity of the A.B. degree awarded in the College of Arts and Sciences."

In consideration of the faculty agitation, which received much press coverage across the state, Governor Howard Mason Gore, president-elect Turner, and President Trotter attended a special meeting of the Board on April 30, 1928. Reconsidering its ruling, the Board rescinded its order of July 2, 1927, with respect to the titling of degrees. Although permitting the College of Education to award the regular M.A. degree, the Board required the college to label its undergraduate degree as a Bachelor of Science in Education.

In February, 1928, Trotter was reelected professor of Latin. As a faculty member, he continued in active service until June, 1939. On March 7, 1940, he died two days before his wife, with whom he was buried.

Chapter 7
1928–1935

The Heavy Hand of Politics

John Roscoe Turner
July 1, 1928–December 31, 1934

IN ONE EIGHTEEN-YEAR PERIOD, 1928 to 1946, encompassing the Great Depression, the New Deal, and World War II, West Virginia followed national political trends by throwing off almost forty years of Republican control for fourteen years of Democratic governors. In a sense, West Virginia University students in 1928 were four years ahead of their elders' change in political affection and thirty-two years ahead of John F. Kennedy's famous primary victory in the thirty-fifth state. In a presidential poll in 1928 for a national magazine, *Independent*, they cast a majority of their youthful votes for Democrat Al Smith, the "wet" and Catholic governor of New York, over Republican Herbert Hoover, the "dry" and Protestant Secretary of Commerce.

The Republican *Morgantown Post* classified on May 17, 1934, many of the sensational educational mishaps affecting the University in the state's new era of political change as "the dirty hand of (Democratic) politics" reaching into the affairs of all public institutions of higher learning in West Virginia. Even excusing the *Post*'s conspiracy thesis and political bias, it was true that by 1932 the Democrats maintained a firm political hold upon West

135

Virginia University, made possible by new governance procedures and the victorious party's need for spoils. In this period, six official University presidential turnovers, dire budgetary restrictions, uncontrolled faculty infighting, and the state's disillusionment with politicians and educational administrators prevailed to such a degree that the West Virginia Legislature deemed necessary additional governing techniques and restrictions, both internal and external, for all higher education institutions. Such efforts, it was thought, might rescue the University from being perceived as just another agency of state government under the direction of West Virginia governors.

WVU in the 1930s and 1940s was headed politically for one of its many heralded "new" eras. Not only had Democratic politicians replaced their Republican counterparts in state government, but the University itself was experiencing a rapid turnover of its old guard faculty, depressed by their loss of power, but more importantly embittered by inadequate retirement compensation. They knew, if the young Turks did not, that the University was both acting and being treated irresponsibly. Yet they may well have accepted the short over the long view and been blind to the need for change. One encouraging sign of institutional progress was that, although WVU was completely whipped by the state's nineteenth governor, Herman Guy Kump, it eventually emerged victorious over the twenty-first chief executive, Matthew Mansfield Neely. Although some of the faculty rightly could claim to have participated in the first struggle, most of the instructional and administrative staff opted for neutrality in the more blatant second contest.

The late 1920s period seemed to begin auspiciously enough for the administration, the faculty, and the students when, in 1928, West Virginia University scored a surprise victory over Pitt. After the team had held Pitt to one touchdown, Eddie Bartrug intercepted a pass and scampered 60 yards to the Pitt 4. On fourth down, Eddie Stump passed to Nelson Lang for a touchdown, and Little Sleepy Glenn's extra point kick provided a 7-6 lead. A safety in the final quarter converted the final score into a 9-6 victory for WVU.

West Virginia University canceled classes in behalf of a victory parade down High Street, headed by the Cadet band and Fi Bater Capper. It was well that the newly elected tenth president, John Roscoe Turner, permitted a celebration that year, for little did he or the onlookers suspect that WVU fans would have to wait until 1947 for another victory over Pitt.

A more favorable omen than the 1928 Pitt victory for West Virginia University as it looked toward the 1930s was the fact that its president was the beneficiary of new governance procedures. In 1927, the Legislature decreed that a single Board of Governors should administer the institution. Seemingly accepting the University's dictum that its educational mission was more complex than that of the state colleges, the Legislature authorized the State

Board of Education to supervise all other institutions of higher education in the state but exempted the University from such control.

The *Morgantown Post* was optimistic about the University having its own governing board. On March 30, 1927, it pictured the former controlling agency, the State Board of Education, as having been since 1919 "the pawn of politicians for interests not conducive to the University's welfare nor the entire educational program of the state. Objecting to delays in decisions affecting the University, a local editor predicted, "If the board of education can't do the proposed work, the board of governors can."

Perhaps the most important factors in determining new governance procedures were WVU's disinterest in entering the West Virginia Athletic Conference (as the State Board of Education had suggested) and the state board's inability to name a successor to WVU's ninth president, Frank Butler Trotter. Newspapers across the state inferred that the true impetus for change was not educational theory at all. It was, they unanimously suggested, alumni distress over the potential downgrading of WVU athletic opponents, plus the Marshall College president's alleged influence over the state board. Both factors, they claimed, had sufficiently aroused University alumni to force the Legislature into providing new governance for WVU.

As of July 1, 1927, the new Board of Governors, sharing fiscal responsibilities with the State Board of Control, first assumed power over the University's organization and operation, including the selection of its president, the appointment and dismissal of personnel, and the creation of new departments and colleges. With structural changes in 1947, the Board of Governors was to guide West Virginia University for the next 42 years. Moving rapidly to assert jurisdiction in its first year of operation, the Board of Governors named Charles T. Neff, Jr., superintendent of the Piedmont district schools, as its secretary; Thurman Arnold, member of the law faculty at the University of Wyoming, dean of the Law School; and Dr. J. N. Deahl, dean of a newly authorized College of Education. The Board also equated the salary of the football coach with that of the athletic director and created a Department of Journalism out of the English Department, but within the College of Arts and Sciences, with P. I. Reed as chairman. By the end of 1927, it was ready to name the new president.

Not only was the changing governance structure of 1927 and 1928 bequeathing a new image to the University, so also was Morgantown presenting a new face to incoming Mountaineers. In the March 10, 1927, issue of the *Morgantown Post*, retiring President Trotter had warned the city to rid itself of three evils confronting students in Morgantown: bootleggers, high living costs, and "fake hotels"; the city, in turn, promised to clean up the "hotels and other public places of doubtful reputation." It attempted other reforms as well. In 1928, Morgantown increased budgetary outlays for the construction and maintenance of streets, sidewalks, alleys, and for garbage disposal and street lighting. In 1927, a city ordinance forbade employment of persons with communicable diseases in eating places, and another protected shoppers strolling the streets by prohibiting "barking and pulling" by merchants. In 1928, an ordinance also required all hawkers, peddlers, and dogs to be licensed.

Yet neither Morgantown nor the University could escape the economic and political fate of both state and nation in the 1930s and 1940s. Beginning in 1927, city officials noted a gradual decrease in business which adversely affected city revenues; and in 1929, the beginning of the Great Depression, precipitous declines in the local coal and glass industries.

Considering the long-lasting impact of the Depression years upon Morgantown, it was perhaps not unconscionable for the community to view the University in the 1930s more as an economic mainstay than as a cultural asset. It was the age of Babbittry, and John Roscoe Turner, the new president, perfectly reflected the times. Being an economist, he pictured in his inaugural address of November 28, 1928, West Virginia University "not an end in itself but a means to an end. Like an industrial agent, it is evaluated in terms of its yield."

First and foremost, in the days of the deepening Depression many of the locals thought that the University was duty-bound to keep its enrollment up, both to insure the well-being of Morgantown landlords and to assist in gaining larger appropriations from the State Legislature. However, Dean of Men Harry Stone warned the community that University enrollment would depend to a considerable extent on the cost of living for students in the city, and if low-priced rooms were not made available, the town might well expect the educational consumers to shop elsewhere. As to proper pricing, the dean suggested that if students bunked two to a room, they should not be expected to pay more than $1.50 per week. Stone's warning was heeded, and within a week of his secular sermon to civic groups, WVU produced a listing of furnished rooms for eighty-six men at prices that Stone considered reasonable and fair. For good measure, Stone refused to place on the University's approved housing list rooms he considered unsanitary or unsafe because of having gas stoves with rubber hose connections. One year later, with little prosperity in sight, Stone was able to report that restaurants and families were now able to offer board at $5.50 per week and to continue rooms at $1.50 per week for a grand total of $7 per week.

Housing for married students was not considered a University problem in that the Council of Administration (the president and his deans) forbade, under penalty of expulsion, marriage among undergraduates. Student marriages, oddly enough, were thought to have an adverse effect on enrollment trends. Especially in view of the increasing number of elopements among students, the Council deemed its harsh ruling advisable because early collegiate marriages turned the parents of many prospective students against the University. With the University considered as acting *in loco parentis,* the Council of Administration reported that many mothers and fathers had expressed the belief that the WVU faculty was too lenient in matters of student behavior. The Interfraternity Council felt compelled to offer its own opinion, one that was even harsher than that delivered by the WVU Council of Administration. After condemning drinking, the reading of immoral literature, and the showing of lewd movies, it contended that "student marriages are undermining the social structure of our nation."

Just as important as offering cheap room and board in maintaining enrollment was WVU's ability to offer both jobs and loans for students. The administration soon recognized that economic assistance was essential if students were to partake of education in the Depression years. Before the 1929 crash, Dean Stone had suggested it would be better if students did not work while engaged in getting a college education. After the 1929 crash, Stone urgently requested civic clubs and other organizations to provide loan funds, any kind of cheap quarters, and opportunities for students to obtain work. He suggested that since few students were skilled workers, any type of odd job, but particularly one that could be depended upon for the remainder of the year, was needed so students could pay their room and board. Waiting on tables, clerking in stores, or procuring other jobs "with definite weekly income" were all cited as ways to help maintain the University's enrollment.

In 1931, the University launched a campaign to raise a revolving emergency loan fund for worthy students. Loans, given for a period of three months, were designed to help students through temporary financial emergencies. To subsidize these loans, the University considered accepting profits from dances and movies, and even entertained the novel suggestion of scheduling a post-season WVU-Marshall football game, the receipts of which would go to the loan fund.

Fortunately, charity did not have to begin at home; it could come instead from the distant federal government in Washington. The University welcomed news that the Federal Emergency Relief Act (FERA) had allotted WVU $3,430 a month for employing 228 students at an average monthly wage of $15 for 50 hours of work. The federal government later decided that 12 percent of WVU's students would be eligible for such stipends. During the Depression years, only three restrictions were imposed on these essentially clerical or custodial student jobs: students married less than six months were ineligible as were those who joined fraternities and those who did not maintain a "C" average in their previous semester's grades.

There was no question that University education was a bargain during Turner's Depression-ridden tenure as president. WVU advertised that a student's textbooks would cost from $10 to $40 a year, and registration fees $75 to $125 if a resident; or $225 to $450 if a non-resident. Board and room cost from $250 to $325 a year, and a student's washing, from $18 to $24 a year. In general, the University estimated "the legitimate cost of a nine months' term of residence at the University from $450 to $800 a year."

Conceiving of the University as an economic mainstay meant that newspaper editors throughout the state very carefully studied the University's enrollment figures each passing year of the Depression. In turn, the University maintained in the *Morgantown Post* of February 27, 1931, the general proposition that "the fact that the University has been able not only to maintain its enrollment but to make a substantial increase in spite of the general business depression indicates the high service it is giving to the state and the esteem in which it is held by young West Virginians and their parents." Morgantown papers endorsed this happy sentiment and, in 1930, the *Post* noted with pleasure on April 5 that the WVU student population came from throughout the state. "It seems clear from a study of enrollment figures over a period of years," it said, "that not many West Virginia students are deterred from coming to the University because of the distance to it from their home."

However, the *Huntington Advertiser* within the week interpreted the University's statistics differently. Noting that Pennsylvania had more students enrolled at WVU than the combined enrollment from 22 West Virginia counties, it stated ominously that "such a situation may or may not be important to the taxpayers of this state." As usual, the *Morgantown Post* had a ready answer for the Huntington newspaper: As the number of students from Pennsylvania was matched by the number of West Virginia students attending schools in Pennsylvania, curtailment of out-of-state residents would produce retaliatory action by other states against West Virginia.

With enrollment gaining by 1935, WVU had become the second largest industry in Monongalia County. With assistance from government subsidies both in the Depression years and in the war years, enrollment figures in the early 1930s were in the 2,000 range; from 1934 to 1941 to the mid-3,000 range. While attendance dropped in September, 1944, to the lowest point of 1,749 students, it rose by 1946 to a total of 4,010 with the first of the World War II veterans taking advantage of the educational provisions of the GI Bill of Rights.

In recreational activities, the University might have produced a feeling of welcome relief in a trying period of disillusioning academic and economic realities had its coaching staff not been as unstable as the University presidency during the same period. In football, within the eighteen-year period from 1928 to 1946, coaches changed regularly every three years: Ira Rodgers, Earle Neale, Charles Tallman, Marshall Glenn, William Kern, and back to

Rodgers during the war years. In this period WVU managed 87 wins, 81 defeats, 14 ties. Unfortunately, Pitt, the formidable rival, won 15 games during the period and conspicuously left WVU its one victory in 1928.

Basketball coaches in this period enjoyed longer tenures, with F. H. Stadsvold extending his reign which had begun in 1920 from 1928 through 1933, Marshall Glenn from 1934 through 1938, and R. A. (Dyke) Raese from 1939 through 1942. However, the war years produced rapid one-year turnovers in basketball coaches: Rudy Baric, 1943; Harry Lothes, 1944; John Lewis Brickles, 1945; and Lee Patton, who first appeared in 1946.

There were hints of the Golden Age of basketball that lay immediately ahead for WVU. At the beginning of the 1928-29 season, the team was outfitted in new uniforms going from "the rediculous [sic] in rags to the sublime in silk." To a sports reporter in the *Morgantown Post* of January 4, 1928, WVU uniforms looked like part of the wardrobe of chorus girls. The loud gold silk trunks with blue "trimmings" and the blue jerseys encircled by two gold bars and "West Virginia" in gold letters were such "outspoken colors" that journalists inferred they indicated a team better than any previous University team. To those denied seats in the Morgantown High School gymnasium, it was welcome news that the basketball team opened their 1929-30 season in the new Men's Field House.

The high point of the eighteen-year period was the "Cinderella team" produced by Raese. Raese's overall record, 55 victories and 29 defeats, from 1939 to 1942, was climaxed at Madison Square Garden on March 25, 1942, when the Mountaineers won the National Invitation Tournament. Prominent among the players were James Ruch, Roger Hicks, Rudy Baric, Scotty Hamilton, Richard "Dick" Kesling, and Lou Kalmar. Patton's 1946 team, which gained 22 victories to 2 defeats, ranked third in the National Invitation Tournament, and fifth in the nation. Considered at that moment as having "the best record in Mountaineer history," it was only a forshadowing of the spectacular coming decade.

In 1929, the Metropolitan Theater showed the first talking motion picture in Morgantown. Within a year townspeople and particularly students were requesting the theater owners to schedule Sunday performances. The *Post* was skeptical and suggested on February 18, 1930, that the city council disapprove, for if permission were granted "the idea would spread in certain parts of the state that Morgantown is a 'wide open' town and many parents would be deterred from sending their children to the University." The Student Council thought the *Post*'s reasoning was inadmissible, and, using reverse logic, it went on record on February 27 in favor of Sunday movies as a means of protecting the University against possible enrollment loss. Said John Phillips, council president and Rhodes Scholar-designate, "There has been so much affirmative comment on the matter, we felt a tangible expression of this sentiment should be made." The Depression itself provided resolution of the issue. The City Council permitted Sunday movies in March, 1931, for the benefit of needy families. The practice was halted on October 9, 1932, but resumed on February 28, 1933.

Whereas movies were popular, University convocation was not. The University compelled freshman students to attend this function, held every Wednesday. On January 8, 1931, local reporters noted that hardly anyone else recognized the event and pondered how to improve upon a requirement meant to "stimulate the creation of that feeling of solidarity and esprit de corps." It could only suggest better speakers and required faculty attendance. When the faculty failed to heed the *Post*'s advice, the newspaper did a headcount of attendance. It found only 5 percent of the faculty and 20 to 25 percent of the students generally attended. "We don't blame students so much," reported the *Post* on September 20, 1932, for the "faculty sets them as bad an example in attending convocation as could be imagined . . . and their indifference over the years has spread to students." If convocation was a total failure, there were, however, other groups working to bring students together. One was the Religious Work Council, responsible for a statistical computation of the students' religious preferences in the 1927-28 fall semester. The findings, in order, were: Methodist, Presbyterian, Baptist, Catholic, and Jewish.

Students believed that their esprit de corps would be better boosted by the erection of a commons or union building to be known as the Mountaineer Lodge than by the continuation of the University convocation. The *Post* of May 14, 1929, agreed with the sentiment for "a university ought to be a democratic community. This can't be realized at a University where fraternity and sorority houses provide the only opportunity for students to meet. Approximately fifty percent of all University students aren't affiliated with any social fraternity or sorority."

A small step was taken in 1930 toward a student union when the Mountain Room, also to be used by other campus organizations, was set aside in the north tower of Mountaineer Field. At the room's dedication, on October 3, 1930, the *Post* suggested that the community back the students in their desire for a student union because "the lack of men's dormitories limits the students in their places to get together."

But when students did get together, the *Post* was not always pleased. Those who questioned mandatory military training at WVU because of religious or conscientious objections were told on February 26, 1935, they must appeal to the Legislature, not to the faculty or the Board of Governors. When University students two weeks later joined with other students across the United States in the one-hour walkout sponsored by the National Student Strike Committee as a protest against war, the *Post* reported with a certain satisfaction that there was no disturbance because the participation was confined to a small group of fifty in Commencement Hall.

Within the University community, the biggest entertainment of all during Depression and recovery years was watching the administrative turnovers. During the eighteen-year period, WVU experienced no fewer than three presidents, three acting presidents, and one acting dean of the faculties heading the institution for very short periods of time. These seven executives were: John Roscoe Turner, July 1, 1928, to December 31, 1934, tenth president; Robert Allen Armstrong, January 1, 1935, to September 30, 1935, acting president; Chauncey Samuel Boucher, October 1, 1935, to August 31, 1938, eleventh president; Charles Elmer Lawall, September 1, 1938, to June 30, 1939, acting president and July 1, 1939, to August 31, 1945, twelfth president; Charles Thompson Neff, Jr., September 1, 1945 to June 30, 1946, acting president; and Dr. J. F. Sly, acting dean of faculties (during Armstrong's acting presidency), May 10, 1935, to July 31, 1935.

In keeping with socio-political-economic events from 1928 to 1946 both in West Virginia and the nation, the tenth, eleventh, and twelfth University presidents were practitioners from the disciplines of economics, political science, history, and mining engineering. While all three presidents had impeccable administrative experiences and degrees, economist John Roscoe Turner seemed particularly qualified and especially interesting. A native son "acquainted with the perils of barefooted boyhood among the blackberry patches of Raleigh County," Turner returned after an absence of twenty-eight years, "once and for all, . . . to the friendly hills of my boyhood."[1] Actually, his term in the unfriendly hills coincided with the very worst years of the Great Depression, and the change from Republican to Democratic political rule in West Virginia. Turner's decision to play both the role of a University president and a Republican politician proved atrocious timing, especially in his seeking election in 1932 as a delegate to the Republican National Convention.

Born in Matville, West Virginia, on February 13, 1882, Turner had been a student in West Virginia Conference Seminary in 1897, where one of his instructors had been Frank Butler Trotter. Earning his B.S. and M.S. from Ohio Northern University in Ada, Ohio, in 1901 and 1903, Turner received his Ph.D. from Princeton University in 1913. From 1913 to 1916, Turner was professor of economics at Cornell University. In 1916, he joined Washington Square College of New York University where he served as professor of economics, head of the department of economics, and dean of the college until his call to West Virginia University. Turner was one of the few WVU presidents who could claim to be a productive scholar. In 1919, Charles Scribner's Sons published Turner's *Introduction to Economics*, an outgrowth of his lectures to classes at Cornell and New York Universities; in 1921, the

New York University Press published Turner's *The Ricardian Rent Theory in Early American Economics.* In 1923-24, Turner was chief economist and chairman of the advisory board of the United States Tariff Commission.

During his pre-presidential visits to Morgantown in 1928, he carefully defined the role for the institution he was to head: "West Virginia University's standards shall be comparable to the highest anywhere, the University shall be of the community as well as in it, and the institution shall not undertake to do everything but to do that which it undertakes in such a manner that a degree which it confers will mean all that it should."[2] He also visualized the University as something of a research arm for the state government, calling for a non-partisan bureau of research where agricultural, industrial, and engineering questions could be considered and findings passed back to the people.

When he formally assumed office in July, 1928, he became even more specific regarding the roles he expected the University to play, and the long, hard road it had to travel in order to attain them. On November 28, 1928, the tenth president of West Virginia University bluntly told more than 5,000 persons at his inauguration that in higher education West Virginia held no enviable rank among the other commonwealths because there was no graduate school in the state. This he meant to correct, and from government officials he had obtained the necessary assurances that a graduate school would be forthcoming.

Finding a well-stocked library an indispensable preparation for a graduate program and commenting that libraries everywhere were reckoned the best gauge of the strength and character of an institution, Turner noted that neighboring Ohio State University with 521,740 volumes and the University of Pennsylvania with 602,000 volumes made West Virginia University with 84,000 volumes look weak indeed. But if the audience believed the sheer weight of numbers in the larger universities called for library collections far in excess of that possessed by WVU, Turner compared the library collection per student with institutions approximating WVU's own size: Dartmouth College, with 2,000 students, had 105 volumes per student; Brown, with 2,035 students, had 142 volumes per student; Johns Hopkins, with 1,543 students, had 177 volumes per student; Princeton, with 2,412 students, had 226 volumes per student. In striking contrast, the president asserted, the WVU Library provided only 28.9 volumes per student.

Being an economist, Turner regaled his audience with other dismal facts and figures: in the United States as a whole, there was one college student for every 212 persons, but in West Virginia, there was only one college student for every 318 persons. "As though contesting for cellar championship," Turner proclaimed, West Virginia stood forty-first from the top among the states, with about one-third of its college students attending institutions outside its borders. Finding the states of Washington and West Virginia equal in population, he noted the former had 10,374 college students; the latter, 4,884.

Distancing himself somewhat from the undergraduate programming which Turner believed had absorbed University personnel for too long in the past, the tenth president directed attention toward establishing a research institution of the first order. As a corollary to this principle, he also believed in the strengthening of the professional schools so that the youth of the state could afford "opportunities as good as the best."

Noting in his inaugural speech that WVU's School of Medicine offered only the first two years of a four-year course, Turner indicated that "to go half the way seems to commit us to the whole journey." In West Virginia, "with the exception of perhaps some five hundred midwives" who would face replacement, Turner believed all would welcome a full-fledged College of Medicine, with the resulting supply of trained physicians.

Anticipating a struggle over the location of such a professional school, Turner discounted the belief that a medical college could only prosper in a large city. He called attention to excellent medical schools in Ann Arbor, Charlottesville, Madison, and Iowa City, and cited the fact that the Mayo hospitals were located in a small town. In a university setting, where outside professional calls and alluring fees were fewer and the associations, equipment, and spirit of research were attractive to scholars, Turner believed major medical schools often were created. "I shall recommend," said Turner, "as soon as appears wise, a full offering."

When Congress passed a bill providing nearly $16 million for veterans hospitals, including $700,000 for a hospital in West Virginia, the time appeared right. Turner indicated that Morgantown was the logical location. Admitting that there were many sites more centrally located than the University campus, he suggested that most visitors had found it necessary "to go around the State to get through it, its central portion being comparatively inaccessible."[3] Since modern roads now made geographic considerations less important, Turner believed the larger consideration for a medical school location was "the affiliating agencies at hand."

He called for the location of the veterans hospital in Morgantown. Operated in conjunction with the WVU medical colleges, such a facility would eliminate the need for state citizens to bear the prohibitive costs of trips to Johns Hopkins, Cleveland, New York, or elsewhere. When it was decided Huntington, not Morgantown, was to be the site of the veterans hospital, Turner experienced his first major defeat. Some forty years later, the decision which had located the veterans hospital at Huntington also spelled defeat for WVU when its supporters could not convince the Legislature and the governor to resist the creation of a second medical college, with special federal funding, if established in conjunction with existing veterans hospital facilities.

As the new year, 1929, began, University supporters were optimistic about their chances to receive the necessary funds for a graduate school, library improvements, and a major classroom addition. Loyalists believed the president's program "had received state-wide support given to few educational enterprises," and Turner himself thought he was operating "within the realm of practicable achievement." Confidently, the tenth president proposed in his first budget: $300,000 a year for the next biennium in behalf of a graduate school; $85,000 as an annual appropriation for library purchases; and $212,250 a year over a four-year period to construct an academic classroom building.

What Turner received was something quite different and unexpected: major cuts in all requested items. In what Turner first called "entirely inadequate" action, the Legislature designated a mere $12,000 for the establishment of a graduate school; slashed the book budget to $25,000; and allocated only $50,000 for the library expansion and nothing for a million-dollar classroom building. Only special efforts by President Turner before the Senate and House Finance Committees increased the building appropriation to $300,000.

Long before it reckoned the Depression itself as a deterrent to increased appropriations, the *Post* noted other unfavorable omens for WVU in the 1929 legislative session. Particularly suspect to the newspaper was a rider attached to the revised budget bill specifying that no part of any appropriation for the University could be used for the maintenance or operation of a University rural high school. The immediate intent of this rider, the *Post* surmised, was to restrict teacher-training activities at the University, thus benefiting the normal schools, and its long-range significance was to undermine the College of Education's responsibility for preparing superintendents, principals, and teachers for the public high schools.

The University was not without defenses. The General Education Board, established in 1903 by John D. Rockefeller to aid education, "without distinction of race, sex, or creed," had offered $150,000 toward the cost of a new high school building.[4] The Cass, Grant, and Union districts of Monongalia County had agreed to impose a levy of the same amount as matching funds. Despite objections of the governor and others to diverting state funds for local uses and the location of the high school upon a site which might interfere with the expansion of the University plant, the *Morgantown Post* correctly predicted on April 27 and July 2, 1929, that University officials would have their way in the matter.

Another bothersome fallout from the graduate school request was the suggestion that if the University entered into full-scale graduate work, it should drop simultaneously all undergraduate endeavors. The *Wheeling*

Intelligencer suggested on September 17, 1929, that the University devote itself entirely to graduate research, abandon its work in arts and sciences, and "thus end its competition with the state's private colleges." The *Post* responded on the same date that the path to a graduate school ran through the College of Arts and Sciences, and that such a college was the center of the organization of a true University. "If the only way the University can get a graduate school is to abolish the college of arts and sciences," it said, "the price is too high, much too high."

WVU's efforts in graduate schooling also produced another suggestion several years later that the normal school at Fairmont be converted into the University graduate school. Said the *Morgantown Post* on October 24, 1934:

It would be interesting to know how any graduate school could be dissociated from the University of which it was a part. Graduate schools make constant use of resources of the University and perhaps use library, laboratories, etc., more than anyone else at the University. It's less a separate school than the top layer of all schools which make up the University. It doesn't have a separate faculty, but draws on all faculties of the University.

Undaunted by the omens of 1929, Turner preferred to interpret the $12,000 appropriated for the Graduate School as a definite commitment of the Legislature to establish a full-fledged graduate school two years hence, and he immediately began his search for a Graduate School dean. He also indicated that he would use the $300,000 appropriation for the erection of a new library building, rather than for an extension of the old, and quickly would find a new use for the old building.

Without delay, Turner began organizing the Graduate School. To the considerable annoyance of the old faculty, he selected an outsider, Stephen P. Burke, as chairman of the Graduate Council. He was research director for Combustion Utilities Corporation in New York City. The Board of Governors endorsed Turner's selection of Burke and organization of the Graduate School into basic groups of subject matter rather than departments. This was done, the Board said, for purposes of economy in the use of University facilities, personnel, and equipment. It also indicated that the Graduate School had the power to conduct two lines of work — to pursue research and investigation with particular reference to the problems of the state, and to train and recommend to the Board of Governors candidates for graduate degrees of Master of Science, Master of Arts, and Doctor of Philosophy.[5]

The four basic graduate groups designated were the Industrial Science Group, the Biological Science Group, the Social Science Group, and the Education Group. The Engineering Experiment Station, including the Bureau of Mines Research, all engineering branches, mathematics, geology, physics, and chemistry, composed the Industrial Science Division. The Agricultural Experiment Station, all agricultural branches, botany, plant pathology, genetics, zoology, and the appropriate branches in medicine comprised the Biological Science Group. The Bureau for Government Research, history, economics, politico-legal studies, and languages made up the Social Science Group. All branches in professional education completed the Education Group.

The heads of the divisions were all Turner appointees: Burke for the Industrial Sciences; Dean Fred D. Fromme of the College of Agriculture for the Biological Science Group; John F. Sly of the Bureau for Government Research, later replaced by Dean Wilson P. Shortridge of the College of Arts and Sciences for the Social Science Group; and Dean Earl Hudelson of the newly created College of Education for the Education Group.

Older members of the faculty were unhappy with these appointments. One was the Dean of Engineering, C. R. Jones, who expressed the opinion: "It seems to be the set determination of the present University administration to complete the task of shelving all of the men who have had active connections with former administrations — the men who have built up the University — and to replace them with unexperienced newcomers of a subservient type."[6]

With a graduate faculty and its administration in place, Turner attended to the next phase of putting the Graduate School on firm footing; gaining the necessary subsidies to attract qualified students. The *Morgantown Post* of June 2, 1930, heaped praise upon those persons and corporations responsible for six fellowship programs in the 1930-31 period: "For coming at this particular moment when so many difficulties are being met in getting the Graduate School established and in operation, they will furnish an encouragement and stimulus greatly needed." This they did, for at the 65th annual commencement, the University conferred the Ph.D. degree upon six graduate students who were possessors of these fellowships.

Believing more gifts would be forthcoming when the Graduate School produced results such as these, the *Post* cautioned on May 15, 1931, that legislative appropriations, not gifts alone, were necessary. President Turner, of course, agreed even though he was cognizant of the impact of the Depression.

For the 1931-33 biennium, Turner recommended almost a million-dollar appropriation for the Graduate School — $455,800 for 1931-32 and $508,300 for 1932-33. Defending himself and his budget request at a student convocation he defiantly said, "Don't tell me we can't afford it. We can't afford to do without it." But he added bitterly, "We have a generous legislature in this state. They multiply institutions and then starve them." In response to Turner's criticism, the State Budget Commission recommended a mere one-sixth of the president's request on behalf of the Graduate School, $75,000 a year for a total of $150,000, and the Legislature chose to appropriate no funds at all. The Turnerian economic thesis that a graduate program "has a state-wide view, ignores sectionalism, and puts the well-being of the state above the interests of any locality," and that "a vote against the graduate school is a vote against the state,"[7] simply went unheeded in West Virginia's Depression years. The state's dwindling resources had to be applied to elementary and secondary schools if those schools were even to remain open.

Moreover, the Turner administration discovered that the desirability of a graduate school, despite seeming official and state press approval, had been taken too much for granted. As the Depression deepened, highly visible enemies of a graduate school multiplied across the state. The *Charleston Daily Mail* editorialized on February 18 and again on March 2, 1931, that it was not a sound policy for West Virginia taxpayers to assume such expenses at any time and marshalled leading educational opinion against the concept. Chancellor J. H. Kirkland of Vanderbilt University was quoted as saying most states had gone too far in furnishing graduate education, that it was not an obligation of the state when the public schools were in desperate need, and that a state might not necessarily derive great benefits from a few young people receiving Ph.D.s. President E. M. Hopkins of Dartmouth College, also listed among the skeptical, questioned the wisdom of the state providing graduate level education. Within the state, others suggested in the interests of true economy that deserving, would-be graduate students, like medical students, be given scholarships to go outside the state.

The budget situation for Turner went from bad to worse during the remainder of his presidency. In July, 1931, he was ordered to effect 8 percent savings; in June, 1932, he was told to cut University salaries by 25 percent. In September, 1932, the Legislature ordered that Turner's own salary be reduced from $15,000 to $7,500 a year, and that the salaries of athletic director Stansbury and the football coach be cut substantially. In preparing budget requests for the 1933-35 biennium, a desperate President Turner stated to the *Morgantown Post* on January 13, 1933, that his recommendations for WVU were "at the minimum to maintain the integrity of the University and protect the capital investment of the state." In this instance, he did not plead for special consideration of the Graduate School.

Behind the scenes, WVU administrative officers made valiant suggestions on how to ward off catastrophe. Dean W. P. Shortridge of the College of Arts and Sciences wrote President Turner:

I believe that I voice the sentiments of the vast majority of the members of the faculty when I say that they would much prefer a cut in salary rather than see any of their colleagues dropped at this time.[8]

As he discerned,

Members of the University faculty cannot transfer to other positions even in good times as easily as a ditch-digger can change from one ditch to another. At a time like this it means professional death and economic ruin to some of our men who may be dismissed by a cut in personnel. At a time when the President of the United States is doing everything in his power to increase employment and raise wages, it does not seem a good time for the University to dismiss men with families dependent upon them when economic ruin would inevitably result.

Despite Shortridge's appeals, Turner found himself forced into both horizontal and vertical cuts. In the main, the president reported, it was difficult to adjust salaries downward because the low level of WVU salaries compared to salaries at other universities dictated utilizing salary cuts as little as possible.

To the House Committee on Investigation of the University, on December 27, 1933, he provided these data on the comparative salaries at West Virginia and other universities: the average professor's salary at representative state universities in the north and middle west was $5,242, at the University of Virginia, $5,375, at West Virginia University, $3,536; average associate professor's salary at representative state universities in the north and middle west, $3,733, at the University of Virginia, $4,030, at WVU, $2,531; average assistant professor's salary at representative state universities in the north and middle west, $3,095, at the University of Virginia, $3,118, and at WVU, $2,351.

Turner also noted that the variety of offerings in a University curriculum, together with limited enrollment, necessarily meant small classes with high per capita costs. This fact, he admitted, had led to criticism of the University, particularly of the smaller professional schools. For good measure, he also recognized that criticism invariably had attended the releasing of staff.

When the final budget bill was approved by the Legislature, the University found itself cut one-third from appropriations received two years before. The impact was devastating. In July, 1933, the University Board of Governors released eighteen faculty members and nineteen others were "conditionally retained provided enrollment warrants and finances permit." A local newspaper reported on July 3, 1933, that average salaries for the faculty fortunate enough to remain were: deans, $4,713; professors, $3,538; associate professors, $2,691; assistant professors, $2,397; and instructors, $1,811.

Yet, considering the odds against President Turner in coping with the budget, he did very well in the Depression era in the construction of buildings: the University Library and University Demonstration High School were built. Additions to Woman's Hall and a dormitory for men were financed through bond issues amortized from operations of the dormitories. He also presided over the opening of the Men's Field House and Elizabeth Moore Hall. In addition, he engaged in planning for the remodeling of the old library building into an administration building, and for a mineral industries building.

Moore Hall, completed in 1928, was named for Elizabeth Moore, principal of Wood-burn Female Seminary that was donated to the state to help begin WVU.

He also was responsible for other campus improvements: an electric clock for Woodburn Hall, an ingenious attempt to solve the traffic problem on University Avenue, Oglebay Hall Annex, the purchase of the 158-acre Kearneysville farm for a demonstration center in the use of sprays and in the picking and packing of fruit, and the construction of tennis courts.

To accomplish a major building program, the administration alternated between seeking new sources of financing and postponing major additions to the construction under way. With only $300,000 allocated for the library, officials decided to adopt a design permitting additions in future years. The first Library unit thus was planned as a three-story structure with space for 350,000 volumes and seating for 430 students. When eventually completed to seven stories, "just two less than Yale, the largest library in the United States," it was to have, said the *Morgantown Post* on June 28, 1929, a capacity for one million volumes and seating for 840 students.

Turner planned for each new building to be designed and located to enhance other nearby buildings and the area it served. The Library was placed on the I. C. White property so as to preserve the trees and to provide a court-yard facing the Law Building, and was flanked on one side by the recently built Chemistry Building and on the other by an undetermined future build-ing. With the Library as the focal point of a second campus circle, the faculty reported itself to the *Post* on July 16, 1929, highly pleased that attention was paid to make the new library "the last word in efficiency, utility and com-fort, characterized by quiet beauty befitting it as the intellectual and cultural center of the University."

Construction of the Library and its new campus setting called attention to the fact that University Avenue ran directly through the campus, causing pedestrian and traffic congestion from the Law Building to the Sunnyside Bridge. Turner proposed to relieve campus congestion by the construction of a vehicular tunnel — a proposal revived, again unsuccessfully, forty years later by President James G. Harlow. The top of the tunnel, designed as a plaza, would unite the campus; the cost was estimated at $93,000. Said the *Morgantown Post* on March 8, 1930, in customary approval:

The problem of improving traffic conditions through the University campus is one that can't be postponed indefinitely. Conditions are becoming worse and no relief can be expected without a drastic proposal such as President Turner's for a tunnel on University Avenue . . . . Relief is needed for motorists and students. Hundreds of students cross University Avenue between classes, traffic is slowed and it's dangerous for students crossing.

When no appropriations were forthcoming for either a bridge or a tunnel, Professor J. B. Grumbein, who succeeded C. L. Brooks as superintendent of grounds in 1932 and retained the position until he retired in 1945, recom-mended a safety island, to become immortalized as Grumbein's Island, with stoplights at the intersection of College and University Avenues. Turner grudgingly accepted Grumbein's proposal, and none of his successors was able to fashion a more ambitious alternative.

The Library was dedicated on November 30, 1931, and on June 7, 1933, Mrs. Guy D. Goff donated Senator Goff's private library of 9,000 volumes to the University, making its total holdings 130,000 volumes exclusive of newspapers, pamphlets, and manuscripts. A year later, the State Education Association established a memorial to honor the life and work of Waitman T. Barbe whereby his private library, which Mrs. Barbe bequeathed to the University Library after his death, could be enlarged and protected, and made more useful to new generations of University students.

On September 14, 1933, the administration announced that it desired to place the offices of the president, the financial secretary, the Board of Governors, the graduate council, the Bureau for Government Research, and two or three deans under one roof, releasing half the first floor in Wood-

Main library opened in 1931.

burn Hall for classroom use. By March 3, 1934, it was reported that of $20,150 needed to remodel the old library, the Civil Works Administration was granting $15,150, with the understanding that the building would be used for both administrative and classroom purposes.

Dormitories could, through student charges, be made self-liquidating. Turner's first attempt at a men's dormitory was made in 1932 when he housed thirty boys in the Boughner house at 540 North High Street. Said the *Morgantown Post* on September 9, 1932, a paper that always welcomed the diminution of fraternity influence in University life: "The opening of men's dormitory at the University this fall, even on a limited scale, may prove to be a significant event in the history of the University . . . Experience has shown that the dorm system, properly supervised and guided, offers the best method of introducing students to university life with the greatest prospect of facilitating adjustments."

The administration, in what President Turner called the University's "most progressive step in a decade," then turned to plans for a new men's dormitory and two additional wings on Woman's Hall, seeking approval for a $400,000 loan from the U.S. Reconstruction Finance Corporation. The U.S.

Public Works Administration (PWA) granted the sum toward the cost of a five-story men's dormitory at the corner of North High and Prospect Streets, housing 360 students; and an addition to Woman's Hall accommodating 150 women. After the plans were drawn, it was found the PWA costs were too low, and that both dormitories would require additional money. Eventually, the PWA granted $625,000 to permit construction, with chief credit for the transaction going to A. B. Koontz, Charleston lawyer and a member of the University Board of Governors.

The University Demonstration High School, first housed in Woodburn Hall and then transferred to the old Dering home at the corner of Willey and Spruce Streets, was opened on September 6, 1925, for eligible pupils from Cass, Clinton, Grant, and Union districts. To state critics of the enterprise, it was the University's bold bid in teacher training, a province of the normal schools, in retaliation for the normal schools' entry into arts and sciences instruction. The demonstration school probably succeeded because, in the Depression, it cost the state nothing. Its new building was the result of an offer by the General Education Board of New York City for $150,000 to be matched by a levy of $150,000 on the districts involved.[9] The building at the top of Price Street was opened in time for the fall semester of 1933.

Despite his success with a building program, however, Turner's days as president were numbered. Perhaps F. N. Sycafoose, delegate from Webster County to the State Legislature, first foresaw Turner's fate, if not necessarily the real reasons for it, when he recommended dismissal because (1) Turner had permitted women to smoke; (2) had permitted the teaching of evolution; and (3) had neglected the work of his office by seeking election as a delegate-at-large to the 1932 Republican National Convention. On July 23, 1932, the Morgantown Republican Party paper was incensed, reminding Sycafoose that evolution was an acceptable and scientific doctrine taught at most universities worthy of the name. It also wanted to know if there was anything incompatible between being University president and exercising the full rights of U.S. citizenship. But rather than investigate these accusations more thoroughly, suggested the *Post*, it would be better to check the mental processes of the Webster County delegate. When the House of Delegates by a vote of 75 to 3 expunged from its records Sycafoose's resolution, the paper was satisfied with the legislator's defeat and hoped the news would "catch up with press dispatches of the introduction of the resolution tending to present West Virginia to the world as another Tennessee or Arkansas."

In the spring of 1934, three events drew attention to Turner's shaky presidency. In March, the State Senate angered Governor Kump by rejecting A. S. Brady as a member of the Board of Control, the fiscal agency that had annoyed President Turner. In April, Governor Kump appeared, on a private matter, before the Board of Governors to discuss growing dissatisfaction with Turner. For public consumption, it was divulged that the Board had considered dividing the duties of the president and had dismissed D. M. Willis as financial secretary. The summer of 1934 proved decisive. In a July meeting of the Board, Turner was provided with only conditional employment for the remainder of the year. In August, Kump requested information from John Baker White of the Board of Control about why Democrats were not receiving jobs on the University campus and was informed that 32 of the top 38 University administrators were Republicans. Only the University chaplain, the dean of the School of Medicine, the director of the Summer Session, the chairman of the Graduate Council, the University physician, and the University nurse were Democrats.[10]

In the fall of 1934, the public was informed of Turner's trials and tribulations. Having lost political favor, Turner next tasted faculty revolt. In September, Dean Shortridge's 1933-34 annual report for the College of Arts and Sciences was spread across the state. In it, Shortridge sharply criticized the consolidation of the Departments of Botany, Zoology, and Plant Pathology into a single Department of Biology administered by the College of Agriculture. Turner had engineered the change the previous year. Shortridge also criticized faculty dismissals, suggesting that in the future no staff member be dismissed without one year's notice. In proposing the creation of a University Senate or some other agency to give the faculty an opportunity to express itself in a form useful to the administration of University affairs, Shortridge in effect was criticizing the president for having abandoned general faculty meetings.

Shortridge considered the work in botany and zoology to be academic, not professional, in nature, and therefore not belonging in the College of Agriculture which, he felt, was enhancing its enrollment at the expense of the College of Arts and Sciences. As to the dismissal of faculty, he believed that inadequate attention had been paid to instructional needs within his college which, he felt, had borne a disproportionate burden. As he described the situation:

The dismissal without notice of members of the instructional staff, particularly those of professorial rank, inevitably produced a feeling of insecurity of tenure on the part of the entire staff which was not conducive to the best results. The character of university teaching is such that individuals cannot do their best work under conditions which foster and promote unrest, uneasiness, or discontent. Reasonable security of tenure has long been regarded as one of the chief inducements attracting men to the life of the scholar. Monetary returns in the teaching profession are generally far below what they are in other lines for men of equal or less training than is required for university teaching. The charm of a relatively quiet life spent in scholarly pursuits at a fair salary but with a reasonable security of tenure has served to attract men of ability and character to the field of university teaching . . . This feeling of security was greatly disturbed by the action taken on July 1, 1933.

Shortridge restricted his favorable news to a few outstanding achievements of certain students trained in the College of Arts and Sciences: Charles R. Sleeth, a German major, who had won a Rhodes Scholarship, and Charles Wise and DeWitt White, whose debate training in the Department of Public Speaking had led to their selection as representatives of the United States in a series of debates with students in British universities.

Other Morgantown residents apprised Governor H. G. Kump of their opinions of the Turner presidency. One was James R. Moreland of the law firm of Moreland and Guy who wrote his views of the University situation to the Governor:

The President has been inclined to advance favorites rapidly, and then as rapidly turn on them and have them dismissed, until some members of the faculty fear executive favor as evidence of danger in permanentcy [sic] of their positions. All of which has undermined confidence, created a spitit [sic] of unrest and uncertainty that is not conducive to good work. This tends to a feeling that long service as a successful teacher, a good research record, and a good character offers no securety [sic] for tenure of office. The Faculty members are used not like co-workers in a great educational enterprise but rather like day laborers under driving bosses, liable to be at any time laid off at the whim of the executive. The marale [sic] of the Faculty is naturally low when advancement seems to go by favor and not by merit.

Only one Faculty meeting has been held in five years. All changes are proposed by an 'inside group' and forced upon the faculty with out discussion. Individuals with ordinary training and ability are brought in at much larger salaries than are paid to those who have already proven their worth. Departments are ripped out of one college and put into another without co-operation or consultation with the heads of departments, so that some who were dismissed should have been retained. Some departments were crippled by dismissals and others were not affected or reduced. None of the persons who have been brought in during the last five years were dismissed, the brunt falling upon those previously employed. Few native West Virginians have remained, and most of the valuable traditions of the school are destroyed. The development of school traditions takes years to build up and can be destroyed in a short time.

In October, new members were appointed to the WVU Board of Governors, with Turner losing his last vestige of support. The Board president announced that Turner's condition of employment would be final retirement as of December 31, 1934. After an all-night session on October 15, 1934, student leaders announced a "restrained and well ordered protest demonstration" against reported plans of the Board of Governors to remove Turner as University president. Their formal statement read: "The demonstration is not a strike. We don't want anybody ousted or anybody put in. To us it is a matter of principle. Our University has been a political football long enough." The following day students paraded on campus with banners proclaiming "Pull Us Out of State Politics," "Unshakeable Our State University," and "The University Before Politics." Many classes were dismissed when

80 percent of the student body participated in the demonstration. But there was one bastion of law and order remaining in the University. The College of Law continued in normal session with law students voting not to participate in the walkout. The state's political establishment also remained firm — Governor Kump's two daughters attended classes.

The public received contradictory statements from Board members and the president on October 16 and 17. Board member A. B. Koontz indicated that Turner's conditional employment had not changed; the Board's president, E. G. Smith, insisted that Turner was retiring; and Turner issued a statement attributing his ouster to politics. The tenth president admitted he had accepted conditional employment, but the minutes of the July meeting, unknown to him, he said, were changed to show he was deposed. He carefully noted for the historical record that he was deposed by a straight Democratic-Republican vote of 4 to 3.

In an effort to enlist the support of young people, Koontz suggested that students had a right to petition the Board and that he was glad to see students take an interest in University affairs. But the Board president implied that, while students were expected to show Turner the respect due a retiring president, they were not to attempt to dictate personnel to the Board despite "the encouragement of their politically minded elders who have axes to grind."

One dean, Earl Hudelson of the College of Education, was convinced that the organization of West Virginia University was "wrong-side-out." He believed that even stronger action than removal of a president was warranted. Seeing the University as "primarily a local, conservative, academic institution," he said the image had been created statewide whereby "we are looked upon as a community of old ladies fussing over petty jealousies and prerogatives and dripping at the jowls with juicy gossip."

To Hudelson, the trouble that had befallen West Virginia University lay not in the Great Depression, but in the fact that it had not seriously offered technical education. "Standards of technical training being what they are," stated Hudelson, meant that "for nine out of every ten students the College of Arts and Sciences should be a service institution rather than the avenue to a degree. For the 10 percent who have no vocational aim and who wish merely to refine themselves or have a college degree, the College of Arts and Sciences is the proper place."

Hudelson was certain that "the fault is not that too many youth are going to college, but that colleges are training youth for a world that is no more." To Hudelson, the University was turning out dozens of science teachers whom it could not place, but was rejecting a proposed curriculum in forestry because money had been allocated to areas that only would turn out more graduates trained for a "bygone day." "We have placed only one and a half French teachers as French teachers in two years; yet the French Department continues to pour out graduates by the score, trained for teaching but destined for idleness," Hudelson observed.

Thus, Hudelson's words made it appear doubtful that even the removal of Turner as president meant that all areas of the University were prepared to practice harmony and high-minded service to the institution. Yet all engaged in academe recognized Dean Hudelson's pragmatism and could not dismiss his words of warning about the training of the generations of World War II and its aftermath: "It is high time we were taking stock of this world's need for trained men and women and adapting our curricula to the situation. We must either discover new outlets for our products and direct them toward those outlets, or we must admit that we have broken faith with the taxpayers and suffer the consequences."

Four Terms for Roosevelt and Four Presidents for WVU

Chauncey Samuel Boucher
October 1, 1935–August 31, 1938

Charles Elmer Lawall
July 1, 1939–August 31, 1945

BETWEEN THE DEPARTURE OF John Roscoe Turner as tenth president on the last day of 1934 and the arrival of Irvin Stewart as thirteenth president in the summer of 1946, West Virginia University resumed its accustomed role of being what the *Morgantown Post* described as the "political football of the state." Its struggle for political independence during the administrations of Presidents Turner, Armstrong, Boucher, Lawall, and Neff was sometimes helped, sometimes harmed by its alumni, staff, faculty, and students. Members of its official hierarchy who achieved major administrative positions in this era and who desired political independence for the University aimed to become its chief executive. A very few were successful, but even when bypassed, they were able to advance their careers in other institutions or in other occupations outside academe as the era moved from depression into recovery and World War II.

In responding to these many administrative changes, the remaining faculty played enigmatical roles in the institutional quest for survival. Yet they felt free to render opinions. As John Roscoe Turner had noted in his in-

159

augural address on November 28, 1928, if one had faith that in a multitude of counsel there was wisdom, one would have been pleased to learn that a new president had been "advised, much advised, and variously advised as to exactly the right way to run the University." Agreeing that the state university belonged to the people, Turner countered that so did the army. "But the university," he warned, "would win no more battles than would the army if it tried to do everything that everybody said."

Many of those administering WVU and the state government seemed to be imitating their federal models on the Potomac both in their admonitions and their assignments. If Franklin Roosevelt had his brain trust in times of domestic and foreign troubles, so did West Virginia University and the thirty-fifth state, and the most ambitious and activist-minded of the faculty were its members. And if the President of the United States had not always restrained his intellectual assistants, neither had a state governor nor a University president forever contained their politically minded scholarly subordinates. The trouble with their counsel was, as Turner proclaimed at the beginning of his administration: "There is much to commend in all this advice. It evidences a helpful spirit. It should be heard courteously and pondered deeply. None-the-less, it all has one fault, just one; it points in too many directions."

What he might have added was that in the Rooseveltian political revolution of 1932, the office-starved Democrats momentarily were pointing in only one direction: to sweep the Republicans out of all national and state offices. As Governor Kump pointedly complained to E. G. Smith of the Board of Governors on April 29, 1935, 80 percent of all employees in the West Virginia educational institutions were Republicans, their political affiliation had been made the basis of their selection, while competent people in other political parties, particularly Democrats, had been denied employment.

The WVU hierarchy was no exception in the cleansing of the Augean stables. For into the Republican administration of John Roscoe Turner stepped three new, bold, and iconoclastic additions to the faculty, Thurman Arnold and Stephen P. Burke, Democrats, and John F. Sly, a progressive Republican. Turning their attention in the years of the Depression from undergraduate education and professional training to service in the state and by giving advice freely, these men projected themselves into the highest realms of the West Virginia establishment. By virtue of their activist West Virginia years and to the envy of their harassed colleagues, they propelled themselves out of WVU and onto the staffs of the most distinguished institutions in the land, Yale University, Columbia University, and Princeton University.

Thurman Arnold set the pace for all other WVU brain-trusters to follow. A native of Wyoming, a member of the Wyoming House of Representatives, and the mayor of Laramie, Arnold, in his original move from West to East, served as dean of the WVU College of Law from 1927 to 1930. Adapting the professional school's program to fit Turner's goal of "building the University into the life of the State," the Princeton and Harvard educated law dean first inaugurated a lecture series of outstanding speakers who were intended to keep the State Bar abreast of the latest developments in the legal profession and students acquainted with authorities in the specialties of law.

With the cooperation and financial assistance of Yale, the dean enabled WVU to begin the collection of the state's first judicial statistics. Within a year of administering this undertaking, Dean Arnold was invited to Yale to become a visiting professor, and the following year was asked to join the faculty. How could he not accept, lamented the *Morgantown Post* on January 29, 1931, because his salary offer was twice that paid at WVU and, in addition, he would be given the opportunity to participate in one of the most progressive enterprises in legal education in the country. The newspaper could only hope that under his successor the Arnold program of judicial collections, of encouraging individual research by the law faculty, of establishing a judicial council in West Virginia, and of consulting with the State Bar Association about legal education would be continued.

Of the three, Arnold, Sly, and Burke, the Law School dean was the most respected by the faculty, perhaps because he was the most successful and because locally he paid attention to what Professor Oliver P. Chitwood was fond of referring to as the Southern amenities of life. As an example of such courtesies, Arnold penned a note to Dr. Chitwood in which he expressed a loss of valued friends in the WVU community as a result of his move to the Yale Law School:

In my scheme of things personal friendships count very much indeed. I like to think about them, and pretend that I have a knack of selecting only first rate people as my friends — persons of character, intelligence, honesty, and loyalty. And I always like to think of you as one of the real outstanding persons on the West Virginia faculty — judged by these standards, which I think are the only things that count.[1]

Others, however, displayed less attention to placating influential faculty members. One was a New York Catholic and outsider, Stephen P. Burke, handed the deanship of the first WVU Graduate School. Burke showed the least teaching inclination but the most service-oriented enthusiasm of the trio of experts making their way in a state of extractive industries. While on the WVU staff, primarily in the administrative capacity of chairman of the Industrial Relations Sector of the Graduate School, he also served as the economic and financial adviser to the Governor and the West Virginia Legislature from 1932 to 1936, as a member of the Technical Board of Arbitration on the Value Correlation of Coals in 1934, and on the Joint Legislative Committee on Social Security in 1935-36. After surrendering the graduate deanship and finding no enthusiasm in the administrations following Turner for an independently directed Institute of Industrial Research headed by himself, Burke retranslated his administrative expertise outside of WVU as research director of the Consolidation Coal Company, as president of the Fairmont Coal Company, and as chairman of the advisory board of the West Virginia Department of Public Assistance. In the 1940s, however, he returned to Columbia where he had received his professional education. In refutation of his critics who believed him not destined for an academic career, he served there as professor of chemical engineering until his death in 1945.

The third individual seeking to enhance the University's contributions to the state while simultaneously boosting his own professional career was John F. Sly, selected by Turner to head the newly created Department of Political Science and to serve as director of the original Bureau for Government Research. In cooperation with the activist College of Law, Sly's Bureau also jumped on the service-to-the-state bandwagon by announcing it was prepared to offer municipalities of the state expert assistance in revising their ordinances. In the early days of the Depression, the director engaged himself in a study to determine where and for what purposes the tax dollar was being spent in West Virginia. Out of this project he recommended a complete revamping of the state's fiscal system. Looking forward to the beginning of a state-synchronized budgeting, accounting, and reporting system in West Virginia, Sly argued that his advice with respect to financial problems, constitutional amendments, and statutory change would mark the beginnings of a permanent economy program, and that nothing else would suffice.

To President Turner's chagrin and Dean W. P. Shortridge's annoyance (given the frequent disappearances of the political and industrial science personnel from the Morgantown campus), incoming Democratic administrations thought highly of Sly and his associates. Even the local Republican newspaper, sensing no political-ideological damage in Democratic professors' efforts to improve the state's economy, informed its readers on June 7, 1933, "As what they did becomes better understood, public appreciation will increase and public prejudice against 'professorial theories' will diminish." Because the professorial estimates of probable revenue yield from the new forms of taxation proved reliable, and because their drafting of measures set a new mark for directness and simplicity, the House of Delegates in turn acknowledged on March 24, 1934, its appreciation of the services of Dr. Sly, Dr. Burke, and their associates. It was believed the Bureau for Government Research had become the state's "unofficial brain trust" because of its advice to governors and to legislators.

It seemed, therefore, only fitting in the political change under way in West Virginia that Dr. Sly be appointed by the Board of Governors "acting dean of the faculties," and assigned a myriad of duties under acting president Robert Armstrong. The faculty was comforted by the Board's election of Armstrong, the faculty member with the longest term of service to the institution. It looked upon the selection of the acting chief executive as evidence that the Board did care about the faculty's role in the institution. Armstrong, who was to die within a year after presidential service, was, however, deemed worthy of assistance. Whether he liked all that he got remains moot.

A consistent Democrat who occasionally ran for office, Armstrong had served WVU for forty years as a faculty member. His interests transcended the classroom; he also had served for years as an instructor of a large Bible class for men in the Methodist Church. Well-known across the state, the literature professor engaged in countless teachers' institutes and high school commencement gatherings. Known for his pamphlets, *How to Know the Bible, Historical and Literary Outlines of the Old Testament,* and other monographs dealing with the study of Shakespeare and the Bible, Armstrong had chosen as his fields of emphasis Victorian literature, the short story, the American novel, and particularly the literature of the English Bible.

Given Armstrong's academic orientation, his extracurricular activities, and his lack of administrative experience, Sly perhaps could be forgiven for changing his own title of "acting dean" to "acting president" in the biographical sketch he submitted to *Who's Who in America.* He indeed was handed responsibility for the budget, for administrative reorganization, and for revision of courses of study. In addition, he was concerned with the utilization of space and equipment, the allocation and adjustment of the staff and the strengthening of University activities peculiar to the economic, social, and scientific life of the state. For good measure, he assisted in compiling and revising regulations governing student conduct.[2]

In carrying out such an awesome assignment, Sly indicated he saw his duty as that of liaison officer between the faculties and the Board of Governors. His approach was to appoint faculty committees to consider the various problems posed by the Board of Governors. In that manner, the primary duty of suggesting solutions rested upon faculty members, leaving Sly in the safer position of being merely the coordinator and compiler of the faculty suggestions for the Board.

Although in some areas Sly utilized committees for his work, in others he proceeded directly, particularly in allocating and adjusting the staff of the institution. Probably because the dean of Arts and Sciences, W. P. Shortridge, had questioned his lengthening absences from the classroom, Sly relieved Shortridge of his deanship and substituted his protege, Carl M. Frasure, as acting dean.[3] Burke, dean of the Graduate School, was also removed from his position, causing the faculty to speculate as to whether Sly was destined to be the next University president, the next dean of the College of Arts and Sciences, or the next chairman of the Graduate Council.

The Board of Governors, however, resolved the question of Sly's future position within WVU, as well as putting an end to his arbitrary administrative procedures, by accepting his resignation within three months of his service as acting dean of the faculties. With considerable circumspection, Sly asked to be returned to his former status as professor of political science and director of the Bureau for Government Research, and, in addition, requested that he be given a year's leave of absence as a visiting lecturer at Princeton. Reporting to the *Morgantown Post* on July 30, 1935, that his work with the faculty committees was completed, Sly said he had produced (1) an equalized, flexible, balanced budget; (2) administrative adjustments laying the groundwork for a new president; (3) an organized faculty; and (4) plans to solve all problems vexing the University. As he saw it, conditions were now right for a new president to be appointed, and a new administration could not escape the promise of a successful future.

Despite the evidence of many victories, the political tide had turned against the "brain trust," the members of the WVU Bureau for Government Research. As of December 15, 1937, the *Wheeling Intelligencer* remarked that in its judgment "nothing of outstanding benefit to the people of West Virginia had evolved from the labor of these thinkers." Criticizing the concept of brain trusts, the newspaper said they "cause lawmakers to shun their duties; theory replaces reality."

The *Morgantown Post* suspected that the *Wheeling Intelligencer* was confusing the WVU professors with the federals, and contrasted the former with the latter as follows:

They [members of the WVU Bureau of Government Research] were fact-finders, not policy makers, and technical experts in preparing estimates and drafting bills. We've yet to find any legislator who feels they caused them to shun their duties; instead they gave them help to perform their duties better.

Despite the *Morgantown Post's* effort to separate state brain-trusters from their federal counterparts and to acknowledge their contributions to the state, WVU's eleventh and twelfth administrations allowed the Bureau for Government Research to lapse until it was reactivated by President Irvin Stewart in 1949. With a certain show of sophistication, the Board of Governors adopted a resolution thanking John Sly and his faculty committees for the work they had done, and granted Sly his leave of absence. Later in the year, on March 10, 1936, it accepted his resignation. The Board thus placed itself on the market for an outsider as eleventh president of West Virginia University.

As they had done in the selection of Turner, the Governors turned to a sitting dean of a College of Arts and Sciences to head the institution. In 1935, they found their experienced administrator at the University of Chicago, an institution which since 1927 had undertaken momentous reconstruction of undergraduate collegiate educational methods and processes. Quickly they named Chauncey Samuel Boucher the eleventh president of WVU.[4]

Before Boucher had committed himself to administration and the Chicago Plan, he had been an historian. Neither pro-Confederate nor pro-Union as had been his predecessors at WVU, Boucher published in the field of Southern antebellum history, and the essence of his intellectual and emotionally neutral research was found in his presidential address to the distinguished Mississippi Valley Historical Association, "In re That Aggressive Slavocracy." Receiving his A.B., M.A., and Ph.D. from the University of Michigan, he had served as an American historian at Washington University, Ohio State University, the University of Texas, and the University of Wisconsin before going to Chicago in 1923 and becoming dean of the College of Arts, Literature and Sciences in 1927. Distancing himself from his predecessors at WVU, Boucher disapproved of a formal inauguration, declaring that although such a ceremony might be pleasant, colorful, and a satisfaction to the pride of one in whose honor it was staged, it was of little value educationally. The Board concurred with an expression of appreciation.

It was probably not so much the theory of the Chicago Plan that interested the Board as the fact that in implementing the plan, Boucher served as constant contrast to Turner. This seemed apparent in his observation that "no educational program can be successfully administered in any institution until and unless the group most vitally concerned with instruction — the faculty — are, in clear majority, in sympathy with the program as a result of a conviction of its soundness."[5] In his first address to the WVU faculty, Boucher disclaimed any intention of forcing the Chicago Plan upon West Virginia University, but he did suggest that the faculty, and not its presidents, might develop its own West Virginia Plan.

Through the technique of faculty consultation, Boucher set to work immediately to correct what he and the Board perceived to have been his predecessor's errors of judgment. He first called for a standing committee on educational policy and practice to receive suggestions for reports and studies from faculty members and to make appropriate recommendations to administrative officers for changes in policy. In addition, he stimulated many more faculty committees into action. Reported the *Morgantown Post* on October 2, 1935, Boucher's challenges "will be accepted by the University faculty which hasn't in the past had full and free opportunities to contribute to University policy."

Boucher conspicuously reorganized Turner's concept of a graduate school and provided for a University Senate. The Senate, composed of all full professors, heads of departments, the registrar, and the president, was granted original jurisdiction over all legislative matters concerning the entire University or activities involving more than one school. Just as the faculty of each school was the legislative body for that school, so the Senate represented the University as a whole. Conceived of as an upper house for all legislative bodies in the University, including the reactivated Council of Administration, the Senate was a new governmental experience for WVU faculty members.[6]

In turn, the Graduate School faculty comprised all who taught courses for graduate students, and this faculty accepted, as its duty, the setting of requirements for admission to the Graduate School and for the awarding of graduate degrees. In 1934, the Board of Governors had abolished the four-divisional graduate council that had respected neither colleges nor departments; now the Board authorized President Boucher to appoint a new Graduate Council consisting of five to nine members with the assistance of the deans of the schools offering graduate work.

No sooner were the Graduate Council and the University Senate in place than Boucher handed one of his most troublesome problems to the Senate for solution: the location and administration of the discipline of biology. After careful study, the Senate recommended that Turner's consolidated biology unit in the College of Agriculture be split up again with the return of botany, zoology, and physiology to the College of Arts and Sciences as a single biology and zoology department. The arts and sciences department would then concern itself with the "pure" aspects of the subjects while other academic units would be devoted to the "applied" aspects. In a spirit of compromise, the Senate suggested a Council of Biology to recommend procedures under which common efforts to promote biological sciences might be undertaken by the University. In calming the embittered College of Arts and Sciences, Dr. Boucher also returned the deposed W. P. Shortridge as dean, and made Carl Frasure assistant dean after consultation with and by a vote of the chairmen of the College's departments.[7]

In addition, the University Senate recommended that the Athletic Board be changed to consist of five faculty, one alumnus, and one student in lieu of the old committee of two faculty, two alumni, two students, and the director of athletics. Behind this suggestion lay the growing feeling that WVU athletics would never be on a sound basis until the stadium debt, created twelve years previously by insufficient private contributions, was liquidated by the state.

As Director of Athletics H. A. Stansbury explained to WVU alumni in their magazine of January, 1936, obligations of the stadium-athletic indebtedness constituted an unbearable embarrassment to the University, particularly with respect to the unpaid guarantees and like obligations. As Stansbury reviewed the dilemma of recent years:

That an educational institution should be in arrears for three or four years on such items as guarantees of $8,000.00 to her oldest football rival, Washington & Jefferson College; $12,000.00 to the University of Pittsburgh; $10,000.00 to Kansas State College, and $15,000.00 to Pennsylvania State College, to say nothing of $21,000.00 to A. G. Spalding & Bros., for the very uniforms that the Varsity teams have worn, and other smaller items of like nature, is a situation probably unparalleled in intercollegiate athletics.

To Stansbury, all financial difficulties had arisen from construction of the stadium. If its costs had been eliminated, "We would today have all bills paid and nearly $100,000.00 in the bank."

In his first year, Dr. Boucher seemingly could do no wrong in his dealings with both athletics and academics. His establishment of a loan fund in memory of his father for University seniors needing funds for fees in order to graduate was well received. Boucher indicated that the fund would be supplemented continuously by honorarium payments he received from speeches given across the state and nation. Beyond this presidential gesture, the faculty was most appreciative of being incorporated into the University's decision-making process. To emphasize its valuation of this new-found role, the faculty tendered a surprise party for President and Mrs. Boucher to mark the close of their first year at West Virginia University. On October 23, 1936, the local paper analyzed the significance of the impromptu social event in three ways: it showed the esteem and affection the faculty had for the University president; it demonstrated the loyalty the faculty granted to the administration as well as its united support of University programs; it served as evidence of a new integrity the faculty had found for itself – the regaining of its self-respect and the demonstration that it could act cooperatively in the discharge of its duties and for the furtherance of the University's service to the state.

Boucher spent the remainder of his short time as president establishing in June, 1936, a College of Pharmacy; changing the name of the College of Agriculture to the College of Agriculture, Forestry, and Home Economics; and presiding over curriculum changes in the College of Arts and Sciences. The College of Pharmacy reflected the University's hope for a future medical school. The second action emphasized work done in home economics, first offered in the College in 1914, and in forestry, initiated as a two-year offering in 1935, and expanded to a four-year course in 1936. Sensing a new state mission for the University in the field of forestry, the *Morgantown Post* observed on March 15, 1937: "If courses in forestry prove as popular as they should be and serve the state's recognized needs for more scientific attention to its forest resources, it will not be long before the college has broadened its contribution to West Virginia's welfare in three important fields."

Boucher's third effort reflected his earlier interest in the Chicago Plan because all WVU arts and sciences students were to take four comprehensive courses covering biological, physical and social sciences, and the humanities. Such courses were seen as an integration and unification of several departmental courses then offered, and students were expected to take comprehensive exams showing a mastery of subject matter.

Considered among the most alumni-oriented presidents of WVU, Boucher presided over the reactivation of the Alumni Association and the establishment of its Loyalty Permanent Endowment Fund with scholarships to be financed with the interest earned. The Alumni Association asked at least 2,000 contributors to give a minimum of $25 each so that $50,000 might be obtained in a relatively short time. Although the early response was disappointing, the Fund had exceeded $1.5 million by 1980.

Although successful in arousing faculty enthusiasm, Boucher occasionally had to squelch student spirit. Denying the use of University buildings and property to undergraduates for football thuses, except in instances where responsible sponsorship was provided, he called for police intervention in his first year when students rushed the local theaters for free entry and dismantled the porches of North High Street residences in their quest for firewood for their thuse bonfires. Throwing brickbats at the police, the students were repulsed only when authorities used tear gas. In his second year, after designating Richard Aspinall, assistant to the president, as the official to whom thuse requests must be made, Boucher pondered aloud to the *Morgantown Post* on October 6, 1936, whether the thuse should be "continued as a grand institution or prohibited as a menace to the University and the community." Charging that the freshman students made "jackasses of themselves" in rushing the theaters, the president threatened drastic action to avoid endangering persons, property, and the "good name of the University." During the remainder of his presidential term, Boucher was never called upon to define the action he had in mind.

President and Mrs. Boucher refocused student interest away from the town and back to the campus when in 1938 they opened the doors of a remodeled cafeteria building from eight to eleven p.m. for dancing in an area designated as a student union center. Equipped with a soda fountain and "mechanical music machines," the new space was available for student activity during afternoons and evenings throughout the school year. Although such space was quickly deemed inadequate for student needs, it did signify that certain social needs were being recognized. Even the *Athenaeum* believed on September 22, 1937, that the old order was passing when it reported that an unidentified girl had sought permission to try out as a University cheerleader and a nonplussed dean of women planned "to seek the advice of several prominent upper classwomen as to whether they considered the requested innovation to be in the best interests of the University."

The advice the dean received and the action she took remained unreported on the eve of World War II. Nonetheless, the *Morgantown Post* speculated the following day: "Could it be possible that the men of the University have reached the place where they can regard with equanimity the prospect that they are to be led on cheers by female students?"

Following the national celebration of July 4, 1938, Dr. Boucher quietly announced his resignation and his acceptance of the chancellorship of the University of Nebraska, "where Mrs. Boucher and I feel that we must accept the call to greater possibilities for service in the field of higher education." The *Morgantown Post* interpreted the larger field to mean 8,500 students, 400 faculty members, and a $12,000 salary at Nebraska as contrasted with 3,500 students, 150 faculty, and a $10,000 salary at West Virginia. The state press, after expressing regret at the now familiar loss of a WVU president, immediately suggested that the next president be more of a West Virginian. The *Morgantown Post* also was so disposed when it remarked on July 11, 1938:

An outsider must spend a period of apprenticeship becoming familiar with the state and its needs. He must become familiar with the University itself. If the Board of Governors can find a man possessing much of this information, it is a valid reason for choosing him over another who must spend years perhaps to reach the other's level in those respects.

On September 1, 1938, the day Chauncey Samuel Boucher's resignation became effective, Charles Elmer Lawall, 47-year-old director of the University School of Mines, became acting president and within a year, president. The *Morgantown Post* noted on September 2, 1938, that the appointment gave the coal industry of West Virginia an opportunity to say that this was the first time in University history that a selection board had recognized the basic industries of the state by choosing as its head a man particularly interested in mineral industries. But more than that, the Morgantown paper was particularly pleased that Lawall commanded a much wider interest throughout West Virginia, one that extended beyond his training of mining engineers at Morgantown. It noted that he was director of the Mining and Industrial Extension Division, for which the whole state had been a campus.

Only through the coal interests was Lawall to make any impact on campus construction. Because of the Depression, the last major academic buildings had been the chemistry and library buildings constructed in 1925 and 1930. With these exceptions, the building program remained stalled for almost a quarter of a century. Given the growing shortages made manifest by World War II, the Lawall administration openly advocated few construction efforts until 1945–46. Rather did it suggest, in addition to finding solutions to the perennial problems of parking and lighting, modernization of existing buildings.

With considerable fanfare, the Lawall administration announced on April 19, 1939, the remodeling of Commencement Hall, which seemed to endorse the *Morgantown Post's* sentiment that extensive improvement of a fifty-year-old building would ensure its service for many more years and would save the taxpayers' money. State funds indeed were saved when it was announced that its modernization would occur through a WPA project at a cost of $40,000, a sum which would provide a new interior floor plan and the installation of plush-covered seats. When rededicated on March 13, 1940, it was given the name Powell Benton Reynolds Hall, honoring the man who had served as vice-president, chaplain, and professor from 1885 to 1910 and who was twice acting president. Tradition also was served when chimes were installed in the Administration Building in the same month.

On May 7, 1940, the Board of Public Works released half a million dollars from its conditional budget for the construction of a mineral industries building at WVU, suggesting that the building be ready for occupancy in 1941 and house the School of Mines, the Geological Survey, the chemical engineering department, and the coal research laboratories. Two days later, the *Morgantown Post* thought it significant that such a building had been demanded from the various sections of the state—from the coal industry, from the mine unions, from the manufacturing industries, and from businessmen in general. In its view,

The source of demands is significant because it shows recognition that the University has large possibilities of being converted into the principal research agency of West Virginia and that its services to the state are as yet largely undeveloped.

That the University was capable of responding to the research needs of the state seemed obvious when WVU scientists became charter members of the seventy-seventh chapter of the Society of Sigma Xi. The *Post* poetically described on March 29, 1939, the chapter's installation as "a merited national recognition of the University's devotion to competent scientific research that will serve to bring together in a learned society of highest standards those faculty and research students of the University who carry the torch of science in the pursuit of truth."

On October 16, 1942, the Mineral Industries Building was dedicated as "one of the finest and most essential additions to the campus in view of West Virginia's vast coal, oil, gas, chemical, and ceramics industries." No institution in the United States, it was argued, "has better material facilities for giving instruction and conducting research into mineral resources." The following year, 1943, the grounds surrounding the Chemistry Building, the Library, and the Mineral Industries Building were reconditioned as a small second downtown campus.

The Lawall administration also secured a $100,000 state appropriation for a Health Center, completed in May, 1942, and a bond issue of $440,000 for Terrace Hall, completed the same year. Reconstruction of the old Wade

Mineral Industries Building was completed in 1942 and later renamed White Hall for Israel Charles White. It houses the College of Mineral and Energy Resources, originally called the School of Mines, and the Department of Geology and Geography.

school building on Beechurst Avenue was accomplished for the College of Education's venture into supervised elementary teaching. The administration also secured the reconstruction of a clay-testing laboratory located between the Field House and the Heating Plant, and purchased small properties in an attempt to stretch the boundary lines of the downtown campus. The *Morgantown Post* particularly was pleased to see that a beginning was being made in the proper maintenance and upkeep of the stadium now that the state had formally assumed the stadium's outstanding indebtedness by appropriating $336,750 to pay off the bondholders.

Following the long campaign of the State Newspaper Council to have journalism students more adequately recognized, the Lawall administration recommended the establishment of one more professional school, a School of Journalism, to replace the department of journalism. The *Morgantown Post* of April 24, 1939, was naturally pleased because, "The chief advantage of a journalism school rather than a department is that a greater feeling of professional responsibility is promoted and developed. . . . Also students should be able to transfer easier. . . . With a separate school of journalism, the newspapers of West Virginia should be more interested in work done here and should cooperate more fully with the school."

With three main objectives in mind, Lawall also established an art department: to provide the practical and technical training for those students with special aptitude for art work; to acquaint the students with the history and appreciation of art as a part of their general and cultural education; and to give academic training for those students who wished to become art teachers in West Virginia public schools. The pragmatic twelfth president also organized a new department for the training of social workers, because "up to this time, it has been necessary for our State Department of Public Assistance to go outside the State for many of its professional workers."[8]

It was in his pursuit of academic freedom and the necessary guiding principles for promotion and tenure that Charles Lawall scored certain achievements, and perhaps rectified errors of due process made in preceding administrations. In accord with the principles of academic freedom and tenure formulated by the American Association of University Professors, Lawall approved the order adopted by the Board of Governors on November 16, 1940, which outlined its endorsement of AAUP principles. He also publicized the Board's statement of policy as of October, 1942. On October 7, 1946, and October 14, 1947, the Board further clarified its tenure policy by placing newly appointed assistant professors on a three-year probationary period, but indicated that in turn it expected from the faculty reasonable notice of intentions to resign.

Lawall was undoubtedly forced to take action by recommendations of an AAUP investigating committee that criticized the WVU record in the cases of Evelyn Dixon and Walter Wadepuhl of the Departments of History and German in 1938. In the disposition of the Dixon and Wadepuhl cases, it was obvious that WVU administrators had not given the two faculty members proper notice of termination. Lawall, however, did not reinstate the two faculty members who were relieved of their positions after respective services of thirteen and twelve years. Rather did Lawall fall back on the Department of History's argument that Dr. Dixon, an English historian, was relieved of duty to make room for a medievalist; and the German Department's opinion that Dr. Wadepuhl, a scholar working on the definitive edition of the works of the poet Heinrich Heine, was relieved because enrollment called for a reduction in faculty teaching German, and beginning German courses were better taught by others who were not research specialists.

It was Allen W. Porterfield, head of the German Department, who, in protesting the possible neglect of Wadepuhl's teaching duties in favor of his research interests, inadvertently indicated that such scholarly pursuits did West Virginians little good. In a letter circulated throughout the campus and the Jewish community in West Virginia, Porterfield wrote to Wadepuhl on June 30, 1939:

You are working on the minutiae of the life (hundreds have done it before) of a voluntarily exiled German Jew who died 81 years ago and who was never anything in his life but a highly gifted destructive journalist and an equally gifted lyric author with a limited field.[9]

The head of the German Department stated that if Wadepuhl had been doing research in law, mining, engineering, political science, business administration, or on virtually any other theme except the one he had chosen, it would have been easy to interest the people of West Virginia in his enterprise. However, since he had chosen Heine, Porterfield advised, "You will find it hard to get this State to go along with you on that and it is the people of this State who pay your salary."

In other academic matters Lawall witnessed the successful effort of the Council of Administration and the University Senate to make it possible for academic colleges other than the College of Education to train teachers. The faculty sought and gained a modification of the Board order of July 2, 1937, which vested full control in the College of Education for all professional teacher preparation, academic teacher preparation, and authority to recommend all applicants for certification to the State Department of Education.

Most of Lawall's administration fell within World War II, and the University was appropriately concerned with winning the war. The University's College of Engineering acted as the leading agency for national defense in West Virginia under the auspices of the U.S. Office of Education when it began training 1,000 men and women in engineering and technical courses for the defense program. The courses were part of the Engineering, Science, and Management War Training Program (ESMWTP). Most of the work in subjects such as machine design, metallurgy, and engineering drafting was offered through the extension division in the industrial centers of the state. The agricultural college, in turn, worked with the state and county agencies engaged in increasing agricultural production in wartime.

As a part of the University's defense program, the R.O.T.C. enrolled 878 cadets in their first two years of training and 140 advanced students in the third or fourth year of training in 1941. Another branch of the defense program, sponsored by WVU since the fall of 1939 in cooperation with the U.S. Civil Aeronautics Administration, was the Civilian Pilot Training Program, with graduates of the program immediately entering the Army and Naval Air Corps.

In addition, the University Council of Administration ordered a streamlined war-emergency program designed to speed up graduation. In its behalf, Lawall called for eliminating Easter recess, shortening of the Christmas vacation, and operation of the University on a six-day week. The University permitted registration of third-year high school and college preparatory students of "exceptional ability"; extended full credit to students with a "C" average who had completed half a term before being called into service; and eliminated the final exam period by substituting tests given during the regular course of study.

The WVU School of Medicine began operating on a quarter system on June 1, 1942. This provided a twelve-month term instead of a nine-month term of two semesters, and thus produced an additional class every three years. Said the *Morgantown Post* on April 13, 1942: "If ever West Virginia ought to consider expanding the University School of Medicine from two to four years, the time is now" as part of the national effort to alleviate one of the nation's most serious manpower shortages. In addition, the School of Medicine, in cooperation with the U.S. Public Health Service and Monongalia County Hospital, trained qualified women students who agreed to remain in the nursing profession for the war's duration.

By the fall of 1943, WVU was training 1,150 men for the armed forces: 300 in aviation, 600 in engineering, 50 in medicine, and 200 in pre-medicine for the Army Specialized Training Program (ASTP). On behalf of the soldier-students, four fraternity houses were leased, the first two floors of the law building were converted into barracks, and the men's dormitory was reserved for the aviation cadets.

Student-soldier activities at WVU received front-page attention in a New York City newspaper, *PM*, on November 18, 1943. The story was headlined: "Soldier Fined for Dancing with Negro Girl — But Officer's Order is Overruled." The details were relatively succinct. Private H. P. Suiter, Army Air Corps preflight student, had attended a dance for aviation cadets at the Hotel Morgan on November 5, 1943. Having won a jitterbugging contest at previous dances, he invited a Negro employee at the hotel to jitterbug with him that evening in the hopes of another victory. Instead, Suiter was denied contest entry and formally charged with conducting himself "in a manner to bring discredit upon the military service by dancing with a colored girl in view of those present." His sentence was deduction of two-thirds of his monthly pay ($50) and restriction to his quarters for the remainder of the semester.

The Eastern Flying Command, to whom final jurisdiction belonged, overruled the 48th College Training Detachment of which Suiter was a part and declared his sentencing illegal because of improper charges. According to *PM*, Suiter's action in bringing an unidentified person, either white or black, improperly dressed to the party was the only possible issue. Although pleased with the final verdict, *PM* viewed the incident as "the most blatant, unfair evidence of capricious, irresponsible Jim Crowism that has come out of the Army in a long, long time." It did not understand why the story was concealed from University authorities and the local community.

By the 1943-44 academic year, the military camp atmosphere within the University was drawing to a close. In 1944, the Army announced it would be ending the pilot training program at the University, and the War Department canceled the Army Specialized Training Program across the nation and at WVU. By 1945, the University enjoyed a short period of peace, but braced itself for returning veterans who desired a college education.

World War II left one outstanding imprint upon West Virginia University: as the *Morgantown Post* reported on October 9, 1942, it "pushed University men out of the footlights and into the wings." As examples of change, it noted that the scholastic and political positions of honor at the University were dominated by women. Particularly, it called attention to the fact that Betty Head had moved from vice-president to president of the student body because of President Pete Yost's enlistment in the Navy, and that the campus newspaper possessed an all-female editorial staff. An event that did not occur even during World War I on the WVU campus took place during World War II when twenty-four girls were auditioned and accepted on September 29, 1943, as members of the University Band.

For the first time in the history of the University, women students outnumbered men students, excluding the soldier trainees. In the 1943-44 fall semester, there were 809 women enrolled compared to 592 men, dominating the statistics in Arts and Sciences, Education, the Graduate School, the Schools of Journalism, Music, and Physical Education. Women also had enrolled in the Colleges of Engineering, Law, Medicine, and Pharmacy, with the only male holdout among the professional schools being the School of Mines. Four years before in 1939, Margaret Buchanan Cole had been named the first woman president of the Alumni Association.

The rise in the influence of women only underscored the drop in enrollment at WVU during the war years. In particular, the war threatened the operation of the College of Law whose students were almost all of draft age. By the spring of 1943, the University enrollment of 1,958 was a 1,007-student decline from two years earlier. The College of Law had fifteen students and was contemplating closing its doors after the 1943-44 semester.

Of the unbroken string of Democratic governors elected in West Virginia in the Roosevelt years, Matthew Mansfield Neely was the only chief executive who had been both an undergraduate student at West Virginia University and a graduate of the WVU College of Law. He had been suspended in 1900-1901 for unruly behavior. As one of the most agile politicians in the state and the nation, his success at the polls seemed to bode well for his alma mater. In his inaugural address as twenty-first governor in January, 1941, he foresaw a most specific and activist role for the University in a state that he admitted was not one of the leaders in the field of higher education. The University, he said, "should be so expanded and perfected that it would be unnecessary for anyone in the state to go abroad for technical or professional training." Not only should it provide finished education in the fine and useful arts, he suggested, but it should afford education in the "liberal and lucrative sciences" equal to that obtainable in any other institution of learning in the United States.

One month after this address, the *Morgantown Post* spoke favorably of Neely's plans for doubling women's dorm space because of the governor's well-known devotion to the University as the state's leading institution of higher learning and his determination to see it become a great university. At the dedication of the Mineral Industries Building, Neely declared again that he intended to see established a full-fledged College of Medicine and a first-rate College of Aeronautical Engineering at his alma mater.

When such programs were not forthcoming to Neely's satisfaction by the end of World War II, the Governor promptly replaced five of the seven members of the WVU Board of Governors. Before the reconstituted Board on June 16, 1944, he dramatically argued that conditions at the University were so bad there should be a change in the University presidency. The data that Governor Neely used were not only garnered by his private staff but were contained, in part, in a damaging petition to him signed by most of the faculty of the College of Engineering and Mechanic Arts. Statistically, Neely demonstrated that only ninety-four of six hundred twenty-two chemists employed in the Charleston area were University-trained, that only 10 percent of the students from the southern portion of the state attending institutions of higher learning were enrolled at WVU, and that a statewide, graduate extension program had not been maintained by the University. The chief executive charged the university president with inability to project himself as a leader among faculty members because of his unwillingness to fight to change inadequate appropriations, and scored him for permitting reversion of legislative monies to the state treasury at the conclusion of the budgetary years. The results of inadequate presidential leadership, Neely assessed, were the sacrifice of WVU's comparable standing with other state universities east of the Mississippi and lack of development of effective educational programs.[10]

Within a matter of days, and after twelve continuous hours of deliberation, the Board agreed by voting four to three to remove Lawall from the presidency. Also accepting Neely's advice, it removed R. P. Davis as dean of the College of Engineering.

Anticipating that Governor Neely would present his "reform program" before the Board, President Lawall had informed the Board that if changes were needed, there were proper ways to bring them about without damaging the University and the high confidence it had enjoyed. "I and the rest of the University staff are ready to join with you and carry out policies of proper changes for the maintenance or advancement of the high standards of the University," he had said via the state press.

But when he understood the full intent of the Board, President Lawall felt compelled to write "If only my personal interests were at stake, I would perhaps feel inclined to resume my work as director of the School of Mines." However, as University president, he informed the Board that he felt it his solemn duty to look only to its best interest and that of the state. Therefore, he concluded, "I cannot temporize or be a party to what is considered at the very least a premature course of action . . . . I am not in a position to submit my resignation as president of West Virginia University."

Although the faculty failed to respond to the packing of the Board, the attempted dismissal of the president, and the stance he took, the state press and WVU students were most vociferous. Staging an immediate demonstration, students issued a formal protest which admitted on June 20, 1944: "We cannot change the minds of a hand-picked board, but we feel we have shown the state of West Virginia the students' sentiments on President Lawall's administration."

Four days later, the executive committee of the student government followed this mass appeal by the student body with an open letter to all West Virginia citizens, calling on them to resist Governor Neely's "dictatorial action." Accusing the Governor of making the University president "a greased pig in the field game of state politics," the executive committee stated that it was opposed to Lawall's ouster because "we believe it is insensible and against our good and the progress of the University." Assessing Lawall as "a capable administrator, an unusually understanding man, and in general the most gentleman-like man on the campus," the student leaders resolved "to fight to the end" to restore Lawall to his rightful position by working with alumni and any other groups who put the interests of the students and the University before "political greed and cunning."

Governor Neely ably defended himself against the student position. "All I want," he impatiently explained to the students on June 24, "is the best educator that can be found in the United States for the salary that West Virginia can afford to pay." Reiterating themes from his inaugural, he emphasized that he desired the opportunities and facilities in West Virginia's highest educational institution be equal to those of any other state so that "our young people will not be sent elsewhere for their education." Although booed by the students as he left the Board meeting, the Governor denied that the actions taken were political and stressed that decisions reached were of benefit to the students. He stood, he said, on previous claims that the

University was not making sufficient progress, that too few students were coming to the University, that too many athletes went elsewhere, and that WVU must exert itself to compete with other schools, especially in "scientific progress and research." Claiming that the University for several years "had been slowly dying of dry rot," he said WVU's loss in student population since 1938 was 500 percent greater than that of Marshall.

The state press agreed with the students who were dismayed by the actions of the Governor and his hand-picked Board. On the day of the student protest, the *Morgantown Post* put forward the almost universal opinion of major newspapers of the state that

. . . something is wrong with a governmental structure that allows a Governor to take over the state university . . . Alumni all over the state are seething with righteous indignation. Public spirited citizens are outraged. The University community is numbed with apprehension and uncertainty . . . We hope that not only the friends of the University but also the friends of decency and responsibility in public government and the believers in a sound and growing system of higher education in West Virginia will counsel together on the best possible way of restoring a tolerable measure of order and security to the University.

Alumni groups, at the behest of students, also sprang into action against Governor Neely's "raping of the University." On June 21, W. P. Lehman, president of the Alumni Association, vehemently protested to the Board of Governors their recent decisions, and alumni groups across the state planned "strong and concerted activity" to have the decision revoked. In answer to charges of enrollment losses made by the Governor, Charles Hodges, spokesman for the Alumni Association, made a one-hour radio address on July 14 over West Virginia stations. The Governor's charges, broadcast Hodges, were "full of half-truths, inaccurate comparisons, and childish complaints." In answer to the Governor's comparison of enrollment statistics at WVU and Marshall, Hodges noted that the University's normal enrollment historically had been 70 percent male, 30 percent female; Marshall's enrollment, 55 percent female, 45 percent male. Naturally, the alumni spokesman inferred, with men drafted for World War II, WVU showed the greater decrease.

As the alumni and student protest mounted, Governor Neely was not without defenders. J. B. Easton, president of the West Virginia Industrial Union, believed the University to be "extremely backward," for he had no recollection of a labor representative ever being asked to speak at the University. Theodore Allen, West Virginia Communist Party member, who attributed the recommendation of a repeal of the state income tax to University brain trusters, suggested that a "purge" of the University was necessary if reactionary ideas of decreasing state revenues were to be demolished. On June 27, 1944, the *Fairmont Times* claimed the Governor was symbolically

Governor Matthew M. Neely

fighting for the people against "absentee landlords," the coal interests, in the administrative upheaval at the University.

In truth, the Governor was his own ablest defender, and in direct imitation of Franklin Roosevelt, he went to the airways to present his case directly to the people. In a "fireside chat" on the state of the University, on July 6, 1944, Governor Neely, "after more than three years of courteously seeking and vainly waiting for University improvement," expressed hope for a bigger and finer school under a "go-getter" president. His duty, judgment, and conscience had warned him "with trumpet voice," he declared, that temporizing should end at once and reform should begin without delay. Reiterating his charges that "priceless persons" had gone from West Virginia high schools to football glory elsewhere, he concentrated on the enrollment losses and the lack of academic achievement, particularly in engineering, as well as the unsuccessful athletic program at the University. He suggested that coal associations which opposed the removal of President Lawall and Dean Davis were motivated by a desire to escape increases in taxes needed to finance the Governor's "reform" programs. "Old-guard" Republicans, he charged, were turning his effort to improve the University into a personal attack against him and against a fourth term for Franklin D. Roosevelt. To demonstrate his deep interest in the state's University, the Governor concluded his emotional address with an offer of $500 a year to the University each year of his life if 999 other West Virginians matched him. In his final appeal for approval of his actions, he suggested:

. . . If you desire that the University be lifted high above the Dead Sea level of inferiority in which visionless greed has long kept it and that it be made a fountain of everflowing blessings for you and your children after you, join me in this important fight for educational reform, and help render an inestimable service to all the average men, women, and children of the state.

The faculty saw the 1944 contest for administrative control of the University in a highly introverted manner. Addressing a cautious statement to the Board of Governors, the alumni and the student body, as well as the people of West Virginia, the faculty sidestepped the claims of either the WVU president to remain in office or the West Virginia Governor to find a presidential substitute. Rather did it express its belief "that the welfare of this institution is of greater importance than are the fortunes of any individual."[11] Maintaining that it would always be outspoken in its stand on any question involving its duties and responsibilities, the faculty nevertheless declined to express an opinion as to the "wisdom or unwisdom [sic] of recent or earlier specific acts of the governing authorities." Rather did it confine its statements and recommendations to policies for the future, for "if this faculty should do otherwise, it would be assuming responsibility where it has no authority, since its advice has never been sought in either the appointment or the removal of administrative officials."

Showing a notable lack of concern with present misfortunes, the faculty asked that in the future it be provided committee contact with governing authorities, requested that the languishing University Senate be reorganized on a parliamentary basis, called for a strong, independent Graduate School, and urged that immediate plans be made for sufficient staff, buildings, and equipment to take care of large increases in enrollment following World War II. The faculty also recommended restoration of salary cuts of 10 to 20 percent made twelve years ago; additional adjustment of salaries to meet the marked increase in the cost of living; correction of inequalities in salaries and wages (including those of clerical and janitorial personnel); promotions and salary increases in accordance with an established schedule; and an increase in the University's supplement to the allowance of the State Teachers Retirement System.

In other words, if President Lawall could provide substantial increases, the faculty would be grateful. Or if Governor Neely's appointee could provide the necessary funds, the faculty would be just as grateful. And even if some unknown seized the reins of power, the faculty would remain expectant of more favorable monetary considerations. Thus, the faculty narrowed its definition of how best to resolve the current imbroglio.

The *Morgantown Post* was discouraged by the faculty's abdication of responsibility in the matter of appointments and removals of administrative officials. It wondered if the Governor's raid on the University had so shocked the faculty that its moral courage had deserted it. In the local newspaper's judgment, the alumni, the students, and the people of West Virginia had the right in this crisis to expect some word of warning from the faculty that the University's integrity had been threatened. With a note of sorrow at the faculty's obtuseness, it rhetorically questioned on July 14, 1944:

With profound regret, we feel compelled to say that in our judgment the faculty has let the University down, let the alumni and the students down, and let the people of the State down. The University cannot scale the mountains until it sets its feet out of the muck and mire. And if the faculty from its preferred position can't see that the University's feet are in the muck and mire, what can be expected from those not so favorably placed?

With alumni and students doing their proper homework, the *Morgantown Post* reasoned that perhaps the courts, if not the faculty, would strike the next blow for freedom.

It was Charles Wise of Charleston, former student body president and later head of the University Board of Governors and the WVU Advisory Board, who saw to it that the courts played their proper role. His vehicle was his own alumni group in the state capital. In testing the validity of the action taken by the Board of Governors in dismissing President Lawall and demoting Dean Davis, the Kanawha County chapter of the West Virginia University Alumni Association contended that when the Board, at its May 27, 1944, meeting, reelected the president and the dean for the 1944-45 fiscal year, the contract was binding on the state, and the Governor could not set it aside.

Dr. Lawall, President Lehman of the University Alumni Association, and Charles M. Love, Jr., president of the Kanawha alumni chapter, joined as plaintiffs in the suit against the reconstituted Board of Governors. Lawall, entering the case in order that all faculty be assured of tenure and academic freedom, said to the *Morgantown Post* on July 8, 1944:

I am joining a group of outstanding people for the purpose of protecting the good name of a fine University, with the hope that it may again be put on and kept on the high plane it occupied before the recent hurried and ill-advised action by a board certainly not familiar with the facts and statements thereafter justifying such action.

The *Post* attempted to explain to its readers why the legal experts had zeroed in on technical and minor matters. The more important question, the packing of the Board, was not to be decided by the courts, it said, because the "Governor is within the law but in defiance of the spirit of the law." Only the Legislature could amend the law and provide, as in other states, the Board with constitutional status. "The specter of political interference in higher education in West Virginia will not be banished until effective steps of some kind are taken to provide permanent protection against a repetition of Governor Neely's ripper tactics," it editorialized.

With the suit to invalidate the Board's order pending in the Kanawha County Circuit Court, friends of the University also asked Circuit Judge J. F. Bouchelle for an injunction to maintain the *status quo* at WVU until judgment was entered. Bouchelle granted the temporary injunction retaining

Lawall in the presidency because he was "a public officer," but denied it to Dean Davis who, he held, was not. In turn, the reconstituted Board, seeking State Supreme Court intervention, questioned Kanawha County Court jurisdiction as well as the circuit judge's injunction. The State Supreme Court declined to take a hand in the University case. Thus was the administrative upheaval avoided while West Virginians took time out to participate in the 1944 national and state elections. In this contest, Franklin D. Roosevelt secured his fourth term as president, Clarence Watson Meadows became twenty-second governor of West Virginia, and Matthew Neely retired, only to be elected to the U.S. House of Representatives in 1944 and to the U.S. Senate in 1948.

In 1945, following a pre-election bipartisan conference in August, 1944, Lawall became secure in his tenure because of the termination of the Neely board which had been denied State Senate approval, and by action of Governor Meadows in appointing an entirely new board which, in April, 1945, rescinded the order of the Neely board for the president's removal.[12]

In September, 1945, the twelfth president resigned to accept a lucrative position with the Chesapeake and Ohio Railway Company, and the secretary of the board, C. T. Neff, Jr., succeeded him as acting president. Neff held the fort until Irvin Stewart arrived in 1946 as thirteenth president of West Virginia University.

As a favorable omen for the Stewart presidency, the Legislature reconstituted the Board of Governors with nine members in 1947. One of the historic provisions of the 1947 legislation stated that "no member of the board may be removed from office by the Governor except for official misconduct, incompetence, neglect of duty, or gross immorality and thus only in the manner prescribed by law for the removal of the Governor or State elective officers."

It had taken West Virginia University eighty years to arrive at political independence. Its chance at self-determination coincided with the conclusion of World War II, causing the faculty to call attention to an immediate problem which might be turned into a golden opportunity:

West Virginia University is probably facing right now the most critical period in its history. Recent federal legislation will enable many thousands of young men and women returning from the armed forces to attend college. One hundred and eighty thousand men and women have entered the armed forces from West Virginia. Of these, it is estimated, ten percent will be eligible to attend school . . . of these, the University, with its facilities for technical training, would probably get half, certainly at least 2,000, with a slackening off of war-stimulated industry, many civilians will also attend college, especially since their families will have accumulated savings . . . If appropriations are not obtained sufficient to retain an efficient faculty and to provide necessary equipment and buildings to enable the University to compete with the universities of neighboring states, the result will be most humiliating indeed.[13]

Part 2

The Land-Grant, Comprehensive
State University

1946–1980

Chapter 9

A People's University

1946–1958

Irvin Stewart
July 1, 1946–August 25, 1958

ALTHOUGH CHOSEN AS THE THIRTEENTH president of the University, Irvin Stewart may have been, from his own standpoint as well as from that of the University and the state, one of its luckiest. Certainly he enjoyed an institutional rarity: one of the longest and possibly most successful administrations in West Virginia University history. The historian Oliver P. Chitwood, who had seen many presidents during his own half-century of service to WVU, surmised, long before Stewart resigned effective August 25, 1958, that no one could make too many errors administering the institution if he combined, as did Stewart and Chitwood himself, Southern, Baptist, and Democratic allegiances.

The cautious Board of Governors, however, used other criteria to ascertain Stewart's fitness. Dr. Vannevar Bush, president of the Carnegie Institution and Stewart's associate in the research leading to the supersecret Manhattan Project of World War II, reported on March 20, 1946, to the Board of Governors that Stewart was an outstanding man, reasonably conservative in viewpoint, and one who "doesn't rub anybody the wrong

185

way." Bush thought a governing board might deem it noteworthy that Stewart had ". . . negotiated 2,500 contracts for him in connection with the atomic bomb project. In no case was there any hard feeling and the manufacturers evidently had great trust in Mr. Stewart and he did not in any way take advantage of the confidence placed in him."

When the Board learned to its possible dismay that Stewart also held allegiances to the Century Club of New York and the Cosmos Club of Washington, D. C., it was nevertheless assured on March 12, 1946, that although Franklin D. Roosevelt and a "pink" editor of *The New York Times* belonged to the former, it did not mean that these memberships branded Stewart per se as a "radical." Convinced that only blue bloods of the two cities were invited to join such fraternities, and that few betrayed their aristocratic upbringings, the Board members relaxed.

The state media, two months in advance of Stewart's arrival, broadcast more detailed biographical material than that deemed necessary by the Chitwood prototype or by a conservative board, emphasizing the appointee's varied administrative experiences. This produced, as one editorial writer archly suggested, numerous contacts with educational, research, and scientific leaders, and organizations of the day which might prove beneficial to the thirty-fifth state. Although his overall career was more governmental than academic and more administrative than educational, the president-elect had balanced his various credentials for institutional leadership by teaching at the University of Texas from 1922 to 1928 and at the American University Graduate School from 1929 to 1932, and in summer sessions at Columbia University, Duke University, and the University of California at Los Angeles.

Associated with the U. S. Department of State from 1926 to 1928 and from 1930 to 1934, and a member of the Federal Communications Commission from 1934 to 1937, Stewart served as director of the Committee on Scientific Aids to Learning, 1937 to 1946, executive secretary of the National Defense Research Committee from 1940 to 1945, and executive secretary of the Office of Scientific Research and Development from 1941 to 1945. In 1946, he became its deputy director. During World War II, he also fulfilled duties as the executive secretary of the Committee on Medical Research in the Office for Scientific Research and Development. The latter experience was perhaps more consequential to WVU's future in the West Virginia health controversies of the 1950s than it seemed to selection committees of the mid-1940s.

Fortuitously for fresh outside leadership, state attention recently had focused upon past educational sins. Just before Stewart assumed the presidency, a Senate Concurrent Resolution of February 26, 1945, directed an interim committee of educational specialists to make a comprehensive study of the educational system of West Virginia, including the institutions of higher learning. George D. Strayer, professor emeritus of education in Teachers

College of Columbia University, assisted by a professional staff and an advisory committee of fifteen representative citizens of the state, completed the survey on December 10, 1945. In light of the limited resources of West Virginia, the committee recommended a single university.

The opportunistic Board in turn, with certain exceptions and reservations, responded that it was in complete and enthusiastic accord with the Strayer findings. The Board recommended that the status and duties of the University president be strengthened so that all other University officers, particularly the comptroller, be made directly responsible to him, and requested that the president attend all meetings of the Board instead of appearing, in accordance with past practices, only when invited. Stewart, in his capacity as president-elect, promptly endorsed the principle that the University president should be present at all meetings of the Board.

Strayer and his associates were aware that recommendations for University advancement could not be quickly converted into actuality and admitted that the state's one university, which had not yet gained total support from all sections of the state, suffered two major handicaps: first, relative isolation in that the institution was far removed from the center of population of the state, and second, "the conditions surrounding the campus in the City of Morgantown" which the educational experts chose not to identify in their report to the public. It remained for the *Bluefield Telegraph* to spell out on November 22, 1947, some of the local circumstances that adversely had affected the loyalty of old grads attending University homecoming events. Bemoaning the fact that the University city was no longer "the quiet, picturesque community it once was," it blamed the Morgantown Ordnance Works for polluting the air and endangering a visitor's sense of smell.

The *Sunday Exponent Telegram* in Clarksburg also worried that Morgantown was "wide open" – with slot machines, gambling dens, and liquor being sold openly to students. If in Morgantown "the racketeers of every kind" are flourishing, the Clarksburg editor wrote on October 26, 1947, parents "should withdraw their children from that school and send them to some other school which is protected."

Reacting against the editorial, "Morgantown Needs Cleanup," Stewart reported to the Clarksburg Publishing Company two weeks later that it was the opinion of a group of student leaders that the Morgantown situation was not such as to constitute temptations to students and that it would be far easier for students to gamble or drink in other West Virginia cities than in Morgantown.

In an early swing around the state, Stewart also capitalized upon the Strayer Report's findings. He told the Charleston Rotary Club on August 23, 1946, that "if the University is to serve the State as it should it must be accepted by all people of West Virginia as the State University and not merely a university which serves the northern part of the state and which other parts have only a passing interest in." At the state capitol, he called upon the people of the state to see that West Virginia had a fine university, one that incorporated an intelligent student body, an adequate physical plant, and a first-rate faculty. "The intellectual capacity of the people of West Virginia is certainly adequate, the physical and financial resources of the state are adequate," said Stewart in his quest for support. "An inferior university," he preached, "is a luxury which West Virginia is too poor to afford."

To enhance West Virginia University's attractiveness, the thirteenth administration initiated several programs highlighting the University, its students, faculty, and academic programs. It thus anticipated in the public relations arena the criticism of the West Virginia Alumni Association on April 28, 1949, that the University was sadly lacking in tradition despite its many years of existence and despite "further fact that it is as rich historically in this element as many other educational institutions of its age and accomplishment." Greater West Virginia Weekend, an event planned to restore such University traditions as Mother's Day, a custom of observance originating in the thirty-fifth state, had been discontinued in 1943 because of World War II. The University promptly resumed its observance on May 10-12, 1946. In 1947 and 1948, mindful of parental influence upon affairs of state and before some of the largest crowds ever assembled on the campus, it dedicated the final day of festivities to visiting mothers.

Borrowing the idea from his native state of Texas, the new and energetic president inaugurated an annual, statewide observance of the University's birthday, February 7. Prodded by Stewart and the Board of Governors, Governor Okey Patteson proclaimed the day "University Day," calling upon all citizens to recognize, through programs and activities of West Virginia University, its contributions to the people of West Virginia. The first University Day on February 7, 1950, set the pattern for future birthday observances. Harold Stassen, former governor of Minnesota and then president of the University of Pennsylvania, keynoted the event.

The first celebration of the birthday also gave Stewart an early opportunity to educate the state's inhabitants to his conception of West Virginia University. In a speech before Charleston alumni, he presented his democratic concept of the type of institution whose birth was being celebrated:

The state university is a people's university. It belongs to the people in a real sense. They can determine the direction and rate of its growth by the way in which they grant or withhold their support. It is an important instrument for assuring that ours shall remain a classless society. The son of the town's hardest worker or of the town loafer, the son of the rich man or of the poor man, the son of the miner, the school teacher, the farmer, the bank president, or the day laborer, if he has the ability, can attend its classes; and he may emerge as tomorrow's governor, judge, legislator, manager of industry, or as a better farmer and as a better citizen. That is a wonderful possibility; and its continuance is one of the strongest safeguards against the substitution for democracy of a political or economic system which would deny that possibility.

Mountaineer Weekend was another feature providing the University a showcase for parents, alumni, and friends, and an opportunity to "multiply the number who regard the University as a dependable and sympathetic agency ever at their disposal," the *Morgantown Post* reminded its readers on February 6, 1950. First inaugurated on November 8, 1947, in the fall of Stewart's second year, it began a new campus tradition. But when the event was translated into a revelry, the question arose as to whether student leaders were taking proper advantage of the opportunity of their heritage celebration to depict traits, characteristics, and a sense of humor of the typical mountaineer. "For our part," lectured a Morgantown journalist on May 5, 1949, "we are not altogether satisfied that the undergraduates are showing as much originality and resourcefulness as they possess in caricaturing the mountaineer as 'poor white trash' who apparently spends all his time carrying a catalog to the outhouse."

Cued in by President Stewart that the University should work to increase the pride of West Virginians in themselves and in their state, the Student Government requested on May 22, 1957, that the University Book Store end sales of all products depicting a tattered hillbilly with "his jug, felt hat, bare feet, and ragged clothes," since the use of such "provokes an unsavory and degrading connotation of our Mountaineer spirit and tradition." Rather did the Executive Council of Student Government believe the true spirit of the mountaineer was exemplified by the coonskin cap, the buckskin uniform, and temperate demeanor.

Stewart, who quietly had been initiating such refinements in costuming and behavior, replied one week later to the student body president with a note of congratulations for his effort to end the representation of the mountaineer as a hillbilly and requested the manager of the University Book Store to withdraw from sale all items of merchandise carrying the imprint of the comic or hillbilly mountaineer. The manager complied, but reminded Stewart on May 28 that a change would be expensive in that the Book Store would take a loss of $300.00. The administration in its quest for new imagery gratefully absorbed the necessary costs.

In November, 1950, Mountain, ranking honorary for men, also sought a role in the new image-making by campaigning for funds to erect on the campus a statue of the Mountaineer in the Daniel Boone tradition. A future governor of the state, then a student official, Arch A. Moore, Jr., solicited $100 from the administration for the campaign and instituted Mountaineer Statue Festival as a means of soliciting from concession and entertainment booths money which eventually would total $15,000, the estimated cost of the statue.

Borrowing an idea from the Golden Bears of the University of California, Mountain honorary created in 1948, at President Stewart's behest, the Committee of 55, which consisted of one person from each county, to provide a direct tie to the University. Acting only at the request of the University president and always in an unpublicized manner, it, too, was an agency meant to stimulate loyalty to the University through its endorsement of University policies and plans across the state.

Of more immediate benefit to the Stewart administration, interested in the inculcation of loyalty to West Virginia University, the Strayer Report advocated changes in the University's governance. Suggesting in 1945 that the affairs of the University had been dominated by "a system of remote control," it called for immediate change because "plural and divided control of the University is prejudicial to the existence of a ranking institution." The first opportunity for progressive educational direction was presented to the voters of the state in the fall election of 1946 in an educational amendment which would have provided the University Board of Governors constitutional status, prevented the removal of its members from office except for cause, and secured to its governing officials tenure in office.

Members of Mountaineer Post 127 of the American Legion, composed of University students recently discharged from service, appealed in the October 30, 1946, issue of the *Morgantown Post* for approval of the amendment, charging that the state's educational system was "incompetent, poorly administered, and in confusion." One of the first college American Legion posts of its kind, it organized itself in 1945 and affiliated in 1946 with a new women veterans' organization to play an important role in University life. Believing "the future of this state is at stake," these veterans characterized opposition to the amendment as insuring the unsavory politics of the past; they suggested approval of the amendment for the benefit of higher education in the state. For good measure, the *Morgantown Post* clarified the veterans' argument by bluntly stating that affirmative action on the part of voters would prevent the continued packing of the University Board of Governors, which so recently "outraged all the people of the state and did untold harm to the University."

Despite town and gown endorsement, state voters did not ratify the educational amendment. Although the Strayer Report had recommended change by constitutional means, the governor, the Legislature, and a legislative interim committee came to the University's rescue with considerable dispatch in the aftermath of the educational amendment's defeat. At the end of 1946, the committee drafted bills which transferred authority over the University that the Board of Governors had shared with the State Board of

Control to the Board of Governors, and the authority over the state colleges
that the State Board of Education had shared with the State Board of Control to the State Board of Education.

On January 9, 1947, Governor Clarence W. Meadows propelled the
Legislature into action with his statement that West Virginia University
"should be THE University both in theory and fact." The lawmakers promptly
enacted legislation on February 25, 1947, which was substantially in line with
the Strayer Report recommendations on the conduct and control of institutions of higher learning. One bill reconstituted the University Board of
Governors, effective July 1, 1947, with nine members serving overlapping
nine-year terms and subject to removal only for cause. Another bill transferred to the Board all fiscal control over the University once vested in the
State Board of Control. Newspapers observed that the new Board would have
greater powers and responsibilities than ever before vested in any of its
predecessors by controlling not only its purse strings, within the limits of
legislative appropriations, but also its educational policies and staff personnel.

With a new board behind him, Dr. Stewart was inaugurated on April
26, 1947, in academic ceremonies in the Field House before 153 delegates
representing the learned societies and other institutions of higher learning
and a crowd of University well-wishers numbering 4,000. It was the first
inauguration of a University president since 1928. The two-day ceremonies
included addresses by James B. Conant, president of Harvard University,
and Vannevar Bush, president of the Carnegie Institution. Both speeches were
broadcast statewide. Bush's description of Stewart as "a leader who will see
the vision, who will think things through soundly, and who will unsparingly
give his best strength as the University and the state go forward," coupled
with Dr. Conant's expressed belief that Stewart had the "patience, strength,
endurance, wisdom, and vision" for the job, sufficiently impressed a local
newspaper editor to believe that "the moment" and "the man" had joined forces
in behalf of both the state and the University. In thanking his two former
wartime associates in the Office of Scientific Research and Development, Dr.
Stewart restricted his own remarks to the obvious: if the University were
to increase its services to the state, it needed more funds from public and
private sources to broaden extension services, strengthen research, and
improve instruction.

With an impressive inauguration, a new governing board, a state government committed to the concept of a single state university, and active efforts on the campus and across the state to establish loyalty to the University,
Stewart faced three matters needing immediate attention. One was the disposition of his immediate predecessor in office; the others, of a more pressing
nature, were housing and an athletic controversy.

When Irvin Stewart appointed C. T. Neff, Jr., vice-president of the

University, he positioned the former secretary of the Board of Governors and most recently the acting president in a role that best reflected Neff's traditional responsibilities to WVU. On May 24, 1946, the *Morgantown Post* called attention to "the dignity, tact, modesty, and competence which Mr. Neff had exercised and displayed in what is surely one of the most difficult of all positions — the acting president of a university," and on October 8 expressed certainty that he would favorably acquit himself by being concerned with "internal administration." As the newspaper saw the situation, President Stewart would be relieved of much of the detail work and could devote himself to the external affairs of the University. Yet when Neff died in 1953, the office of vice-president was allowed to lapse, and when Louise Keener succeeded Neff as comptroller, the internal affairs of the University fell wholly under the control of the Deans of the respective colleges. Although the University was expanding in faculty, students, and academic programs, the Stewart years thus showed one of the leanest administrative structures in the history of the institution.

Rapidly increasing enrollments at all colleges and universities after World War II also affected West Virginia University. On August 3, 1946, Stewart sounded the keynote of a housing drive: "The University is desperately in need of all living accommodations available in Morgantown or in outlying communities." Noting that original fall enrollment estimates of 4,500 had reached 6,000 and could peak at an even higher figure, the president signified, to the possible dismay of many a faculty member, that the University was prepared to schedule classes from 8 a.m. to 10 p.m. and throughout Saturday if necessary. Enlisting all church, civic, service, labor, and veterans organizations to appeal to their members for housing for University students, the new president dramatically led the way by making available half of the second floor of the president's home to five war veterans who would pay regular dormitory fees directly to the dormitory office for their palatial accommodations.

A block-by-block canvass of Morgantown homes, a doubling of students in all dormitory rooms, the conversion of lounges into sleeping quarters, and the federal government's gift of 150 trailers and surplus barracks, which were converted into one hundred apartments, made possible a record enrollment of 6,010, almost twice that of any previous session in the University's history. The breakdown of students was revealing: men outnumbered women 4,717 to 1,293, an almost 4 to 1 ratio. When the *Morgantown Post* declared on July 31, 1946, that it was one's patriotic duty to help resolve the housing crisis, it defended its choice of an adjective by suggesting that "if they were good enough to fight for us, they are good enough to share the shelter of our roof if we can find a place for them." The newspaper had accurately

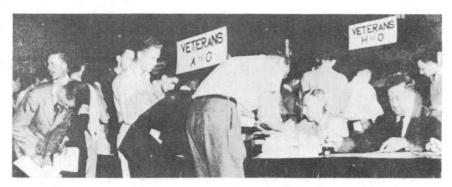

GI Bill flooded WVU and other institutions with World War II veterans who other-wise couldn't have afforded a college education. Many of them were married and lived in surplus Navy barracks reerected below University High School in an area that became known as College Park.

assessed the character of the student body, for 60 percent of the 1946-47 enrollment were veterans.

Throughout the Stewart years, which embraced not only the post-World War II era but also the Korean conflict, veterans represented a significant percentage of the total student population, ranging from a low of 11.9 percent to a high of 64.7 percent. From the top enrollment of 6,735 students in 1948, figures sagged to 4,421 in 1951. When Stewart finished his presidency in 1957-58, enrollment stood at 6,216, 200 more than when he began in 1946. In the dozen years of his administration, the percentage of nonresident students ranged between 10.1 percent and 13.5 percent. Students coming from Morgantown and adjacent areas produced the highest in-state enrollment figures, but every county in the state was represented in the University's enrollment during each of the postwar years. With respect to the number of degrees awarded, the twelve-year period netted almost the same number of undergraduate degrees as had the previous seventy-six years, and more than double the number of master's and doctor's degrees awarded since the University's founding.

Appeals by University spokesmen in behalf of Morgantown housing for both students and faculty and for more dormitories, especially for women, continued until the 1949-50 academic year, when officials judged that the University population had stabilized. Throughout the postwar era it was argued that the University had been negligent in its previous forty years in failing to provide dormitory rooms for all women who wanted them.

In the controversy over more dormitory construction for women, a con-dition aggravated by the fact that in this period the University required that women be housed in WVU facilities, Dr. Stewart possibly foresaw the 1960-70 period when state universities across the nation would abandon to local entrepreneurs their traditional role of student landlords. Before civic groups, the president emphasized the need for private rather than state or federal monies as the stimulant to dormitory construction. The University's first priority, he patiently explained on December 1, 1949, was finding funds for instruction because "we cannot do both on appropriations we are likely to get from the Legislature, and rightly or wrongly I feel the emphasis must be put on spending tax funds for badly needed instructional facilities." He said he agreed with the thinking of the Board of Governors that using public funds for instruction and private funds for living quarters was the only realistic policy available to those governing a West Virginia educational institution.

One of Stewart's first tasks after assuming the presidency was to solicit money from the private sector. Addressing the West Virginia Chamber of Commerce on October 5, 1946, he urged future investors, "if you have faith in the West Virginia of tomorrow, you may confidently spend your money at the University." He said that the University was understaffed and inadequately financed, and he emphasized on November 16 that in addition to the support the University obtained from state government, "business and industry in the state should make substantial contributions toward the improvement of the research facilities at the University."

It did not take Stewart long to become specific in his drive for dollars. Speaking at the closing session of the West Virginia Coal Mining Institute on August 1, 1947, he urged industry to contribute $100,000 a year for the next five years to support "an initial program of coal research at the University." He said, "it's to the benefit of industry itself to see that young men of the type who meet qualifications for these scholarships (which would be provided by the contributions) are attracted to the profession of mining engineering and are assisted in preparing themselves for that profession."

Taking a harder look at Stewart's chances of enlisting private money, a *Morgantown Post* journalist recounted on October 24, 1949, that before Stewart's regime, the University had made ignominious efforts to endear itself to wealthy citizens but had failed in most of its attempts—notably when it freely but vainly gave Oglebay Hall its name in hopes it would be remembered in the will of the late Earl Oglebay. In like manner, in expectation of monetary remembrances, the University had awarded questionable honorary degrees that netted more strikes than hits. Because of a long-standing tradition of non-support, the Morgantown editor suggested that newspapers which overcame the non-contributing habits of their readers were deserving of Pulitzer prizes. As a general proposition, because of the belief that tax-supported institutions met their needs through legislative appropriations, the doubtful journalist suggested that those who wanted to see the University raised to higher standards should concentrate their efforts on the Legislature at its biennial budget sessions.

Despite journalistic rebuff, Stewart persisted. Not only did he suggest that West Virginians approach dormitory construction as private individuals and not taxpayers, but he also described on January 20, 1950, the way it might be expedited. He observed that the gifts to the West Virginia University Alumni Association's Loyalty Permanent Endowment Fund were by contributors whose small bequests, when added together, made possible solutions to problems that one meager gift alone could not satisfy. On June 5, 1950, when Fred G. Wood, retired Beckley coal operator, willed 517 acres of coal land in Raleigh and Wyoming counties, a bequest expected to net $200,000 in royalty figures per year, Stewart dwelt on the principle of remembering WVU in wills rather than the actual sum received from Wood.

When the University received a $3,770.30 gift for the establishment of the Andrew Delmar Hopkins Scholarship in Entomology, the six donors of the sum requested that the money be invested in stock of the American Telephone and Telegraph Company, with the income to be used in making scholarship awards. When a legal opinion from Assistant Attorney General Robert E. Magnuson on February 12, 1954, indicated that the West Virginia Constitution prohibited the state from becoming "a joint owner, or stockholder in any company or association in this State or elsewhere," Stewart pressed for establishment of the West Virginia University Foundation. Set up on December 3, 1954, the Foundation was intended by Stewart to provide greater freedom to the University in developing ideas and encouraging programs for which legislative support was not yet ripe. The Foundation, it was suggested, could provide, among other things, salary supplements to distinguished professors, support for scholarly or other research projects, publications, lectureships, scholarship and loan funds, and purchase of special equipment.

In a final accounting, for each of the twelve Stewart years, the total gifts and bequests for scholarships, research and teaching grants, loan funds, and miscellaneous purposes moved from $20,000 in the first year to $500,000 in the twelfth year for a grand total of $1.5 million. In a four-year period, the WVU Foundation had received gifts in cash or securities with a value in excess of $136,000.

That Stewart had called attention to private giving did not mean that little heed was given to public subsidy. In the matter of legislative support, he was able to increase considerably the sums awarded the University. In state appropriations, the Stewart administration went from a low of $2,940,891 in 1946-47 to a high of $6,297,850 in 1957-58. All income available to the University increased during the Stewart administration from $5,960,962 in 1946-47 to $21,657,223 in 1957-58.

Whereas Stewart's search for private housing and private gift-giving led him to the concept of the WVU Foundation, Inc., his initial search for a solution to the athletic controversy of the 1940s directed him into West Virginia University's greatest era in sports which included the "golden era" of WVU basketball. It was not that he desired unusual success on the gridiron or the basketball court, areas of greatest concern to some alumni. As he expressed his own view on the subject:

Every institution likes to see its athletic teams successful. Its friends hope that it will win more games than it loses. However, since a win for one team represents a defeat for its opponent, the total of victories and defeats will balance. For a properly scheduled institution over a period of years, the number of victories should approximate the number of defeats.[1]

For good measure, he added:

West Virginia University likes to win athletic contests, but is not unduly concerned over losses to teams representing comparable institutions. A well-played game, with good sportsmanship on the part of players, coaches, and spectators, is a credit to an institution. This philosophy is thoroughly consistent with the place of intercollegiate athletics as part of an educational program rather than a side show.

In the fall of 1946, Stewart's first year, there was widespread criticism of the University's athletic program. Complaints involved unsuccessful past seasons, Athletic Director Roy M. Hawley, Football Coach William F. Kern, who had just returned from World War II to resume the head coaching duties, and the sources and methods of awarding athletic scholarships.

In response to the growing publicity on the matter, President Stewart appointed on December 19, 1946, a special committee composed of alumni and others "to study the organization for the conduct of all phases of intercollegiate athletics at West Virginia University, to suggest whether improvements are feasible, and, if so, to recommend ways in which the improvements may be accomplished."

On March 1, 1947, the committee recommended that control of all University intercollegiate athletics be vested in a new University Athletic Council subject to the supervision of the University president and the Board of Governors; that the athletic director be budget officer and chief executive officer of the council; that the council control, supervise and approve budgets, schedules, the granting of athletic awards, the formulation of policies, the approval of practices, and the nomination of personnel employed on management and coaching staffs. The council was expected to resolve differences of opinion and define areas of authority between the athletic director and the coaches and to respond to public questioning about the athletic program.

The committee also recommended that Coach Kern and Director Hawley be retained. It reported that state appropriations and athletic gate receipts had never been used for distribution as athletic scholarships, although it acknowledged that voluntary contributions had been made for scholarship purposes by "numerous prominent and respectable citizens of the state." Seeing "no inherent wrong and no rightful objection to such assistance," the committee recommended that the administration of such funds be vested in a single, responsible agency independent of the department of intercollegiate athletics or any of its personnel.

On April 26, 1947, the Board of Governors issued a directive which followed, for the most part, the special committee's recommendations. A new council replaced the former nine-member, faculty-dominated Board of Intercollegiate Athletics, a body the investigating committee maintained could not exercise proper authority over sports because of its limited powers. In its place the new council was composed of four faculty (one of whom was the dean of the School of Physical Education acting as chairman), two alumni members appointed by the president from nominees of the executive committee of the Alumni Association, one student, and one member of the Board of Governors appointed by its president. As Stewart put it, "the new Athletic Council quickly established effective control over the athletic program, and the reality of University control in that area has not since been questioned."[2]

Kern's 1946 team had managed a 5-5 record, and his 1947 team, captained by Gene Corum, posted a 6-4 record, including a victory over Pitt, the first since 1928. Nonetheless, he resigned shortly afterwards and was replaced by Dudley S. DeGroot, a former All-America lineman at Stanford. Aided by quarterback Jimmy Walthall and co-captain Vic Bonfili, DeGroot's 1948 team recorded 8 wins and 3 losses, capped by a 21-12 victory over Texas Western in the Sun Bowl, providing WVU its best football record in a decade. After a poor season in 1949, DeGroot resigned.

Art (Pappy) Lewis, former head coach at Washington and Lee University and assistant coach at Mississippi State, took on the assignment as WVU's twenty-fifth coach in 1950. Slowly, the WVU football picture changed from one of defeat to victory, undoubtedly helped by the University's entrance into the Southern Conference. Lewis's 1952 team ranked tenth nationally in total offense and seventh in total defense, and star end Paul Bischoff became the first WVU player named to a major college first-team All-America squad since 1925. The 1953 team posted an 8-1 record, won its second conference championship, but lost to Georgia Tech in the Sugar Bowl. The 1954 team was 8-1 and again won the conference championship. Another conference crown and an 8-2 record were posted by the 1955 team, which ranked second nationally in total offense and eighth in total defense and boasted such stars as quarterback Fred Wyant, halfbacks Joe Marconi and Bob Moss, and linemen Bruce Bosley and Sam Huff. In 1956 the football team posted a 6-4 record; in 1957, a 7-2-1 record, and, for the fifth time in a row, remained undefeated in Southern Conference competition. In 1957, guard Chuck Howley received many post-season All-Star selections.

The first year of President Stewart's administration was the second year for basketball coach Lee Patton. Patton posted a 19-3 record in 1946, earning the Mountaineers a return engagement to the National Invitation Tournament. Senior Leland Byrd earned All-America honors in 1947. In 1947-48, West Virginia finished 17-3, and in 1948-49 had an 18-6 record. Patton's 1949-50 team dropped to 13-11, and tragedy struck — at midseason Patton was injured in an automobile accident on his way to the Penn State game in February. He died on March 7.

Robert N. (Red) Brown succeeded Patton, having been recruited from Davis and Elkins College where he had served as athletic director and head coach of all sports. His team, aided by 6'9" Mark Workman, finished with an 18-9 record, and in 1951-52 the team soared to a 23-4 mark. Workman earned All-America honors, and WVU was ranked ninth by the Associated Press. Brown surrendered his coaching duties to become the University's athletic director.

Fred Schaus, captain of the 1947-48 and 1948-49 teams, returned to his alma mater as Stewart's next basketball coach. His first year, 1954-55, saw WVU winning the first of six consecutive championships in the Southern Conference. The 1955-56 team won 21 and lost 9, with "Hot Rod" Hundley establishing a WVU scoring record as a junior, averaging 26.6 points per game. At the end of the year, Jerry West, from Cabin Creek, West Virginia, and East Bank High School, one of the most sought-after high school stars in the nation, announced his decision to attend WVU.

In 1956-57, Hundley and junior standout Lloyd Sharrar took the varsity team to a record of 25 and 5, with Hundley receiving All-America recognition. The 1957-58 season was Schaus' best with 26 wins and 2 losses, and included the Kentucky Invitational Tournament championship. This was the most prestigious mid-season tournament of the late 1950s. Although the team lost in the NCAA tournament, the Associated Press, United Press, and International News Service ranked the Mountaineers Number One in 1958.

Stewart might have downplayed the importance of sports, but nonetheless during WVU's "golden era" of basketball, 1946 to 1960, teams coached by Lee Patton, Red Brown, and Fred Schaus posted a composite won-lost record of 289-88. This winning percentage of .764 was second only to the University of Kentucky, which won five national championships in the same period. From 1946 through 1959, the football record showed 82 wins, 56 losses, and 3 ties, a percentage of .592. In individual terms, the brilliance of All-Americans Leland Byrd, Mark Workman, Rod Hundley, and Jerry West on the basketball court was mirrored on the gridiron by such standouts as Bob Orders, Bruce Bosley, Sam Huff, and Chuck Howley.

The Board of Governors believed, somewhat in contrast to Stewart, that such outstanding athletic activity merited attention from the state's appropriating authorities. As their October 22, 1955 minutes record, "Discussion revealed the unanimous feeling on the part of the Board that a new policy of presenting two complimentary tickets to athletic contests to members of the Legislature had been well received."

To this policy, Stewart reluctantly agreed. But in striking contrast to the Board's enthusiasm for sports, he continued to speak out against undue importance being placed on athletics. In an address before the Kanawha County Alumni Association on February 7, 1950, he disassociated himself from fostering a "big-time" athletic program for the University when he said:

Popular interest in intercollegiate contests is natural and desirable. High enthusiasm in victory and deep despair in defeat are understandable; but the individual who would magnify the athletic program until it imperils the real business for which the University was established is not an asset in the long run no matter how fervently he protests his loyalty.

No doubt the successful formation of a new athletic council coupled with frequently outstanding athletic records enabled Stewart to direct his attention elsewhere, notably to the University's physical plant and buildings which had been grossly neglected for several decades. An immediate answer to social needs, first demonstrated in the acquisition of trailers and barracks for married student housing, was duplicated when the Stewart administration turned to the post-World War II surplus property disposal program of the federal government. Two temporary buildings acquired in 1947 and 1948 became a cafeteria and a student union. The student union building, formerly a recreation center at a naval base in Virginia, provided the ever-increasing student body with a bowling alley, ballroom, snack bar, little theater, table tennis, shuffleboard courts, and other needed space where meetings and social events could be held. With William D. Scott assuming direction on January 15, 1948, the student-named Mountainlair was opened on May 15. At first, admission was charged for many of its activities, but by 1949 students insisted that the practice be dropped in favor of an activity fee collected from all registered students.

The concept of a fee, once established, would not only support the original but also future Mountainlairs. Looking toward the day when the present, but temporary, Mountainlair would be replaced and acting upon a student referendum, the Board of Governors in 1955 adopted a fee of $3.00 per semester to be paid by each full-time student toward the eventual construction of a new student union building. Imposition of the fee was authorized specifically by the Legislature. Until funds were adequate to permit construction, the money was invested in U.S. government securities. In March, 1958, the fund exceeded $55,000.

Under the federal property program, the University also acquired in 1948-49 an experimental farm of 150 acres in Mason County and an experimental forest of 495 acres in Randolph County (the Tygart Valley Farm). A summer camp for engineers of 53.5 acres in Preston County (Camp Russell Love Morris) was added in 1950.

Because the immediate postwar era with its doubling of the student population not only overtaxed the University dormitories but also called attention to the University's limited acreage and inadequate construction program of the 1930s and 1940s, Stewart appointed a faculty committee to prepare recommendations that he could present to the Board of Governors on the nature and priority rankings of needed buildings. In the summer of 1947, a poll of department heads indicated the University's greatest deficiencies were in academic structures: classrooms, laboratory space, library. Unless these were quickly provided, they said, the research and instructional needs of the University could not be met. The University president and the Board of Governors agreed. When a $2.7 million appropriation was released in August, 1947, Dr. Stewart announced the first purchase of property in his administration: parcels of land between University and Beechurst Avenues which would serve as a site for three major buildings to be completed in the next two years — a general classroom building, a biology building, and a physics building. Fronting the Field House across Beechurst Avenue, the four buildings were referred to as a needed and necessary quadrangle of learning. In 1949, the Board acquired additional Beechurst Avenue property as a site for a new building for the School of Music.

Using the occasion of a University birthday celebration, the Board of Governors named the classroom building Armstrong Hall in honor of Robert Armstrong, who had been associated with the University as both student and teacher, as head of the English Department, as University chaplain, and as acting president. It was believed that Armstrong Hall, although temporarily housing the education faculty as well as the language and economics faculties, would become the new center of the College of Arts and Sciences.

On September 28, 1950, the Board named the new biology building Brooks Hall, "a perfect name," said the *Morgantown Post*, "for it's seldom that four brothers are all associated with their native state and the University in the way the four Brooks brothers were associated with West Virginia, the University, and the biological life of West Virginia." Armstrong and Brooks halls opened in 1950 and 1951; the unnamed Physics Building in 1952, the unnamed Music Building in 1954, and a University Book Store in the basement of the Law Building was in operation by 1958.

During the Stewart years, the original campus saw limited purchases for academic and dormitory purposes. To aid in the accreditation of the teaching program in forestry, and as quarters for the Department of

Agricultural Engineering and the Division of Forestry, the Board of Governors purchased and remodeled in 1946 a four-story building adjacent to the Stadium. In 1947, the Board acquired a brick residence adjacent to the University Library which was used successively as a dormitory annex, offices for the School of Music, and a faculty club. Agricultural Extension, the Department of Nursing Education, and the Speech Clinic were located in a three-story frame building on Spruce Street acquired in 1949. The nursery school of the Division of Home Economics and the Department of Agricultural Economics were housed in four houses on Price and Prospect Streets.

More substantial building included a new dormitory for women and the purchase of property north of Men's Hall as a site for a new dormitory for men. By creating a superstructure on the Library, its stack capacity was doubled and additional reading rooms and carrels were added. In the general area of maintenance, new boilers were installed in the heating plant, new balconies and bleachers were added in the Field House, lighting was improved in the Library, Reynolds Hall, the Administration Building, and in classrooms and laboratories across the campus. Fire stairs were placed in Martin and Science Halls, classrooms added to the Armory, additional laboratories fitted into the Chemistry Building, and extensive repairs and new seats provided for the Stadium.

The State Road Commission's construction of Monongahela Boulevard linking Morgantown and Star City in 1948 led the University in that year to acquire by condemnation proceedings the Krepps and Dille farms. The new road would provide easy access, University planners suggested, to the two adjoining farms that totaled 260 acres. When on June 21, 1948, Judge Charles Baker overruled a special plea by the farms' owners who sought to show that the Board of Governors had not proved the necessity for seizing the land, he took occasion to note, "The University Board of Governors, through testimony of its witnesses, shows need for more room now and in the future, and presents a well thought-out plan for future expansion." With condemnation proceedings successfully ordered, the Board of Governors next gave consent to the annexation of the Dille and Krepps farms by the city of Morgantown.

The Board engaged C. F. Cellarius, Cincinnati architect and campus planning expert, to survey the campus and indicate a master plan for growth. Aided by committees of the State Planning Board and the faculty, Cellarius recommended that the farms serve three principal purposes. A site west of Beechurst Avenue, leveled by the highway construction, was designated for baseball and softball fields, horseshoe pitching, tennis courts, an archery range, football practice fields, and other physical activities. Also west of the highway, fifty acres of steep and wooded hillside, from the athletic fields down to the Monongahela River, were reserved for a University Arboretum.

Such property, campus officials announced on May 22, 1950, during Commencement Week, would feature native trees, shrubs, and other plants in the natural setting of an "outdoor laboratory," an area useful not only for student instruction but also as a place of educational interest for thousands of West Virginians not well-versed in the plant resources of the state. The site east of the highway was reserved for the Colleges of Engineering and Agriculture and Forestry.

As Cellarius foresaw the University's progress along Beechurst Avenue, which paralleled the Monongahela River, he estimated that it would not be too many years before the University would have to abandon the present football stadium in favor of a new one on the outskirts of town where adequate parking facilities would be available. However, the *Morgantown Post* pointed out that "a new stadium is far down on the list of priorities. It's simply a thought for the future."

To be freed from the confinement of fifty acres on the Downtown Campus through the addition of two hundred acres on Morgantown's outskirts was indeed a challenge to University planners. It was also an invitation to Morgantown real estate speculators. The Board, however, indicated its tactics on February 7, 1950, when it

Resolved that because of excessive prices asked for property needed to permit the expansion of the University in Morgantown, and in light of the failure of commissioners in condemnation proceedings to establish reasonable prices when the University has resorted to condemnation, the Committee on Campus Plans is requested to include in its study and recommendation to the Board the feasibility of transferring a portion of the University's teaching program to another campus to be acquired in some other part of the state.

It explained its threat as well as accomplished its strategy when it added: "The principal end sought is to bring the University's requirements for additional land in Morgantown to such proportions as can be satisfied by purchases at reasonable prices."

With a third campus to be devoted to a medical center, the creation of a second campus called for decisions of the highest order and, as always, with particular attention to traffic flow. These decisions were quickly forthcoming. The second campus would be used for the professional schools of the University, as would be true of the third campus, and thus alleviate the movement of undergraduates between campuses. Statewide campaigns were launched to impress West Virginians with the need for new buildings for engineering, agriculture, forestry, and home economics. The State Society of Professional Engineers, the University Alumni Association, and state organizations interested in agriculture were enlisted and directed by a three-man campaign committee set up in each of the state's fifty-five counties. And just as the medical school would be financed by a totally new method never before used in West Virginia or for that matter by any state university, so also would the planned professional buildings on the second campus, rapidly becoming known as the Evansdale Campus.

On June 2, 1956, reacting to a proposal by President Stewart, the Board of Governors recommended that the Legislature authorize the issuance of $10 million worth of revenue bonds for the Colleges of Agriculture and Engineering. This was deemed necessary in view of the demonstrated inadequacy of appropriations for constructing and equipping new buildings from surplus revenues only. The step was taken pursuant to an act of the 1956 Legislature which authorized revenue-bond financing of the proposed construction by providing for the creation of a University capital improvements fund in the state treasury. Into this special fund student fees would be placed for the purpose of bond retirement, a concept new to the state. Although there was experience in the use of rentals for the building of dormitories, student fees never had been used to provide academic facilities at WVU or at any other state university.

When the University successfully had met the legal challenges to this unprecedented legislation, other states followed. The concept enabled West Virginia University to supplement inadequate physical plants and to plan for the future, instead of facing denials for construction money by the Board of Public Works and the Legislature which, from the standpoint of the institution, too often had conditioned their allocations upon treasury surpluses.[3]

The arrangements for engineering and agriculture had come none too soon. On June 13, 1956, a $1.4 million fire gutted 54-year-old Mechanical Hall, home of the Departments of Civil, Aeronautical, Electrical, Mechanical and Industrial Engineering, as well as the Department of Buildings and Grounds. Representatives of the Fire Marshal's office termed the fire accidental and indicated that their probe revealed no negligence on the part of anyone. President Stewart endorsed their findings, noting: "Mechanical Hall itself was an old building, the fire hazard of which was recognized in repeated requests over more than a decade for funds to replace it."

On the day following the fire, Dean Chester A. Arents of the College of Engineering established offices in the Physics Building, and all students who took classes in Mechanical Hall were reassigned to other classroom buildings. By the end of July, the University had received bids for the construction of two prefabricated temporary buildings to be financed partly by the fire insurance on Mechanical Hall. Some equipment that had been salvaged from the ruins was to be placed in the new quarters. The College of Engineering announced plans to offer its complete engineering program in the fall semester, utilizing laboratory sharing with the School of Mines and the Departments of Chemical Engineering and Physics.

With financial backing assured for the construction of the professional schools upon campuses that then seemed to possess unlimited acreage, Stewart had achieved a special place in University history. Yet he would have been the last to suggest that he had fulfilled the many requirements of an exacting job to the satisfaction of all.

One of his failures, though not for the lack of trying, was convincing the Legislature of the importance of higher faculty salaries. The Strayer Report had indicated that the salary scale was far below that of comparable institutions. On October 25, 1946, Stewart said, "an institution which cannot attract and hold at least its fair share of able young men is definitely on the downgrade." On February 21, 1949, the Board of Governors reported to Governor Patteson that the University was "in the lowest 8 percent of comparable institutions in the North Central Association of Colleges and Secondary Schools in the average salaries of the instructional staff." Near the conclusion of Stewart's presidency, John E. Brewton reported in his 1956 survey of public higher education in West Virginia that the average salary of the instructional staff in all institutions of higher learning in the state was low. Fringe benefits from the State Teachers Retirement Program, in which University faculty were placed with public school teachers, were too low when compared with benefits available to college personnel in institutions elsewhere. Sabbatical leaves, authorized by the Legislature in 1953, never were granted because of lack of funding. Not until 1956 was the University staff covered by the federal Social Security System, and not until 1957 were payroll deductions for group insurance authorized. The situation for the clerical and maintenance staffs was worse.

Dr. Stewart addressed a memorandum to all deans and directors on July 29, 1948, which indicated his intent to put the money for faculty where it would do the most good:

It has come to my attention that some of you may be preparing your budget estimates for the biennium on the basis of a percentage increase in salary generally applicable to all members of the staff. If any dean or director is making his plans along this line, he should change his philosophy immediately. You gentlemen are expected to exercise discretion, to recognize exceptional merit and to reward it. In all probability, there are members of our staff who should receive no increase because the calibre of their work does not justify an increase in salary. In all such cases I shall expect you to have the courage to recommend that no increase be made. At the other extreme I expect you to recognize merit which should be rewarded. Placing all staff members on the same basis in the recommendations for promotions is a matter easy of mathematical application, but any person who submits his budget on that basis is falling down on his job. I shall expect from each dean and director a budget based on merit which he is prepared to defend.

In academic programming, Stewart practiced little innovation. The pattern of the schools and colleges changed but slightly with only the College of Commerce carved out of the Department of Economics and Business

Downtown Campus in 1955.

Administration in 1952, and the Potomac State School's name changed to Potomac State College of West Virginia University in 1953. As a result of medical pressure in the state, a School of Dentistry was established in 1953. Following the adoption of a resolution by the House of Delegates requesting such action, undergraduate training of teachers for elementary education was included in the program of the College of Education in 1951. With legislative approval in 1953, the University entered into contracts with Ohio State University and Oklahoma State University whereby WVU students were admitted for the study of veterinary medicine at those institutions.

Again in response to recommendations from professional groups in the state, the prerequisite for admission to the College of Law, to become effective in 1959, was changed from a requirement of three years of college work to the possession of a bachelor's degree from an approved college. The four-year program in pharmacy was advanced to five years, also effective in 1959. The Bureau of Business Research was established in 1949 and the Bureau for Government Research was reestablished that same year. An Institute of Industrial Relations was created in 1956. A Graduate Center of Science and Engineering in the Kanawha Valley was endorsed by the Board on May 31,

1958, while a proposal that a single board to govern all public institutions of higher learning to replace the existing separate WVU Board of Governors and the State Board of Education for all other state institutions of higher learning was rejected by the Board on August 29.

In combating the State Auditor, Edgar B. Sims, who wished to bring the University under strict state control, Stewart and the Board of Governors eventually won out in their twelve-year struggle, but not without confusion, delays, additional labor and expenses that interrupted the president's penchant for maintaining a smoothness of operations which he considered the mark of an efficient establishment. On April 10, 1950, Sims refused to pay the hospital and medical expenses for injured University athletes from an athletic fund derived not from state appropriations but from ticket sales and athletic fees. Although the State Auditor had been overruled by the Supreme Court in a similar case in June, 1939, he based his refusal in the Stewart years on his assumption that it was an unconstitutional act to use state funds to benefit individuals. The Supreme Court favored the University on May 23, 1950, upholding the contention that the action in assuming hospital and medical costs followed a practice of long standing and represented a part of the cost of maintaining the athletic department and the athletic program of the University.

When the University reemployed, on a part-time basis, persons who had been granted prior service allowance under the teachers retirement program, Sims withheld their pensions on October 5, 1949, contending that the state should be reimbursed the amounts paid in salaries for the half-time teachers before they could qualify for their retirement benefits. Again, the State Auditor was in conflict with rulings both by the State Teachers Retirement Board and the State Attorney General, and again the Supreme Court upheld the University's statutory authority to reemploy retired teachers for part-time work.[4]

In 1953, the State Auditor decided that the University need not belong to the North Central Association of Colleges and Secondary Schools and withheld its membership dues. Having joined the regional accrediting association in 1926 for purposes of establishing and protecting standards, West Virginia University again appealed to the Supreme Court for its right to continue as a member. On June 8, 1954, that Court unanimously ruled that the State Auditor had exceeded his authority in matters of University concern.

Like his predecessors and his successors, Stewart failed to solve the University's traffic and parking problems. On October 3, 1947, the *Athenaeum* called upon the city to assign patrolmen to Grumbein's Island to protect students from drivers "who delighted in charging down upon groups of students, forcing them to sprint for safety." About the only concrete attempt to alleviate the parking situation was the installation of a campus parking permit system in 1950. Permits, costing $10 a semester, were supposed to reduce the number of cars on campus.

Considering the era which preceded his own administration, President Stewart was understandably proud that in his own presidency there had never been a suggestion of political interference with the institution. He complimented the four governors whose regimes coincided with his own for completely respecting the position of the University.

Yet when the *Daily Athenaeum*, reacting to the 1956 West Virginia primary election campaign, suggested on April 17, 1956, that "there is every reason to believe that another administration run by the statehouse crew would do little to improve the state government" and alluded to reports of kickbacks to state officials for the rewarding of contracts, of Liquor Commission employees freeloading off the state, and the State Road Commission's hauling the "right" voters to the polls, the University administration and the West Virginia University Board of Governors overreacted.

Disclaiming any responsibility for or sympathy with recent *Athenaeum* editorials, the Board expressed regret at their publication and extended its apology to persons attacked. The Board of Governors emphasized that the University always had abstained from any action which might have been interpreted as involvement in political matters and added that "it is basic to sound operation of a state university that it refrain from participation in politics."[5]

The disclaimer amused the *Charleston Gazette*. Noting that the *Athenaeum* was paid for by deductions from student tuition and advertisements, it believed the paper was free from Board of Governors' jurisdiction. In truth, argued the *Gazette* on May 3, 1956, all that the members of the Board managed to convey, "correctly or incorrectly, to everyone in the state" was that "board members stood in trembling fear of reprisals" from the state administration. To the Charleston paper, the WVU Board was simply "childish in disclaiming its part in the student rap at the statehouse."

The Stewart administration proved scrupulous on other fronts as well: a restrictive attitude regarding faculty members' political allegiances and political activities; a harsh policy regarding students' religious scruples against compulsory military training; and a moderate position on students' desires to participate in the national phenomenon of panty raids. Without hesitation, the Stewart administration accepted in 1954 the U.S. Supreme Court ruling on integration of the races in the nation's schools.

With his term of office coinciding with the Cold War with the Soviet Union and the hot war in Korea, Stewart was forced to confront some West Virginians with high anxieties about subversion. This was an era that encompassed the political antics of Senator Joseph McCarthy of Wisconsin and the U.S. House of Representatives' Committee on Un-American Activities.

It was also a time tempting some politicians and organizations to suggest that Communists had infiltrated all levels of the schools and the government throughout the nation.

Stewart acknowledged this state of affairs in the early days of his presidency when he wrote the Board of Governors on November 3, 1947: "There is building up over the country an atmosphere conducive to witch hunting, and I assume that the University will be one of the places where some people will try to find witches." Always one to anticipate trouble before it struck the school, Stewart first established a faculty committee whose members "are above suspicion themselves and who have the confidence of their colleagues." To these peers, he proposed to refer all reports of communism on the part of members of the faculty. In indicating the nature of their duties, he told the committeemen as well as the Board of Governors that on his part, "I would recommend the dismissal of any member of the faculty who is a Communist, because I believe that Communism requires intellectual dishonesty incompatible with serving on the University faculty."

Assuming this stance, which also had the concurrence of the Board of Governors, Stewart indicated he was nonetheless expecting the University to resist unreasonable requests which might violate the principle of academic freedom in the classroom. In speeches across the state, he tempered his disapproval of communism with insistence that University students must be taught the facts of that political philosophy and the faculty must present the facts about, as well as encourage classroom discussion of, the principles of communism.[6]

His preparedness strategy against potential academic witch-hunting came none too soon. As if on schedule, the State Federation of Republican Women's Clubs and *The Jefferson Republican* of Ranson, West Virginia, requested on January 11, 1948, an investigation of alleged communistic activities at the University. Stewart's reply, to early and later demands of this nature, was that if claimants could produce solid information instead of rumor or innuendo, he would see that the proven facts would be considered by proper authorities. But solid information of this nature never was presented, as he undoubtedly expected would be the case. West Virginia legislator Rush Holt, who had achieved a certain national reputation in searching for possible subversives, learned that two University faculty members had been cited by the House Committee on Un-American Activities for having linked themselves to organizations which, in the Committee's definition, were highly suspect. The president responded to the finding by permitting the individuals concerned to answer the allegations; the Board was satisfied with the faculty responses; thus, the record remained intact in the Stewart years that no faculty member was discharged for alleged Communist sympathy.[7]

Yet the Stewart administration never lessened its defenses against charges of communism. In 1950, with McCarthyism at its peak, Stewart, in a memorandum to all budget officers on September 30, 1950, strongly reiterated his view that there was no place for Communists on the staff of West Virginia University. Noting that for some time it had been WVU policy to query prospective appointees to positions carrying tenure about their views on communism, the president indicated that it now seemed desirable to take further steps to minimize the likelihood of appointing a communist. By administrative fiat, he ordered that all future appointments be conditioned upon a prior signature by the prospective appointee to an oath that read:

I, _____, do hereby affirm that I do not advocate the overthrow of the Government of the United States by force or violence; that I am not a member of the communist party or any other political party or organization that advocates the overthrow of the Government of the United States by force or violence.

To Stewart this oath was similar in content to those required by the federal government for major positions. Thus, he seemed to be saying, WVU was resisting pressures in accordance with established procedures found effective by impeccable establishments outside the state.

This stance was reconfirmed when the House Committee on Un-American Activities requested on June 9, 1949, lists of textbooks used in the social sciences. Although Stewart honored the request, it was not until after the American Council on Education had advised compliance. In his informative note of June 20, 1949, to the Board of Governors on the matter, Stewart said:

Strictly speaking, I assume that the separation of powers between the state and the national government is such that the House Committee has no proper jurisdiction over the University. In spite of that fact, my inclination would normally be to supply the desired information to any committee of Congress. The House Committee on Un-American Activities falls in a class by itself by the way in which it has used its official position to smear private individuals without giving them an opportunity to appear before the Committee. It is quite possible, for instance, that the Committee may have some private list of volumes with some points of which the chairman of the Committee may disagree. It would be in keeping with past performances of the Committee to publish a list of institutions in which one or more of those volumes was used as text, with a thinly veiled inference that the institutions using the volumes were hotbeds of communism.

In a somewhat related manner, particularly at the time of state and national elections, Stewart also had to define the degree of political activity permissible to members of the University community. Drawing a distinction between a staff member's candidacy for office and his advocacy of the election of another, Stewart, in response to specific questioning by a faculty member, saw nothing wrong with a staff member seeking election to a national nominating convention of either party; seeking election to serve on a county or state party executive committee; writing or delivering speeches on behalf of announced candidates; or serving on election day as a party watcher at polling places or transporting voters to the polls either on a paid or unpaid basis.[8] As he wrote the Board on January 30, 1952, faculty members "have an obligation as citizens to participate in political campaigns in any manner which will not adversely affect the University . . . I do not believe that we can expect staff members to be political eunuchs."

On September 15, 1952, Stewart admitted to Governor Okey L. Patteson that the general proposition that University faculty and staff members possessed the same political rights and responsibilities as other citizens might mean that the exercise of such rights would embarrass the University as a result of poor judgment on the part of staff members. Stewart assured the Governor, however, that the right to engage in partisan political discussions did not apply in the classroom. In a memorandum to the faculty two days later, Stewart drew even tighter reins by stating that under no circumstances should any University obligation be neglected or University schedule altered to permit a faculty member to participate in such political discussions. In particular, he warned, no class meeting should be missed even though a colleague might be willing to act as a substitute, nor should the time of any class meeting be changed.

Stewart philosophically concluded in 1952 that decisions on such matters were such that "no matter what one does, it's wrong." Six years later, shortly before leaving the presidency, Stewart approved, with Board concurrence, part-time Law Professor Robert T. Donley's acceptance of an appointment to the State Supreme Court. Donley accepted the appointment only on condition that Board Resolution 702 denying reappointment to employees running for state or federal offices be held not applicable to a judicial position. The Board and Stewart waived the ruling, Donley accepted the appointment, ran for reelection and was defeated, and returned to his position with the College of Law. Yet during this same period the Board refused to reappoint a county extension agent who was an unsuccessful candidate for State Commissioner of Agriculture.[9]

While liberal with Donley who, as the first contributor to the WVU Foundation, Inc., had initiated in 1954 the Edward G. Donley lecture series in law, the Board struck an illiberal position with students who had chosen for themselves the roles of conscientious objectors. When two local preachers, the Reverend Normal L. Harsh and the Reverend Fred Bowman of the Church of the Brethren, appeared before the Board to seek support of their request that conscientious objectors be exempt from ROTC requirements, the Board, in refusing the request, strongly stated in its minutes of May 28, 1955, "that there be no waiver of the military and air science requirements for students objecting to military training on religious grounds, inasmuch as it is reasonable to require that able-bodied boys who desire to study at a land-grant institution learn how to defend their country by force of arms if the occasion should arise."

For good measure, the Board noted that the state of West Virginia had provided a number of colleges where there was no ROTC program and that students objecting to military training on any ground were free to attend those colleges.

With respect to students who participated in panty raids on the women's dormitories and sorority houses, however, the Stewart administration took the position that such episodes undoubtedly were only influenced by the wave of similar raids on other campuses. One such episode occurred on May 20, 1952, and was vividly described by Vice-President Neff who found himself as the sole administrative officer charged with campus law and order as Stewart was off campus making a commencement address at Marlinton; Joseph Gluck, director of student affairs, was making a commencement address at Buckhannon; and the dean of women was ill.

Neff rounded up forces from the Superintendent of Buildings and Grounds and solicited the aid of the city police as a further protective measure when he became aware of an assembly of students on North High Street. Following the explosions of firecrackers, a bugle call sounded and the formation advanced on Terrace Hall. In his personal account of May 22, 1952, to Stewart of an "arduous evening," he reported:

At the south end of Terrace Hall, girls were hanging out the windows, encouraging the raiding party. The place by then was teeming with raiders . . . I advanced through the crowd into Terrace Hall and drove out as many of the mobsters (stupid so-called students) as possible. However, they were swarming like bees at this time. It was suddenly realized that Terrace Hall was being vacated by the raiders, and I discovered that they were making a charge (if a charge includes stealing goods) on Woman's Hall.

Off campus, the position was that the raids were student pranks with nothing inherently vicious about them and were therefore not a matter of serious concern to parents. On campus, both the student government and the administration sought to forestall recurrences and to afford restitution to persons suffering financial loss from pilfered lingerie. To the public, Stewart offered the following press release on May 22, 1952, combining both stances: "From the facts presented to me it is clear that part of the blame rests with a few girls whose taunts encouraged the boys to enter the dormitories. The fact that the episode was conducted in a spirit of fun does not alter the fact that it was both unimaginative and incredibly stupid. The more mature and intelligent students share the administration's regret of this incident."

To the Board, both Vice-President Neff and President Stewart expressed gratification that the police who were present did not try to stop the raiders. "In my opinion," said Stewart, "this was good judgment, as it would have changed the character of the raid into a brawl by the students and the police."

When the long-established doctrine of separate but equal educational facilities was rejected by the U.S. Supreme Court on May 17, 1954, in the *Brown et al.* v. *Board of Education* case, Stewart wrote on May 21 to the office of the Attorney General pointing out that WVU before the recent ruling had admitted only West Virginia Negroes to the graduate and professional programs not offered at West Virginia State or Bluefield State Colleges. He asked the two pertinent questions: (1) Whether West Virginia University should now admit West Virginia Negroes to courses of study offered either at West Virginia State or at Bluefield? (2) Whether there was any obligation to admit out-of-state Negroes to any of the University programs? (At the time, WVU admitted out-of-state white students and foreign students to all its programs except those in the School of Medicine.)

In answer to Stewart's first question, the Attorney General on June 1, 1954, stated that WVU should admit any person who applied for admission, regardless of race, provided that such applicant fulfilled all of the requirements then prescribed for entry. He also was of the same opinion that no prospective out-of-state student could be refused entry because of his race so long as he met the requirements set forth for out-of-state students generally.

Stewart promptly informed the president of the Board of Governors that he was putting the ruling into immediate effect for the Summer Session. "It is probable," he said on June 2, "that we shall have one or more Negroes in our classes in the elementary school and in the University High School. If this is the case, these will probably be the first Negro children to attend public schools on a non-segregated basis in West Virginia." And without incident, West Virginia University, in contrast to its southern neighbors, was integrated as a result of Stewart's prompt, but unadvertised, action.

Although the integration of WVU caused no public furor, the awarding of unearned doctorates to non-students caused a certain stir. Toward the end of the Stewart presidency, West Virginia University saw fit to honor John L. Lewis, long-time president of the United Mine Workers of America Union, with an honorary degree. On that occasion, the *Huntington Advertiser* recalled the beatings, bombings, and bullyings that occurred in West Virginia coal fields as a result, it said, of Lewis's efforts to unionize miners. "In its relation with employers," the paper continued on May 3, 1956, "the miner's union has probably been more ruthless, more arbitrary and more grasping than any other labor organization in America. But it is ridiculous to say 'union' when what is meant is a one-man dictatorship. This is the man upon whom our state university chooses to bestow its highest honors."

The Charleston Gazette argued that Lewis's degree was long overdue; so did the *Huntington Herald Dispatch* in an open letter to Lewis. To Lewis, honor was meant more for the union than for himself; his interpretation of the award was "possibly because I was never incarcerated in West Virginia." For West Virginia University and for Irvin Stewart, it marked a new direction in the awarding of honorary degrees.

With studied precision, Irvin Stewart had for twelve years faced the dangers of a University presidency and merited a well-earned retirement from administration. On June 1, 1957, the University Board of Governors accepted "with regret and reluctance" Dr. Stewart's resignation as president, effective June 30, 1958. The Board had known for some time of Stewart's desire to return to teaching, and a resolution adopted on April 26, 1952, made it possible for one holding full-time administrative responsibilities to assume other duties such as teaching. Since 1952, Stewart had held the title of professor of political science. Only two other presidents in the University history (Trotter and Purinton) had remained at the institution following their tenure as its chief executive officer.

In no like period of University history, noted the *Morgantown Post* on June 3, 1957, was a physical plant doubled "with the end not yet in sight" and a comparable growth in the number of teachers and students sustained. But perhaps even more significant than building or population count, the *Post* believed, was that Stewart had wrought a change in the way of thinking about the University, and produced optimism for the future and a growing awareness of the support the institution must receive because it was West Virginia's university. For his part, Stewart graciously acknowledged the Board of Governors' leadership as "outstanding in its quality and unselfishness"; the faculty as able, enthusiastic, and unfailingly cooperative; the students as responding well to their opportunities; and the alumni as awakening to their interests in the institution. Stewart was pleased to acknowledge that "evidence is multiplying of a mounting public realization of the importance of the University and its program."

To Stewart, a certain period in University history had ended. With the timetable set for building the Medical Center and the agricultural and engineering facilities on the new campuses, he believed the next phase was about to start. He suggested that the president who was to have the major responsibility for enacting the new phase should be in on the planning. "It would not be in the best interests of the University for me to start in on the next steps in that program and then leave before it was completed," Stewart observed.

Chapter **10**

1946–1958

In Sickness and in Health, Till Death Do Us Part; The Inviolate University Campus

Governor
Okey Patteson

As of June 30, 1948, an unencumbered balance in the West Virginia treasury showed an excess of $28.5 million. This embarrassment of riches set the stage for innumerable requests throughout West Virginia, perhaps causing politicians of the highly sectionalized mountain state to wish for deficits rather than surpluses. Bracing themselves for their constituents' requests, the executive and legislative branches of the state government had not long to wait.

Fortified for battle with the ammunition of charts and tables showing major student enrollment increases from all counties of the state, the West Virginia University governing board had a ready answer. In behalf of all the state's inhabitants, it called for the immediate expenditure in the 1949-51 biennium of about $17 million to satisfy a much-needed University building program. About three-fourths of its request was earmarked for the undergraduate and graduate sciences: engineering, agriculture, physics, and medicine. The smaller proportion, about one-fourth, it designated for the Library, the School of Music, an arts and sciences classroom building, and dormitories. The budget request was

214

well-conceived. In a sense, it was returning the University to the original terms of the Morrill Act of 1862 by emphasizing for a Legislature largely concerned with furthering the extractive industries of the state the more practical, vocational, and therefore more highly visible aspects of higher education.

Dealing a body blow to the University building requests, the council of the State Medical Association simultaneously advanced on October 15, 1948, its long-time objective of providing state residents a complete, in-state medical education. It recommended that the University's two-year School of Medicine be expanded to four years, and, in addition, that a four-year dental school be created. It also suggested, without further delay, an appropriation of more than $6 million to finance the proposed schools, and, in defiance of a concept of one unified state university located on a single campus, that the two schools be located in Charleston.

Irvin Stewart, respecting the strength if not the wisdom of the West Virginia medical lobby, classified his remarks on the subject of its earlier subcommittee recommendations to the WVU Board of Governors as confidential. Noting that the demand for admission to medical schools normally outran available facilities anywhere in the nation, Stewart questioned the Association's proposition that young West Virginians "are entitled to receive a medical education in this state to the same extent as training is now given those seeking an education in other professions and businesses." He also doubted the Association's prediction that graduation from a medical school in West Virginia would induce a larger number of doctors to settle in the state. "It is my impression," Stewart confided, "that place of internship is a more important factor, but I recognize that as a layman I may be misinformed on the point. New Jersey has no medical school, yet has no reported shortage of general practitioners." For the moment, both the circumspect WVU president and the cautious governing board issued no public broadsides attacking the medical proposals.

With respect to maintaining the status quo of a two-year program for its medical students, West Virginia University had worked out a plan with the Medical College of Virginia at Richmond which both neighboring states had come to view as economically favorable to their interests. Under an agreement of January, 1944, West Virginia University annually sent to the Medical College twenty students who enrolled in its junior class. Their eligibility for admission, promotion, and graduation was in accordance with the regulations of the Medical College as the entry requirements of West Virginia students were identical to those for Virginia students.

For the privilege, the University agreed to pay the Medical College for each session at the time of registration $1,000 annually for every student enrolled. A minimum payment of $17,000 per session was exacted for instruction in each junior class and a like sum in each senior class, even should the enrollment in either class, or in both, drop below seventeen students. In addition, West Virginia students paid the Medical College the same tuition and fees charged to Virginia students. Diplomas awarded students under the coordinated plan bore the signatures of the officials of both WVU and the Medical College of Virginia. The agreement, running for five years from January, 1944, to January, 1949, was subject to automatic and continuous renewal at five-year intervals unless either party, two years before the end of a five-year period, gave notice to terminate the agreement.

This WVU medical plan often was referred to by states without university medical centers as the best way to resolve the high costs of medical education. WVU presidents seemed satisfied, and President W. T. Sanger of the Medical College of Virginia believed it very worthwhile. As he saw it, the arrangement increased the size and significance of the Medical College and enhanced Richmond's standing as a medical center in Virginia. The plan called for no capital outlays, and increased revenue permitted the strengthening of the teaching staffs. As both institutions were highly cooperative, he saw no problem in relation to curriculum organization. When consulted by the governor of West Virginia in the growing controversy over medical education about the effectiveness of WVU's two-year medical program, Dr. Sanger reported that students from West Virginia were exceptionally well-trained and always ranked high in their classes.

Finding such an agreement suddenly unacceptable to West Virginia physicians, Irvin Stewart rushed to address their professional society in July, 1948. Speaking before the assembled State Medical Association, Stewart asserted that the initial cost of a medical college would approximate at least $19 million, and that such an expenditure would necessarily endanger the currently proposed budget for the University building program. Available funds would be spread so thin, he asserted, that the small outlays would not be effective anywhere in the state. His trip was in vain. In the immediate post-World War II era, the idea of a state medical center proved popular throughout the state. At the right time, the doctors had made their request and the state seemed ready to listen and possibly comply. Nonetheless, the popular, budget-minded Stewart had single-handedly made the public assertion that unless a sound and continuing method of financing such a project could be found, which would not impose great hardships on an already inadequately financed institution, West Virginia University could not accept the new responsibility.

In a poll of Democratic and Republican candidates for the next Legislature in 1948, aspirants for public office overwhelmingly favored a four-year medical school. When both political parties endorsed a four-year medical college, and the American Legion went on record favoring the proposal,

Two-year School of Medicine was located in this building.

Stewart next carried his go-slow message to yet another professional group. Before the West Virginia Petroleum Council, he declared that the $17 million request by the University for its building program was based on "the belief that the people of West Virginia will be prepared to support the University adequately when they know what support is needed." Speaking before a group vitally interested in the state's mineral resources, he argued that areas of knowledge and expertise already established at the University, and of direct benefit to them, should be strengthened first. Then, with their support and the provision that the state could find additional revenue sources, he would agree to a four-year medical school.

Stewart next carried his campaign directly to the state's future chief executive. Writing identical letters on October 1, 1948, to both the Democratic and Republican candidates for governor, Okey Patteson and H. S. Boreman, Stewart reviewed the recent history of capital expenditures at West Virginia University. Noting that the Mineral Industries Building completed in 1942 had been the only classroom-laboratory building erected on campus since the Chemistry Building had been completed in 1925, he contrasted the needs of an enrollment of 2,143 students in 1925 with the needs of the 1948 enrollment of more than 6,700 students. Because he had no assurance that the acute requirements of the larger student body would be met, he informed the candidates that the Board of Governors was not now prepared to take a position with respect to the establishment of a four-year school of medicine since it had no information about the source of the large sums of money needed for such an endeavor. The candidates gave Stewart no assurances that they recognized the merit of his pleas.

Coming to Stewart's rescue, the Board of Governors issued an October 30, 1948, press release that said consideration of a medical center would be given "if and when it appears that funds for the required capital expenditures and operating costs therefor shall be available without prejudice to the needs of existing programs being carried on in the University's established academic and professional schools and colleges." On January 27, 1949, the Board noted that "all parts of the University should be located at the seat of the University in Morgantown."

Prompted by the Board's declaration for a unified academic campus, a *Morgantown Post* editor one week later prophetically wrote that the desire for a four-year medical center now sweeping the state would end as a conflict among ambitious communities that would like to capture the medical college. When his own publication led the pack of those criticizing the council of the State Medical Association for recommending that the medical school be relocated, he helped his own prediction come true. Documenting the fact that only rarely was a new medical school affiliated with a state university established in a city different from the one in which the parent school was located, the editor suggested that no city in West Virginia was large enough to furnish adequate clinical hospital facilities for a university medical school. He therefore questioned whether the argument in favor of Charleston, that only the capital city had the necessary hospitals for teaching purposes, was valid.

Other newspapers joined the issue. *The Raleigh Register*, although believing that the medical school should be located in Morgantown, played it safe. If for some reason the medical school went elsewhere, as had the state capitol itself on several occasions in West Virginia history, the paper suggested in mid-October, 1948, that Beckley, with two general hospitals, a veterans hospital, and a tuberculosis sanitarium, was an ideal choice. As predicted, Huntington and Wheeling newspapers approved the Medical Association's recommendation for a medical center, but argued that their cities should have been specified instead of Charleston. Charleston newspapers promoted the capital city, and found no reason to argue with the wisdom of the medical men who made up the council of the West Virginia Medical Association.

When Governor-elect Okey Patteson added his endorsement to that of the council for a four-year medical school, Morgantown spokesmen thought it advisable to call attention to the Monongalia General Hospital situated on a county-owned tract that would be made available to the University when and if the medical program at the University were expanded to four years. Because this hospital, with its nurses' training program, had been in successful operation for many years, it was argued that the state would be handed a long-established clinical program.

To the displeasure of the University, bills to divorce the School of Medicine from the University and move it to Charleston were introduced in January, 1949. Referring disdainfully to "a small group of doctors acting in the name of the State Medical Association," Morgantown advocates contended on January 28 that when legislators obtained the facts and "weighed the new financial burden versus existing University needs," they would have difficulty in supporting such legislation. If not for the temporary surplus in revenue, suggested a *Morgantown Post* editor who supported the current building program of the University, not even a Medical Association council would have dared urge this new venture on the state at this time.

Across the state, the issue of location had been joined and the political impasse made necessary a more formal interchange of views. At a joint public hearing on February 8, 1949, sponsored by both the House and Senate medical and health committees, the principal supporters of all cities, but particularly those of Morgantown, Charleston, and Huntington, were given opportunities to advance their positions. Dr. D. A. MacGregor, chairman of the West Virginia State Medical Association's fact-finding committee, advocated Charleston because of its larger population and its availability of clinical and hospital facilities. He believed that a first-rate medical school could function only in a center of population ranging from 200,000 to 250,000 people. Dr. W. T. Sanger, president of the Medical College of Virginia in Richmond, was one of the chief upholders of Huntington. Perhaps reflecting his own situation in the Old Dominion vis-a-vis the medical school in Charlottesville, he, too, favored a metropolitan area for the location of the school because it would furnish a greater number of specialists and medical patients. In contrast with the environmental situation at Charleston, he assessed that Huntington had a quiet atmosphere and was free of atmospheric pollution.

Editor Brooks Cottle of the *Morgantown Post* led the fight for the medical school's establishment at Morgantown by arguing that "if you start scattering the University around, you not only will endanger the medical school but the University as well." In contrast to Sanger, he drew in particular upon the University of Virginia's experience and other state institutions' histories, as proof that medical schools could operate successfully in smaller communities. Supporting Cottle, William Thompson, a leading member of the WVU Board of Governors, presented letters to the committee which indicated that best results could be expected by locating the medical school at Morgantown. Faithfully, he reiterated the original Stewart position that, unless the medical school could be uniquely financed, the University's overall effectiveness as an educational institution would suffer.

Sectional animosities within the state momentarily abated when the

Legislature passed a Senate-sponsored resolution calling for an interim joint committee of both houses to study the school proposal and report in 1951. It was understood by all that Governor Patteson wanted an appropriation for the four-year medical school made at the 1951 session. Granted this reprieve, Morgantown felt more relaxed because of recent news releases favorable to its cause. It was reported that current resolutions on a medical center by the American Medical Association's Council on Medical Education and Hospitals and the State Dental Association had specified no particular site, and that the council of the State Medical Association had withdrawn its active support of Charleston. The State Nurses Association also had gone on record as being opposed to any nursing school that would not be a part of the University. The State Chamber of Commerce publicly questioned the expenditures required for a four-year program and the Charleston Chamber of Commerce declared its belief that a medical school was not necessarily a substantial community asset and that its location should be determined solely by the consideration of the greatest good to the state.

The WVU Board of Governors then issued a definitive statement on its position. It recognized the need for a medical school; it favored the establishment of a medical school if necessary funds were supplied; it believed such a school should be on the University campus; and it reminded the Governor of the Board's own prior obligation to existing schools of the University, which should be met before assuming responsibility for a medical-dental program. To Morgantown, the Board on February 18, 1949, "had taken a position of the highest educational statesmanship."

Believing that able senators and delegates had been appointed to serve on the Legislature's interim committee, Morgantown spokesmen, strengthened by the Board's declaration, readied themselves on March 17 for the struggle ahead by making certain that the city's population figures for 1950 were not "misreported so as to give a misleading picture of the size of the community and its ability to furnish clinical material for medical education." Morgantown residents were further comforted to note on August 6, 1949, that President Stewart, as well as presidents of the medical, dental, and nurses associations, had been appointed to sit on the advisory committee to the legislative interim committee. It was believed that the committee showed good judgment in appointing out-of-state medical deans as its consultants.

WVU proponents, however, had too hastily assumed that out-of-state experts would flock to the banner of the University city. The findings of two experts in the field of medical education who made independent surveys for the committee did not favor Morgantown. Unfortunately for University interests, Dr. H. G. Weiskotten, dean of the Medical School at Syracuse University, and Dr. Wilburt C. Davison, dean of the Medical School at Duke University, preferred the larger population centers of West Virginia as sites for a new medical center, and Dr. Alan Gregg, director of medical sciences for the Rockefeller Foundation, believed to be friendly to the University at Morgantown, was unable to participate as consultant to the committee.

On the other hand, Dr. W. R. Berryhill, dean of the University of North Carolina School of Medicine, emphasized to the interim committee on February 6, 1950, that since progress in medicine was dependent upon close association with the basic sciences, a medical school could best forge ahead when it was in close proximity to an institution of higher learning. In addition, he felt that not only would administrative clearances and daily collaboration between the dean of the Medical School and the president of the University save hundreds of hours of time, but it would promote mutual understanding and confidence that often were lacking when two academic units were separated by a hundred or more miles. To Berryhill, the centralization of administration, which incorporated accounting, purchasing, maintenance, and servicing, lessened the duplication of departments and staff, lowered the cost of servicing, maintenance, and administrative supervision, and promoted economy of operation.

The legislative interim committee also gained information from Dr. Roy R. Kracke, dean of the Medical College of Alabama in Birmingham, who favored locating a medical school in a metropolitan area, and studied the North Carolina Survey Report, the Missouri Survey Report, and the Florida Survey Report, all recent instances of legislative action where new medical schools had been joined with state universities located in small towns.

Delegates from all twenty-nine county and regional societies were present at a specially called meeting of the House of Delegates of the West Virginia State Medical Association on November 19, 1950, at the Stonewall Jackson Hotel in Clarksburg. After a three-hour discussion and debate, the delegates unanimously voted not to make any recommendation about the site in the belief that the legislative interim committee would best decide the proper location for the institution where state funds could be spent most economically to secure the best possible facilities and greatest benefits for the largest number of citizens. Nevertheless, the Association's House of Delegates recommended on November 21 that the proposed medical and dental schools be created as part of West Virginia University.

Such action, however, did not deter two former presidents of the Association, Dr. Thomas G. Reed of Charleston and Dr. Thomas Bess of Keyser, from appearing before the legislative interim committee meeting in Charleston on December 5 to point out the disadvantages of establishing a four-year school of medicine in a small community on the periphery of the state as well as the advantages of selecting a centrally located site in an area where there was a large population. Nor did it prevent Dr. Frank J. Holroyd of Princeton, West Virginia, upon formally assuming the presidency of the

State Medical Association on January 1, 1951, from suggesting in his presidential message in the January issue of the *West Virginia Medical Journal* that the vast majority of physicians and dentists were in accord with the proposed relocation of the School of Medicine to Charleston.

On January 16, 1951, Governor Patteson called for the necessary legislation for medical education which he believed should be administered by the University. In deference to the uses being made of the treasury surplus, he suggested that a new tax of one cent a bottle on soft drinks be used as a means of financing the medical complex. The next day, the legislative committee responded favorably to the Governor's request.

The excise tax on bottled soft drinks and syrups, as recommended by the Governor and then later enacted by the Legislature, resolved the problem of providing revenue for the construction, maintenance, and operation of four-year schools of medicine, dentistry, and nursing at West Virginia University.[1] Originally supported by some bottlers and opposed by others, it had two immediate effects: it permitted the bottling industry to raise the currently established price of five cents for bottled drinks to ten cents, and it enabled the Legislature to collect $3 million annually for the medical center. In addition, retail vendors were allowed an average commission of 12.5 percent for collecting the tax, the largest commission on tax collection granted by West Virginia.

The solution to financing the medical school called for the University's position on the special taxing arrangement. This Stewart repeatedly stated over the years: the medical program required an assured income in a large amount specifically dedicated to the purpose and not competing with other University needs; the University did not ask for the soft drinks tax but admitted that, in operation, the tax produced satisfactory support for the medical education program; if the tax were ever to be repealed, the repeal should come after, and not before, a substitute producing at least the same amount dedicated to the same purpose appeared on the statute books.[2]

In his January 16 message, Governor Patteson had cited three major issues: there was to be a medical school administered by the University and there would be adequate funds for its establishment, the only remaining problem was location.

Faced with conflicting recommendations from medical educators and the survey reports of states that recently had established four-year medical centers, one view favoring without qualification the location of a medical school on a university campus and the other view insisting upon its location in a metropolitan center, the committee recommended on January 17 the establishment of four-year medical, dental, and nursing schools under the supervision and control of the Board of Governors of West Virginia University. Five members favored locating the school in Morgantown, and five members favored Charleston. Thus, the committee found it impossible to make a specific recommendation concerning the school's site. The division within the committee closely paralleled the split within the Legislature, where it was suspected that a majority of the members of the House of Delegates favored Charleston and a majority of the Senate wanted Morgantown.

The stalemate only whetted the appetite of the University now that it had won on the issues of control and of adequate financing. On January 29, 1951, Monongalia Senator Don J. Eddy presented for legislative consideration the opinion of Dr. Alan Gregg, director of the medical science division of the Rockefeller Foundation. A most influential and politically skilled medical administrator, Gregg was the expert witness who, because he had been out of the country, had not been able to present his recommendations before the legislative committee. As he had in the past, Gregg supported the concept of affiliating a medical school with the state university on a single campus. In a report made on the University of Missouri, Dr. Gregg had stated that "the growing fringe, the advancing frontier of medical science may safely be assumed to be dependent upon contact with the natural sciences — indeed contact is too weak a word — coalescence would better describe the relationship." Such coalescence, he wrote, may be anticipated only if the medical school were situated in close physical relationship to other university departments, such as physics, chemistry, biology, psychology, and anthropology. When states such as Missouri needed to train more doctors for practice in rural areas, Dr. Gregg suggested that it needed doctors accustomed to and contented with life in the smaller towns. Large cities, he suggested, set before medical students the attractions of city practice, of early specializing, of migration to the still larger cities, and of something nearer to commercialism than could survive the test of rural practice.

Dr. Gregg also opposed the location of a university medical school in a large city because he knew of none that had not experienced at least one serious quarrel between the university and the powerful professional leaders of the city. As he strongly put it, "unless your university medical leaders are resigned to offering teaching positions in return for support and collaboration of clinicians with few other claims to attention, they may well prepare themselves for a decade of pressures and political maneuvers. Usually if appointments are made *quid pro quo* and at a distance from the university, the character of the school depends on forces only slightly under the university control." With regard to West Virginia, Dr. Gregg took off the gloves when he analyzed the report made by Dr. Wilburt C. Davison, dean of the Duke School of Medicine. In rebutting Davison's claim that contacts between faculties of the academic basic sciences and the medical school were limited, and that friction and misunderstanding were the usual results, Dr. Gregg wrote: "I should think such difficulties, like those of having bad neighbors, come from the quality of the neighbors rather than their nearness. The institution of matrimony runs similar risks, yet with good management matrimony can produce results not to be obtained by monasticism."[3]

As the time for decision grew near, the *Morgantown Post,* in reviewing the state's attitude toward a medical school on March 8, 1951, found no papers, except *The Charleston Gazette* and the *Charleston Daily Mail,* supporting the removal of the medical school to Charleston. The Clarksburg papers and the *Fairmont Times* appeared to be largely quiet on the subject; the Huntington papers were only concerned with Charleston's efforts "to capture" the medical school as a community asset. On the other hand, the *Post* was pleased to discover that Beckley's two papers, the *Post-Herald* and *The Raleigh Register,* as well as the *Parkersburg News,* had been strong in defense of the unity and integrity of the University. General apathy about the underlying issue, which the *Post* defined as making the University first-rate, was widespread. The Huntington paper added a discouraging note by saying, "We think it a fair summary of daily press' attitude to say that at least one half of the papers haven't thought the question important enough to call for comment or take any firm editorial position."

On March 9, 1951, the Legislature decided that West Virginia should have a four-year program of medical, dental, and nursing education administered by the University Board of Governors at a site to be selected by Governor Patteson and financed by a special soft drinks tax. Requiring the Governor to determine the location by July 1 undoubtedly prevented a bitter deadlock between the two houses because the House of Delegates continued to lean toward Charleston and the Senate toward Morgantown. Yet the final and evasive action taken by the fiftieth Legislature was not without preliminary skirmishing. The House's original legislation had called for the Governor to determine the site with benefit of a seven-member advisory committee. The Senate modified the House's legislation by striking out the advisory committee. Senator Eddy of Morgantown next moved that the Governor appoint a twelve-member advisory committee which would include the nine members of the Board of Governors. As this was too obvious a ploy, the suggestion was rejected, and the Senate adopted the House bill, as amended, to let the Governor make a choice without special counsel.

Promising to make a careful study before reaching his decision, Governor Patteson asserted the day following the passage of the House bill, "I absolutely have not in any manner committed myself as to the location of the school, and I have not given any thought to a proper site." Indicating that he would consult with the Board of Governors, the State Medical Association, and other experts, he said that he had first opposed a bill granting location power to the chief executive but then felt it best "to sacrifice myself" rather than lose the school.

Once it had been decided that the Governor would make the decision, all newspapers were in a quandary. Said the *Morgantown Post*, "For the first time since the medical school became a subject of debate, we're at a loss to know what to say." It feared, however, that the Governor was predisposed toward Charleston. *The Charleston Gazette* claimed that the only motive of the group favoring Charleston was to increase the number of the state's doctors; *The Raleigh Register* knew that "Morgantown IS THE SITE"; the *Parkersburg News* suggested to the Governor that he choose Morgantown as the site to "go down in history as the 'Father' of the Medical College at West Virginia University on the historic campus at Morgantown."

After Cottle and other members of the Morgantown delegation met with the Governor on May 7, it appeared to them that "politics would not play a role in his decision." To them, Patteson would not hesitate to put the medical school at Morgantown if he could be certain that adequate "clinical material" was available for teaching purposes. Never surrendering the fight, Cottle next called attention on May 24 to the 18,000 catalogued volumes which constituted the medical collection and again raised the question of the cost of duplicated services if the medical college went elsewhere.

The Charleston Chamber of Commerce, saying on May 31 the location of the University medical school in its city would not "in any manner constitute dismemberment of the institution," believed that such a location "would be of great value in intensifying and developing interest in the southern part of the state." The Morgantown editor scoffed at such reasoning. Carried to its logical extremes, this idea that the physical parts of the University ought to go to the people meant giving the College of Agriculture to Lewisburg, the College of Engineering to Wheeling, the College of Law to Clarksburg, Cottle argued.

Before his announcement on June 30, 1951, Governor Patteson spent a final week in conferences with chambers of commerce and other organizations interested in presenting their arguments in behalf of the school's location. He also consulted with out-of-state experts and read many letters from interested citizens throughout the state, which he assessed in conjunction with all the reports, data, and briefs that had been submitted formally. Acknowledging that in accepting the task, he would be "the goat," a position he clearly disliked, Patteson reported that he nevertheless "burned the midnight oil" and reached the definite conclusion that the logical and best place for the location of the medical school was Morgantown.

Governor Patteson noted that the most recent trend across the United States was to erect medical schools and associated university hospitals on the campuses of state universities. Particularly was he impressed by the comparative cost studies of state-supported schools, which showed that more expensive schools were found in large cities than in small cities, that the cost of operating a medical school separate from the principal campus was substantially greater than the operation of a medical school attached to the principal campus of the university, and that medical schools in small towns had achieved distinction with relatively low unit cost and with great efficiency. He particularly noted data which rebutted the contention of those who maintained that a medical school must be located in a metropolitan area to obtain sufficient clinical patients because he understood that no matter where a medical school was located, the evidence was overwhelming that a medical school must build its own teaching hospital to supplement existing facilities.

To Patteson, dismemberment of West Virginia University would be a violation of a century-old policy, one that earlier had prevented relocation from Morgantown of the College of Law and the School of Music. If the Medical School were located elsewhere, suggested the Governor, then it would be natural for the Pharmaceutical Association to recommend that the School of Pharmacy be moved to the location of the Medical School. Following such logic, it might seem feasible, added Patteson, that people in the Eastern Panhandle might ask for the College of Agriculture because that area contains some of West Virginia's best orchards and farms.

Because operating a medical school is big business, the Governor felt that it was essential for the state to practice all possible economy when undertaking its establishment. To move the medical education program from the University would require the state to make provisions for a certain number of non-medical courses at the new location. In Morgantown, the Governor was assured that the University could meet the needs of the medical students in chemistry, physics, biology, bacteriology, physiology, and anatomy. He also believed that in behalf of new developments in industrial medicine, psychiatry, and general mental hygiene, the University could provide medical students with access to strong departments of sociology, economics, psychology, and philosophy.

Since by-products of atomic energy were expected to play an important part in medical therapy, Patteson assessed the resources of the University as best able to bring to students the latest in atomic progress. The West Virginia University Library, with its many expensive reference works and files of periodicals, would be used by both medical and other students, thus preventing the duplication of library facilities.

Noting that the faculty of the two-year School of Medicine was directing advanced work for a number of students in non-medical fields, Patteson documented the fact that the University would be required to surrender that part of its graduate program, or supply additional faculty at great cost, if the School of Medicine faculty were located elsewhere. Furthermore, he added, it generally was conceded that living costs were much less in a university town, with its dormitories and other provisions for helping student life, than were the costs in a more metropolitan area. The Governor suggested that the life of the University campus, consisting of a good recreational program as well as cultural and educational facilities, would benefit the Medical School, and the Medical School and the University would both benefit from an interchange of students, faculty members, physical facilities, and ideas.

As to the uniqueness of the Morgantown location, Governor Patteson was able to discover advantages for a medical center that its own inhabitants had overlooked. The Governor noted that the Hopemont Sanitarium for tubercular patients was only 34 miles from Morgantown; a veterans hospital at Clarksburg, 44 miles; the Weston State Hospital for all types of mental cases, 68 miles. The mineral baths at Berkeley Springs, the emergency hospital at Fairmont, and the chronic disease hospital at Wheeling were the only medical facilities of their type in the state and all were closer to Morgantown than to either Huntington or Charleston.

Actual experience, Patteson argued, proved that when medical schools were divorced from university campuses, rivalry developed and often politics entered the medical school. Most certainly, he said, politics never should be allowed to affect such a vital institution as a school of medicine. But perhaps most important to the Governor was the fact that the taxpayers would be saved large sums of money by utilizing already existing facilities at Morgantown. To duplicate these on a new campus was an unjustifiable waste of money.

Knowing that Charleston, Huntington, and other cities making bids for the medical center would be disappointed, the Governor reported that he was assured of their full cooperation and help in connection with the medical school, regardless of location. Typical of those who accepted in good faith the Governor's decision was the State Medical Association. The editor of its journal stated in the August, 1951, issue, "Now that Governor Patteson has decided upon a location for the Medical School, let's all get behind it and work to make it a success."

Within the first week of July, 1951, major newspapers across the state fell in line with the decision. *The Charleston Gazette*, admitting it was naturally disappointed, stated in a front-page editorial "we are inclined to agree with most of the reasons he [Patteson] has given for the selection of Morgantown." The *Parkersburg News* referred to the "wise, prudent, and popular decision by the Governor," and it was certain that the Governor and the people of West Virginia never would regret the judgment he made. The *Fairmont Times* said that establishment of a medical center was far more important than its location and believed that the Governor's reasoning on the latter was hard to refute. "The Governor's statement, without the slightest taint of ghost writing," said the *Morgantown Post*, "will take its place as one of the great papers in the archives of West Virginia, a truly historic document."

The *Huntington Herald-Dispatch*, still believing that its city's claims were in some ways the strongest, stated that "one would have to be narrowly partisan and proudly chauvinistic to fail to recognize the compelling persuasion of the overall case in support of the selection of the University campus." The *Charleston Daily Mail* felt that to challenge the Governor's choice "would be ungrateful and only revive sectional rivalry." *The Wheeling Intelligencer* believed the Governor's decision "probably meets with the approval of most people."

In a radio address to the people of West Virginia on July 2, 1951, Patteson confessed that when the fight over the site had first developed in the 1949 Legislature, he had not believed that Morgantown could support a medical school. But during the 1951 legislative dispute, he realized that he knew very little about requirements for establishing medical schools. Undertaking to study the problem and approaching the issue "with an open mind," he had concluded that "the logical and best place for the location of the medical school is Morgantown."

Once the good news was in, the University moved quickly to realize on its campus a medical center that would serve the entire state. The Monongalia County Court transferred to the state 85 acres, which was added to an adjoining 55 acres owned by the University to form a 140-acre site for the complex. The administration selected a building committee composed of faculty of the two-year medical school, employed consultants for dentistry and nursing, initiated discussions with health professions educators, and retained the architectural firm of Schmidt, Garden, and Erikson of Chicago to prepare an overall plot plan for the site and preliminary plans for the building. In addition, members of the faculty building committee and members of the University Board of Governors visited other institutions "to broaden their scope of sophistication and observe new practices."[4] James A. Hamilton Associates, hospital consultants, of Minneapolis, Minnesota, were retained to make a survey of the state's needs in health services. The firm concluded that the area of the new center, which contained 385,000 persons located within a 30-mile radius of Morgantown, could well support a hospital of sufficient size to satisfy teaching needs.

From these deliberations emerged the concept of a basic sciences facility and an associated teaching hospital. Architects for the buildings were C. E. Silling and Associates of Charleston, West Virginia, with Schmidt, Garden, and Erickson of Chicago as associate architects. James A. Hamilton Associates again served as hospital consultants. Within the Basic Sciences Building were to be housed the first two years of the medical education program, the complete dental education program, the School of Nursing, a library, an auditorium, and the College of Pharmacy.

In the fall of 1952, the WVU Board of Governors decided that construction must allow space and facilities for entering classes which would contain 60 medical students, 50 dental students, 50 nursing students, 40 pharmacy students, 25 medical technology students, 12 occupational therapy students, 12 physical therapy students, 12 X-ray technology students, and six dietetics students — a total enrollment of 1,200.

The Board determined that the teaching hospital would provide 520 beds, of which 330 would be general acute, 140 chronic, and 50 rehabilitation; that outpatient clinics should be capable of handling 45,000 visits per year; and that the overall structure should be integrated under one roof to provide for exchange between clinical and pre-clinical staffs, laboratory workers and clinicians, and the staff and students of the various schools. In arriving at these findings, the Board of Governors declined on October 24, 1953, the offer of the Monongalia County Court of Monongalia General Hospital for use as part of the WVU Medical Center.

The Board of Governors also decided to construct the heating plant first, followed by the basic sciences facilities, and the teaching hospital. Ground was broken for the heating plant on December 9, 1952. The initial cost was $1,092,680, but a subsequent expenditure of $331,858 was needed to complete the project. Bids for construction of the Basic Sciences Building were opened August 31, 1954; the construction price was $10,889,035, with an additional allowance of $1,388,071 for built-in laboratory equipment. Construction began in the summer of 1954. The teaching hospital contract was signed July 3, 1957, in time for more than $2 million in federal funds under the Hill-Burton Act to be allocated to the project. Hospital construction began in the summer of 1957. In 1958, the Legislature appropriated additional revenues to make the grand total for the hospital $15,897,777, including the fixed equipment. Of the total project cost of $31 million, all but $5.6 million came from the soft drinks tax. Additional legislative appropriations from the state's general funds totaled $2,800,000; federal contributions from Hill-Burton funds and a Health Facilities Grant amounted to $2,800,000.

The Basic Sciences Building was completed in the summer of 1957, and in September the two-year medical program moved in as well as the first class of dental students in the history of West Virginia. The first class of nursing students entered upon completion of hospital construction in January, 1960.

The total net income from the soft drinks tax amounted to $28,755,321 in the nine-year period of construction. Therefore, on only two occasions did the construction costs outstrip the income, necessitating additional legislative appropriations. President Stewart's advice thus had been accepted by the state. West Virginia University not only was to administer the Medical School on its own campus, but also the Medical Center's budget was not to impinge upon other programs of the state's only university.

Victory in obtaining the Medical Center doubtless had its satisfactions. But keeping it in operation became as arduous as achieving its creation. For the Stewart administration and all successors discovered they were cast in an annual battle to ward off the repeal of the special pop tax. Having achieved their increase in price and gained their concession of a large commission to collect such a tax, bottlers suggested over the years that deficits, not profits, had resulted for the soft drink industry in West Virginia, and that the burden of supporting the Medical Center should no longer be their special province.

By September 17, 1954, the *Charleston Daily Mail*, believing that enough time had passed to measure the effect of the special tax, "which has been anything but beneficial to the soft drink industry," questioned West Virginia's "Eenie, Meenie, Minie, Moe" theory of taxation — "Moe" being "the industry that just happens to be available for some new form of tax discrimination." In 1956, the West Virginia Bottlers Association opened an all-out campaign for the repeal of the penny pop tax. Where heretofore the bottlers had centered their attack strictly on repeal of the pop tax as discriminatory and harmful to their business, their campaign now was enlarged to bring about a modernized tax system, built upon a fair and equitable tax basis.

West Virginia University, in responding to the possible plight of a particular industry and the need for additional monies for the Medical Center, repeated and refined over the years the following positions: that a campaign to repeal the pop tax without an adequate substitute was a campaign to kill the medical education program and with it the chances for adequate medical, dental, and nursing services for West Virginia; that the University held no brief for any particular tax and would recommend to the Bottlers Association or any other business organization that they might propose a substitute tax for legislative consideration; that the tax originally was proposed by bottlers to help them break the nickel price line; that the revenues collected to support the Medical Center were from consumers and were not taken from the bottling industry because it never had possessed them; that there had not been a stated intention, if the soft drinks tax were to be repealed, that the price of soft drinks would be reduced to the consumer by that amount; that, if the soft drinks tax were to be repealed, there would be a loss of $4 million in the state's revenues and a corresponding increase of that amount to the industry beyond its original gains.

With the Legislature upholding the special pop tax as the only likely source of revenue to promote the health and well-being of West Virginia, President Stewart could only remark to J. E. Decker on April 18, 1952, that "the soft drinks tax clearly places the burden of the support of the expanded program upon the consumers of soft drinks, just as a large part of the support of the public schools comes from cigarette smokers."

Medical Center

From the Banks of the Monongahela to the Banks of the Potomac, Part I

Elvis Jacob Stahr
February 1, 1959–January 25, 1961

FROM THE LATE FIFTIES to the late sixties, West Virginia University was affected more deeply than usual by developments emanating from both the national and state scene. As had been the case a hundred years earlier when the thirty-fifth state was created, the Morrill Act passed, and the University first opened, decisions of the federal government seemed to offer the best possible approaches to relieve the economic distress of West Virginia, and, in turn, to provide for the well-being of its comprehensive, land-grant state university. If a century earlier it had seemed expedient to be for Lincoln and the Republican Party, it now seemed pragmatic to join forces with the new Democratic leadership taking over from Dwight Eisenhower.

On January 2, 1960, John F. Kennedy, the first Roman Catholic to be seriously considered for the Presidency since Alfred E. Smith, announced his presidential candidacy. West Virginia soon discovered it was destined to figure in making the Kennedy bid a successful one. In the important May 10, 1960, West Virginia primary, the Massachusetts politician garnered 60.8 percent of the presidential preference vote, and, in securing

232

236,510 votes to Hubert Humphrey's 152,187, knocked his most serious contender in the primaries out of the race. The press stressed the significance of the urban, Catholic candidate's decisive triumph in a rural, Protestant state, and concluded that his nomination and election were imminent. On July 15, 1960, John F. Kennedy and Lyndon B. Johnson became the Democratic Party's presidential and vice-presidential candidates, and on November 8, 1960, they won the national election. At the same time, W. W. Barron, a Democrat, captured the state prize in the West Virginia gubernatorial contest, replacing Cecil Underwood, a Republican, as the chief executive.

Indebted to West Virginia for endorsing his candidacy and appalled by the poverty he encountered in the state, President-elect Kennedy appointed on December 5, 1960, a special 23-member task force to consider federal programs for economically depressed areas of the country. The task force report, submitted on January 1, 1961, recommended an area redevelopment program and urged that Appalachia receive special priority. In 1961, Congress responded with passage of the Area Redevelopment Act, authorizing $394 million over a four-year period, 1962-1965, for loans and grants to depressed areas, an act not without interest to educational institutions. On April 9, 1963, President Kennedy established a Presidential Appalachian Region Commission which described Appalachia as "a region apart — geographically and statistically," noting that its most serious problems were low income, high unemployment, lack of urbanization, low educational achievement, and a comparatively low standard of living. West Virginia had long urged that such action be taken; the state, its people, and its university expectantly awaited results.

Thus on November 22, 1963, the thirty-fifth state felt special grief about the death of Kennedy, the thirty-fifth President of the United States. But the Mountain State fortunately was not forgotten by his successor. On January 8, 1964, President Lyndon B. Johnson in his State of the Union message called for an "unconditional" declaration of "war on poverty in America." By August, 1964, Congress had appropriated almost a billion dollars to alleviate poverty and had authorized ten separate programs under the supervision of the Office of Economic Opportunity. A separate proposal was submitted to Congress on April 28, 1964, calling for a comprehensive program to relieve poverty and to develop economic resources in the depressed ten-state Appalachian Mountain region. Although failing passage when first introduced, the bill became law on March 9, 1965.

These actions by Presidents Kennedy and Johnson, and the Congress came none too soon for West Virginia, the only state that lay entirely within the Appalachian region. As a result of the census report of 1960, West Virginia awoke to the fact that it had suffered a population loss, caused not by a declining birthrate but from out-of-state migration by its own people trying to escape the state's severe economic depression. In 1950, West Virginia had a population of 2,006,000; in 1960, only 1,860,000. By 1964 it was estimated that West Virginia's population would drop to 1,797,000. Consequently, the state's strength in the electoral college diminished from eight to seven votes and it lost a seat in the House of Representatives.

The portrayal of West Virginia as having never recovered from the Great Depression was enhanced in the public mind with the publication in *The Saturday Evening Post,* on February 6, 1960, of an article by Roul Tunley entitled "The Strange Case of West Virginia." Quoting migrants who had fled the state since World War II in search of work, the author concentrated not only upon the factor of unemployment, "consistently the highest in the nation," but also upon "its second-rate roads, its ugly auto dumps, its polluted streams, and its dearth of good restaurants and hotels," which created the spectre of the state as "remote, backward and dangerously provincial." Implying that West Virginia was less like Switzerland and more like Afghanistan, one critic was quoted as saying "West Virginia rocks on a sagging front porch while her neighbors drive by in shiny new cars," and another referred to the West Virginia migrants as "shoeless, shiftless, beer-swilling clods who wouldn't go to a church that didn't use rattlesnakes in the service."

At this moment of adverse national publicity and faced with extraordinary faculty mobility and a more than doubling of its student population, West Virginia University hesitantly entered the age of the multiversity, when it seemed that money needed for teaching, research, and service was far more likely to come from Washington, D.C., or from foundations located on the Atlantic or Pacific seaboards, than from the state capitol in Charleston. Given the economic signals from the Kennedy and Johnson economic-social programs, WVU began to refashion itself accordingly.

In that crucial time period, the University acquired administrative leadership, faculties, and even students who fancied themselves keen interpreters of the federal scene. That high-ranking University personnel were astute cannot be doubted because two presidents (bracketed by three acting presidents) within less than a decade joined the national administrations of Kennedy and Johnson on the banks of the Potomac rather than continuing to administer higher education on the banks of the Monongahela. Even Irvin Stewart, residing on campus as professor of political science after his twelve-year presidency, caught Potomac fever before his retirement in 1967. In 1962-63 on a three-semester leave, he served as the first director of telecommunications management in the executive office of the President.

Although Stewart's intention had been to resign the WVU presidency effective June 30, 1958, the Board of Governors, unable to decide on his successor, had persuaded him to remain in office for an extra two months. Granted leave to conduct a one-year's study of developments in political science under the auspices of a Ford Foundation grant, the thirteenth president could be held no longer. By August 3, 1958, the Board was able to announce that Elvis Jacob Stahr, Jr., vice-chancellor of the University of Pittsburgh, would become the University's fourteenth president on February 1, 1959, and that Clyde L. Colson, dean of the College of Law, would serve as interim president from August 26, 1958, to January 31, 1959.

Stahr's credentials were impressive. A native of Kentucky and a 1936 graduate of the University of Kentucky where he majored in history, Stahr had achieved the highest grades in that institution's history. As a Rhodes Scholar, he spent three years at Oxford University winning three additional degrees, and acquired upon his return to the United States a diploma in Chinese language from Yale University. In World War II, he served overseas for more than two years, rising in rank from second lieutenant to lieutenant colonel in the infantry. At the end of his military service, he practiced law in New York City, but forsaking Wall Street in behalf of his native state, he accepted appointment as dean of the College of Law and later became provost at the University of Kentucky. Concluding this period of initial educational administration, he was named one of the "Ten Outstanding Young Men in America" by the U.S. Junior Chamber of Commerce. During the Korean conflict, Stahr was a special assistant to the Secretary of the Army, and in 1956 executive director of the President's Committee on Education Beyond the High School. At the University of Pittsburgh he was vice-chancellor for the professional schools when West Virginia University beckoned. Although his services were needed at Pitt through the 1958-59 fall semester, the University of Pittsburgh chancellor allowed his vice-chancellor one day each week at WVU to acquaint himself with the school and the state before Stahr assumed presidential office at the beginning of the spring semester.

The aspect of Stahr's appointment that caused the greatest press attention was not the man himself but his salary of $30,000 a year, which made him not only the highest salaried chief executive in University history but also the highest paid public employee in the state. The *Morgantown Post* worried that the stipend might be used against him, as well as the institution itself. In a state whose per capita income was far below the national average, the *Post* sought to undercut criticism by declaring on August 16, 1958, that "the University can't have much of a future if its value to the State is placed so low as to put a bargain tag on the presidency." On August 5, *The Charleston Gazette* had thought otherwise and charged the Board of Governors, in ignoring the advice of the Board of Public Works, with having committed the Legislature "to an expenditure for which there's no precedent in state history." Claiming that the Board "has put itself above other branches of the government in the way it conducts its affairs," *The Gazette* compared what it considered a salary indiscretion with the board's "extravagant" transformation of a $15 million medical school into a $30 million project. When Governor Cecil Underwood also indicated that he believed that an increase in WVU presidential salary was "inadvisable," the issue became sufficiently news-worthy to haunt both Stahr and the University throughout his presidential tenure.

Stahr, as had been promised, promptly began his visitations to the cam-pus and to the state to prove he was worth the price the Board of Governors had placed upon his head. In his first visit with West Virginia newsmen on August 7, he charmed if not surprised the Morgantown contingent by declar-ing that the University had "a beautiful campus" and that he expected to speak soon in all parts of the state in order to make friends for the University. On September 8, in the capacity of a "freshman" who had much to learn about the University, he humbly joined with Colson in greeting the University's entering class. On October 3 in Parkersburg, he asserted before the West Virginia Press Association that the state must provide conditions in which a "university in fact" can exist. In the 1958 fall issue of the *WVU Alumni Magazine,* Stahr declared that unless the people of the entire state wanted a university of which they could be increasingly proud, "they do not want me, because I shall devote all of my energies to continuing the upward momentum begun under Dr. Irvin Stewart's great leadership." Before Fair-mont civic groups on November 14, the president-elect maintained that "the future of West Virginia will depend very greatly upon the future of West Virginia University," because the state's ranking institution heavily influenced, for better or worse, the quality of all education throughout West Virginia. On several of his visits throughout the state, Stahr took the occasion to repri-mand the author of the *Saturday Evening Post* article for implanting false ideas about the great state of West Virginia. On this, if not on all positions taken, he received tremendous applause.

Once having completed his obligatory swing around the state, Stahr for-mally began his presidency on February 2, 1959. He seized the occasion to highlight the University's most recent achievement, the Medical Center, by announcing a major breakthrough in his first staff appointment: Kenneth E. Penrod, assistant dean of the School of Medicine at Duke University, who would serve as coordinator of Medical Center affairs, effective July 1.

As it had done in the past on such occasions, the *Morgantown Post* pondered the new chief executive's problems if for no other reason than "a change in University presidency doesn't always mean a new chapter in Univer-sity history." Since Stahr had arrived in West Virginia at a time of deep reces-sion, the paper figured that obtaining adequate appropriations, especially for faculty salaries, would be his most difficult assignment. Stahr indicated as much himself. The building program, the *Post* believed, would continue its present momentum, and because of new funding principles was not as great a problem as finding money for salaries.

No one seemed interested in suggesting that if a portion of student fees could be directed into buildings, they might just as easily be channeled into instructional salaries. However, the paper was encouraged at a later date, on March 9, 1959, to note that Governor Underwood was expected to sign into law a bill to raise an additional $3,300,000 for state colleges and the University by imposing a new $50 per semester entrance fee for students in addition to their regular tuition. Two-thirds of the bill's revenue would be directed for construction of new buildings and the remainder for faculty salaries. Yet when the final appropriation was passed, the Legislature provided only a 5 percent salary increase across the board for all institutions of higher learning. President Stahr reported himself to the student newspaper on March 17 as somewhat dumbfounded that WVU salary increases had been equated with salaries at the state colleges.

In truth, Stahr had been very concerned about the effect of the substantial boost in student fees imposed by the Legislature. "We'll just have to hope for the best as far as enrollment is concerned," he wrote to one member of the Board on March 1, "but I see no way in which the Board might do anything now to reduce the total impact for next fall." Stahr's solution was to make strenuous efforts to build up both scholarship funds and student loan funds, and to try to interest the Benedum Foundation in doubling their scholarship grant "in the light of the doubling of fees."

Just as Irvin Stewart had surrounded himself at his own presidential installation with colleagues from the Office of Scientific Research and Development, Elvis Stahr provided five men representing significant phases of his own professional life to be present at his inaugural ceremonies. The honor guard was composed of Edward H. Litchfield of the University of Pittsburgh, whom he had served as vice-chancellor; Frank Pace, Jr., chairman of the board of the General Dynamics Corporation and former Secretary of the Army, with whom he had served during the Korean War; Robert T. Rinear, executive vice-president of the General Precision Equipment Corporation, with whom he had practiced law in New York; Herman Lee Donovan, president emeritus of the University of Kentucky, under whom he had served as law dean; and Courtney C. Smith, president of Swarthmore College, a fellow Rhodes Scholar at Oxford University from 1936 to 1939. A festive inaugural dinner on the evening of October 2, at which each of these men spoke, was carried by closed-circuit television through four different dining rooms on three floors of the Hotel Morgan to 880 guests. Adding to the occasion was the presence of Governor Cecil Underwood and Judge Elvis Stahr, Sr., of Hickman, Kentucky, and joining in the tribute at the largest dinner gathering in Morgantown history was President Dwight Eisenhower who dispatched a telegram from his Oval Office praising Stahr's service to the nation and to the educational world.

Stahr's banner year was 1960. As he explained the background of the success to the Board of Governors on February 10, 1960:

I feel that our efforts in making personal contacts with the legislative leadership of both parties just prior to the opening of the Legislature have paid off. They all stuck by us when the going got tough. I should also add that many and probably all of the members of the Committee of 55 really went to bat, and this, too, helped greatly. In addition, the two finance committees were extremely generous in the time they accorded me for hearings, and I was able to get across with facts and figures, and not just an emotional plea, a pretty full picture of the University's needs.

The administration announced that a $5 million building program would be launched in the spring to provide additional housing for women students and for faculty at the Medical Center. On January 18, the *Morgantown Post* could not resist further suggestions by opting for dormitories for medical students and dormitories for agriculture and engineering students who took classes on the Evansdale Campus. On February 5, Stahr upstaged the *Post* by suggesting a bigger library. As his first year in office closed, Stahr listed the administration's past accomplishments as the initial construction of the Engineering and Agricultural Sciences Buildings, completion of University Hospital, opening of the dental clinics, and installation of a new nuclear reactor.

In contrast with the 1959-60 budget for which he was only partially responsible, President Stahr on May 28, 1960, pronounced his budget of 1960-61 a forward-looking one, enabling the University "to make progress in some fields and prevent its losing ground in most others." It was a pleasure for Stahr to report that the budget permitted increases averaging 10 percent for faculty and professional staff, 8 percent for clerical and maintenance staffs, and establishment of a student counseling service, a personnel office, and an accelerated program in coal research. The budget also promised new staffing for the College of Commerce which would lead to a graduate program and a department in business administration, the hiring of a horticulture professor who would serve as University landscape architect, additional staffing of the medical school and hospital, and establishment of a School of Nursing.

Flushed with victory over the 1960-61 budget, Stahr came forward on October 13, 1960, with ideas for the 1961-62 budget request: an $18 million building program that would provide a forestry center; a complex structure that would incorporate a student union, adult education center, field house, and auditorium; a communications-arts center; a College of Commerce building; an elementary laboratory school; and a home economics building. Also on the fiscal ledger, he positioned several million more dollars for cam-

Engineering Sciences Building, completed in 1961.

pus housing, the library, and a 10 percent increase in personal services for academic and administrative salaries.

Stahr moved quickly to announce major administrative and faculty appointments and, in so doing, indicated the nature of pressures upon WVU in the decade ahead: staffing of the Medical Center, appointment of major administrative officials, and a restructuring of the President's Office. He had begun in early 1959 by naming Penrod coordinator of the Medical Center; before the end of the year, he selected Donovan H. Bond, associate professor of journalism at WVU, first director of University development. In 1960, he appointed Ernest J. Nesius, associate director of the University of Kentucky Agricultural Extension Service, dean of Agriculture, Forestry, and Home Economics; Harold J. Shamberger, former member of the WVU Bureau for Government Research, assistant to the president; Dorothy M. Major, Indiana University, dean of the School of Nursing; Dr. Clark Sleeth, assistant to the retiring Edward J. Van Liere, dean of the School of Medicine.

With considerable skill, Stahr raided the University of Minnesota for additional major medical faculty by selecting men in number two positions in their respective specialty areas at that institution: Dr. Bernard Zimmermann, outstanding visceral surgeon and leader in the field of cancer surgery, became chairman of the Department of Surgery; Dr. E. B. Flink was named chairman of the Department of Medicine; and E. L. Staples, assistant director and fiscal officer of University of Minnesota hospitals, was appointed administrator of the WVU teaching hospital. In 1961, Stahr set in motion the following appointments: Dr. J. F. Golay, dean of faculties at Roosevelt University, was named dean of the Graduate School; Dr. Q. C. Wilson, chairman of the Journalism Department at the University of Utah, dean of the Journalism School; Dr. Carl Frasure, chairman of the WVU Department of Political Science, dean of the College of Arts and Sciences; and Dr. Francena L. Nolan, Pennsylvania State University, assistant dean and director for home economics.

With respect to Golay's position, Stahr had in mind the combination of a graduate deanship with an academic vice-presidency. To the WVU president and the Board, the union of the two would produce three advantages: the attraction of a high-caliber man to the graduate deanship, the additional authority which would upgrade and give meaning to the graduate deanship, and the assistance the chosen individual would give to the president in the general supervision and leadership of the overall academic program of the University. It was agreed in a special Board order on April 13, 1960, that the new and important position would be called "Provost of the University."

In addition to capturing personnel in a tight academic market, Stahr created a university relations committee to coordinate the public relations efforts of the University, established an Office of Personnel and named Thomas Wall, assistant director of personnel at the University of Pittsburgh, its head; and instituted a student counseling service, with James Carruth, associate professor of psychology, as its first director. The School of Nursing formally was established in 1960. New duties and responsibilities were implied when the School of Physical Education and Athletics was renamed the School of Physical and Health Education, Recreation and Safety.

Not only was the Stahr administration providing extended services to the state through the University, it also was implementing strategies whereby educational instruction would be carried directly to its people. The Kanawha Valley Graduate Center of Science and Engineering was retitled the Kanawha Valley Graduate Center of West Virginia University, implying that offerings of other than a technical nature would be made available. The 1961 Legislature authorized a two-year branch of the University to be opened in Parkersburg so its residents could begin work leading toward a University degree. As the *Morgantown Post* explained on June 7, 1961, the Parkersburg branch would be self-supporting, operating much like the Kanawha Valley

Agricultural Sciences Building, completed in 1961.

Graduate Center where those enrolled would be considered regular students of the University. When coupled with Potomac State College of West Virginia University at Keyser, the University seemed to be compensating for its Morgantown location and validating the slogan of the Stewart administration, "The state is our campus." The University also expanded its services by leasing from the State Conservation Commission, on a 99-year basis at an annual rental of $1,000, 7,532 acres of Coopers Rock State Forest, which was renamed West Virginia University Forest.

During his administration, the activist president followed his predecessor in giving attention to the inculcation of student loyalty to WVU, as well as to fostering friendship between WVU and the state through extension teaching and services. When a student fees committee questioned the propriety of an allocation for the debate team which represented a small proportion of the student body, Stahr responded by guaranteeing the team an annual budget of $2,500 for the next four years. After all, he insisted to the *Morgantown Post* on December 11, 1959, "A strong debate team is just as important to the University as a strong football team." But majorities, as well as minorities, had their special assignments. In an open letter to the student body, Stahr invited all students to assist him by contacting legislators during their Christmas vacation. If legislators became conscious of the deep interest of the students in University affairs, Stahr emphasized, they would be more impressed by the seriousness of the institutional needs.

The Morgantown press approved the enlistment of student advocates in University causes. Believing that too much formal protocol was followed in informing the public of the University's fiscal needs, one editor maintained that the ordinary citizen was reduced to knowing little of the institution's plight. This was because the Board of Governors presented overly complex figures to the Board of Public Works, which, in turn, presented obscure computations to the Legislature. Too often, the figures were meaningless to a public uneducated in statistical techniques. The paper congratulated Stahr for briefing the students, taking them into his confidence, and suggested the campaign extend to the faculty and alumni as well.

Not only did Stahr use the press to address students but, through the same medium, students communicated with each other, as did thirteen Army and Air Force cadets who protested compulsory ROTC training. In an open letter to the student body in the *Daily Athenaeum* of April 28, 1960, the cadets editorialized that "militarism in any form whatsoever is not to be desired, and consequently we believe that the present system of compulsory ROTC constitutes an undue infringement upon our rights." They urged all like-minded students to join them in their demonstration against assembling in formation, believing that the student body would be able "to correct this deplorable situation."

Colonel W. E. Roberts, head of the Military Science Department, passed the problem to the central administration. Stahr reminded the cadets on April 29 that the military training requirement was provided under the laws of West Virginia and the regulations of the Board of Governors. Eligible students, he proclaimed, had knowingly undertaken the obligation of military training by accepting admission and enrolling as students at a land-grant institution. He urged that their approach to the problem be restructured "in a more thoughtful way" than by a protest which he characterized as no more than students' attempts "to evade their own lawful obligations." So ended, for a brief time in the 1960s, efforts to challenge compulsory military training at WVU.

Stahr's first year of mild student protest was not quite over. When University officials announced that only Ph.D. degrees would be formally awarded at the 1960 commencement, three seniors protested the lack of recognition being accorded those who had met all requirements for their hard-earned bachelor and master's degrees. This time the *Morgantown Post* agreed with the students when it asked on May 10, 1960, "What sort of reward is it to march seniors to the Field House, hold them as a captive audience, and then have them and their parents 'sneak around' to various colleges to receive their diplomas?" Enrollment statistics, however, were on the side of the Stahr administration. From 1958-59 to 1961-62, enrollment had advanced from 6,278 to 7,514. Time did not permit presentation of diplomas to more than 1,300 degree candidates coming forward in the early 1960s.

With reference to growth in student enrollment, Stahr was soon to couple his belief that out-of-state students should be welcomed to WVU with the new medical school's serious need for qualified candidates who were failing to materialize within the state. The president first broached the subject of modifying 1937 University regulations of admitting only West Virginia students to medical school before the West Virginia State Medical Association. Sensing that the professional society now disapproved of its long-standing policy, the Board of Governors adopted new regulations on August 29, 1960, by carefully stating that qualified West Virginia residents would receive first priority but that unfilled class spaces would be provided "exceptionally qualified applicants from other states."

Whereas both the Turner and Stewart administrations had advocated a Mountaineer statue as a symbol for West Virginia University, the Stahr regime was responsible for three additional campus attractions. One was the installation of the University's first Festival of the Fine and Lively Arts, a 34-day accent on the arts beginning March 1 and continuing through April 3. Across the campus lawn in front of Woodburn Hall were strung evidences of the students' handiworks in painting and sculpture. In a response of March 15 to the display, the *Morgantown Post* was glad to note that the basketball court was not the only floor upon which University students excelled and called attention to the musical production of *South Pacific* as an important dramatic ingredient of the festival days.

With an assist from Sigma Delta Chi, society of professional journalists, and Associated Women Students, and, to the discomfort of the Department of History's chairman whose offices were beneath the clock's mechanisms, the chimes of Woodburn Hall's tower were reactivated on December 8, 1960, to bring forth Christmas carols. Student body officials, with an assist from the First National Bank of Morgantown, began a campaign to transport the mast from the U.S.S. West Virginia from Seattle, where the Navy was dismantling the distinguished World War II vessel, to the University campus. On March 17, 1961, the mast, landlocked in the middle of the campus as a memorial to World War II veterans, was warmly welcomed by a crowd of students, townspeople, and at least one pacifist. During the speeches by representatives of the town and gown organizations responsible for the dedication ceremonies, the unidentified pacifist slowly raised his sign above the crowd. The sign foreshadowed the younger generation's growing disillusionment with war as an instrument of national policy. It read: "Let this mast stand as a symbol of the illness of mankind."

As a part of the Greater West Virginia Weekend and Mothers' Day Sing, a new tradition was instituted when the Board of Governors designated an award to honor those who had rendered the University long and distinguished service. Titled "The Order of Vandalia," its appellation was borrowed from a name proposed before the American Revolution for an area roughly corresponding to the present state of West Virginia which some land speculators wished detached from the original colonies as a fourteenth member. Three Charleston residents, Charles Hodges, who had served as president of both the Board of Governors and the University Alumni Association; Arthur Koontz, former president and member of the first Board of Governors which was created in 1927; and Houston Young, past president of the University Alumni Association and founder of the Loyalty Permanent Endowment Fund, received illuminated scrolls and bronze medallions as the first recipients of the award.

But to many, success in sporting events was a more powerful weapon for stimulating loyalty than academic performance or ceremonial occasions. The athletic situation in the Stahr years was one of triumph in basketball and defeat in football. In 1958-59, the basketball squad posted a 29-5 record and marched into the NCAA tournament finals, losing out in the final moments of play to California, 71-70.

The 1959-60 season marked the true end of an era in WVU basketball history. The team's record was 26-5, and the Kentucky Invitational crown was returned to Morgantown along with the sixth Southern Conference championship. Jerry West was listed on every All-America team in the country. He established a new WVU scoring record of 29.3 points per game and a rebounding average of 16.5. Coach Fred Schaus' sixth University team finished as the school's best in every category of scoring: it averaged 89.5 points per game, 46.3 percent field goal shooting, and 71.4 percent free throw shooting; it set a single game record of 117 points in a Southern Conference tournament win over William and Mary; and it hit 100 or more points seven times in the season.

Better facilities for the team seemed in order as thousands of ticket buyers were turned away from a Field House with seating for only 6,500. Stahr indicated he saw in the future a new basketball home by 1964, located on the Evansdale Campus, costing $5 million (from legislative appropriations and private donations), and seating 12,000. However, he qualified his approval of the project by stating on July 21, 1960, "It had first priority after $12 million worth of construction needed now." Nevertheless, Schaus was thought to have spurned an alluring offer from the University of Washington to remain at WVU the year before because of the promise of better accommodations for his basketball team.

"Not suggesting that athletics need de-emphasis or that they don't play a proper part in the University's growth and development," the *Morgantown Post* of July 7, 1959, had gone on record against a costly field house. But it saved its greatest criticism for those who had suggested that the football program could be improved by building separate dormitories for members of the varsity athletic squads. "A few universities which enjoy little recognition beyond their football teams have done this," it reported, but their examples were not worth emulating. There were simply more pressing needs for the University, the editor stated, than the creation of "athletic menageries." Yet none could deny, the football program needed help of some kind.

Art (Pappy) Lewis's last two years as football coach in the Stahr regime were uncomfortable. Although his 1958 team remained undefeated in conference play, the overall record was a poor 4-5-1. The tie game proved, however, to be of historic interest because it represented the last time, for many years to come, that the Mountaineers did not lose to Penn State. The 1959 team was Lewis's last, a 3-7 record including lopsided losses to Maryland, Syracuse, and Southern California, and unexpected defeats by Boston University and The Citadel. Yet Lewis managed to close his career with a spectacular win over heavily favored Pitt, 23-15.

Unswayed by the victory, the Athletic Council voted unanimously not to rehire Lewis. Following a meeting with the Board of Governors, however, President Stahr issued on January 18, 1960, a lengthy six and a half-page statement approving his conditional reappointment. Although he did not rebut their findings, the president nonetheless insisted his action was not "a rebuff" to the Athletic Council. In turn, this was characterized as a "skin of your teeth" reappointment by the press because Stahr had written, "We expect the coach to do his job in such a way as to rebuild steadily the confidence in him . . . which we believe has been diminished for some years. If he cannot do this in a reasonable time to the satisfaction of both the Board and me, I am authorized to demand his resignation."

As a result of Stahr's pronouncements, the football coach was no longer referred to as "Pappy" but as "Skin of Your Teeth" Lewis. Nonetheless, Lewis indicated he wanted to stay at the University, expressed confidence he could keep the University strong in football, and denied bitterness over the controversy. However, Stahr felt compelled to issue on February 2 a new statement of confidence in Lewis and to reiterate to Lewis "and now anyone else that the question is settled and Lewis is coach." Lewis managed to open the 1960 spring drills, but resigned before their conclusion to accept a professional coaching job with the Pittsburgh Steelers. Having won more football games than any other coach in WVU history, Lewis left WVU with a 10-year record of 58 wins, 38 losses, and two ties. Twice his teams had lost only one game in a season, and his 1953 team had played in the Sugar Bowl. Upon receiving Lewis's resignation on April 18, Stahr immediately appointed his assistant, Gene Corum, acting coach. On April 21, Stahr named Corum head coach because "the appointment was enthusiastically received by the Athletic Council, heartily concurred in by the athletic director and me, and unanimously approved by the Board of Governors."

The year of athletic resignations continued. On August 22, 1960, Stahr announced that George King, assistant to Schaus for two years, was now the University's new head basketball coach. Schaus also departed for professional coaching — with the Los Angeles Lakers of the National Basketball Association. He left behind a six-year record of six straight Southern Conference titles, 146 wins, and only 37 losses.

In minor sports, West Virginia University was also beginning to attract interest. Posting an 11-2 record, Coach Bob Means' 1960 rifle team, whose member Bruce Meredith was named All-America, finished second in the nation. In 1961 the rifle team, featuring two All-Americans, Bruce Meredith and Bob Davies, finished first nationally. The 1961 WVU baseball team, despite losing Paul Popovich to the Chicago Cubs, captured the first of four consecutive Southern Conference championships in 1961 and the wrestling team, with records of 9-2 in both 1959 and 1960, also won titles in the Southern Conference. Although weight lifting was not a WVU sport, John Kantor, representing the University in national competition, was declared national collegiate 191-pound champion in 1961.

Successful football and basketball coaches who had produced golden years were not the only administrators leaving West Virginia University. *The Charleston Gazette* reported on January 14, 1961, that President-elect John Kennedy intended to nominate Stahr as Secretary of the Army, an appointment that would complete his selection of service chiefs under Robert S. McNamara, newly named Secretary of Defense. The *Morgantown Post* complained bitterly, the same day, "Whatever may be the larger good in this appointment, it can only be regarded as a severe blow to West Virginia and its University." The paper considered the affairs of the University to be in such a transitional period that "to take the helmsman's hands off the wheel even for a moment" was hazardous. For good measure, it listed the challenges facing the president of WVU: the Medical Center was about to begin full operation, the new Evansdale Campus was almost ready for occupancy, a large building program was still in progress, and the University's budget for 1961-62 was ready to undergo legislative scrutiny. Months later, it remained unreconciled to the loss, contending on May 16, "West Virginia needs Elvis Stahr as president of the University more than the United States needs him as Secretary of the Army."

To lessen the shock of such a short presidency, Stahr explained to the supporters of the University on January 14 that he had not sought the appointment "in any way whatsoever" and that there were "reasons from the standpoint of both the University and my own situation which would have impelled me to decline it had it not been placed squarely on the basis of duty to the country." The Board of Governors requested Stahr on January 16 to accept a leave of absence rather than resign, and it expressed in a press release "its confident hope that Stahr would return to head the University after discharging his responsibility to the nation." The Board's confidence was either misplaced or merely a brave public display because on June 6, 1961, it was compelled to accept Stahr's resignation. As Stahr explained the unhappy predicament that forced his definitive resignation, he could not afford, nor could the nation afford, that he make himself an automatic "lame duck" as head of the Department of the Army by fixing a specific time when he would return to reassume the WVU presidency. Therefore, there was no way out for him or for the University but to cut the assignment for good.

With Stahr's departure, the Board again turned to the faithful and experienced Clyde Colson for help during an administrative hiatus. Preliminary inquiries ascertained that former President Irvin Stewart saw no compelling reasons to assume the presidency and thus violate his original rationale for resignation and that Kenneth Penrod was desperately needed to continue directing the Medical Center. Within the small administrative heirarchy, the choice fell to Colson. However, Colson made it clear that he considered his duties as acting president to be of short duration by calling attention to two facts: he was not relinquishing his responsibilities as dean of the College of Law, and he was positively curtailing the speechmaking activities of the President's Office. Decrying his abilities as a public speaker, and indicating his disinclination toward "road work," he pointed out that he had suffered a heart attack in March, 1958, five months before his previous five-month term as Acting President.

It was a difficult year for Colson. In view of the state's adverse economic condition, the University itself cut by about one-half its request for additional money from the Legislature. The acting president admitted the University's need, but indicated it would simply tighten its belt and "do first things first," among which was to scale down its faculty pay raises from 10 percent to 5 percent.[1] Colson was pleased to acknowledge, however, that increases in appropriations permitted the institution of a new supplemental retirement program covering that portion of faculty and staff salaries not already covered by Social Security and the State Teachers Retirement System; a large increase in the appropriation for equipment; and a 25 percent increase in appropriations for current expenses.[2]

During Colson's administration, West Virginia University ceased to be the state's only university. Marshall College made its bid to join WVU in university status. At first, because of little interest shown in the state press, a Morgantown newspaper confessed on January 17, 1961, that it had no idea how seriously the Legislature would consider changing Marshall College's name to Marshall University.

Stahr, flying from Washington to Charleston for a special meeting with legislative leaders and the University Board of Governors, made a special plea to kill the measure granting Marshall university status. His statement before both groups was that "West Virginia needs and can have one excellent University and one excellent College. She neither needs nor will profit from two universities of low rank." His advice, which he thought particularly acceptable because he was no longer connected with West Virginia University, was dispatched by Acting President Colson to all members of the Committee of 55. In response to the growing political activity of WVU, the *Charleston Daily Mail* charged on February 3 that University officials were unduly alarmed by the spectre of a college assuming new status because whatever its name, Marshall's future remained under strict control of the Legislature. The Morgantown paper comforted itself with the knowledge that the *Wheeling News-Register,* and all Beckley, Fairmont, Clarksburg, and Martinsburg papers were in opposition to the *Charleston Daily Mail* and Huntington newspapers in their promotion of Marshall College.

As the decision neared, the *Morgantown Post* noted on February 25 that support for a name change included legislators who wished to submit to West Virginia voters a liquor-by-the-drink amendment. The alliance of the "wets" with those desiring a university in the southern part of the state, declared the Morgantown paper, lent substance to the charge that the decision before the Legislature had been converted into the question, "Is it to be Bourbon University or Marshall by the Drink?" According to the *Post,* "If the purity professions of Marshall blitzers have misled any West Virginians into believing the name-changing maneuver is anything less than a well-organized scheme to scuttle the state's system of higher education for the interests of Huntington the evidence now shows the lengths to which the campaigners would go to achieve their ends."

Marshall College achieved victory on March 1, 1961, when it became Marshall University. Its president pledged not to work for a "big institution" but for one "with a great intellectual challenge."[3] Huffed the *Morgantown Post* the following day, there remained only one thing to be said about the Marshall affair: legislative action did not end the matter because "despite repeated statements that Marshall wants to be only what it already is, but under the label of university rather than college, Marshallites will be most unhappy and most frustrated if this proves to be true."

That 1962 would be a better year seemed possible when the Interfraternity Council listed "scholastic improvement" as its number one goal. Said the *Morgantown Post* on May 5, cognizant that fraternities were on the defensive because of the generally unsatisfactory academic standing of their members, "We hope the University fraternity program will contribute to students getting more out of colleges, and the colleges getting more out of the students." This pious remark set the stage for the next WVU presidency.

Colson was able to point to increases in enrollment, in undergraduate and graduate degrees granted, and in extension courses. He recorded "notable firsts" in the School of Nursing enrolling its first class, in the granting of the first degrees of Doctor of Dental Surgery, in the admittance of the first patient to University Hospital. Aware that 1960-61 was another year of transition for the University, he believed in his concluding report as acting president that "Despite the obvious difficulties inherent in such a situation, every effort was made to continue the progress which has been under way since 1945."

From the Banks of the Monongahela to the Banks of the Potomac, Part II

Paul Ausborn Miller
January 1, 1962–August 15, 1966

THROUGHOUT 1961, CLYDE COLSON suffered acting presidential imprisonment twice as long as he had previously, but by the end of the year the board was able to offer him relief. It announced that Paul Ausborn Miller, provost of Michigan State University, would be West Virginia University's fifteenth president, and would assume the duties on January 1, 1962. The delay until the new year was caused by two factors: Elvis Stahr was compelled to surrender his leave of absence and officially resign the WVU presidency to continue as Secretary of the Army; and a person had to be found who could measure up to the exciting Stahr. The initial publicity surrounding the selection of the new president indicated the way in which Miller initially would surmount "the tough act to follow."

Although born in East Liverpool, Ohio, Paul Miller considered himself a native son of West Virginia. In an educational sense he was, because he was graduated as valedictorian of a small West Virginia high school and received a Bachelor of Science Degree from West Virginia University in 1939. In addition, he qualified for native status by having occupied the position of county agricultural agent in Ritchie and Nicholas counties from 1939 to 1942. After serving as a first lieutenant in the Army Air Corps in World War II, he received his master's and doctorate in anthropology and sociology from Michigan State, an institution that first had attracted his attention when he participated there as a victorious member of the WVU boxing team. At Michigan State from 1947 through 1961, he rapidly advanced from professor of sociology to director of the Cooperative Extension Service, to vice-president of off-campus education, to University provost. One book, *Community Health Action*, two technical monographs, and forty articles enhanced his academic standing and made him all the more acceptable as a chief executive of a land-grant institution that recently had undertaken the responsibility of a medical center.

The fact that Miller was only the third president of West Virginia University to have received some part of his formal education in its hallowed halls sharply differentiated him from his immediate predecessor, who had obtained his graduate degrees abroad. Other dissimilarities that could be considered attributes as well as subtle distinctions were carefully noted by the state press. The new president told of working his way through WVU with limited help from his parents by waiting on tables at a fraternity house and by serving as a student assistant in biochemistry. Miller spoke of acquiring his higher degrees at Michigan State with the needed assistance of the GI Bill. With studied reference to his own lean student days, he remarked at his first statewide press conference, "We must find a way to help the patched-pants student." And, "We have an obligation both as faculty and citizens to help him get through college."

Editorial response to his selection and to his well-publicized attitude toward patched-pants students in a poverty-stricken state was most favorable. Not only was it pleasing to welcome home a former graduate whose wife, Catherine Spiker, was a native of Harrisville, it was also encouraging, said the *Sunday Gazette-Mail* in Charleston on November 19, 1961, to hear him admit that "No University with uplift ambitions should try to make itself a second Harvard. It should seek an individuality built upon the needs of the area it serves." Because Miller favored relating WVU directly to West Virginia and the Appalachian plateau, *The Wheeling Intelligencer* was confident on November 8 that "he brings to the task of administering our highest institution of learning an understanding of our people, our problems, and our potential denied a man with no West Virginia background." In a more direct and personal manner, the *Fairmont Times* on November 8 put the matter in blunt editorial language, "Those who know the president-designate concede that he lacks the 'glamour' of his predecessor, Secretary of the Army Elvis Stahr, Jr. This will not necessarily be a handicap."

Because of the variant public images of the fourteenth and fifteenth presidents, press speculation centered on whether Miller would be accorded the elaborate inauguration so recently tendered Stahr. The answer was a somewhat studied and elaborate negative. After proper hesitation, Miller announced he would not wear "The President's Robe," especially designed for his predecessor's inaugural. Made of royal blue faille, trimmed in heavy gold brocade, designed in England after the pattern of traditional chancellors' robes, the academic costume had excited much public attention and admiration three years earlier. In lieu of the ostentatious costume, Miller indicated his preference for his own customary black doctoral gown. He explained on April 11, 1962, to a sympathetic student body, "I've worn this robe in all of my academic ceremonies and it has too many sentimental values to be set aside."

On April 21, 1962, the *West Virginia Hillbilly* commented approvingly on the simple and democratic character of the Miller inauguration and judged that the Board of Governors had wasted both money and time on the previous inauguration by welcoming one who too quickly answered the "siren call of the New Frontier in Washington." The editor mused that whereas West Virginia exports of natural resources had been on the decline, the exportation of human resources was at an all-time high, with teachers leaving West Virginia for Maryland and Florida, and industrial workers departing for Ohio and Michigan. Therefore, he speculated, the Board of Governors' solution to a quickly vacated presidency was "a native more or less, who, though not born in West Virginia, lived here, went to and boxed at WVU." It was, explained the *Hillbilly*, "the use of a native, so to speak, to keep the import from being an export."

But Miller also was able to convey yet another picture of himself. It was a more discriminating characterization of a sophisticated, dynamic, and benevolent conceptualizer who had returned to awaken the provinces. The sociologist-president suggested that he came to West Virginia, not because he was an alumnus or a native son, but because he sensed there was an opportunity at a particular institution to change its character. After all, he maintained, he was to be viewed first and foremost as a professional in the field of higher education, an attitude which seemed to negate either sentimentality or romanticism as explanations for his move. As for the cynical speculation that the WVU presidency would serve as a springboard to still higher positions, Miller mildly reprimanded such analysts by suggesting on April 11, 1962, that as provost of Michigan State, he had been sufficiently successful to produce those results if such had been his ambitions.

As to his real motivation in accepting the position, and the direction his presidency might take, he dropped his clues quite early in his administration. Speaking on January 29, 1962, before the Living Resources Forum in Morgantown, he maintained in one of his first formal addresses that:

Most states seem to form into distinctive regional areas. I prefer to call them industrial-agricultural regions. If you look at them closely you will discover that they organize about a city and that the surrounding territory is integrated uniquely by the nature of natural resources, terrain, transportation, marketing systems, productive facilities, occupational structure, job markets, population factors and trends, and the stage of economic and institutional development. More and more, I believe, will universities like West Virginia University have to define and understand these industrial-agricultural regions, and then arrange their resources and program planning in accordance with them.

Since Morgantown was not one of the state's largest urban complexes, Miller's thinking that the University needed major reorganization, if not relocation of some of its parts, was either missed or ignored by local analysts. That he had always carried with him, even as a student, a critical image of the University was revealed many months later. Speaking before the Presbyterian Men's Panel of Morgantown's First Presbyterian Church on October 9, 1963, he foresaw a formidable task ahead of him in reshaping West Virginia University because:

. . . both the State and the community, over much of the last 96 years, haven't been quite sure just what it means to have a great university, nor what a difference a great university may make to both a state and a given community. It is not a very happy fact that for most of the history of WVU, students came and went without undue intellectual excitement, attended classes in a small number of relatively old buildings, in an institution operated on quite modest budgets with salaries paid in the mines and in industry throughout the community exceeding in many instances the salaries of the faculty. During those long years, few, if any state universities suffered more.

Within a presidency that would encompass the centennial celebration of the Morrill Act, West Virginia's statehood, and almost extend to the University's one hundredth birthday, Paul Miller did not intend to view such events — as had the early founders of West Virginia and its university — as an opportunity to slip a liberal arts curriculum into a school designed for vocational and technical purposes. Rather did he see himself, in the University's annual report of 1962-63, as presiding over the culmination of the land-grant movement in education which recognized that all work was dignified and worthy of continuous improvement by educational institutions and that citizens should have educational opportunities commensurate with their abilities, regardless of income or social position. To Paul Miller, throwing wide its doors to the citizens of the state, West Virginia University was to become the catalyst for solutions to problems that had delayed the state's development for much of its first century.

In his efforts at a new definition, Miller assumed that his responsibility as president was to change, quite radically, the status quo, through re-education of all who were concerned with West Virginia University. On many occasions, notably in preparing annual reports to the Governor, the Legislature, students, parents, alumni, and other University supporters, Miller used his presidential pulpit to preach the dynamic purposes of West Virginia University and all state universities as he saw them. With considerable approbation, he recognized that such institutions shared three primary functions: teaching, research, and service, and he therefore assumed them all capable of solving social and economic problems at national, regional, state, and local levels. His decision was not whether to act but how to act, while preserving a certain uniqueness for West Virginia University within the land-grant system.

Although occasionally recognizing that much had been accomplished at West Virginia University since World War II, he characterized past institutional efforts as having resulted in stronger loyalties to academic disciplines rather than to institutional goals, of building up the physical plant but reducing "the companionship of learning," and of simply trying to make the institution resemble other state universities. Calling for innovation rather than conformity in October, 1965, Miller summoned forth a "new university" which would generate interest and support. In a sense, he resembled an earlier sociologist-president of WVU, Jerome Raymond, who attempted to push an unwilling nineteenth-century institution into the twentieth century. Yet Miller could on occasion be respectful of the past and was prepared to acknowledge to the thirteenth president of WVU at the end of his own presidency:

I believe I know enough about the life history of an academic institution to know that Irvin Stewart made this place a University. Even today, as we plan our physical expansion on the new campuses, and feel pleased about the capital improvements program, of all persons I could not overlook that the fundamental ideas were worked out by you. In a very real sense, both Elvis Stahr and I have only elaborated what you set in motion over years of magnificent leadership.[1]

The new West Virginia University, in assuming the role once assigned to the University of Wisconsin in a frontier state, would be an island of competence within Appalachia, a land Miller characterized in October, 1965, as being "of great beauty scarred by exploitation, great natural wealth undercut by intellectual deprivation, great opportunity retarded by obsolescent institutions." But how could this role be subsidized? As he saw it, tax revenues to the federal government exceeded its needs, while the opposite was true of state and local governments. Therefore, it was only logical that public universities would become the intermediaries between funds from the national level and planning programs at the state level. And what more deserving depository was there than the federally created state university?

By October, 1966, West Virginia University, in Miller's mind, suffered several weaknesses that might negate the purpose he had envisioned for it.

One was the long-standing tendency to fragment into unrelated departments, schools, and colleges. Another was the lack of an institution-wide communication system which would provide a means of working toward consensus on major issues of development. As noted by others both before and after Miller, the University also suffered the disability of an unusual location on the northern perimeter of the state, and because of the underdeveloped transportation systems within the state, had not made a sufficient commitment to the educational needs of every corner of West Virginia. The tendency to spend disproportionate amounts of time on such physical problems as traffic control rather than strengthening the institution's academic programs was another debility that Miller was determined to erase. As Miller explained his philosophy to a faculty member:

West Virginia University needs more tension, more fire, more conflict over ideals and ideas. The University is terribly compartmentalized, with unusual organizational inefficiency. But this observation is not to be confused with the contributions of conflict to social groups — and indeed as a necessary prerequisite to freedom.

   In fact, my concern with more viable faculty government, and a belief that general studies and specialized topics must be placed in tension with each other, are cues to my hopes for a more vivacious campus. Especially in universities, the price of peacefulness (as I have had to remind trustees from time to time) is mediocrity.[2]

By appointing on May 8, 1962, and October 12, 1965, two major University planning committees chaired by his provost, John F. Golay, and asking each school and college to review its own ten-year programs, Miller planned to draw upon these self-studies to provide a framework of change in the years ahead. What Miller had in mind, and what review committees faithfully endorsed, was the creation of centers for learning and study that would coordinate the skills and knowledge of many professions, many arts, and many people. Similar to, though more ambitious than, Stewart's idea of visiting committees, Miller grandly conceived of areas where the layman and the professional would share experiences and seek to understand each other's viewpoints.

   Since his strategy as outlined in his inaugural address called for a massive reorganization of the internal structure of the University to foster "interdisciplinary cooperation and coordination," Miller preferred to start in those areas where present University capabilities showed the possibility for creating "true eminence" and where federal subsidies and private foundation money combined with state appropriations would most likely underwrite the cost of such predetermined successes.

   Because of the expressed interest of the Kennedy and Johnson administrations in Appalachia, Miller sought as his major contribution to consolidate miscellaneous local and regional concerns into a West Virginia University Center for Appalachian Studies and Development. His original thrust at innovation was, however, imitative of his own educational and administrative experiences at Michigan State. With modifications, divisions directly supporting the Appalachian Center comprised all the extension services of the University such as the Cooperative Extension Service, the General Extension Division, and the Mining and Industrial Extension Service. Also included were the off-campus centers, the Parkersburg Branch and the Kanawha Valley Graduate Center. Overseas commitments, consisting of cooperative ventures with the U.S. Agency for International Development to establish an agricultural college in Tanzania as well as the staffing of agricultural colleges in Kenya and Uganda, were regrouped in the Appalachian Center in the international programs unit, whose costs were underwritten by AID and the Rockefeller Foundation. Research resources for statewide application became a unit within the Center known as the Office of Research and Development.

To analyze local problems and involve area residents in achieving development goals, statewide development centers were established in Keyser, Weston, Beckley, Charleston, Parkersburg, and Morgantown. In cooperation with other state agencies, the centers, really spin-offs from the Appalachian Center, conducted workshops, conferences and clinics, and sponsored cultural activities and short courses. Within these centers, attention was focused on such basic concerns as the state's nonrenewable resources, such as coal and petroleum, and its renewable resources, such as farm and forest products. The state's chemical production, its travel and recreation potential; and its human resources, including labor economics, occupational skills, and continuing education, were all considered within the province of the Appalachian Center.

In time, the ever-enlarging Appalachian Center grew to encompass an Institute of Water Resources and an Institute for Labor Studies, to serve as administrator of the National Youth Science Camp in Pocahontas County, to train counselor aides and youth advisers for the U.S. Department of Labor's program for disadvantaged youth, and to supply all West Virginia counties with state technical assistance as defined by the Economic Opportunity Act of 1964.

To most observers, this grandiose educational project failed within a few years. Defenders of the experiment placed the blame upon the federal government's de-emphasis of uplift and poverty programs made necessary by the escalating costs of the Vietnam War. It also was argued that the federal Appalachian program focused on highway construction rather than upon centralized administration of a University's extension services. To these setbacks was added the burden of proving to those who were the opponents of the concept that expenditures in off-campus activities were not to the detriment of on-campus educational needs. To many in academe, the sociological needs were expressed in a language retranslated by competing disciplines as hopeless jargon and unrealistic objectives for the thirty-fifth state.

If Miller's pet project did not receive universal approval, other educational ventures were viewed more favorably by the public and the University family. Because it was expected to emphasize the state's art and culture, the Creative Arts Center, a new academic mix of art, music, and drama, was conceived as a companion piece to the Appalachian Center by the administration and as necessary support of the fine arts by the faculty. As a further anchor to the Appalachian Center, the Center for Regional Social Studies (to become the Regional Research Institute) was created as an independent research agency to underscore the University's programs in social and economic studies. To avoid parochialism which could affect regional research, it was carefully noted that area studies, both domestic and foreign, were legitimate concerns within the framework of the regional studies program.

In view of the establishment of the Medical Center, one of the most obvious academic areas capable of sustained progress was biological science, which was fused with the medical school to create an Institute of Biological Sciences (to become the Graduate Institute of Biological Sciences). More or less a holding concern for expected federal grants, and not unlike the grand design of amalgamating the biological sciences into the agricultural college once envisioned by President John Roscoe Turner in the 1930s, the Institute like the Appalachian Center never quite achieved the purposes for which it was designed. In the years ahead, grants from the National Institutes of Health and other comparable agencies were more apt to go directly to the Medical Center than to the Institute of Biological Sciences.

Moving into the area of natural resources in December, 1963, the Miller administration emphasized forestry education which was considered of special concern in a state "where much of the land is better adapted to forest growth than to any other purpose." Into this project entered, in interdisciplinary lock step, the College of Engineering and the College of Agriculture and Forestry.

These four, the WVU Center for Appalachian Studies and Development, the Creative Arts Center, the Institute of Biological Sciences, and the Regional Research Institute, were the major creations within the first half of Miller's projected ten-year program of new interdisciplinary efforts. The second half of his administration saw the beginnings of a new movement in three more areas, and suggestions and expectations in two more colleges.

In 1965, the College of Human Resources and Education was created. Organized on a divisional basis, it included a Division of Education which comprised all the programs formerly conducted by the College of Education with the exception of counseling, reading, and special education; the Division of Clinical Studies which brought together counseling and guidance, the developmental reading program, speech correction and audiology, rehabilitation counseling, and special education; the Division of Home Economics which was transferred from the College of Agriculture and Forestry because of its new concern with the family, the home, and the basic social sciences; and the Division of Social Work which was transferred from the College of Arts and Sciences. The College of Human Resources and Education also included the Human Resources Research Institute, designed to augment research and scholarly productivity in each of the program areas and to establish stronger ties with the basic supporting disciplines, especially sociology and psychology. In response to the need for "a university-wide source of stimulation, leadership, and coordination of the curricular and co-curricular learning experience," Miller also created in October, 1965, the Office of Student Educational Services, which was to manage activities previously designated as Student Affairs, as well as the student union, financial aids, the foreign student office, and veterans affairs. The educational aspects of all student housing, on and off campus, as well as the Counseling and Health Services and the placement office also fell under its jurisdiction.

Before his administration came to a somewhat abrupt end, Miller indicated he had interdisciplinary visions extending beyond the boundaries of the Morgantown campus for both the College of Law and the College of Arts and Sciences. As he pictured the future of the state and the future of the University on January 28, 1964, the Kanawha Valley was the key to the development of both because: "Almost one fourth of the State's population is there, its center is our principal seat of government, and its great concentration of research-based industry gives promise of continued expansion."

So intrigued was the WVU president with the concept of more direct linkage of the University to the Kanawha Valley that he assigned key faculty members to explore new academic relationships that WVU might develop. An original committee composed of Dean Chester A. Arents, Engineering; Dean Thomas C. Campbell, Commerce; Dean Carl Frasure, Arts and Sciences; Provost John F. Golay; and Vice-President Ernest J. Nesius developed the first planning paper — "Report of the Study Made on the Feasibility of Expanding the Graduate-Research Center in the Kanawha Valley."

The study, issued March 8, 1965, concluded that the establishment of a graduate-research center in the Kanawha Valley was a primary goal of the citizens of the valley and the state for the attainment of a centralized industrial locus bordered by the state's major streams and new highway intersections. Recognizing it as the Ruhr of the U.S. chemical industry, it saw this section of the Appalachian region as rich in natural resources but low, proportionately to other regions, in the numbers of trained persons and library resources. Noting that the Appalachian region represented 10 percent of the U.S. population, the report documented the educational fact that, except for the universities at Pittsburgh and Morgantown, the center of Appalachia was without more than minimal graduate-research facilities.

The report went to the Executive Committee of the WVU Board of Governors which concluded it would be impractical to transfer all or part of the College of Engineering to the Kanawha Valley. Instead, it thought that consideration might be given to developing a public affairs center rather than a center for strict scientific orientation. This might entail consideration of moving such University units as the College of Law and related departments that could support the public affairs concept.

In the fall of 1966, Miller appointed Golay, Nesius, and Librarian Robert F. Munn to prepare the statement; Golay insisted that Dean Paul L. Selby, Jr., be included as a committee member as was Dean Frasure of the College of Arts and Sciences, whose college would be most affected. These five, prodded by the president, produced the working document.

For several years, a new law building had been one of the priorities in the University's construction plans. Earlier, Miller had suggested to the West Virginia State Bar what he would do with the old Law Building, but not necessarily where he would locate the new one. "We will very shortly be out of space in our downtown main library," he said on October 11, 1963. "The present College of Law building with very modest renovation could very well become an annex and reading center for the main University library."

It took but a simple combination of two factors, the proposed building of a new law school and the alleged need for the University to service the Kanawha Valley, to encourage Miller in October, 1966, to support an interdisciplinary Law and Public Affairs Center in the Charleston area, with the College of Law at the core of graduate-level programs. The location was considered logical because an emphasis on legal education and public affairs "at the seat of state government would be especially appropriate to the state's development" and, in addition, would show evidence that the University was giving more attention to the educational needs of the Kanawha Valley. Such a suggestion, when coupled with the fact that a proposed building for the College of Law still remained undesignated on the Morgantown campus, caused a furor in the local press.

"Surely there must be something wrong with the grotesque report that the University Board of Governors is giving serious thought to the dismemberment of the University on the eve of its 100th birthday," responded the *Morgantown Post* on May 9, 1966.

Nonetheless, the President's Office put forward its working paper proposing establishment of the Law and Public Affairs Center two days later. It had six major premises. The first was that an obvious clinical area in which the law school should have an effective practical training program was in advocacy before the courts. In the Kanawha Valley, the paper suggested, there was to be found an abundance of litigation spread through various trial and appellate courts. Secondly, in dealing with regulatory agencies and the state bureaucracy, a location in the state capital would provide on-the-spot opportunity for field work and the observation of government offices and functions. That disciplines in the Center would have firsthand knowledge of the legislative processes of the state became the third premise. The fourth point dealt again with the inaccessibility of Morgantown to most areas of the state. The Kanawha Valley Center also could meet the large potential demand for a program in business administration. And, finally, Charleston, as the seat of government and the largest city in the state, was the point of convergence for the primary transportation systems of the state.

The law faculty was not impressed, seeing no merit in severing the College of Law from the main body of the University and combining it with a limited number of existing or prospective graduate programs 200 miles south of the Morgantown campus. Having engaged in clinical training to the extent it deemed consistent with a sound program of legal education, the law faculty asserted that advantages for clinical training in the Kanawha Valley were specious and "the move to such an environment would constitute regression to a trade school concept of legal education." It sought to remind the president and the Board of Governors that "a college of law is a professional school, not a trade school, nor part of a university extension program."

One professor of law, Willard D. Lorensen, complained to the Board of Governors that Miller's proposal "runs contrary to the enlightened progress of legal education in this nation." He wrote:

The faculty of the College of Law represents about six-tenths of one per cent of the licensed legal talent of the State. It is no waste of human resources to insist they be scholarly rather than service-oriented, and that their environment reflect such a choice. The law student spends twelve years in practice for every year in the College of Law. This ratio offers abundant opportunities for the development of practice skills. It is folly to substitute service for scholarship. It is even worse to substitute activity for learning. But such are the goals of the proposal.

Professor Jerome S. Sloan of the Law School, in the *Daily Athenaeum* of May 12, 1966, questioned directly Miller's reasoning about the matter and indirectly Ernest J. Nesius's influence in peddling the new educational concepts. To Sloan, Miller's explanation "cannot be based in terms of mere expediency (to get money for the University in the future) without either yielding to the implication that the Legislature simply does not or will not support the University unless they have a toy to play with in Charleston, or that you are unable to get the funds needed from that admittedly simple body."

Law Center, completed in 1974.

Nor could Miller's explanation, said Sloan, be based upon the need to reform the outlook of the Law School because "the latter, though it needs doing, will not be done by moving the Old Turks to the New Sodom." What Miller must do, argued Sloan, was assure everyone that Nesius's Appalachian Center would not be involved with the new center.

Jumping into the fray on June 16, 1966, the West Virginia Law School Association opposed the separation of the College of Law from the University community on the grounds that it would disrupt and delay the present plan for the construction of a new building for the College of Law; the amalgamation of the College of Law with other schools or fields and the integration of the student bodies would in all probability result in the institution being removed from the approved list of the American Bar Association and losing its accreditation by that body; since the proposal apparently contemplated a substantial enrollment of part-time or night students, the law faculty, already understaffed, could not operate on a "second shift" basis; clinical study was readily available in any one of the county seats, and observation of state government, if vital, could be accomplished in a two- or three-day field trip.

The State Bar generally was not impressed and agreed in substance with the public and private criticisms of relocation. In keeping with the general sentiment of the state, the Board of Governors began to distance itself from the project. According to the *Dominion News* of May 13, 1966, those who said they had not yet taken a stand on the issue were President Charles C. Wise, Jr., of Charleston, Secretary Ralph J. Bean of Moorefield, Forrest H.

Kirkpatrick of Wheeling, Okey B. Glenn of Williamson, and Douglas K. Bowers of Beckley. Vice-President Albert B. C. Bray of Logan was in favor, Mrs. Gilbert Bachmann of Wheeling was leaning toward the center, James Swadley, Jr., of Keyser voiced "definite reservations," and Thomas L. Harris of Parkersburg was unavailable for comment. It was later clarified that Dr. Harris was in strong opposition. Thus the Board, at first encouraged by the project, left it to the president to dismiss the venture.

As to the College of Arts and Sciences, Miller twice asked administrators to furnish him with a new view of the College. Clearly, during the Miller years, the College had already changed, mostly with the loss of various programs. It lost drama and parts of speech to the Creative Arts Center and social work to the College of Human Resources and Education, barely preventing sociology and psychology from joining the latter creation. Many of the basic sciences had been reorienting themselves toward such designs as the Institute for the Biological Sciences. Moreover, it seemed as if some of the social sciences were headed toward the proposed Center of Public Affairs in Charleston. Rumors abounded that the College would be divided into a new College of Communications, where English, journalism, and the remnants of the Speech Department would be housed, and into separate Colleges of the Humanities and the Physical Sciences. To many, the plans simply awaited the retirement of Carl Frasure as dean of the College of Arts and Sciences before the college would be dismantled completely. Yet such was not its destiny. It was not that the College's strength was too great; it was because Miller left before completing his grand design.

Whereas his design encompassed new centers of learning, there were smaller pieces to be fitted into the jigsaw puzzle of innovation. In its annual reports, the Miller administration referred to some transformations as major, and others as minor. Among the latter were the creation of a separate Department of Philosophy (philosophy had been a part of the Department of Psychology) supported by grants from the Claude Worthington Benedum Foundation; a program of religious studies, supported by The Danforth Foundation; a consolidated Department of Foreign Languages replacing several language departments; a new division of statistics within the Department of Mathematics; a core curriculum consisting of 36 credit hours in the liberal arts and sciences required of all undergraduates entering in 1964; and the inauguration of a limited honors program. Oddly enough, the Departments of History, Chemistry, and Economics, because they were adhering to suggestions made by their national professional organizations, were singled out as having made significant advances. Within the Graduate School, attention was directed to a graduate program in Latin-American studies and the inauguration of a doctoral program in economics following a successful program of faculty recruitment in the College of Commerce. A suggestion for the creation of distinguished faculty positions, later known as Benedum and Centennial professorships, was made.

The Miller administration also brought about a new Computer Center (which had assimilated the old data processing center), an Office of Admissions separate from the office of the registrar, the Office of University Relations which coordinated the public relations program, news and information services, publications, and radio-television broadcasting; the first educational television station in West Virginia; a 10-week Summer Session replacing several short terms in order to have year-round academic programming; and an Office of Physical Planning.

All of these arrangements required serious physical planning and dictated a reconstruction of the President's Office. At the close of his own administration, President Irvin Stewart had admitted that since the postwar growth of the University had taken place under a single president, much of the information required for decisions or recommendations remained in his sole possession. Because the University was destined to become much larger and more complex, he suggested that future presidents lacking a background in institutional development should have additional administrative assistance.

In his short tenure, Stahr had just begun to change the concept of the President's Office before he suddenly vacated it, but he appointed Harold J. Shamberger as Assistant to the President and he suggested that John Ford Golay, graduate dean, be given larger administrative duties. However, Stahr departed before Golay arrived and Miller determined Golay's duties. Golay had a background similar to Stahr's. A graduate of the University of Southern California, he, too, had been a Rhodes Scholar and had received from Oxford University his B.A. with honors from the School of Philosophy, Politics, and Economics, as well as his master's and doctoral degrees. During his time away from the United States, he had seen military service in World War II with the Royal Air Force as a flight lieutenant. After the war, he had served as the executive secretary in the office of the U.S. High Commissioner for Germany in Bonn, and as chief of the American section, Allied General Secretariat, and secretary-general of the Allied High Commission. Upon his return to the United States, he had published *The Founding of the Federal Republic of Germany, 1958,* and had served as dean of faculties and professor of history at Roosevelt University in Chicago. With special interest in the political and constitutional history of modern Britain and Europe, he held faculty rank as professor of history at West Virginia University.

When Miller assumed his duties at WVU, he elevated Golay to the new position of provost, a position considered the president's deputy for academic affairs, and retained Golay as dean of the Graduate School. Three vice-presidents, falling under Miller and Golay, were also named: one for the Medical Center; another for the Appalachian Center; and the third for administration and finance. In addition, Miller appointed a director of Student Educational Services, who was also an assistant to the provost, and three presidential assistants, one a principal assistant, executive manager and later acting director of university relations; another an assistant for special affairs; and a third to study legislation on education and promote "college awareness" programs and also serve as director of admissions. Great as the extension of the President's Office seemed under Miller, it was destined to continue to grow with his successors.

Physically, the campus also changed radically during Miller's time to underscore the concept of new centers of learning. Both the 1963 and 1966 Legislatures reaffirmed their belief that tuition could be used to pay off bond issues for new capital improvements, although such bond issues were not to exceed $20 million. By June 30, 1964, through bond issues based on dormitory operations, construction of residence halls for more than 900 students began on the Evansdale Campus. (These became known as Towers 1 and 2). Also begun was the Forestry Building, which was aided by a grant of $958,000 from the U.S. Area Redevelopment Administration. The first phase of a five-year schedule of repairs to Mountaineer Field was also started that year. It was to include a new press box, masonry patching, waterproofing, and painting. In cooperation with General Electric Company, West Virginia University installed a new outdoor lighting system on the campus. Most important, the Miller administration began a five-year conquest of the Morgantown Golf and Country Club. Year by year, new acreage acquired from the country club filled in the land gap between the Evansdale Campus and the Medical Center. The renovation of the Chemistry Building also was initiated and culminated in a research addition to the Chemistry Building in 1968 at a cost of $2.9 million.

As a part of physical planning, several planning committees decided that the only major new construction on the Downtown Campus would be a new student center and that what was in store for the old campus was a thinning of its obsolescent buildings. Down came Reynolds Hall, the Armory, and the Physical Plant shops; the Health Center was moved up University Avenue to make way for the Mountainlair and its parking garage, which were completed in 1967 at a cost of $6.6 million. At the same time, the president vacated the President's House on the Downtown Campus in favor of residential living.

The Creative Arts Center was scheduled for completion in three phases with each corresponding to one of its threefold academic interests — music, drama, and art. The first phase, devoted to music, was completed in 1967-68 at a cost of $7 million. Evidence of further University commitment to the fine arts was displayed when an auditorium and music unit at Potomac State was completed in the same year at a cost of $1.2 million. By 1968, two additional dormitories (to become known as Towers 3 and 4) were constructed

Allen and Percival Halls and the President's Home on the Evansdale Campus. West Virginia native woods were used in the paneling and floors of Percival Hall, which houses the Division of Forestry and which was completed in 1965. It was named for W. Clement Percival, who headed the forestry program from 1934 to 1966. Allen Hall, home of the College of Human Resources and Education and the School of Social Work, was named for James E. Allen, the West Virginia native who served as U.S. Commissioner of Education and New York Commissioner of Education. It was completed in 1969.

on the Evansdale Campus, but by that time the original concept of a seven-tower dormitory was shelved. Henceforward, it was assumed that private construction could handle the dormitory needs of West Virginia University.

On the drawing boards at the close of the Miller administration were facilities for educational television, a new field house to cost $7 million, and an addition to the Forestry Building to cost $3 million, which would house the College of Human Resources and Education. Somewhere at a site still undetermined would be the new law building.

With the University now expanding at a rapid pace, especially on the Evansdale Campus, Miller considered new arrangements for transportation among the campuses. Expressing an interest in a monorail system on October 21, 1965, he nevertheless discounted obtaining one for WVU because "in this terrain monorail installation and operation would result in enormous costs to the University and the state."

Just as Paul Miller advocated major changes in order to realize, if not broadly interpret, the original meaning of the Morrill Act, so also did he initiate a transformation of the patched-pants student body of West Virginia University. In his inaugural address, he had forcefully stated that "the new president will insist that our campus life aim for a high level of decorum and taste." This the new president thought was exceedingly fitting and proper "since the issues of our state and country are so grave, the support of working people so hard to come by, family sacrifices so great that it would be intolerable for him to look aside from the loose and open practice of the minor vices." Although departing from the founding fathers' insistence on a liberal arts education, he tended at the outset of his administration toward reinforcing their emphatic demand that students exhibit adult behavior.

Little more than a month after Miller's formal inauguration, the *Daily Athenaeum* reported on May 10, 1962, that student conduct rules were being tightened and that life might well be all work and no play. For one thing, Miller did not respond favorably to a short work week. Rather did he visualize a University open six days a week, running classes from 7 a.m. to 10 p.m. if necessary. Sororities and fraternities were ordered to close the bars in their houses, an action which was only the first step in a reassessment by the Miller administration of the entire Greek system on campus. He warned that the Greek world was "a vestige of an older and more immature day in university life" that was currently "alternating between trying to find a new ideal and getting in the way" of the administration's reordering of priorities. Contending that the system needed help in defining a radically different mission than the one it then followed, he predicted on October 21, 1963, that "unless such mission is found, the system must be gracefully led aside so that the main business of the University will not be delayed."

Conspicuous in the traditional behavior of fraternities and sororities was a failure to pledge blacks or foreign students, and the *Daily Athenaeum* on November 11, 1964, felt compelled to investigate this social phenomenon. It found that while no sorority had pledged a Negro in campus history, presidents of at least half of the University's eleven sororities would condone non-white membership "if the right girl were to come along." All fraternities seemed to feel that fellow members should be chosen on an individual basis, that the social issue should not be "forced," and that assigning members to a fraternity in behalf of "forced integration" would wreck the purposes of the organizations.

Not only the WVU president but also the University Senate was disturbed by such discrimination and debated a resolution on February 9, 1965, that the University should withdraw recognition and support, either direct or in-

Creative Arts Center, costing $10 million, houses programs in art, music, and theatre. It includes a 1,420-seat Concert Theatre, Opera and Studio Theatres, and two art galleries.

direct, from any sorority, fraternity, or other student group or association which, through its constitution or bylaws or any other governing document, denied membership on the basis of race, color, religion, or ethnic origin. The *Athenaeum* sought Greek reaction to the Senate proposal. Eight sororities would not comment, indicating that information on the matter could be obtained from their national headquarters. Sixteen of the eighteen fraternity presidents stated that their national organizations already had eliminated all discriminatory clauses from their constitutions.

On April 6, 1965, a past president of the WVU Board of Governors, Forrest H. Kirkpatrick, challenged Greek leaders to "develop culture, insight, and stability of character" in an address to the Greek Leadership Conference. Exhorting them not to be satisfied with the clatter of petty rituals, he urged them to strive to build a better society and not to use their college years as a time to escape from the pressures of the modern world.

In the fall of 1965, University officials forbade Kappa Alpha Fraternity to fly its well-known Confederate flag from the chapter house, at football games, thuses, or on any other public occasions. This first had been demanded by the athletic department, but the KA's response was to unfurl their familiar symbol in full view at the WVU-Syracuse game on November 13, 1965. When ordered by University authorities to wrap their flag in moth balls, Kappa Alpha grudgingly complied.

One charge of discrimination quickly led to another. By the time of Miller's departure, Bettijane Christopher, student representative on Panhellenic Council, expressed the hope that the Greeks could meet the challenges of an integrated society. Suggesting discrimination in American society was not confined to race, she asked on May 13, 1966, why there were no women in the Mountaineer Marching Band? The campus ministry joined the Reverend Michael Paine in suggesting on January 27, 1967, that Interfraternity Council and Panhellenic representatives be removed from the Student Cabinet pending the opening of Greek organizations to Negro members. Another campus minister suggested that such acts as picketing segregated barbershops might make excellent duties for Greek pledges.

In some respects, the fraternal organizations could be counted on to battle discrimination. The Panhellenic Council was on record on October 25, 1962, as asking students not to patronize Pike's Restaurant because it was the only establishment in Morgantown discriminating against Negroes and foreigners. Four days later, the Associated Women Students' Executive Council also suggested a boycott because it felt that other restaurants with leanings toward racial discrimination might be dissuaded from taking a stand similar to Pike's.

It remained for a Negro student, Michael Woodson, to identify the kind of life blacks led in the University city when he stated on November 23, 1967, "I can't even get a haircut in this town." He calculated that because of the white Greek system, 100 Negro students on campus enjoyed no social life. "Once in a while," he said, "we Negroes get together, but we have to go to the Holiday Inn to have a party. For one thing, there is a shortage of Negro girls on the campus, and most of the guys have no dates. So they sit around and drink beer. That's all we can do."

The Miller administration had judged the times correctly. It was not long before the Interfraternity Council invited University fraternity presidents to a meeting to discuss steps to remove racial discrimination from the Greek groups following an earlier meeting with Council members and Negro students. The rush system was revised, permitting blacks to sign up for rush and to consider all fraternities. Under the new system, candidates also were not required to furnish recommendations as a prerequisite to membership invitation. Following these agreements, a Negro student spokesman announced on April 21, 1968, "The fraternities have come up with more concrete and sincere proposals than the other organizations we've confronted."

Before the arrival of the 1970s, the first predominately Negro but integrated fraternity, Kappa Alpha Psi, was expected to receive its charter on the WVU campus. Initiated on April 30, 1969, by blacks who were previously undergraduates at Bluefield State College, the chapter was designed to give "Negroes a group to belong to" if they "wanted to enter the Greek system." Earlier, on January 27, 1967, the University had denied permission for a Negro sorority on the basis of a ban forbidding any segregated group on the campus.

Sports during the Colson-Miller years enjoyed moderate success. The Mountaineer footballers were 4-6 in 1961, 8-2 in 1962, 4-6 in 1963, and 7-4 in 1964, earning a bid to the Liberty Bowl. In 1965, the record was 6-4. Coach Gene Corum's gridders won the Southern Conference championship in 1962, 1964, and 1965.

In basketball, West Virginia displayed greater consistency and success: 23-4 in 1961, 24-6 in 1962, and 23-8 in 1963. In 1964, however, George King's squad slumped to 18-10 and lost to George Washington in the Southern Conference tournament. All-America Rod Thorn spearheaded the 1962 and 1963 basketball teams to Southern Conference championships.

The Mountaineer baseball team won four consecutive Southern Conference championships from 1961 through 1964, and centerfielder Bill Marovic was named on the All-America team in 1964. West Virginia also won Southern Conference championships in wrestling in 1964 and 1965.

In other sports, WVU produced winning cross country teams in 1962, 1963, and 1965 under coach Stan Romanoski; introduced soccer as a sport in 1961; posted an 8-1 record in gymnastics in 1963; captured the Southern Conference crown in track and field in 1964; and continued its domination in national rifle contests. The 1962 riflemen, who finished fourth in the country and first in sectional standings, posted a 13-2 record. Lewis Rowan was named All-America. Jack Writer and Dean Bahrman were both named All-America in 1964, and that team won the national championship. The 1965 team, third in the nation, featured All-Americans Jack Writer, Dean Bahrman, and Andy Holoubek.

In his inaugural address, Paul Miller declared that the University was destined to grow, for "it dare not do otherwise in a state which ranks first among others in the population proportion of college age youth and forty-sixth in the proportion of those who are in college." Within a decade (from 1957-58 to 1967-68), the WVU student population more than doubled—from 6,184 to 14,888. This enormous increase required budgetary changes of major proportions if new faculty were to be recruited and old faculty retained.

Miller called attention to the rise in enrollment on many occasions. Speaking before the Board of Public Works on December 9, 1963, in behalf of his 1964-65 budget, he pointed out that University grant funds from foundations, both private and federal, were far too low. "This is true," he said, "simply because our staff members have teaching loads almost twice those of their counterparts in the leading state universities." Characterizing this as false economy, Miller noted that the University suffered from having too few senior professorships with the time and resources for scholarship and research which would attract the badly needed outside support. He also reported that the average WVU salary for all ranks was 11 percent below that of all land-grant institutions, and West Virginia needed to make a major effort in salary improvement because "average academic salaries for the entire country are increasing at the annual rate of 7 percent."

At the midpoint of his administration, Miller reminded the Legislature on January 21, 1964, that, in the four years since 1959-60, undergraduates had increased 27 percent, professional enrollment by 53 percent, and graduate enrollment by 85 percent. He pointed out that the 1963-64 increase of 24.7 percent in graduate students over the previous year topped all universities in the United States. Yet, beginning in 1961-62, salary increases for West Virginia University, which had been 16.4 percent in 1961-62 dropped to 8.1 percent in 1962-63; 6.7 percent in 1963-64; and 5.4 percent in 1964-65. In the same period, Miller called attention in January, 1965, to the fact that undergraduate enrollment had risen 50 percent and graduate enrollments had doubled.

Not only was Paul Miller fighting the perennial appropriation battle, he also was combating the national problem of how to attract and hold new faculty members. Realizing that faculty with children had left the community because of dissatisfaction with Morgantown schools, Miller made a dramatic pitch for improvement at a time when a new superintendent of schools was being selected. Speaking before the University Senate on October 13, 1965, he pledged that the University would provide the difference between the maximum amount the Board of Education could allocate and whatever sum a first rate "educational statesman" might demand to become the new superintendent of schools.

Miller wrought two other changes in promoting a more favorable atmosphere for the faculty. Upon his recommendation, the Board of Governors on November 6, 1965, permitted members of the faculty and staff to run for and serve in elective public office at the municipal, county, state, and federal level. Those who did run for or serve in public office where such offices were obtained in partisan elections had to disassociate themselves from the University, on a temporary basis, through obtaining leaves of absence without pay. The second concession was a new Faculty Constitution. Accepted by the University Senate at its meeting on October 12, 1965, it was adopted by the full Senate membership by a referendum in November, 1965. The Board approved it on February 5, 1966.

Other disputes occupied Miller's last year in office, particularly the recurring proposal that all institutions of higher learning be placed under a single state governing board. Having been appointed chairman of a committee set up by the Legislature to study the need for coordinating higher education in West Virginia, Miller had been sitting on several proposals which recommended consolidation. One of the more feasible, he reported, was a board of regents which would have a limited, twofold purpose of presenting an overall higher education budget to the Legislature, in a "united front" effort by West Virginia institutions of higher learning, and giving approval to new programs at any state college or university. Miller was cool, however, to the notion that West Virginia University's control should pass to a single board. Blasting such a proposition, he predicted that this would transfer control of higher education into the hands of professional administrators. "Lay government," he contended on December 8, 1965, "is essential and provides a buffer between the colleges and their integrity and all the problems they face."

By 1966, rumors had it that Miller would leave WVU by the end of the academic year. Speculation as to his successor centered on the three vice-presidents, Harry Heflin, Ernest Nesius, and Edward G. Stuart. By June 29, 1966, *The Charleston Gazette* was suggesting that Miller had become frustrated trying to cope with "West Virginia provincialism" and that haggling with state officials over appropriations, plus the recent controversy over moving the Law School to the Kanawha Valley as part of a new graduate center of public affairs, were tempting him to accept some federal appointment. By July 6, the press reported that Miller was to succeed Francis Keppel as Assistant Secretary of Education in the U.S. Department of Health, Education, and Welfare. The Board of Governors accepted with regret Miller's resignation effective August 15, and appointed Harry B. Heflin, vice-president for administration and finance, acting president.

Although quitting his post, Miller offered advice to his successors by enumerating what he considered to be four "needs of the future":

1. A higher level of state support in recognition of graduate and professional programs.

2. Long-term stability in the financing of the Medical Center.

3. Legal and administrative measures to increase the flexibility of the Board of Governors in budgeting appropriated funds and to reduce impediments to efficient administration.

4. Accelerated planning and action between the city of Morgantown and WVU in order that community services and attractiveness might achieve standards normally found in university communities.[3]

Upon Miller's departure, the *Morgantown Post* reported on July 11 that "troubled waters at the University quieted down over the weekend to be followed by a period of such serenity that you'd hardly know the place." This was due, it said, to the appointment of Harry B. Heflin as acting president, "a man fitted for the position," to the fact that the Board of Governors was not transporting the Law School to Charleston, and to the green light given by the Board for preparation of plans for a new Field House.

Yet not all alumni were serene, and some pondered the too frequent disappearances of WVU presidents. As one wrote to the Board of Governors:

For a President to give up leadership of a great University to accept a junior cabinet position in one of the youngest and least important of cabinet secretaryships is clearly a reflection upon the university, its program, and its salary schedule. I note also that Dr. Elvis Stahr accepted the position of Secretary of the Army, one for which he was not particularly qualified by training, remained in the position less than one year and then accepted the presidency of a large university.[4]

The departure of a president and the ascendancy of an acting president who had received the blessings of his predecessor seemed not a bad omen when it was reported on July 11, 1966, that the University had just received the largest gift in its history, a $500,000 endowment from Mrs. C. S. May for research in human reproduction and family planning, and that the University had led the nation in 1965 in increased support from alumni. The Development Office received $720,000 in the first year of its existence; bequests passed the million-dollar mark in 1966. The University announced on August 11 that a conditional million-dollar grant from the Benedum Foundation was to be used for bringing "academic excellence" to the University by means other than new physical facilities. In behalf of such money, to be translated into distinguished professorships, the University was expected to raise $200,000 in each of the next five years. In addition, Joseph Arkwright, coal pioneer of Monongalia County, established on May 5, 1967, a $50,000 trust fund with the Alumni Association's Loyalty Permanent Endowment Fund, which would provide $2,000 annual scholarships in mining engineering.

Not all problems disappeared with Miller's departure, and Charleston's interest in possessing a part of the University hardly diminished. Despite the sidetracking of Miller's law and public affairs center in the Kanawha Valley, which even Governor Hulett Smith opposed, the Governor nonetheless supported an expansion of the graduate center in the Kanawha Valley and suggested that colleges other than WVU might be of assistance. "I believe we must have a center," he said on July 15, 1966, "but perhaps there should be a joint effort to expand it with the help of the proposed Board of Regents on higher education." Disagreeing with Miller, who desired that the University assume total responsibility for graduate training and its expansion throughout the state, the Governor emphasized, "there's need for a larger facility so that the great population of the valley has a chance to get advanced degrees." Three days after the Governor's pronouncement, West Virginia educators took heed. Top administrators of West Virginia and Marshall Universities met in "private meeting," reported Robert Munn, who had as-

Acting president during WVU's centennial was Harry B. Heflin, who also came out of retirement in 1981 to serve as the eighteenth president for four and a half months.

sumed John Golay's duties in graduate education, "to see if a sensible arrangement can be made for graduate work in the Kanawha Valley," and if the center was capable, to offer a full complement of courses in business, chemistry, and engineering.

When it was reported on December 5, 1966, that the federal government might pay one-third of the cost of setting up a state graduate center in Charleston, State Superintendent of Schools Rex Smith pronounced its establishment as certain if "both West Virginia University and Marshall University were involved in the center." Yet the following day the *Morgantown Post* advised caution in such intercollegiate experiments by editorializing, "The state's present facilities for higher education in tax-supported institutions are so short of being adequately financed that in enlightened self-interest it cannot wisely divert any available funds for creating another institution of poorly defined purposes and hastily drawn specifications." Before his term as acting president was over, Heflin added his support on March 17, 1967, to the graduate center concept. "We're talking about starting a center in cooperation with another state college to get more graduates enrolled in one way or another," he said.

Heflin's endorsement foreshadowed official Board policy and the decision of the 1967 Legislature to appropriate $350,000 for the Kanawha Valley Graduate Center. This was to be followed by a legislative appropriation of $450,000 for fiscal 1968-69, with the stipulation that "a sufficient amount of this appropriation shall be used to reduce the tuition and registration fees in comparison with those at West Virginia University for the same purpose." At a meeting on April 14, 1967, the Board of Governors issued a cautious statement concerning the West Virginia University graduate program at the

Kanawha Valley Graduate Center. Recognizing that the primary duty of WVU was to provide the optimum educational opportunity for all citizens of West Virginia, as well as acknowledging the prime importance of a graduate program of excellence on the campus at Morgantown, the Board stated: ". . . a graduate center in the Charleston area with the same high quality course offerings, and of greater scope is in the best interests of the state as a whole, and for West Virginia University."

Therefore, it approved a proposed plan for WVU to offer about five times as many graduate credit classes in the fall of 1967, and planned classes in the engineering sciences, business administration, public administration, education, human resources and development, and other supporting sciences. It agreed that all graduate credit courses taught would be associated with established curricula leading to advanced WVU degrees.

Deciding to invite representative leaders in the Kanawha Valley to serve in an advisory capacity to the WVU Board of Governors in formulating a long-range plan for the Center, it included in its statement that, "Aware of the interest held by other higher education institutions, the Board places much stress on effective cooperative relationships between WVU and the nearby colleges and Marshall University."

In looking to the future, and also sensing a need for cooperation, Dr. Heflin predicted to the Board of Governors on April 15, 1967, an increased competition for appropriations, especially between WVU and other institutions of higher learning. In particular, he noted an important political fact of life: the number of legislative representatives in Cabell and surrounding counties exceeded those in the northern areas. As a former administrative official of West Virginia institutions other than WVU, he therefore spoke in favor of an increased number of graduate centers in the state and the need for cooperation with Marshall as well as other educational institutions, both state and public.

Throughout the year, Heflin kept the public informed about the University's constant expansion. The opening of an $8 million student union, Mountainlair; a $3.5 million addition atop the $2.5 million Forestry Building to house the College of Human Resources and Education; and leasing of Mont Chateau for staff meetings, social activities, and the housing of official visitors, and its possible ultimate development as an educational center for adult education programs, were evidence that the University continued to expand its facilities.

A $642,439 grant for the construction and expansion of the Parkersburg Center, encouragement of WVU space research, approval by Washington of plans for building a $1,045,748 educational television station and assignment of Channel 24 UHF in Morgantown, and a five-year training grant total-

Mountainlair, the student union.

ing more than half a million dollars from HEW's Division of Air Pollution, making the University one of the largest graduate air pollution control training centers in the United States, were signs in Heflin's one-year presidency that WVU had become a major recipient of federal government largesse.

The acting president scored his highest marks, however, on University budgeting for the 1967-68 academic year. Utilizing visitations by the State Board of Public Works and the Governor, whereby state officials might obtain a "visual impression" of the University's growth and needs, an expanded enrollment, which in 1966-67 stood at an all-time high of 12,255, and nostalgia for the WVU centennial which occurred in 1967, Heflin first suggested to the state Legislature's interim committee and the Board of Public Works an increase of $4.5 million over the previous year's appropriation. When his request was trimmed to $3 million in the first go-round with the Board of Public Works, the *Morgantown Post* reported on December 30, 1966, "That's about as well as you can do," and, although the increase was tentative, it did represent a "tremendous personal tribute to the brilliant job done in Acting President Harry B. Heflin's budget request."

By January 18 of the next year, a more confident Heflin was stating "we must have the full amount we asked for, for it was a modest proposal." Using six student leaders who appeared before legislative committees on February 2, the administration impressed the state's representatives with its contention that the University needed full support for the "University is unlike all other state schools." At the University's centennial celebration, Heflin stressed on February 14 the need for fulfillment of the University's "potential for greatness" before three former governors (Barron, Underwood, and Patteson), the current Governor (Smith), and 375 distinguished guests, including former presidents Stahr and Stewart.

When the University's final appropriation of $19,747,000 was approved, the *Morgantown Post* reviewed Heflin's accomplishment in arithmetical terms on March 15, 1967: with the previous budget at $16.1 million, the new appropriation was a 22 percent increase; Heflin had requested $20.6 million; the Board of Public Works had allowed $18.5 million; the Senate had recommended $19.72 million; and the House had recommended the final $19.747 million, only $853,000 less than the acting president's original request. Harry Heflin thus established himself as the ablest of all acting presidents in WVU history by obtaining the largest percentage increase in the battle for legislative appropriations.

The overall University budget, while satisfactory, did not mean that internal divisions of the appropriated amounts were pleasing to all. Studies by the acting provost and his staff indicated, in the Board of Governors' minutes of April 14-15, 1967, that over the years budget allocations to academic units tended to favor those units stressing research and/or public service rather than teaching. For example, the College of Arts and Sciences taught 53.2 percent of the weighted student credit hours yet received less than 36 percent of the total amount allocated to the schools and colleges in 1966-67. On the other hand, the College of Engineering taught 7.9 percent of the hours but received 16 percent of the allocation. The corresponding figures for agriculture were 5.04 percent and 15 percent. But whatever the differentials in faculty-student ratios compared with the operating costs of competing academic units, the new WVU pay scale showed that professors' salaries could extend from $9,000 to $12,000; associates from $7,500 to $10,500; assistants from $7,200 to $9,350; and instructors from $6,600 to $7,700.

Heflin's year was a successful budget year, but it also captured attention because it was the official centennial year. It even obscured the 1966 football record of 3 wins, 2 ties, and 5 losses, which followed an unsettling 1965 year in which the Mountaineers won their first four games and were leading the nation in most offensive statistics before running into Virginia, who stopped them 41-0. Although winning the Southern Conference crown, the team only managed a 6-4 season.

Following the 1965 losing season in basketball, and the departure of George King to become head coach at Purdue, youthful Raymond (Bucky) Waters assumed control of the young and inexperienced 1966 team and produced a surprising 19-9 record, including wins over nationally ranked Duke, Maryland, and Syracuse. John Lesher, Ron (Fritz) Williams, and Carl Head led the Mountaineers.

The 1966 rifle team captured its third national championship, the Southern Conference crown, and the Kansas State Invitational Rifle Tournament, the largest rifle invitational yet assembled, and placed Jack Writer, Dean Bahrman, and Andy Holoubek on the 1966 All-America team. In 1966, Coach Steve Harrick won his 300th baseball game at WVU, and the team posted a 26-7 record with one tie. The 1966 swimmers posted an impressive 11-4 mark, for WVU's second winning record in swimming history; the wrestlers, despite a 4-8 season, won the Southern Conference title for the third consecutive year, with John Luckini named the league's top wrestler; and Coach Charles Hockenberry's golf team was 11-4.

With more basketball than football victories, sports enthusiasts clamored for a new field house, but the University Senate on June 20, 1967, questioned the wisdom of constructing a basketball arena. Recommending that no action occur until a new president had had time to review overall University building plans, it objected to the Board's having approved the field house as the only building in a $20 million bond issue. Since a classroom complex, a library, a law building, and possibly an administration center were stalled, although they were incorporated in the bond issue prospectus, Dean Carl Frasure of the College of Arts and Sciences expressed concern that the field house project might eat up half of the bonding money for new buildings. Dean Thomas Campbell of the College of Commerce labeled the Board's action the "height of folly" considering the University's other building needs. Only C. P. Yost of the School of Physical Education defended the arena by declaring that it was "academic in nature" and not just "an athletic show place." The Board agreed with Yost, and called for bids on the new field house before the arrival of the new president.

If the faculty preferred to forget the actions that were to make the WVU Coliseum inevitable, the Centennial Year, with its theme, "From Changing Knowledge to Enduring Wisdom," made Heflin's one-year presidency memorable. Symposia on "The Lessons of History" and "Frontiers of Science" brought to the campus such distinguished speakers as Arthur Schlesinger, Jr., Oscar Handlin, and Jesse Stuart; the University's Festival of Ideas considered "Sex on the Campus" with William Masters and Virginia Johnson lecturing at the Medical Center; and politicians such as Jay Rockefeller, Arch Moore, Jennings Randolph, and Hubert Humphrey considered the subject, "Why West Virginians Despair." As part of an International Awareness Series,

Richard C. Hottlett, CBS correspondent, reported on Vietnam; the University hosted the national convention of the Intercollegiate Association of Women Students; and Dr. Heflin announced on April 12, 1967, that within a year or two the University would name five distinguished professors to Centennial Chairs.

Centennial celebrations aside, speculation centered on whether Heflin in one year could in any way equal the changes wrought by Miller in five years. Since the Miller administration had been clearly oriented to social action and had believed that it held both a responsibility and opportunity for the University to play an active role in programs designed to improve the welfare of the people of West Virginia, it was doubtful that the Heflin administration could appear more dramatic.

But Miller's and Heflin's provost, Robert Munn, believed that the Heflin year had in many ways surpassed the preceding administration's five. To the provost, compiling his 1966-67 report to the president, more important developments had occurred in strengthening the academic program in Heflin's tenure than in any year in recent memory. Most important, he believed, was the acceptance by the great majority of the faculty of three basic principles: that the University's first responsibility was to make certain that undergraduate instruction was of the highest possible quality; that the university did not have and was unlikely to obtain the resources to develop and maintain high quality undergraduate instruction plus a wide range of high quality doctoral programs; that so far as doctoral programs were concerned, the University should select a limited number of programs which seemed particularly relevant to West Virginia and concentrate its resources on them.

In keeping with past events in University history, the statement of general principles on the part of the administration was worked out in the context of a specific issue: the desire of the Department of Philosophy to be permitted to grant the Ph.D. degree, which it claimed had been a promise of the Miller administration. The Heflin administration said no on February 8, 1967, basing its case on the fact that the University could not afford a program requiring the addition of a number of faculty members to a department with very few majors and only two or three graduate students.

The Department of Philosophy, through its chairman, Joseph F. Lambert, saw the issue in terms affecting not only its own interests but the interests of all other academic units. Noting that there were two principal types of colleges — the traditional one pursuing knowledge for the sake of knowledge, and the technical school promoting training in specific technical trades, Lambert foresaw on April 11, 1967, WVU being oriented more and more toward a polytechnical school with an emphasis on training persons to solve specific technical problems of the state. To Lambert "the new WVU program was unwisely unconventional, confusing and impractical; the new WVU policy was unreasonable and its financial policy suspect."

Ten colleagues, from areas other than philosophy, agreed, finding the drift inconsistent with the recently published report of the West Virginia Commission on Higher Education recommending that WVU be the center of graduate education in the state, and inconsistent with the conventional and traditional idea of a university as an institution whose purpose was the disinterested pursuit of knowledge and truth.

Asserting that academic policy problems do not spring from financial difficulties, the embattled academics in a direct communication to the Board of Governors charged:

At West Virginia University they stem partly from philosophical conflict between the faculty and the administration over what constitutes a university. One thing is clear, however; a polytechnic institute is not a university. A real university is more than a polytechnic institute. Until recently the university had been making headway toward the goal of providing the people of this state with a 'true' university preparing students in all areas, both undergraduate and graduate, for the challenges which await them. We are concerned and mystified by the circumstances under which the policies and promises leading toward this goal were changed. What we wish is only continued development of the University along lines which will permit it to fulfill its commitment as an academic institution not only to the State of West Virginia but also to its students, to the nation and to the wider worlds of scholarship and science.

To Munn, this group represented a small, but vocal minority, and he was pleased to report, by almost unanimous faculty support — except on the part of the Philosophy Department — the decision was reached not to approve the new doctoral program. What was most important to Munn was "the mature level of faculty discussion and its recognition of the need to bend every effort to make the most intelligent use of limited resources." This came about, he said, when the minimum grade-point average for admission to the Graduate School was raised from 2.0 to 2.5; a more searching review of proposed new graduate courses was undertaken by the Executive Committee of the Graduate School; a recommendation was made for abolishing eight master's degree programs which had failed consistently to attract students; and establishment of University-wide doctoral programs, drawing on staff and equipment of existing departments and administered by Graduate Deans' committees, rather than the creation of new departments, was agreed upon.

The University was not alone in its budgetary restrictions on new and old programs. The armed forces groups, realizing that the new volume of students was greater than the number of officers it could muster to handle such programs as ROTC, suggested that the military program on campus be made voluntary. The acting president and the Board of Governors agreed. One alumnus, when hearing of the change in policy, protested to Heflin on June 21, 1967:

It is not just the changing of a required to an elective course; normally, that is admittedly a pedagogical decision. It is the principle of, as stated in the press, submitting to the misguided, the discontents, the parlor-pinks, the chronic complainers, the beatniks and all of the other off-color and non-descript loud mouthed groups, many of whom are fronting for the international communist conspiracy whether with or without their knowledge. Some of these types have no consideration for their country and will protest anything just to be 'against.' We had a few of this type when I was in the University. This country was founded on the principle that ALL able-bodied men should prepare themselves to protect and defend their homeland. The ROTC program is a means to assist to this end. The Communists have bragged that they will bury us. If we keep on submitting to them and letting them whittle away at our basic concepts as we continually are doing – they will do just that.[5]

Heflin acknowledged the alumnus had made many good points with which he personally agreed. Yet he felt constrained to note on June 22 that "WVU is not in the forefront in this change for most other land-grant institutions have already made it." Noting space requirements and officer requirements were just too much to handle between 3,000 and 4,000 men in the freshman and sophomore classes, he could only appreciate the concerns which had been expressed.

With the successful celebration of the University's first one hundred years and an above-average budget allocation for the coming year, speculation increased that Acting President Heflin would become president the following year. Dodging such questions at news conferences, Heflin appeared unconcerned about the position. However, the Student Legislature, the governing body of University students, asked the Board of Governors on March 31, 1967, to appoint Heflin to the presidency on a long-term basis.

The students' request was not to be honored. In a surprise announcement on May 21, the Board announced that 55-year-old James G. Harlow, dean of the College of Education at the University of Oklahoma, would become the University's sixteenth president. The Board noted that Acting President Heflin had removed himself as a candidate for the presidency early in the search. A ten-year period, consisting of two presidents and three acting presidents, had ended.

Simultaneously, former President Irvin Stewart, serving as professor of political science from 1958 to 1967, announced his retirement. Ordinarily reticent to comment about events since leaving the WVU presidency, he permitted himself one final observation before his departure for Washington. At a Faculty Honors Convocation on March 7, 1967, he said:

West Virginia University has a competent, hard working administrative staff and an able Board of Governors. They merit high marks for the work they have done and are doing. Nevertheless, I venture to suggest that, in common with their opposite numbers in other universities and as a part of the never-ending review of University goals, they take a fresh look at where we are and where we are heading in the matter of funds from Washington. The mere fact that money is available from Washington or that someone has an idea for which support money might come from Washington is only the first, and in many respects the least important, of the factors to be considered.

Chapter 13

1967–1977

Into the University's Second Century: Gadgets and Governance

James Gindling Harlow
August 16, 1967–June 30, 1977

BELIEVING IN 1933, the year in which he completed his bachelor's degree in mathematics and his master's degree in physics from the University of Oklahoma at the age of 21, that he would become "an electronics hotshot," James G. Harlow, sixteenth president of West Virginia University, later admitted to *The Charleston Gazette* on October 15, 1967, he had made a mistake in vocational timing. Finding himself during the Depression unable to get any closer to electronics than selling vacuum tubes in a basement of a hardware store, the young Oklahoman quickly opted for high school teaching in Seminole and Oklahoma City before serving in the Navy during World War II.

From 1934 to 1941 and 1946 to 1948, he served as editor of the Harlow Publishing Corporation whose principal businesses were the printing of law books and high school textbooks. This assignment came from a family business begun by his father, Victor, a country newspaper editor who had migrated from Missouri to Oklahoma to rescue the family fortunes by founding a regional political magazine called *Harlow's Weekly*. Not only did the publishing concern provide an income

282

supplement to his high school teaching, but it also enabled Harlow to write several high school teaching aids in algebra, mathematics, and science, and thus establish himself.

Concluding his naval service with the rank of lieutenant commander, Harlow became an instructor and later assistant professor of physics at the University of Oklahoma, and also filled in for a year as associate dean of the University College and dean of the College of Arts and Sciences in a period of rapidly increasing veteran enrollment. In 1951, with student population slackening, he entered the University of Chicago, where he obtained a doctorate in education, and then served as a research associate and associate professor of education. Lured back to his native state in 1957 by a group of businessmen to direct the Frontiers of Science Foundation, he was asked midway through the year to become dean of education at the University of Oklahoma, a position he held for ten years.

At the age of 55, Harlow responded to West Virginia University's call. His age caused a *Martinsburg Journal* editor to surmise at the time of Harlow's formal inauguration on September 14, 1968, that the sixteenth president was obviously not "in the category of his two immediate predecessors who seemed to be merely 'using' WVU as a stepping stone in advancing their personal ambitions." The *Morgantown Post* concurred and was of the opinion that "after the recent short-termers who held the office and left it when they couldn't resist the lure of more prestigious positions, Dr. Harlow offered a promise of more stability and more direction for the University." Harlow himself implied he had not sought the University presidency, and that it had found him at a somewhat advanced age for beginning such services when he said to *The Charleston Gazette* one month later: "I would never look for a state university presidency. I never have. I think anybody who isn't afraid of one isn't safe with one."

Both during an early visit to the campus and during his first state press conference on June 22, 1967, the president-elect disarmed reporters by speaking more of Oklahoma's university than West Virginia's and by declaring that any statements on the latter were not at the moment "hampered by either information or responsibility." Nevertheless, he reported that he was "looking forward to working with a bunch of pros who really know what's going on." He also disarmed the residents of Morgantown as well as the academic community when he remarked, "A University's relationship to its community is like a marriage. It is not friction free but is involved in a mutual activity from which neither can escape." At his first convocation on September 6, 1967, Harlow was also to disconcert the students by humorously commenting that all it really takes to be a university president is "a touch of grey hair for a look of distinction and a mild allergy for a look of concern."

Casting himself and Mrs. Harlow as representing the wave of the future—

the time when nature-starved people would be clamoring to move to West Virginia from overcrowded and riot-torn cities — the president manufactured another bond with West Virginia. He recalled that John Steinbeck's *Grapes of Wrath* had cast Oklahomans as the Appalachians of the 1930s and 1940s, and that he was, of course, an Oklahoman. He also remembered that Pare Lorentz, a former WVU student who is considered the father of documentary films, had captured the drama of the Oklahoman migration in a world-famous film, *The Plow that Broke the Plains,* and that Oklahomans had deeply resented that an outsider, an itinerant West Virginian, had created the epic. But since Oklahoma had survived her notoriety, he avowed, West Virginia would survive the criticism and satire about the state and its people both at home and abroad.

With his professional education background, his publishing experience, and his love of electronics, the transplanted Oklahoman surprised no one, including the *Daily Athenaeum* of June 22, 1967, by being interested in making higher education aware of "the application of programs, learning techniques, audio-visual and computerized learning." The Board of Governors quickly caught the Harlow vision when they, too, predicted in their 1969 report the following for WVU's second century: the disappearance of traditional group lectures as a method of transmitting information, and their replacement by electronic devices, including closed-circuit television, films, slides, tape recorders, and computer consoles. It perhaps was disappointing, after such recommended mechanical build-ups had taken place, to learn six years later from the North Central Association of Colleges and Secondary Schools' Visitation Report of April 8-10, 1974, that the most frequently encountered academic complaints by students involved the televised elementary biology course.

One of the president's first purchases for the University was a new IBM 360-75 computer. Harlow hailed the action in his 1970 report to the Regents as "one of the most significant steps taken by West Virginia and West Virginia University in recent years." The professional staff realized a new day had dawned when the University, under Harlow's prodding, contracted with Arthur D. Little Company to conduct a fiscal survey before adopting a new management information system. Harlow was able to report to the Faculty Assembly in the fall of 1969 the immediate results of his new management information system: a computerized payroll system saving numerous hours of clerical drudgery; a computerized master personnel file replacing a dozen splinter files, which he characterized as redundant in parts and inadequate in their entirety; a computerized budgeting system permitting the comptroller to produce a monthly report of account balance within a week after the end of each month; and a manual for budget officers containing among other things a compendium of administrative policies and procedures.

The faculty, hearing of the above mechanical goodies in lieu of Paul Miller's exhortations for the University to bring about societal changes, must have known that they were facing another presidential transition. They would have been even more certain of change if they had known that within a few years Harlow would request that the name of Paul Miller's Center for Appalachian Studies and Development be conservatively recast as the Center for Extension and Continuing Education. He notified Chancellor Ben Morton on November 4, 1974, that, "The current name of the unit does not appropriately relate this unit to West Virginia University nor does it indicate that the unit performs a University function. The proposed name 'Extension and Continuing Education' are titles that are generally accepted throughout the country as being representative of the extended functions of land-grant universities."

He also noted, with disapproval, that after the establishment of the Center for Appalachian Studies and Development, the federal government had established the Appalachian Regional Commission for the economic and social development of the entire Appalachian region. The similarity in the two names, if not in the divergent functions, had caused considerable confusion, Harlow asserted, both within and outside the state. The North Central accreditation team put a past endeavor in more discreet terms when it provided in its 1974 Visitation Report the definition that "The Appalachian Center was an ambitious concept which has been carried out on a much more modest scale than originally envisioned."

Perhaps because Harlow had confessed ignorance of West Virginia University and admitted that he hated to leave Oklahoma "very, very much," *The Charleston Gazette* on August 27, 1967, gratuitously presented the new chief executive with a "civilian view" of the institution he now headed. The paper was compelled to furnish such a picture, it said, because it worried that Harlow's limited association with the university he was to lead, had been restricted so far to the people inside the organization and to the community in which it resided. As he began his presidential duties, *The Gazette* asked him as the first cardinal principle of faith to discount Morgantown's suspicions that the evil big city of Charleston was trying to steal the University and move it piecemeal to Kanawha County. It begged him to believe that southern West Virginia felt only the deepest concern about the school, and wanted it to grow, prosper, and become a center of scholarship and learning to which it could send its sons and daughters to develop their intellects.

With reference to the preceding Miller administration, *The Charleston Gazette* especially bequeathed its own critical version of the present state of the University to the inexperienced and untried president. It listed its "many questionable programs, tucked away all over the campus, expending funds that could be better used elsewhere." As the sixteenth executive unearthed the superfluous projects from their secret hiding places, it asked him not to worry about "that curious organization called the Appalachian Center," for now that "one of those periodic bursts of up-by-the-bootstraps activity," to which West Virginians were prone, had extended the University's services into every corner of the state, the administrative unit had finally settled down mainly as a resting place for county agricultural agents.

It informed Harlow that the main interest of most West Virginians was in the football and basketball teams, and that athletic success was indeed beneficial when requests for funds were made to the Legislature. It suggested that the University's Board of Governors was truly one of the most prestigious bodies in the state, but cautioned its new executive officer that its members guarded their prerogatives jealously, perhaps took themselves too seriously, and unnecessarily undermined public confidence by handling public affairs in private.

To *The Charleston Gazette*, West Virginia University was and should be the preeminent higher educational institution in the state. But the paper believed that it had never quite fulfilled its proper role. That could be accomplished, *The Gazette* maintained, if the University emphasized less its enrollment figures, concentrated more on a higher quality program for fewer undergraduates, and dutifully strengthened its graduate education facilities. The University's overall appearance, the paper added, would be more pleasant if Harlow could persuade architects to abandon "the Early Missile Site designs" used for new buildings on the Evansdale Campus.

There is no evidence that Harlow directly replied to *The Gazette*, but early actions indicated he at least might have taken the architectural and athletic advice as seriously as he was to accept the admonitions regarding the Appalachian Center. He quickly faced the issue of rejuvenating the facilities of the physical education units. Minimizing his own impact upon the decision-making process in the matter of WVU sports, Harlow told the *Daily Athenaeum* on June 22, 1969, "I don't think a change in the name of the University president will make any difference in athletics." Although he personally preferred trout fishing in a secluded area to spectator sports, he found nothing wrong with big-time athletics. "It's popular," he said to *The Charleston Gazette* on October 15, 1967. "We get big crowds in the stadium. This is fine as far as I'm concerned. I think we ought to do whatever we do as well as we can. I would be embarrassed to have the least effective state university football team in this area. I would rather close it down than not have a good one."

No sooner was Harlow in command of the campus than he faced the issue of a new basketball arena. For his edification, the *Morgantown Post* of September 22, 1967, listed the various opinions about the Board of Governors' awarding of an initial $8.864 million contract to a Charlotte, North

Carolina, firm to build an all-concrete building of rounded, mushroom design. One view was that since the original cost would quickly exceed $10 million, there was a serious question whether half or more of the available building funds should be assigned to a single facility. Other opinions ranged from Law Dean Paul Selby's belief that the ultimate decision on priorities in constructing campus facilities belonged to the faculty, to the University Senate's recommendation that field house construction be delayed, to the *Morgantown Post's* cautionary advice that everyone had been heard from on the matter of WVU's next building project except those who would pay the bill: the students and their parents. The local newspaper noted that the need for classroom space was acutely short: that the English Department held classes in six different buildings; that commerce classes had increased 47 percent in the past three years and could no longer be squeezed into their allotted instructional spaces; and that introductory biology classes ranging to 700 persons each were taught in a downtown theater.

Feeling compelled to respond to the charge of an increased enrollment pressing upon academic facilities, Athletic Director Robert N. Brown replied: "I sympathize with all departments. I will be the first to admit classrooms are needed and many divisions are overcrowded. But on the other hand, the Physical Education and Athletic Department has long outgrown its facilities. The department has waited patiently for priority in building. We could have pounded our fists and ranted about our needs years ago and I am well aware of the dire situations in many divisions. But I do believe most firmly the arena is urgently needed."

The *Morgantown Post*, under new editorial direction, agreed with the athletic director. Two days earlier it noted that throughout the state thousands of basketball fans were shouting, "Build that arena." It suggested that classrooms be assigned top priority only after the arena bids were approved because an immediate basketball arena "will do more to further cement the wonderful relationship that now exists between the people and their University than all the classrooms and offices we can build."

Although Acting President Heflin had refused to commit himself to a coliseum at such construction costs, the Board of Governors and President Harlow agreed with the sports enthusiasts by forwarding a recommendation to the Legislature for the new arena at Evansdale, causing the *Morgantown Post* of September 25, 1967, to characterize their actions as a "courageous and progressive decision that will serve this state well." After the guarantee of Coliseum construction and upon further reflection, the *Post* apologized for the short shrift given to Dean Selby's proposed Law Center. When the law dean elaborated upon his earlier criticism by suggesting that the University had lost $3.5 to $5 million in federal funds by not designing the athletic arena to take advantage of government aid, the paper concurred on October 24, 1967. The *Post* suggested that the Board of Governors take such matters into consideration in determining priority of other facilities to be constructed out of the $10 million building kitty that now remained.

Before an assembly of the faculty on April 13, 1976, Harlow capped his contribution to WVU's athletic buildup with the boast that "The last 10 years have been the best 10 years of football in the last 50 years of WVU's life." He enumerated eight winning seasons, participation in three bowl games, and the fact that in each of the previous ten years WVU had been among the top 20 teams in the nation in at least one of the basic game statistical indexes. In order to better the record of the past decade, Harlow called for "significant changes in physical facilities and in funding of the WVU football coaches — the head coach, at least."

Noting that financial incentives were missing for teams playing at Morgantown before only 34,000 people when they could play at home or elsewhere before 55-60,000 spectators, he estimated that the stadium was inadequate in size and badly in need of structural repair. In addition to deploring the home of Mountaineer football, he suggested further needs, particularly a large enclosed area, or "shell," for indoor football practice during inclement weather and for use by the track and baseball teams. Drawing upon his experiences at Oklahoma, which he was wont to do throughout his term, he emphasized the need for better funding for coaches and for television. The University, he pointed out, needed expensive air time in western Pennsylvania and eastern Ohio to recruit athletes.

Believing the missing element in major sports build-up for WVU lay in its financial support, the president suggested that the coal money from West Virginia could produce what the oil money from Oklahoma had provided the Sooner State in necessary capital. "You'll note that I omitted the impact upon academic programs," Harlow pointedly told his faculty audience, and "the omission was deliberate." However, the president half-jokingly suggested that his sixteen years at Oklahoma "make it possible for me to state that it is not at all inevitable that big-time football will upset the academic effort of a university, though I'm sure that in some cases it has."

There seemed only one fallout in the state from Harlow's program of sports' aggrandizement. Whenever expensive games improvements occurred at West Virginia University, Marshall was quick to notice. Extremely sensitive to the fact that WVU avoided contests with other state institutions, Marshall charged neglect of her own facilities and contended that the Legislature favored WVU.

No sooner did Marshall vent its grievances than, at the initiative of President Harlow, a new chapter in the relationship between the two institutions was drafted at a meeting between the two presidents. In a joint statement

The WVU Coliseum, home of the School of Physical Education and Department of Intercollegiate Athletics.

on December 20, 1967, Dr. Harlow and Marshall's President Stewart H. Smith announced a cross-listing of graduate education courses at the Kanawha Valley Graduate Center. Credit for those taking equivalent courses under the other university's program was now permissible and available at either school. In addition, the presidents agreed to cross-list and exchange credit of all equivalent graduate extension courses in southern West Virginia. "I am delighted to work with WVU in this joint education adventure," said Dr. Smith, and "I appreciate the initiative taken by Dr. Harlow in making this cooperative effort possible." Dr. Harlow replied, "This new collaboration is in the best tradition of higher education in America. I hope it is merely the opener for a much greater cooperative endeavor between Marshall and West Virginia University."

However, one member of the WVU Board of Governors, Thomas L. Harris, reported to Harlow on November 9, 1967, his own ever-increasing anxiety about developments of the graduate center in Charleston which "was supposed to be a simple graduate school to take care of engineers who have

B.S. degrees in the employment of industrial companies in the Charleston-Huntington area." But now, according to Dr. Harris:

We find ourselves with a real graduate center in Charleston, so termed, extending out and reaching for a large number of students who are in the undergraduate level . . . . This situation has given me a great deal of concern because it is drawing money away from the University and from our graduate center there. The appropriations are going to be increasingly larger in Charleston and will diminish the appropriations in Morgantown. I may be hooted at with this idea, but I am watching it grow progressively . . . . It is a well-known fact that Charleston wants to get everything possible in the State in that vicinity, and, unfortunately, they have a large group of legislators in that area, four of the members of the Board of Governors come from that area, and the whole picture gives me no little concern.

President Harlow responded to Harris on November 22 that indeed the population in the Kanawha Valley could not be denied over any length of time. "There will be graduate instruction provided in the Valley in any case," warned the president, "and, for West Virginia, the best development will come under the wing of West Virginia University, which can provide staff, know-how, library, and professional accreditation." To Dr. Harris, Harlow offered small comfort when he further suggested, "Probably the center will become independent of Morgantown some day — but that's a distant day, and other conditions will probably be operative at that time."

The Morgantown paper was convinced that complaints voiced in Huntington and in Charleston about the snubbing of Marshall by WVU now would be laid to rest by evidence that the two were cooperating in the Kanawha Valley Graduate Center, and it even suggested that if and when Marshall became a consistent winner in basketball, the University should schedule Marshall, which was done in 1978.

The early unwillingness to sponsor joint sports events recalled the historical lack of coordination created by the 1947 plan for two separate systems of higher education in the state: one, all institutions of higher learning under the Board of Education except the state university, and the other, West Virginia University under its own Board of Governors. Toward the end of the Stewart administration, the John E. Brewton Study of 1956 had recommended a State Board of Higher Education to absorb the two boards. In the Stewart administration, measures introduced in the Senate and the House of Delegates in 1957 for educational unification never were reported out of the education committee of either house. In the Stahr administration, such measures again met the same silent treatment in 1961.

Obviously, however, if the two boards were to withstand criticism, they needed to provide evidence of a cooperative attitude in matters of higher education. From 1956 through 1968, they manifested such a spirit through a joint committee of the West Virginia University's Board of Governors and the State Board of Education. This vehicle satisfied the Legislature for awhile, served the purposes of the two boards by maintaining the status quo, and effectively stopped the introduction of bills aiming for statutory control of West Virginia's higher educational institutions by a single governing board. During an inactive period of the joint committee, roughly from 1964 through 1968, a West Virginia Committee on Higher Education, sponsored by Governor Hulett Smith and chaired by WVU President Paul Miller, studied and made recommendations concerning the state's higher educational system. Its final report, published on October 31, 1966, after Miller's departure, reopened the issue of educational coordination by recommending a Board of Governors for the eight state colleges, a Board of Governors for Marshall University, retention of the Board of Governors for West Virginia University, and a coordinating board known as the West Virginia Board of Regents.

In 1967, the West Virginia Senate passed a measure to accomplish the goals set forth in the report. While its powerful finance committee recommended passage of a bill to create a coordinating Board of Regents, it rejected additional institutional governing boards. The House of Delegates, however, failed to consider the legislation suggested by the Senate.

Dr. Harris, a member of the WVU Board of Governors, wrote candidly to Harlow on November 9, 1967:

I, frankly, am not in favor of a Board of Regents for West Virginia at this time. I feel that it is going to be at the expense of West Virginia University. Last year when this thing came up, I was the only member of the Committee on Higher Education that dissented, but I did not dissent until I had discussed it with Dr. Stewart, Dr. Stahr, Dr. Heflin, the President of the University of Oregon, and the majority of the committee of the Senate of West Virginia, Henry Held of the Ford Foundation and George Harrah of the Rockefeller Foundation.

All of these people did not think it was a good thing for the University. It would limit the academic freedom on the part of the President and place the Board of Governors in more or less of a clerical position as everything coming from the University would have to be approved by the Board of Regents down to the most trivial thing. I have felt that it would hamper the President and the Board could not give him any relief . . . . The worst part of the whole deal is that they would be, with the exception of the Chancellor, political appointments.

Governor Smith, in his 1968 State of the State address to the Legislature, reaffirmed his desire for a coordinating board. Bills reflecting the Governor's intent failed to clear the finance committee of either house. But for the first time since 1956, a bill calling for the creation of a super board of higher education was introduced in both chambers. From retirement emerged Irvin Stewart, now living in Washington, D.C. In a letter to influential persons around the state, which was given wide circulation in the Legislature, Stewart cautioned on January 26, 1968, against the creation of "an administrative monstrosity which would constitute a continuing obstruction to the progress of education in the state." Describing the multiple-board concept as the worst proposal for reorganization suggested in the past two decades, the still influential educator advised:

In my opinion the continuing autonomy of the University under its own Board of Governors who can devote their full attention to the University and who do not share responsibility with any other administrative body is the best way to advance higher education in West Virginia.

Nonetheless, the 1968 gubernatorial campaign kept the issue alive with Democratic and Republican candidates, James Sprouse and Arch Moore, Jr., supporting the creation of a governing board for Marshall University. In a last-ditch effort, the Joint Committee of West Virginia University's Board of Governors and the State Board of Education quickly reactivated itself as the 1969 legislative session neared. When both boards issued a joint statement pleading with the upcoming Legislature not to tamper with the existing administrative setup for higher education until those directly involved had a chance to make their own study and submit their own conclusions, the *Morgantown Post* on December 19, 1968, rescinded its criticism of the Board of Governors for having failed to speak out on the single-board concept.

Bills to accomplish a changeover to a super board, some incorporating and others excluding the multiple-board concepts, were introduced in the West Virginia Legislature in January and February, 1969. On February 4, the finance and education committees of the House and Senate in a joint session heard presentations regarding the coordination of higher education from the state's prominent educators, including President Harlow of WVU.

President Harlow, making it clear that he spoke only for himself, offered three suggestions to the committees: one, that the joint committee of the two boards make whatever changes in higher education the Legislature felt necessary; two, that the Legislature set up a new board to assume the State Board of Education's responsibilities; three, that the Legislature create a single Board of Regents governing all public institutions of higher education. Attacking the concept of multiple boards, Harlow called attention to their poorly defined responsibilities and the absence of limitations of geography or political party guidelines upon appointments to the various boards.

Suggesting that professional administrative sentiment favored a Board of Regents governing all higher education under public support, and that it was the least expensive arrangement, Harlow tipped the scales toward the one-board concept. Certainly House Speaker Ivor Boiarsky noted the opportunity presented by the WVU president, when he implored the finance committee to send to the floor some bill which would reorganize the administrative structure of higher education in West Virginia. To one observer on the scene it appeared that the opposition of West Virginia University supporters, who had previously blocked all attempts to reorganize higher education, became fragmented and ineffective after President Harlow endorsed the one-board concept.[1]

Local Morgantown papers attempted, half-heartedly, to stem the tide moving toward the super board. The *Morgantown Post* of February 7 expressed the opinion that since most state college presidents supported a super board, they must see it as a chance to help their schools at the expense of the University. Also rising to the defense of the state university, Monongalia County citizens on February 13 forwarded resolutions to Governor Moore indicating their opposition to the creation of a single board, their approval of the status quo in matters of higher education control, and their support for retention of the soft drinks tax as an exclusive funding item for the University Medical Center.

Yet Harlow's action had weakened such efforts. Conforming to Harlow's statements, the *Morgantown Post* found itself saying on February 17, "Although the one Board of Regents proposal isn't particularly objectionable, the need for it is a mystery and the evils it will cure are even more obscure." When one of the Monongalia representatives voted for the Board of Regents bill, the paper on February 21 styled the action a political necessity in order to prevent the passage of a multi-board bill, which conceivably would be more damaging to the University. Finally, the newspaper argued on March 6 that it was necessary to be for the one-board bill to prevent passage of a measure that would have channeled the pop tax for the University Medical Center into the general revenue fund.

When the bill creating the Board of Regents passed both houses on March 3, 1969, President Harlow praised the action: "This certainly is a milestone in the history of West Virginia education. It has great possibilities. I hope we can realize them." Speaking before the University faculty members a month later, he said there was no reason to view the new educational development with alarm. Noting that there might be some changes as a result of the new board's direction, he contended it would be good to work with a group that would have knowledge of the total higher educational program in West Virginia.

Before the change in governance, WVU had experienced one of the biggest construction booms in its history: the Creative Arts Center, Mountainlair, Allen Hall, the Chemistry Research Laboratory, two more dormitories, and the new Coliseum. In addition, it had in the works the proposed law building, an intensive care addition to University Hospital, and the second phase of the Creative Arts Center.

After the change in governance, construction at WVU slowed to a snail's pace and Harlow saw his two favorite projects scuttled: the Grumbein Island tunnel proposal and the computer-library complex. Speaking before a combined meeting of the Morgantown Rotary, Lions, and Kiwanis clubs on November 7, 1969, he warned that the portion of city growth attributable to University construction and student increase was about over. Noting that only the Law Center was due for construction in 1970, he even suggested that the new Board of Regents might decide to halt growth in the student body.

Changes other than a decided slowdown in construction and a possible enrollment curtailment were in store for the University. In an effort to bring all schools in line on the amount spent per student, percentage increases for Marshall University, the state colleges, and the new community colleges took place while percentage declines were instituted for the University. A tabulation of the percent of higher education state general revenue expenditures allocated to WVU showed that whereas the Heflin administration in 1967-68 had secured 50.75 of the total amount for WVU the Harlow administration consistently dropped in percentage terms year by year: 1968-69, 47.01 percent; 1969-70, 46.85 percent; 1970-71, 46.10 percent; 1971-72, 43.19 percent; 1972-73, 42.50 percent; 1973-74, 42.28 percent; 1974-75, 40.44 percent. Only a slight upturn was registered in 1975-76, with WVU procuring 40.88 percent, and in 1976-77, 41.06 percent.[2]

As the Board of Regents began to codify procedures under which all state universities and colleges were to operate, one of many early issues disturbing WVU, other than the all-important funding formula, was the manner in which promotion and tenure would be awarded to faculty members. Reviewing the policy decision drafts of the Board, one university administrator, Jay Barton, sensed that in the categories of research, teaching, and service by which faculty were considered for rewards, the new procedures centered on an "almost fanatical concern with teaching as the only professorial effort worth rewarding." Admitting his objection sounded strange coming from an officer titled Provost for Instruction, he nonetheless felt compelled to point out that the new policies were "heavily biased toward conditions and situations in small colleges in the State rather than the University."[3]

The Board did not endorse Barton's sentiments, and in its promulgations effectively undercut research and service as prerequisites for promotion and tenure. This, coupled with instituting review procedures of each recommending unit's verdict, caused an unfavorable opinion by the North Central accrediting review team, which endorsed Barton's view more than the new processes instituted by the Board of Regents that liberalized the gaining of tenure and promotion for all schools under its control.

WVU suffered not only loss in income and a dilution of measurement standards for faculty, but loss of its statewide centers. WVU affiliation with the Parkersburg Center ended on June 30, 1971, and the following day the school became Parkersburg Community College, reporting directly to the Board of Regents. The Kanawha Valley Graduate Center was removed from WVU control and management on July 1, 1972; henceforward the University's only branch was Potomac State College at Keyser where local opposition forced the Regents to abandon plans to convert it into a community college.

Losing control of its satellites throughout the state and policy control in a number of internal matters, Harlow asserted before the Faculty Assembly in his semi-annual State of the University address in 1973 that West Virginia University had been converted "from essentially a self-governing community of scholars to one very tightly controlled from the outside." In pinpointing the changes in governance, WVU's president referred directly to the establishment of the West Virginia Board of Regents on July 1, 1969, and the appointment in February, 1970, of WVU's first off-campus boss, Chancellor Prince B. Woodard. "WVU is now merely one of 14 institutions operated under Chancellor Woodard's direction," reported Harlow, "and the WVU president now gets his orders directly from the chancellor, who both issues instructions and reports board decisions and policies." For edification of the audience, Harlow counted off 29 directives and much updating and changing of the old Board of Governors' orders that had taken place after May, 1971.

Harlow also noted changes in his own office. Through various committees and councils, he observed that Chancellor Woodard kept in touch with campus constituencies such as the faculty and students so that "the chancellor and board are getting WVU information from many other sources than the president." With presidents left only general disciplinary and police functions, staff appointments, and basic budget management, Harlow commented that "the WVU president's decision-making functions have, during the last three years, moved from primarily discretionary functions to primarily ministerial functions. Under earlier presidencies, it was the other way around."

Unreported to the faculty was the evidence that over the years the correspondence between Harlow and Woodard deteriorated in the matter of mutual respect and trust. On December 16, 1971, Chancellor Woodard informed Harlow that full-time equivalent student enrollment credit hours on the Morgantown campus were inflated, and that after proper amendments to the budget material were made, he would discuss with Harlow the financial impact of the enrollment decreases. On April 5, 1972, Harlow bitterly complained to Woodard that the cancellation of part-time help would provoke a disaster at WVU and that a no-growth position in extension and research for the second successive year would "say things" to the WVU staff that the Chancellor and the Board perhaps would not want to have said. Charging that recent proposals by the Chancellor reflected an effort to channel new money into student-related services, especially into instruction, Harlow remarked that "This is indeed a commendable effort especially for those institutions of West Virginia higher education whose function is almost wholly instruction. For your only comprehensive university, however, it is an effort which will produce a disaster."

The president was not alone in feeling discomfited, if not sometimes humiliated, by the changeover from the Board of Governors to the Board of Regents. On December 17, 1972, the Senate Executive Committee recommended to the Senate that approval be given to appoint a special committee to examine broad problems of University governance and to report its findings back to the Senate. Among considerations motivating the recommendation were "changing patterns of University control by central boards and legislatures." At the outset of the exercise, the Senate was more than agreeable to receiving input on the subject.

Appointing an ad hoc committee of two political science professors, one professor of law, one economist, and the president of the student body, the Senate placed into existence on January 15, 1973, a new university governance committee which spent the rest of the semester interviewing primarily officers of the University administration. When its findings were readied on June 12, 1973, they therefore were viewed as expressing the sentiments of WVU officialdom, if not necessarily the Senate itself.

Picturing West Virginia University as having long enjoyed semi-autonomy and the preeminent position among institutions of higher education within the state, the committee characterized the 1969-73 years of very close external control and supervision over all aspects of the University's functions by the Board of Regents "a traumatic experience to personnel of the University accustomed to exercising a greater degree of professional discretion, judgment, and authority, and to participating in a consultative capacity in the formulation of policy decisions by the governing board."

The committee said the more serious criticisms made had arisen from the Board of Regents' apparent decision to function as an administrative agency that tightly controlled and operated the institutions on almost a day-to-day basis in a nondifferentiating pattern through a very small administrative staff reporting only once a month to the Board in formal meetings. The committee noted: "Fears were expressed that all state institutions of higher education will eventually be cast by the Board of Regents' policies into a single uniform mold with a leveling and stultifying effect."

For good measure, the committee listed nine of the more serious criticisms made of the Board:

1. It had requested too much information too soon on short notice from institutions not equipped to gather and submit reliable data with the speed desired.

2. When a request for Board action or approval was denied, no explanation or rationale for the rejection was given.

3. There was insufficient prior consultation with interested institutions before detailed guidelines or policy bulletins were issued.

4. The Board staff was very small and many doubted its competency to handle so many minute details of the internal affairs of the institutions.

5. Too many controls had been placed on academic programs and programming, with the result that, "It's astounding that a community of scholars should be instructed not to think about new programs without prior Board approval."

6. Decisions on appointments and promotions were not a province of the Board of Regents and should be left to the institutions and their faculties.

7. Funding formulas based on FTE (full-time teaching equivalents) short-changed graduate programs, which by their very nature were more expensive than conventional undergraduate programs.

8. There was evidence of little institutional input into the Board's decisions.

9. The Board's staff did not possess the requisite technological competence and experience to make meaningful evaluations of a large proportion of the grant applications submitted from West Virginia University to funding agencies.

Before the University Senate was made aware of the criticisms, the Chancellor and members of the Board of Regents were forced to consider these WVU complaints. According to the Board President, Frederick P. Stamp, Jr., the Board of Regents first was made aware of the report when members of a legislative committee studying the organization and administration of the Board cited statements from the report in an open legislative hearing. In a letter to President Harlow, an exasperated Stamp disputed all charges of the committee that had been provided the Legislature and asked that this refutation be provided all members of the University Senate Executive Committee.

The Board President, carefully cataloguing all criticism, rebutted all charges in numerical order:

1. When requested data could not be provided in a reliable manner, such data were not used for planning purposes by the Board.

2. Whenever the Board denied an institutional request (which was seldom), the president of the concerned institution had been fully advised of the reasons.

3. Prior to the adoption of policy matters, the Board had always sought

the advice of the Advisory Council of Public College Presidents, which met at least ten times each year.

4. The Board staff was indeed small, did not handle minute details of an institution's internal affairs, and had delegated to the president such responsibilities.

5. No member of a faculty had been instructed not to think about new programs, and the president was only required to inform the Board when an institution began to plan for additions or deletions to academic programs.

6. The Board had delegated to the president of each institution full responsibility for all hiring, setting of salaries, and promotions of all personnel on his campus.

7. The Board's funding formulas for instruction always had reflected a recognition of the high cost of graduate programs.

8. The Board had given extensive consideration to advice, proposals, and recommendations from all advisory groups.

9. Only grant proposals relating to new academic programs had required prior approval by the Board before submission by the institution to a potential funding agency, and these involved an extremely limited number of proposals.

Harlow placed the Board's refutations before the Senate Executive Committee on October 29, 1973. In a reply to Stamp three days later, Harlow and the Executive Committee beat a hasty retreat when the president wrote that none felt competent to respond in detail to the Regents' comments on the report of the ad hoc committee on University governance because, "None of us was privy to the hearings of the Ad Hoc Committee, to the writing sessions, or to the editorial sessions which produced the final report, and the report was presented to the Senate during my absence from the office due to illness."

With no assistance forthcoming from the president or the Senate Executive Committee, the ad hoc committee absolved itself. In company with the WVU president and its own executive committee, the University Senate, which had commissioned the report, adopted none of the recommendations set forth. Mike Connor, former student body president and member of the committee on university governance, stood alone in his advocacy of further pursuing the question of governance. As he saw it, in his undated letter to members of the West Virginia University Senate:

A decision not to adopt the Report and/or a significant change in the structure of University governance would be, in my opinion, both self-defeating and hypocritical . . . . My only hope is that the Senate-commissioned study will not be filed and forgotten. It would be a great disappointment to see the Senate default on this important issue by maintaining its already ineffective status quo.

Despite the fact that Harlow both viewed and admitted his own presi-

Dedication of Mountaineer statue in front of Mountainlair in 1971.

dency as reduced in power and now defined essentially as an in-house position rather than one concerned with the external affairs of state, Harlow had continued to expand the presidential office by incorporating into its staff a provost for planning, a provost for instruction, a provost for research and graduate studies, and a provost for administration and finance. In describing the unique arrangement, he stated in his 1970-71 annual report that the many-provosted office "marks final operational transition from the one-man presidential responsibility used by most universities in day-to-day operation to operation by a presidential team. It is an organizational response to the highly publicized loads of today's university presidency."

In the early days of his presidency, a few of those destined for provostships were then titled vice-presidents. In a speech before the Charleston Rotary Club on December 8, 1967, Harlow noted that he had referred to two vice-presidents in the course of his talk. "As you know," he said, "vice-presidents are a disease of large organizations; they multiply endlessly, and are controlled only through the greatest effort. We already have five at WVU, and we'll shortly have a sixth."

In 1974, the North Central Association looked upon the organization of the central administration, with six provosts serving as staff to the president, but with none having line responsibility, as unusual. It noted that such an organization created some confusion as to which officers were empowered to make certain decisions, that it was frequently perceived as slow to react, with many faculty believing the central administration was overstaffed.

But despite this rebuff, Harlow's office continued to grow. On the eve of his departure from the presidency, Chancellor Ben L. Morton wrote to Harlow on July 7, 1976, about receiving general complaints of a "fairly major augmentation and reorganization that has transpired in two provost offices." Understanding that two associate provost positions had been created, the Chancellor agreed the president had the delegated authority from the Board to make such modifications. "However," he asked, "one does have to wonder, why now?"

With a change in the chancellorship in 1974 (Prince Woodard to Ben Morton), the Harlow administration fared a little better both in appropriations and in construction. Capital construction monies were expended on such items as air conditioning for the central Library, an electrical service-underway and substation for the hospital, steam lines on the Evansdale Campus, fire escapes for Stewart Hall and the central Library, and remodeling of the historic buildings in Woodburn Circle.

During these years, the Harlow administration did achieve the largest federal expenditure of money on a single University project ever obtained in the institution's history: the Personal Rapid Transit System. Before the first phase of the operation was completed, costs had soared to $128 million on a project originally envisioned as costing $18 million, and the story of West Virginia University's computer-directed "people mover" system attracted international attention.

The PRT was the brainchild of Samy E. G. Elias, an Egyptian-born professor with a bachelor's degree in aerospace engineering from Cairo University and advanced graduate degrees in engineering from Texas A & M and Oklahoma State University. Confounded by the traffic jams in the University city upon his arrival in 1965, Elias proposed in the federally financed seminars on mass transit at WVU and to the U.S. Department of Housing and Urban Development in June, 1967, that an automated, computer-controlled, aerially designed and elevated transit system replace the University's bus system by linking WVU's Downtown Campus with the Evansdale Campus and the Medical Center.

During an eighteen-month transition from Lyndon Johnson to Richard Nixon, accompanied by the creation of a new federal department and agency, the Department of Transportation and the Urban Mass Transportation Administration (UMTA), Elias impatiently waited for an answer to his proposal that the national government aid small cities, as well as the large urban centers, in their efforts to convince the inhabitants to minimize the use of automobiles. With no communications forthcoming from the newly created and staffed agencies, the professor took his problem to President Harlow, who, in turn, contacted the district's veteran congressman, Harley O. Staggers, for assistance.

Staggers, chairman of the House Interstate and Foreign Commerce Committee, President Harlow, and Professor Elias, now chairman of the WVU Department of Industrial Engineering, consulted directly with John Volpe, U.S. Secretary of Transportation, about the possibility of a mass transit demonstration project for the University. Volpe, eager to translate into action theoretical transportation alternatives for the automobile-loving, gas-consuming American public, was enthusiastic. The project looked good: its educational advocates were convincing because Harlow displayed a scientific bent and Elias was an experienced transportation specialist who had developed a method for using computers to schedule buses in several major American cities. And it certainly could not be wrong to undertake an experiment in the home district of a congressman whose committee helped determine allocations for the new Department of Transportation.[4]

On June 20, 1969, UMTA announced that, with a University matching contribution of $32,600, it would finance a $100,900 feasibility study for a mass transit system for the University community. In March, 1970, UMTA added $20,000 to the grant. The University study, completed that summer, recommended a mass transit system consisting of six stations, 100 computer-controlled, driverless vehicles with speeds up to 30 mph, and 3.6 miles of guideway, with the Alden Self-Transit Systems Corporation of Bedford, Massachusetts, which had a prototype of such a system already available, as the producer. The estimated cost was $18 million, with the University absorbing $4.5 million (in land costs) and UMTA $13.5 million (in construction and operating costs). By linking the Downtown Campus of the University and the city of Morgantown, which had few parking places for automobiles and was experiencing severe traffic tie-ups, to giant parking lots at the Coliseum and the Medical Center, such a system would reduce traffic congestion, aid the school in its tight class scheduling problems across unconnected campuses, and serve as a demonstration model for towns and cities throughout the United States.

No sooner did public officials announce the actuality of the PRT for WVU and Morgantown than the Department of Transportation decided that its agency, UMTA, rather than the University, would stage and control the experiment. Perhaps this was deemed necessary because the PRT represented the first effort by DOT to apply technology and management techniques borrowed from the aerospace industry to a major rapid transit system. Funding the People Mover as one of its own research and development projects, the newest federal department in a President's cabinet relegated Elias to the role of consultant, cast aside the Alden Self-Transit system the University had recommended as systems manager in favor of Cal Tech's Jet Propulsion Laboratory (JPL), and appointed the Boeing Company as vehicle designer. When JPL quit as systems manager in April, 1971, because of cost controversies, DOT in July named as the new systems manager the already involved Boeing Company, which had just narrowly lost by congressional action the supersonic transport contract.

By 1971, the original $18 million cost projection had soared to an estimated $37.4 million. Facing congressional uproar, UMTA scaled down the PRT to three stations and 2.2 miles of guideway at a projected lowered cost of $28.3 million to help Boeing meet an October, 1972, dedication date. The reduced system, which would permit students to travel between downtown Morgantown and two campuses, now was referred to as Phase I and would be charged to UMTA's budget for research and development; Phase II, which would approximate the original plan of permitting students to travel to all campuses but would not begin until Phase I was completed, was expected to be financed from the agency's capital-grants assistance program. Volpe, a tight scheduler, had insisted at the original announcement of the project that he would be a passenger in one of the vehicles one year later.

President Nixon also was operating under a tight timetable. To demonstrate its commitment to urban areas, the Nixon administration settled on an October 25, 1972, official opening, with Nixon's daughter, Mrs. Tricia Nixon Cox, in attendance, a date significantly only two weeks before the national presidential election. With crews working around the clock for several weeks before Tricia arrived, the PRT did open.

In retrospect, James G. Harlow was to note in the September 8, 1975, issue of *Railway Age* that the PRT simply was not operationally ready at the dedication, but "there was a considerable political component in the time schedule that was forced on it, and the time schedule did interfere with sound engineering practice." He recalled that on its dedication date its vehicles were "bread-boarded" in, and everything "jerry-rigged" in order to transport political passengers in the trial before the television cameras.

Contemporary observers were far quicker to pass political judgments at the moment of the actual dedication than were the dignitaries who had assembled on the platform in the fall of 1972. On October 25, 1972, the *Daily Athenaeum*, for example, saw the ceremony as primarily a political rally because of the presence of so many politicians, the daughter of the President, the anti-war protesters who were heckling the speakers, and the Young Republicans for Nixon who were attempting to silence the hecklers.

Following the colorful ceremony and speeches, President Harlow accom-

Personal Rapid Transit System, a national research and demonstration project funded by the U.S. Department of Transportation, connects downtown Morgantown and the WVU campuses. The PRT features driver-less, computer-directed cars powered by electricity.

panied the dignitaries on an experimental ride. Unfortunately, the three vehicles traveled only a mile down the guideways instead of the required 2.2 miles, and the car carrying Professor Elias and members of the press crew broke down and had to be towed off the track. The press demanded explanations for failure. One associate administrator, Robert A. Hemmes, who was later fired, offered one to *The Washington Post* on June 2, 1974, "We tried to build the system before we had fully designed it. It's called 'concurrency planning' which is taken from the A-bomb program and means you design all the pieces and hope it fits together later. So we designed the guideway, before we had the vehicles."

The year 1973, following the dedication, was relatively quiet with respect to the project, as the Boeing Company returned to testing. However, it discovered the need for many changes, and these proved expensive. UMTA announced that the reduced system, known as Phase I (A), with its three stations (Walnut Street, Beechurst Avenue, and the Engineering complex),

2.2 miles of guideway, five vehicles, research and development software, and test evaluation, would nonetheless be completed June 30, 1973, at a cost of $40.4 million, and that Phase I (B), with a complete demonstration and all vehicles in operation over the three-station, 2.2-mile system, would be available for acceptance testing in 1974 at an additional cost of $19.4 million. The two phases, (A) and (B) together, with a request for a federal grant for operating assistance in its first year, had now escalated to a cost of over $64.3 million, with WVU to take over Phase I of the system in 1975.

By 1973, the Department of Transportation, faced with unfavorable attention in the press, was tiring of the project that *The New York Times* had described as a classic monument to technical miscalculations and political expediencies. New staff members, in turn, were doubting the wisdom of continuing the project beyond Phase I (A) and (B). Robert Clement, DOT's undersecretary, candidly stated in *Engineering News-Record* of November 29, 1973:

Early, in the beginning of this department, too much emphasis was placed on creating toys without any question of whether there would be a specific market for the project. It's no secret that this Administration is dissatisfied with Morgantown. It's another toy. In no way are we disenchanted with PRTs. But we are very disenchanted with Morgantown.

Another dissatisfied staff member, appalled at the price escalation of the project, suggested to *The New York Times* on April 13, 1974, that for a much smaller cost the agency could "give up plans for the transit line and issue every student an electric golf cart for travel on the elevated guideway." When that was rejected, the next proposal was to use "Disneyland-style tram trains" on the guideways.

As the University became aware of DOT's desire to complete Phase I and disappear from the project, its spokesmen began to formulate reasons for the project's extension. Most of them centered on the costs of operation that would fall upon the University with an incomplete system. Phase I, University spokesmen pointed out, would serve only an estimated 3.5 million passengers per year compared to an estimated 14.5 million persons who would use a completed system. Because Phase I served only a minority of students, the University could not levy a toll on all students. In addition, the University still would have to maintain an intercampus bus system. Observers carefully pointed out that the Phase I transit system had failed to reach either of the two destination points, both large parking areas, visualized in the original scheme.

An agreement between WVU and DOT concerning Phase I of the PRT project stated that upon its successful completion, the University essentially had the right to accept or reject the system — if rejected, DOT would be obliged to remove the system and restore the site to its original condition.

DOT administrators charged that WVU was threatening to invoke a breach of contract before any known violation had occurred. Believing WVU was involved in an effort to secure the system's extension, DOT suggested that the sum of $7 million would be better expended for demolition than for the completion of Phase I of the system which the University might expect.

The University rested its case for not permitting DOT to remove itself from the project after completing Phase I on the incomplete nature of the experiment. It faced DOT in a war of nerves by also suggesting demolition because it would be better to have nothing than just Phase I. To the press and to Congress, Harlow was particularly adept in his remarks that "the system as it now stands will satisfy neither of its prime objectives. It won't handle Morgantown's traffic problems and it won't serve as a viable test nationally of the value of PRTs."[5] He chastised those who originally had over-promised the PRT's capabilities, as well as those who now thought in terms of small expense when he said: "It was going to be very much of a worldwide first that was going to do everything from hauling freight around Tokyo to uplifting the black ghetto in New York. The money it would take for the government to finish this project is trifling compared to what it spent without blinking on the Vietnam War." Pretending that the University was quite willing to have Phase I demolished, Harlow bitingly said that: "We're quite willing to have it removed. Because of political considerations, we're so far removed from the original concept of providing a system to compete with the automobile that all we have left is a test track for some hardware."

A compromise between DOT and WVU was essential, and administrators from DOT were the first to give. Said Frank Herringer, who believed that the differences could be worked out: "I hope we can reach some kind of compromise. I certainly don't want to tear this thing down. That wouldn't help Morgantown. It wouldn't help the University. And it would be throwing away 64 million dollars." Suggesting that if the University would accept something less than a six-station system, build some new parking lots, and run a few shuttle buses to the farthest part of the campus, Herringer believed that the agency would be able to help with a capital grant. In May, 1975, UMTA agreed to complete a five-station system and provide 33 more PRT cars at an additional cost of $63.6 million. The University agreed to abandon the proposed Coliseum station.

By 1977, three things were certain about the PRT experiment. First, James G. Harlow, who liked scientific projects, had been given a project tremendously satisfying to one so inclined. Second, the money expended on the project by the federal government made up for the lack of money currently being expended on the University by the state government. And, third, as the *Dominion News* had predicted on September 25, 1970, in the early stages of the PRT development, "the eyes of the United States and indeed the world will be focused on the University city in the next few years as the urban transportation 'People-Mover' is designed and put to a test."

In 1977, however, it was still uncertain as to who would pay for its operating costs. Such costs were estimated at $1.3 million a year, far greater than the University bus system cost of $200,000. They were not acceptable to students, who had indicated on several occasions they did not wish to bear them. When the Board of Regents presented a request to the Legislature for a special subsidy on March 20, 1977, the House and Senate said they were not interested. It remained to be seen if state government would come to the rescue of the project by underwriting the fares, as the federal government had previously come to the rescue by constructing the PRT.

An Era of Radical Change:
Close Encounters with a New Kind of Student

IN THE FIRST YEAR OF the Harlow presidency, Jennings Randolph, senior U.S. senator representing the thirty-fifth state, paid glowing tribute to college students in West Virginia institutions whom he saw as wholesome young people who thought clearly and knew why they were in residence. Into the *Congressional Record* he inserted an editorial from the University's student newspaper entitled, "How long are we going to allow leftist infiltration to mock "This Is My Own, My Native Land?'" as evidence of their Americanism, conservatism, and erudition. The University city's like-minded evening newspaper, the *Morgantown Post,* on November 6, 1967, applauded the senator's praise of diligent young scholars, joined in a salute to the students, yet grudgingly and circumspectly withheld total approbation with the modifying phrase, "or at least a part of them."

Within a matter of months, the outgoing West Virginia Board of Governors sought to prepare the incoming West Virginia Board of Regents for "an era of radical change" when it captured the current campus mood with its valedictory statement of June 29, 1969: "Students have already acquired substantial freedom and responsibility; they undoubtedly will achieve more."

University administrators and governing boards seemingly were aware that students outside West Virginia, who had been shaping the educational policies of their institutions from Columbia University in the east to the University of California at Berkeley in the west, inevitably would influence their counterparts in West Virginia in ways foreign to Senator Randolph and older residents.

The WVU educational hierarchy cautiously moved to accommodate its institutional family of parents, alumni, faculty, students, and friends from within and without the Mountain State to a more modern world of alienation, where the younger generation might on the one hand become activists in an attempt to rectify or modify the inequities of the entire world, or, on the other hand, withdraw from life's participation through the use of marijuana, LSD, heroin, or other mind-blowing drugs. As best they could, administrators readied themselves for the onslaught of the student of the late sixties who entertained new modes of conduct, behavior, language, dress, and hair style, and remained skeptical of all authority, whether religious, parental, or educational.

To provide parents, alumni, and friends a vision of the wide diversity of students found on university campuses in the late sixties, the new *West Virginia University Magazine* in its 1969 summer issue splashed in full color on its cover an assemblage of mods, hippies, playboys, activists, and squares. Explaining that the posed photograph made no attempt to show the proportion of such groups to the mainstream of the student body, the editors also made certain in their notes to readers that readers not necessarily assume that the models' true personalities or interests were revealed by the clothing or the hair styles they wore.

The response to the cover was understandably mixed. In the fall issue of 1969, one reader was pleased to know that the colorful and realistic portrayal of students on the front cover meant that money appropriated for the University was not totally confined to a perpetuation of nineteenth-century ideals. Another was certain the cover would shake up "some of the old grads" but recognized that the student portrayal honestly reflected changes taking place all over the country, even including West Virginia. A third, who believed that "the lack of acceptance by people of people who are different" was the country's current weakness, was convinced that the cover was designed as "a plea for the acceptance of such differences."

But there were others of an opposite opinion who asked that their free subscriptions to the magazine be canceled and informed the University of the withdrawal of their support. One "old grad" wanted to know if, in placing the hippies in the forefront and the clean-cuts in the background of the posed photograph, the University was signaling its preferences for certain kinds of students, and disdain of others. If the intent was "to arouse the Establishment from its apathy," suggested another subscriber, the magazine had achieved success because one of its alumni was quickly rushing to the medicine cabinet for the aid of a Rolaid after witnessing the campus scene.

Following World War II, WVU had only 6,000 students, including many mature veterans. President Irvin Stewart easily contained trouble by his personal and informal involvement with a Council of Student Administration and his rapport with student leaders. President Paul Miller had acknowledged growing student and faculty dissatisfaction with the segregation practices in American society by openly questioning and forcefully modifying the roles played by the elitist sorority and fraternity factions on campus. Similarly, Acting President Harry B. Heflin had anticipated public discontent with the escalation of the war in Vietnam by ending compulsory ROTC training for University males, a decision unthinkable to President Elvis Stahr, who, on his way to becoming Secretary of the Army, could not have personally afforded compromise on the military provisions of the Morrill Act establishing land-grant institutions.

In his early stewardship, President James G. Harlow, with an eye on the new rules of dispensing federal aid to education so that minority rights would be protected, carefully reaffirmed the University's stand on civil rights by asserting there would be no discrimination in University housing or dormitories. University policy was clear, he said. "We are nondiscriminatory in everything we do, as far as it is organizationally possible." Noting on May 28, 1968, that he would try to solve problems or conflicts before they became critical, whether they emanated from the student body or the better-organized maintenance staff, he distanced himself somewhat from personal confrontation when he appointed the Reverend Stacy Groscup, a local Methodist minister, to the special position of University ombudsman.

In an editorial entitled "The University's attempt at philosophical equality," the *Dominion News* on September 15, 1970, praised Harlow's "prudent" action in calling attention of students and faculty to what he called "days of special concern." The president requested the faculty to excuse absences and to avoid scheduling examinations or field trips on February 21, Malcolm X's assassination; March 27, Good Friday; April 4, Martin Luther King's assassination; April 20, the first day of Passover. Ten years later, the University Senate was still debating the validity of University-recognized "days of special concern," with Professor Armand E. Singer suggesting to the University Senate on April 9, 1979, that it might be sacrilegious to mix religious holidays with days to honor people who stood for certain causes. However, the Senate reaffirmed the observances selected the decade before, but suggested further study on the matter because black students might not still maintain "a continuing concern for observing the birthdate of Malcolm X."

Harlow also appeared in the guise of an up-to-date executive when he declared on April 15, 1970, to the *Dominion News* that "no issue touches our lives more personally than environmental pollution." Appointing a University Council on Environmental Pollution, approving an inter-disciplinary course on "Man and His Environment," asking the Coal Research Bureau in the School of Mines to suggest ways of reducing air pollution, and prohibiting the burning of trash, Harlow committed the University to the elimination of its own environmental pollution "in the shortest possible time." As a first priority, he called for converting the Medical Center heating plant from coal to natural gas. In the 1970s, however, in a period of natural gas shortages and Arab oil embargoes, Harlow quietly and temporarily resumed the use of coal. If Harlow in the early stages of his presidency was to minimize ecological disadvantages in his policy decisions, he was to max-imize the conversion to coal in later years as advantageous to students in that calendars providing for an extended break between semesters to con-serve natural gas were not as necessary at WVU as they were on other univer-sity campuses.

But the more pragmatic decisions of his later years as president were not the original portrayals in his early years as the up-to-date chief executive officer of West Virginia University. A national campus tension study on March 19, 1970, lauded West Virginia University in its late 1960s attempt to reduce the probability of student dissatisfactions. The appointment of a black student adviser in 1969, the naming of students to serve on all search committees for new academic deans, as well as the appointment of innumer-able student representatives to a variety of University committees, seemed evidence of a new kind of representative democracy at the state university, all carefully displayed in the University's annual reports of those years.

The student newspaper noted that as a result of Harlow's responsiveness there were black studies courses, black cheerleaders, and an increase in the percentage of black employees. Attention was directed to his approval of controversial speakers despite off-campus opposition, and his endorsement of a limited pass-fail system for students. Said the *Daily Athenaeum* on August 6, 1970, "Harlow obviously believes in debate and discussion and change, but within a democratic framework."

One such opportunity for student discussion lay in WVU's Free Univer-sity, a series of non-credit evening courses on campus that later influenced the development of multi-disciplinary courses and produced modifications in the core curriculum. When members of the Board of Governors and several alumni indicated that they were somewhat concerned about the Free Univer-sity, Harlow quickly put their fears to rest when he wrote one of them on December 31, 1968:

I must confess that I do not see much threat in the 'Free University.' This is not the far-left Free University of New York City; it is merely a series of evening meetings staffed by volunteers drawn mostly from our own faculty, though some outsiders are involved, and so far as I can tell, they are much closer to the old faculty-student bull sessions which you and I knew so well than they are to the radical 'Free University.' I regard them as curriculum probes and I think that some very good things might come out of them, if we don't get too excited.

In all probability, freedom-loving students were more personally pleased with the Harlow administration for lifting the curfew hours than they were with innumerable committee assignments, wearisome tasks best relegated to faculty who received remuneration for such routine services; a stand on civil rights not particularly bothersome to a student body containing a small percentage of blacks; an enumeration in the school calendar of days of concern; or with the president's original clarion call to rid the University of pollution. The Associated Women Students, backed by other campus organizations, fought for and won the battle for an identical privilege of a no-hours policy long enjoyed by male students at West Virginia University. Responding to the female vote of thanks, Harlow said via the *Morgantown Post* of April 23, 1969, "I am heartily in favor of the principle that men and women students should be governed by the same regulations. The principle of equal rights for women and men, with no discrimination, is a hope for the future of West Virginia University."

The outgoing Board of Governors was not as heartened by the change as the president. Forrest Kirkpatrick, speaking for the Board's Committee on Educational Policy and Planning, believed the president's modification of hours for women, as announced on April 23, 1969, violated a Board directive, was illegal, and directly contradicted the intent of a majority of the Board. Harlow was stunned and properly apologetic. His abject excuse to the Board was that he had interpreted its decision of April 19th to accept his recommendation for broadening the Board's statement of non-discrimination to include non-discrimination in regulations with respect to sex. This meant, he thought, that the Board intended to take no action in the matter of women's hours but had passed discretionary action to him. Expressing deep regret for misreading Board intentions, President Harlow promised to attend more closely to Board sentiment in the future.[1] No doubt the University president, with the ending of Board of Governors' control, was comforted by a decision concerning the regulation of students' hours that had been reserved for him and all other presidents of public colleges and universities by the new Board of Regents. Then he discovered that there was, after all, minimal public reaction to the daring policy.

The liberated women of the University began to achieve victories on other fronts as well during the Harlow years. Responding to the efforts of

Marjorie Dean and Charlotte Rolston who threatened to sue their law faculty advisers, Dean Paul Selby of the College of Law recommended on February 13, 1970, that the two professional legal fraternities accept female law students in order to retain University recognition. In accordance with an April, 1972, memorandum from President Harlow, the all-male marching band opened its ranks to any University student. Nineteen women immediately applied for membership and Don Wilcox, band director, reckoned the change cost $14,000 for new uniforms and equipment.

In 1973-74, women students broadened intercollegiate athletics when the Mountaineer schedule for the first time featured women's teams in tennis, basketball, and gymnastics. Even the tradition of all-male managers for sports teams ended when in the spring of 1973 the baseball and track teams boasted female managers. At home baseball games, the audiences had accustomed themselves to four bat girls. Within the Southern Conference, WVU had been pioneering in "creeping liberation" for several years by utilizing women on both its varsity rifle and swimming teams, and in enticing outstanding high school female rifle shots to the highly ranked University rifle team by reserving scholarships for women.

By the mid-seventies, after the student body had upset a trend by electing a student body president who didn't belong to a social fraternity for the first time in twenty-nine years, it completely broke historical tradition by electing for the first time a woman, Lea Anderson, as its president. Running on a platform calling for programs to ease discrimination against student spouses, Anderson had an easy victory after a difficult campaign. "My campaign posters were defaced and I had late night obscene phone calls," Ms. Anderson remembered, but it made victory for her all the more meaningful.[2] Without equivocation, the new student body president believed in equal pay for equal work, and equality of the sexes.

Students also showed keen interest in having beer sold in Mountainlair, particularly when student government scouts discovered that beer had been made available to students in the nearby Jesuit institution, Wheeling College.

The Board of Governors on December 16, 1967, said "no" to beer on campus in a decision announced in January, 1968. Responded the *Beckley Post-Herald*, January 17, 1968, regarding the action "from a bunch of old fuddy-duddies" that had made fools of themselves: "They had a golden opportunity to encourage the students to stay on campus and under proper supervision to enjoy a beer. So they muffed it but good. The students will spread out all around the campus for miles and more of them will get into trouble (driving, if not otherwise) than would have been the case."

The change in control from the Board of Governors to the Board of Regents provided students with a new opportunity to press the Mountainlair beer sale issue and harass the administration. The president reported to the new Chancellor in the fall of 1971 that he was in agreement with the position of the WVU Advisory Board as reported on April 19, 1971, "which is to say that I am opposed to the sale of beer on the University campus or on other University property." But a telephone call from Chancellor Prince Woodard on September 17, 1971, disclosed that a higher authority, the Board of Regents, had resolved to authorize beer sales on the campus of public colleges and universities "if when and in the manner authorized by the President of the institution," although no reference whatsoever had been made to the president's recommendations and opinions on the sale of beer at a recent open meeting of the Board. Faced with the Chancellor's verdict which had blown his cover, Harlow responded to his administrative aides that he now had no alternative but to authorize the sale of beer.[3] But students had to await the 1980 decade before beer was permitted in dormitories. Not until January 18, 1980, was an Evansdale tavern opened in the snack bar of the Towers Residence Halls.

Student independence did not always mean total separation from the University parent. By a one-vote margin, journalism faculty recommended separating the *Daily Athenaeum* from the School of Journalism. A majority of the faculty had become increasingly embarrassed by what they considered to be the *DA's* radicalism and believed it no longer could serve as an effective educational tool. The vote was also affected by the fact that the faculty sought relief from supervisory duties because of the increase in journalism enrollment.

DA editors and a minority of journalism faculty believed the separation was an administration plot to abolish a troublesome student newspaper. After the faculty vote, the *DA* was placed under a student-faculty Committee on Student Publications, and, despite the early prophecies of doom, continued to prosper as an independent student newspaper.

President Harlow began to come into confrontation with activist students when, in connection with Vietnam Day on October 15, 1969, he declared on September 26 that he and the University were without a position on the moratorium observance. In response two days later, the *Daily Athenaeum*, discovering that it was as skilled in phrase-making as the University president, entitled one of its editorials of the period: "James G. Harlow — When the Name on the Door Should Mean More."

Even if the University president did not agree, the student newspaper believed it a moral imperative that the University community take a stand against the war in Vietnam. Calling the moratorium observance an imminent priority because it served as a protest against the war, American involvement in distant lands, and the needless death of both Americans and Vietnamese, the paper argued that one could not remain silent on issues which caused such widespread death and violence. It demanded the right of all students to be absent from classes on such a solemn occasion.

Harlow refused cancellation and informed the local chapter of the National Vietnam Moratorium Committee, "The University will not coerce those who don't agree with the committee's position in observing its proposed moratorium, nor will it coerce those who share the position of the committee." He also declined to take a personal stand, saying, "I do not take positions on public issues because the public does not separate me or my office from the institution." Among other demands he denied was the lowering of University flags to half-mast. The student newspaper flatly disagreed with presidential neutrality and found it refreshing to see so many students involved in campus and national issues. "Courage in one's convictions has become evident at WVU this fall," it said on October 14, 1969, and "students are informed as they have never been before, and they care as they never have before."

Sensing trouble, the more conservatively oriented local newspaper, the *Morgantown Post*, on October 1, 1969, believed the time had now come to identify the radical elements on campus, and to ponder the possibility of confrontation on campus. It listed four obviously "radical" groups that might propel violence: the Mountaineer Freedom Party (MFP); the Student Activist League (SAL); the American Civil Liberties Union (ACLU); and the Young Americans for Freedom (YAF). The first three it designated as left wing, to which might be joined the Graduate Society and the History Society. The last it viewed as a right-wing group whose members, the editor said, were prepared "to crush the hippies and their communistic takeover." It offered other definitions of the group: the MFP, the least radical, wanted more rights for blacks and the abolition of grades; SAL believed in the "politics of confrontation"; the ACLU was the most clandestine organization which took its battles to court. As to whether confrontation would result, the paper did not know, but it quoted Scott Bills of the SAL as saying, "I really don't see the possibility of a student riot here. Our purpose is to radicalize the campus, but though I don't eliminate any possibility, I sincerely doubt there will be a confrontation here."

Despite the *Morgantown Post*'s show of worry, the October 15 moratorium at WVU was without incident and confirmed the opinion of student activist Bills. A movie, "In the Day of the Pig," a "Teach-In," lectures at a "Freedom School," a fast and vigil on Memorial Plaza, followed by a memorial service and the placing of a wreath in honor of the dead on Courthouse Square, a concert for peace, and a candlelight service comprised the events.

Outside reports were also made of Moratorium observances across the United States, and Morgantown did not escape notice. Nicholas Von Hoffman, syndicated news columnist, accompanied CBS crews to the WVU campus, as the network prepared "a piece showing that the great unhappiness even had gotten to this campus of obedient children." Von Hoffman readily agreed that even here were to be found a small but respectable percentage of people "on this football and fraternity campus" sick enough about the war to manifest their feelings.[4] Von Hoffman disagreed with his television colleagues, however, that the WVU community was doing "new" things because the war issue was affecting their lives. Admitting that he did see the erosion of some discipline, a few changes which were more advanced on other campuses, and that "long hair, sideburns and beards" had arrived in Morgantown, he still spotted as symptomatic of clinging to "old" ways many girls in jumpers and boys in sta-press pants. Such costuming persisted, Von Hoffman believed, because "this is a campus where the Greeks dominate, a campus of the '40s and 50s." Von Hoffman summarized:

This place strikes you as still essentially authoritarian. You imagine that students prefer to memorize and give back on exams. You can see that even at the pre-Moratorium mass meeting where most of the speakers were didactic sounding members of the faculty. Such a meeting would be impossible at, say, the University of Michigan.

Nonetheless, Von Hoffman was encouraged by some things he witnessed in Morgantown. The moratorium statements of the Interfraternity Council president bespoke of the life which had taken hold of the more avant-garde campuses, and the fraternity crowd had not yet beaten up the Moratorium sponsors because they did not want to be seen as "a bunch of empty-headed snobs." To Von Hoffman, the local scene demonstrated that Washington's men of power had to learn that getting angry at the population was an inappropriate response to challenges of their authority.

Harlow, however, was not amenable to Von Hoffman's advice not to appear authoritarian or aloof. He issued on January 26, 1970, a statement which sternly warned, in effect, that any student attempt to disrupt University business as usual would "call into question a student's right to continue his enrollment." Although the University welcomed responsible and constructive criticism, he said, any effort to disrupt the University or coerce its officials would bring prosecution as well as suspension or expulsion to the students involved. The University Senate unanimously approved the president's statement within the month. The statement also was endorsed by the Board of Regents. Actually, the campus remained contented for a little while longer with Harlow principally channeling direct requests to himself from the SAL to the Student Government Association. In the meantime, by means of an intra-fund transfer, the president readied himself with new defense equipment for his office; two built-in siren alarms.[5]

Although the quiescent student body showed little interest in storming Harlow's inner sanctum, campus opinion on national issues remained constant. In mid-April, WVU students took part in a nationwide student vote on what action the United States should take with respect to its Vietnam foreign policy. Of the 597 students who voted, 288 called for immediate troop withdrawal from Vietnam, 184 for gradual withdrawal, and 44 for escalation of the war.

Again, national events broke the serenity of many college campuses, including WVU. During the first week of May, which coincided with final exam week at WVU, Ohio National Guardsmen fired into a crowd of demonstrators at neighboring Kent State University, killing four students. At Jackson State, a few days later, Mississippi State Police shot two black students. Across the country, protesting students reacted to these violent events with demonstrations. At WVU, an early morning vigil was held on May 6, focusing on four crosses erected on Memorial Plaza in memory of the four slain Kent State students.

By the morning of May 7, the small midnight crowd had increased. According to one reporter from the *Dominion News*, traffic tie-ups, violent rhetoric, and an on-campus shouting match between demonstrators and more conservative students broke the calm of the day. By noon, demonstrators carrying a mock coffin containing the effigy of President Harlow marched to Stewart Hall. The march had been triggered by Harlow's non-response to an unsigned May 5 request to condemn the Cambodian invasion and the Kent State killings.

Stopped at the locked doors of Stewart Hall, the students demanded entry. Security policy permitted three representatives from the crowd into the building to meet members of the University administration. Not accepting the advice of the students that an endorsement of their request would disperse the assembled crowd, Harold Shamberger, assistant to the president, refused to issue any statement in the name of the president. The students who had been selected for entry also discovered the door to the President's Office locked, and were informed that he would be absent for the rest of the day.[6] Receiving the news of a fast-departing president by those admitted into the administrative sanctum, the demonstrators took their coffin and effigy to Grumbein's Island for burning.

Harry Ernst, director of university relations, clarified presidential purposes for the University establishment. Noting on May 7 that the president had made it clear he would meet with no one under the threat of coercion, and that his appearance at that moment might actually trigger a riot, Ernst added: "President Harlow doesn't normally issue statements on socio-political issues because his views inevitably become those of the University in the public mind. West Virginia University belongs to all of the people of West Virginia who hold diverse views." Harlow's earlier statement to the effect that the University would not tolerate disruption of its activities was repeated, plus an expression of the University's regret to the townpeople for the inconvenience caused by disruption of local traffic.

It was a long seventh day of May before the crowds dispersed. "We're staying in the streets because we're not satisfied with the bullshit we're getting from the University. The streets belong to the people," one demonstrator shouted.[7] A few faculty members seemed in agreement. William Haymond, chairman of philosophy, although taking a stance against violence, also said: "We've got to protect ourselves against repression." Believing that student dissidents were fair game for the "bootlicking pigs," Haymond announced he was canceling all of his finals and giving all his students As for the semester as a demonstration against the national administration.

Local newspapers, while conceding the misfortune, still heaved a sigh of relief on May 7. The *Dominion News* believed, "It's to the great credit of all concerned that the violence-inviting radicals did not succeed in creating a general riot and tragedy." It trusted that the town and the University would keep cool and not give in to emotion in troubled and tension-filled times. Offended by the "filthy language" it heard, the paper desired University authorities to determine who the "law-insulting riot seekers" were and expel them.

The next day, May 8, crowds of identical numbers assembled on the University Campus, following a peace rally on the Courthouse Square. After some debate, 100 students marched on Woodburn Hall and tore up some ROTC manuals. The assemblage then surged to Stewart Hall to repeat their May 5 demands to Harlow. Again unable to see the president, they drifted back onto University Avenue and blocked traffic. As determined counterdemonstrators descended from fraternity houses, the shoving and shouting escalated. Governor Moore called in state troopers to aid the local police.

Arriving on campus at 4:40 p.m., the State Police firmly announced their determination to clear Grumbein's Island and University Avenue of pedestrians. Making two sweeps of the street only to have the demonstrators return to their stations after the police had passed, the troopers used tear gas to disperse the crowd. When the gas cleared, the crowds again regrouped, necessitating a truce between police and demonstrators: the troopers would leave the campus and the students would clear the streets. When State Police loaded into buses to demonstrate their half of the bargain, the crowd cleared the streets to honor their commitment to the truce.

Because of their handling of the situation, the police won the praise of all concerned, with the University president calling them "superb." The *Dominion News* agreed, believing that their offer to leave gave demonstrators a way to save face and avoid possible injury. No injuries or arrests resulted from the confrontation. Damages were estimated at only $50 to $100. Later

State Police clear demonstrators against the Vietnamese War who blocked streets in the Grumbein's Island area in the Spring of 1970. (Photograph by Richard P. Rogers for Monticola.)

in the evening Harlow provided a summary statement of May 8, 1970: "Unpleasant events like that today come and go in the lives of universities. We are fortunate that no one was injured and property damage was minimal. I believe that the cleavages among University groups revealed by the circumstances of the last few days are shallow enough and narrow enough that the University community will be able to heal them."

The following day, with demonstrators relaxing on the lawn at Woodburn Hall and the troopers spending their day at the Evansdale State Police barracks, Harlow's observation had merit. With the last final exams slated that day, it was expected both students and police would return home.

On May 17, on a quiet campus now vacated by students and faculty, WVU awarded more than 3,000 degrees to undergraduates, graduates, and professional students at its 101st commencement. The light-hearted spirit of reunions, it was reported, was disturbed by only one dismal chord, the words of President Harlow at the alumni luncheon: "I can tell you bluntly and explicitly that West Virginia University will face for a minimum of ten years trouble of the type that has befallen colleges and university campuses across the nation. We will need the support of our alumni more than ever before in the history of the school."

Following commencement, mop-up action began. After a May 21 interview with the University president, Haymond was removed as chairman of the Department of Philosophy "as a result of your display of emotional incompatability with administrative assignment."[8] The philosopher informed the press on June 26 that he planned no appeal, contenting himself with the statement, "What we were doing in the streets was good for the University, but it was not necessarily good for the administration." He continued to teach as a tenured professor of philosophy. A June 5 University News Service release disclosed that six unidentified students would be given a June 24 hearing before a University committee on student discipline on charges of destroying University property and disturbing University activities.

The six students eventually identified themselves as Scott Bills, Steve Stepto, Mike Weber, Dan Bucca, Peter Cowan, and Tom Scott King. They asked for delay in the hearings that they wanted made public, and they requested that they be provided with an attorney. Part of the group later obtained counsel: H. John Rogers of Wheeling, joined by the well-known advocate of civil liberty, William Kuntsler, who suggested there was strong evidence that disciplinary hearings were being used to curb dissent at West Virginia University.[9] The administration performed an abrupt about-face. Because of a possible violation of state and federal statutes and because some of the students were not under University regulations at that time, WVU officials let it be known on July 6, 1970, that the University hearings were "held in abeyance."

Bucking responsibility to those outside WVU, the University then requested civil authorities to consider prosecuting the students. However, Joseph Laurita, prosecuting attorney of Monongalia County, bucked it right back. In his opinion, the student matter remained a University administrative problem, otherwise a criminal warrant would have been obtained by University security police. A statement on behalf of the six students called University actions an admission that the administration had acted in disregard of student rights, a political maneuver to attempt further to intimidate student activists, and called for President Harlow's resignation.[10]

The summer remained busy. A concerned citizens committee was formed on July 16 to obtain petitions calling for the firing of "radical members" of the University. Many seemed to agree with the father of one of the "Morgantown Six," who claimed that his son had turned into a degenerate because of radical University professors. Supporting the view that the blame rested with the faculty, the VFW commander was assigned the task of presenting a petition to Chancellor Woodard of the Board of Regents. Randolph and

Tucker county petitioners added to the request that radical students be dismissed from the University.

As the 1970-71 school year neared, the Board of Regents released a new code of student regulations and a general framework within which individual institutions would issue their own rules. It was noted by the *Daily Athenaeum* on August 13, 1970, that a college president's powers to expel or suspend students and to close schools were for use only in case of major disruptions. Harlow saw the new regulations as a reaffirmation of basic West Virginia law; the student body president viewed them as "a progressive step for education in this state"; and Scott Bills called them "blatantly repressive in nature." Harlow also announced, with respect to the new school year, that "we will deal with campus unrest when it arises," the University would try to be "rational" in handling such problems, and daily communication would continue to exist between campus security police and the city and state police.

The year remained uneventful, with the University administration's efforts at discipline judged a failure, and its prophecies of "doom and gloom" unfulfilled. Two of the Morgantown Six were admitted to graduate school on the recommendation of a five-member appeal board, after the University originally had denied their admission. The WVU student protest rally on the anniversary of the Moratorium observance was peaceful. Yet Harlow had indicated on the eve of the Moratorium little optimism about chances for a lull in campus unrest. He appealed to the faculty on October 14, 1970, to have "courage and faithfulness" during periods of disquiet he felt would follow. He pictured the University as "under attack from within and without" and observed that "more serious than terrorism are the lines of distrust not only from student to faculty, but faculty to student."

In fact, in almost every subsequent annual State of the University address, President Harlow alluded to a discouraging climate surrounding higher education. Believing that campus disturbances had disaffected the public, he foresaw in October, 1971, a sharp decline in "the humanistic view of education," a distrust of the college degree, and a sharp rise in "establishment pressure for manpower output." But again his worry about campus unrest proved unfounded. Whether to his satisfaction or dissatisfaction, the campus observed moratoriums, Watergate, and national elections with great propriety.

The student newspaper reinforced Harlow's observation that WVU now had a new kind of student who perhaps mirrored national concerns and interests as the result of the momentous social, political and economic changes since World War II. With approval, it noted on April 19, 1973, a bill allowing universities to hire lawyers to represent students in certain matters. It solicited opinions from WVU officials about whether a new status, brought about by the students' own liberated thinking and their push for more individual freedom, had been achieved. In noting the ending of curfews for women, and the granting of permission to drink beer on campus, to wear shorts to classes, and to visit in men's residence halls, the *Daily Athenaeum* contacted Betty Boyd, associate dean of Student Educational Services (SES), for explanations. She saw the more relaxed regulations stemming from a new theory that education was now viewed as a right, whereas it formerly had been considered a privilege. She believed the restrictive rules for women had been for the old-fashioned purpose of creating a "lady-like atmosphere on campus."

Gordon Thorn, associate director of SES, on the other hand, saw the change in life style as directly related to the declining importance of the Greek system. He believed that "fraternities and sororities may not have changed fast enough with the growth of the campus." Once the Greek system provided more freedom and closer ties between goups of students in their houses, Thorn noted, but now apartment living, offering fewer restrictions and more individualism than the Greek houses, was the more popular choice.

Herman Moses, associate director of residence halls, believed that the student body of the early seventies "looks beyond the outer veneer of personal appearance and more closely examines that inner being in mankind, which is an approach not enough students took one or two decades ago." This sentiment was echoed by Robert Robards, director of housing, who was certain a new student had emerged, if only for the reason that "within the last five years, the students have become human beings rather than just numbers in the administrators' eyes."

On matters unrelated to housing or to drinking beer in Mountainlair, the student newspaper felt that few real changes had occurred. For example, it considered the plight of the homosexual. Believing that the state had no right to determine the morality of the people it represented and that the University, in turn, should not deny certain groups basic rights, it called on February 28, 1973, for official recognition of The Homophile Awareness League (HAL). The University's position that it could not recognize the organization because of existing West Virginia state law was unacceptable to the newspaper because it viewed a state law of 1868 as limiting what consenting adults could do in bed as strictly antiquarian and inadmissible. The Associated Women Students, like the *DA*, also felt that the ultimate in individual freedom had not been achieved. Expressing on February 2, 1972, a need for a women's interest group on campus until discrimination against women was totally eliminated, the AWS president called attention to the fact that the birth control referral center had not yet materialized nor had self-defense courses been initiated.

On other occasions, the *Daily Athenaeum* was not so sure life at WVU had changed, or that students desired change. Impatiently it asked on October 28, 1971, "Why haven't more students taken part in drives by local ecology groups? How many know what SAAP and WV-SPRIG mean? What about subjects relevant to today that haven't even gotten off the ground at WVU?"

Sensing a shift in attitudes in the seventies, the *DA* believed the students' top priority had become high grades. Admitting that achieving a satisfactory grade-point average did take much time, it betrayed a shift in its previous ideological position by observing that several years before students had found time "to join with a handful of activists to riot for a useless and absurd reason." Pleading with students to get out of an apathetic rut, it cried: "Register to vote, write a letter, answer a poll, make a phone call — don't make our generation another silent majority."

But activism on the campus by the end of the decade restricted itself to the minutiae of class-scheduling, the quality of food services, and the hijinks of throwing toilets, bathtubs, and furniture out of student dormitories at the end of the spring semester. Harlow handled these issues with both dispatch and detachment. One decision, pleasing to both students and faculty alike, was Harlow's dropping of the Tuesday-Thursday-Saturday class schedule in favor of Tuesday-Thursday classes on 75-minute periods.

When Chancellor Ben Morton telephoned Harlow for an explanation of WVU dormitory damage at the end of the 1975 school year, Harlow downplayed the incidents. He admitted on June 10, 1975, that destruction of property at the dormitories was unpleasant and reprehensible, but it should not be allowed to discredit the vast majority of WVU students, or to raise questions concerning a year which had been one of the most productive and most pleasant of his years at WVU. This was because he had found the student body as a whole industrious and cooperative, with stress and conflict at a minimum.

But adverse publicity continued, attracting the media, particularly *The Chronicle of Higher Education*. It was reported that the dormitory vandalism particularly shocked citizens in the Charleston area.[11] On May 27, 1975, *The Chronicle* estimated damages at $50,000, and summarized the destruction: ripped-out sinks and toilets, smashed windows, destroyed locks, and burned furniture. Attaching not too much importance to the activity, Harry Ernst, director of university relations, had stated on May 15 that, "Such senseless destruction, especially at the end of the school year, has been characteristic of young people's behavior for decades and it has been increasing recently on large campuses across the country."

Its effect, he stated, would be to raise housing fees for incoming freshman students in the future. For good measure, the administration decided to post signs in the dormitories that destruction of state property was punishable under the laws of West Virginia.[12]

By the summer of 1975, continued charges of apathy and a profile of the freshman class indicated that Harlow's fearful prediction of ten years of trouble was wide of the mark and was more in line with his original assessment of a state university's student body. A majority of WVU freshman students assessed themselves as middle-of-the-road (54 percent compared to 51.6 nationally); liberals comprised 30.4 percent compared to 31.9 nationally; and conservatives were 12.9 percent compared to 13.9 nationally. Only 2.7 percent of the entering class indicated they were either far left or far right.

Modifications in the curriculum became a large order of business in the internal workings of the Harlow administration. After a year-long deliberation by a Senate subcommittee on the University Core Curriculum, the committee chaired by Professor John Stasny recommended that: (1) the University renew its commitment to general education; (2) a significant portion of the students' efforts in general education be devoted to multi-disciplinary courses focusing on the current problems, issues, and concerns of society; (3) the Core program be administered as a University-wide effort; and (4) a Faculty of University Studies be identified to carry the major institutional burden of the Core program. The University Senate accepted the first three recommendations and denied the last in the spring of 1970.

In the name of relevance, a few of the following adaptations materialized: Social Sciences 1 and 2 were revised to focus on such problems as race and poverty; the College of Engineering introduced for freshman students an experimental, problem-solving course entitled "Engineering Design"; a new Department of Statistics and Computer Science was established in the College of Arts and Sciences, and its new Academic Advising Center was made available to the entire University; individualized instruction in the learning center of the College of Human Resources and Education was expanded and living-learning seminars were offered in the dormitories; the School of Medicine adopted a satisfactory-unsatisfactory grading system to replace the traditional letter grades, and the experiment, with limitations, was adopted in other academic areas; an individualized bachelor of arts degree program allowing for interdisciplinary study was permitted within the College of Arts and Sciences as was credit by examination for selected courses; the Department of History added black history, labor history, urban history, and women's history to its curriculum and considered a program in archival administration; the Department of English offered courses in black literature, women's literature, and advanced to a Ph.D. program; graduate programs permitted a knowledge of statistics and computer techniques to equate with, and often replace, foreign language as a research tool; psychology courses were developed so that students could proceed at their own pace and largely determine their own grades. Across the University instructors adapted themselves to new audio-visual aids. All departments made themselves and their courses available to evaluation by students.

In effect, the University was belatedly doing what student leaders had recommended ten years earlier, just before President Harlow assumed office. Along with his counterparts across the nation, Harlow's contributions to campus life, which for the most part were forced upon him by the hesitant attitudes of two boards and the state and federal governments, were judged too little and too late by the troubled students of the late sixties and seventies.

Chapter 15   Into the Nineteen Eighties

Gene Arthur Budig
July 1, 1977–June 30, 1981

A ROTUND MAN WHO ABHORRED physical exercise, James G. Harlow reluctantly presided over the greatest expansion of athletic facilities in WVU history. He asked the Board of Governors to reconsider its plans for the 14,000-seat basketball coliseum, with an eye on making it a more versatile facility. The Board declined. He urged the Board of Regents to approve the construction of the Evansdale Library before the Natatorium. The Regents instead responded to student pressures and built the swimming-diving facility first. He suggested a modest renovation and expansion of old Mountaineer Field; instead the Legislature and the Governor initiated construction of a new $20 million Mountaineer Field and a $4.5 million shell building. At state universities, intercollegiate athletics has a life of its own that presidents and governing boards can hope to influence but rarely control.

In 1967 when WVU prepared to enter its second century, the West Virginia Legislature and the WVU Board of Governors judged that it was the proper time to build the Coliseum. The timing seemed perfect — the WVU basketball record was 19-9 in 1967-68. But the

325

Mountaineers slid to a 12-14 record in 1968-69, the first year of scheduling after leaving the Southern Conference and their first losing season in twenty-five years.

When Duke University offered WVU head basketball coach Bucky Waters its head coaching position, the increasingly unpopular Waters quickly accepted. He had the lowest percentage winning record of any basketball coach at WVU since World War II, a .631 figure, with an overall record of 70 wins and 41 defeats.

The final game played in the old Field House against Pitt in 1970 also ended on a sour note when their arch rival bested the hosts. Little was it then suspected that the WVU record in the old Field House of 374 victories and 77 defeats, an unbelievable .829 percentage produced in more than forty years of competition, was not to be matched in any single season in the new Coliseum during the Harlow years.

A return to success in basketball seemed possible when in 1972 Leland Byrd, former WVU basketball All-American, was chosen as athletic director to succeed Robert L. Brown, who reached the mandatory retirement age of 65 for WVU administrators. Nonetheless, both the 1972-73 and 1973-74 teams posted 10-15 records, the worst since 1938. At the end of the 1973-74 season, Sonny Moran, who had succeeded Waters, resigned as head basketball coach. His overall record of 57-68 in four years was the poorest of any multi-year coach since 1907.

As it had in selecting Leland Byrd, WVU reached into a glorious past to find a former basketball player who might restore lost lustre to the failing sport — Joedy Gardner, co-captain of the 1957-58 WVU squad, which posted a 26-2 record. Gardner did stop, momentarily, the losing seasons. In 1974-75, he managed a 14-13 winning record; but in 1975-76 he barely improved with a 15-13 season. In 1976-77, however, Gardner's team showed marked improvement, with Tony Robertson averaging over 20 points a game and the team posting a final record of 18 wins and 11 losses. In that year, the Mountaineers surrendered their short-lived independence by becoming part of a new conference, the Eastern Collegiate Basketball League, which included traditional rivals Pitt and Penn State as well as Villanova and Rutgers.

In 1977-78, the team's record slid to 12-16, and with the advent of the Budig administration, Gardner became the only head basketball coach openly fired in WVU history. His four-year record of 59-53, although above .500, was not the kind of performance for which the Coliseum had been built nor was it one deemed satisfactory to those with long memories of basketball victories from World War II to the Vietnam War.

With respect to football, it was Harlow's proud boast to *The Pittsburgh Post-Gazette* on April 27, 1977, that the WVU football team had a better won-and-lost record during his ten years as WVU head than during any previous administration, with the Mountaineers winning 69, losing 50, and playing one tie. In addition, the team appeared in bowl games on three separate occasions, and on only two occasions during the Harlow years did it post losing seasons.

The difference between basketball and football fortunes seemed to be a matter of coaching talent. Jim Carlen had become head football coach in 1966, and his enthusiasm and optimism appeared to regenerate the football program at about the same time the basketball program went into decline. In 1967, Carlen brought WVU back to a winning record, if only a modest 5-4-1 season. It marked the team's last year in Southern Conference competition, and Carlen's conference record was 3-0-1. The 1967 team, noted for its defense, recorded three shutouts and allowed no more than three touchdowns in any one game for an average yield of 11.7 points. Losing only to Penn State, VPI, and Kentucky in 1968, the team finished with a 7-3 record.

In 1969, Carlen was able to produce the finest football season in Mountaineer history since the undefeated 1922 season. The team rolled up a 9-1 record, losing only to Penn State. The team was invited to the Peach Bowl in Atlanta where it defeated the South Carolina Gamecocks 14-3 in a heavy rain. In four years, Jim Carlen had compiled a 25-13-3 record, and became of prime interest to other schools. Shortly after this win, Carlen resigned to take on the challenge of bringing Texas Tech up to a competitive level in the rugged Southwest Conference.

Harlow turned to Carlen's top assistant, Bobby Bowden. In his first year, Bowden compiled an 8-3 record, but among the three losses was one to Pitt; although WVU had led the game 35-8 at halftime, it permitted the Panthers to score 28 points in the second half. In 1971, the Mountaineers compiled a 7-4 record, and an 8-3 mark in 1972 was good enough for a return trip to the Peach Bowl. Facing North Carolina State, the Mountaineers were beaten 49-13.

In 1973, the WVU record slipped to 6-5 and in 1974 the team had to win two of its last three games to finish 4-7. The year 1975 started successfully with WVU victories over Temple, California, Boston College, and Southern Methodist. Coach Bowden, who had been "booed and hung in effigy" a year earlier, was now being congratulated, because WVU had vaulted into the top 20 teams in the country.

In a nationally televised confrontation with arch-rival Pitt, WVU won one of the most exciting victories in its history. With three seconds left in the game, sophomore placekicker Bill McKenzie nailed a 44-yard field goal to give WVU a 17-14 victory. It set off one of the wildest celebrations Morgantown had ever seen. Crowds jammed city streets, and 45 persons, mostly students, were arrested for disorderly conduct. The biggest disturbance was at Sunnyside, an area of the city bordering on the Stadium, where students built a fire for their use in the middle of University Avenue. It was also arguable that excitement at University football games was heightened by the 300-member Mountaineer Marching Band, which conveyed a sense of excitement and enthusiasm. Because of the mood it set, a mood which enhanced the crowd's overwhelming Mountaineer spirit, the band was and always would be considered, said the *Daily Athenaeum* on November 13, 1975, "The Pride of West Virginia."   .

An 8-3 record and national exposure against Pitt secured a third Peach Bowl bid. Meeting North Carolina State again, a fourth-quarter touchdown pass from Dan Kendra to Scott MacDonald lifted WVU to a 13-10 victory and WVU's first national ranking in some time (the final UPI poll ranked the Mountaineers seventeenth).

The second bowl victory lost WVU its second consecutive football coach — Bowden departed for Florida State. He left WVU with a 42-26 record, and one of his aides, Frank Cignetti, was named his successor. Cignetti was doomed to four unsuccessful seasons and his contract was not renewed.

If the Golden Age of basketball had called for a new Coliseum at the beginning of the Harlow administration, the conclusion of the second best era in WVU football at the close of Harlow's reign seemingly dictated a refurbished stadium. The Harlow administration proposed that the Legislature appropriate $10 million to renovate Mountaineer Field and add 10,000 seats. The local Elks Club had a grander idea — it convinced the Legislature of the need for a brand new stadium. On the last day of the legislative session of 1977, the Legislature approved a $60.3 million measure authorizing the financing of a $20 million football stadium and a $4.5 million shell building at WVU, balanced off politically by a new basketball and indoor sports complex at Marshall and new buildings at three state colleges.

Responding to a stunned University, which had not asked for but had been given a multi-million dollar athletic construction kitty, Governor John D. Rockefeller IV met with WVU officials to determine what action he would take concerning the newly endorsed sports complex. While gathering pro and con opinions on the proposed structure and location of a stadium, he toured proposed sites.

Although the stadium issue was now considered "up to Jay," it was reported on April 26 that President Harlow hoped that Governor Rockefeller would sign the bill calling for the new football stadium even though he foresaw "a number of problems that still haven't been solved." Since the legislators "have acted in the method they feel best, I have urged Governor Rockefeller to sign the bill," the WVU president stated.

While in the act of approving, Harlow also remembered the University's more modest proposal. By way of a disclaimer to the new proposal, he recollected:

The 300-member Mountaineer Marching Band, which is called "The Pride of West Virginia," entertains at football games and gives a fall concert. It also makes several appearances each year in different areas of the state.

We never considered a new stadium when we decided to ask the Legislature to upgrade the football facilities. We believe it more practical to renovate than build a new stadium in a place not as easily accessible to students. We proposed $10 million to add 10,000 new seats to Mountaineer Field; the new stadium costs $20 million and gives us only 5,000 more seats than renovation.

The lame-duck president also expressed displeasure with the Chancellor, the Board of Regents, and the Legislature by interjecting the comment:

I've felt disappointed that the Legislature and Dr. Morton did not work closer with the University in deciding to go ahead with the new stadium. Dr. Morton never told me prior to Legislative approval that he favored the new stadium project. He never asked me my opinion.

As he contemplated his own departure from the University, the president foresaw four major problems with the stadium decision that he left for his successor: (1) the disposition of Mountaineer Field; (2) the severe traffic problems caused by an out-of-town site; (3) the problem of adequate access roads; (4) the approval of the Morgantown Planning Commission.

During the gubernatorial campaign of 1976, the Governor had agreed with his Republican opponent, Cecil Underwood, that Mountaineer Stadium should be renovated; with Harlow's endorsement, Rockefeller adopted a new position. Calling a media conference to announce his decision on April 28, 1977, Rockefeller stated that his choice had narrowed to "whether to veto and stop progress . . . or sign and create an atmosphere of progress and pride." Convinced that the renovation and expansion of Mountaineer Field "cannot be done effectively," the Governor opted for approving the $60.3 million construction bill. Taking his cue from Harlow's worry over student accessibility to the stadium, Rockefeller extended his remarks to negate the "distant" Mileground site, which, though "most popular" to the out-of-town visitors to the game, was also the "most expensive and the least effective" from the standpoint of students' needs.

In behalf of WVU's building program, Rockefeller trod one extra mile. Noting that many feared that a long-delayed library project on the Evansdale Campus was jeopardized by money allocated to the athletic construction projects, the Governor declared he would make certain that a new library, costing $4 million, remained a priority item in the University building program. In reply to the criticism that $20 million might not prove enough to build a new stadium, he said, "if it costs more, so be it; we'll raise more." He added that the University should have "a first-class facility and a first-class library" and urged that the University and the Board of Regents "get on with it and begin planning."

Indecision about the stadium's location caused the Morgantown critics of new stadium construction to regroup when it was announced that the new facility would be located on the golf course between the Medical and Law Centers. The choices had been narrowed to the golf course, the Mileground, and the Coliseum area.

The Morgantown City Council, the Morgantown Planning Commission, the Monongalia County Commission, and the Monongalia County Medical Society came out in opposition to the golf course site. When the *Charleston Daily Mail* heard of the opposition, it wrote in exasperation on December 4, 1977:

Morgantown opponents to that site began to make noises as though they owned the university, an affliction that has stayed with Morgantown residents through the generations that followed its founding more than 100 years ago.

Some of this assumption of a proprietary interest in a state institution by local residents — who own it no more than the people of the other 54 counties — can be overlooked. But in Morgantown with the new stadium it is getting a little bit ridiculous.

Condemning the action of interest groups, including the League of Women Voters who entertained the "weird" reasoning that the stadium should be planned as an asset to Morgantown as well as to the University, the Charleston paper declared, "That is getting rather parochial."

Despite all attempts to change the legislative and executive decision to build a new stadium and to determine the site selection, the governmental will prevailed. On May 23, 1978, *The Charleston Gazette* announced that the stadium bids would be opened in January, 1979, construction started in the spring of 1979, and the stadium ready for use by September, 1980. Although no modifications were entertained, Governor Rockefeller appeared to be making amends, or at least living up to a previous compromise, when he appeared on campus on July 13, 1978, for the ground breaking of a long-delayed $4.2 million library to be located between the Agricultural Sciences and Engineering Sciences Buildings on the Evansdale Campus. While in Morgantown, Rockefeller also announced that he had designated the University as a Mining and Mineral Research Institute, thereby making the school eligible for federal mining research funds under new federal strip mining laws. To Rockefeller, WVU "must and will be the leader in this nation for coal and energy research."

The declining fortunes of football and basketball, and the decision to fund a football stadium were but a few of the depressants facing Harlow in his last year. Of most immediate concern to the faculty was evidence that in salaries WVU ranked last among 13 comparable state institutions belonging to the Southern Regional Education Board, while West Virginia's state colleges fared far better, ranking fourth among nine other states with similar institutions.

Perhaps indirectly referring to the budgetary fate of WVU and the success of other state institutions of higher learning under the central board, Harlow reminisced in his last year of service at a bag luncheon sponsored by Phi Delta Kappa, education graduate honorary, that he would remember most clearly his difficulties with the new Board of Regents as the low-point of his administration. Central boards, he said, had two defects: first, they tended to standardize excessively, wiping out "little differences" necessary between institutions; second, being far removed from the institution's activities, they did not realize their inability to direct certain areas of university operations. Defining two systems of authority in operation at the university level, he cited first the legal one, extending from the Legislature down to the Board. Unacknowledged by the Board, he implied, was the second, the technical authority, based on the tenure and knowledge of the faculty members, with which the Board should not be concerned. He also complained that university presidents did not have access to the boards because "chancellors have set themselves between the presidents and the boards."

The President, who once was described by a colleague as a man gifted with "the information and consistency of a McNamara, and the self-deprecating humor of a Kennedy,"[1] remained negative and pessimistic in his final state of the University address before the Faculty Assembly on April 27, 1977. Harlow predicted that WVU faculty salaries would remain average or below average for the next five years, and the unpopular image that universities had gained during the past decade would linger. However, he believed, the best thing about the University situation was the condition of West Virginia itself. To Harlow, there was no question that the state would have a large and prolonged boom based on coal. His concluding prediction was that the construction of a new football stadium might lead the University "into a very serious operational and financial problem." In resigned fashion, he stated his administrative valedictory, "the legislature giveth, the legislature taketh away, and those of us who work in the state listen carefully to it."

The campus community and the state were shocked to learn of Dr. Harlow's death from a heart attack on March 10, 1978, less than a year after his retirement. Remembering Dr. Harlow for a new generation of students, the *Daily Athenaeum* editorialized on March 14:

Dr. Harlow's private manner made him a whipping boy among editorial writers. He often found himself criticized, not because his opinions were intolerable, but because he rarely expressed an opinion at all.

In later years, Dr. Harlow became somewhat of a mystery figure. He preferred to handle University matters in a private manner, which cut down on his being seen or heard about campus. Students could go through four years of school and see their president only twice — freshman orientation and graduation.

A search for a new chief executive by a new governing agency, the Board of Regents, called forth a listing of the credentials of the institution itself. As WVU geared itself for the 1980s and a new president, it was able to advertise its sixteen schools and colleges as being in strong head-count condition. At the end of the 1970s it reported an undergraduate enrollment of almost 15,000, and a graduate and professional enrollment of almost 7,000 — a total of 22,000 students. It further refined its computations by noting that two-thirds of the enrollment was from all 55 counties in the state, and one-third from 48 other states and 70 foreign countries. Thus did WVU shed an earlier reputation of an institution so badly located that it could service only Monongalia and neighboring counties in northern West Virginia and southwestern Pennsylvania.

Among the WVU colleges, the College of Arts and Sciences was easily the largest with more than 8,000 students. The College of Human Resources and Education followed with slightly more than 4,000; the Colleges of Agriculture and Forestry, Business and Economics, and Engineering slightly under 2,000 each; Creative Arts Center, 885; College of Mineral and Energy Resources, 589; and the College of Law, 378, rounded out the college totals

Evansdale Library.

at almost 19,000 students. The Schools of Pharmacy, Journalism, Nursing, Dentistry, Social Work, Medicine, and Physical Education contributed in ascending order from 210 to 597 students, a total of slightly under 3,000 students. Projections showed a strong yearly and cumulative percentage increase by the 1980s in the health science enrollments.

By the end of the 1970s, WVU was composed of two Morgantown campuses containing 89 buildings on 801.1 acres valued at $263 million and connected by the Personal Rapid Transit System. Although losing two of its branches, it retained Potomac State, a junior college at Keyser, and added the Charleston Division of the WVU Medical Center and the Wheeling Division of the School of Medicine. It also maintained five off-campus graduate centers at Jackson's Mill, Parkersburg, Keyser, Shepherdstown, and Wheeling. In addition, it operated the State 4-H Camp at Jackson's Mill, ten experimental farms and five forests throughout the state, and a geology camp in Greenbrier County.

Capital expenditures in the 1970s were dominated by athletic facilities: a coliseum at $9,682,957; a natatorium at $1,651,000; and a projected football stadium and shell building at $25,000,000. The professional schools of law and medicine achieved the next biggest considerations of capital outlay, with the Charleston Medical Education Building in 1977 at $6 million, and the Law Center in 1974 at $4.5 million. Extension and computer services were next with the purchase of Knapp Hall, the new home for continuing education, in 1976 for $1.25 million, and the Computer Center in 1970 for half a million dollars. Certain older buildings acquired extensive changes in the late 1970s and early 1980s. Martin Hall was renovated in 1977 at a cost of $1.4 million and Woodburn and Chitwood Halls were renovated in 1980 at a cost of $6 million. Stansbury Hall's reconstruction the same year cost $1.25 million. Colson Hall, renovated at a cost of $1.7 million, now serves as a branch library and home of the West Virginia and Regional History Collection.

WVU's budget for 1977-78 was estimated at almost $148 million from all sources of funds, with about $42 million coming from state general revenue funds. Such figures excluded Potomac State, but incorporated the soft-drink tax from state revenues for about 5 percent of the total. In expenditures, colleges and schools received 41 percent, followed by 16 percent and 15 percent for WVU-wide support services and hospital operations. Libraries received 2 percent, which enabled their collections from 1970 through 1978 to move from 1,025,780 to 1,622,671 volumes, of which 898,133 were books, 57,943 microfilm reels, and 666,595 were other microforms.

Such were the conditions awaiting a new president and a new decade. None was considered a bad omen because hundreds applied for the position. Because of the comprehensive nature of WVU, Gene Budig, president of Illinois State University, accepted the institution's seventeenth presidency. At 38, he became the youngest executive to head a land-grant university in the nation and WVU's youngest president since 1901 — an immediate contrast to his predecessor who was 55 when he accepted the WVU presidency.

Born in Nebraska, Budig received his undergraduate and graduate education at the University of Nebraska. In his first major position outside his home state, he became president of Illinois State University in 1973.

To reporters who wondered why Budig would leave his $47,000 post at Illinois State for the $43,500 job at WVU, the new president explained to the *Daily Athenaeum* on January 11, 1977: "At West Virginia there are Schools of Dentistry, Journalism, Medicine, Mining, Agriculture, Pharmacy, and many others. These are all lacking at ISU, where the prime emphasis is in business, education, arts and sciences, and the applied sciences." As one who was seeking a more demanding assignment, he also noted that there were 182 program areas at WVU and only 55 at Illinois State, and that there was much more emphasis on graduate education at WVU.

Assuming office on July 1, 1977, Budig quickly laid the groundwork for his administration. As a top priority he planned "an aggressive effort to tell the state of West Virginia more about its comprehensive land-grant university" in a visit to all 55 counties where a case could be made "for building a partnership between the state and the University."

In bringing the WVU message to the state, Budig incorporated what administrators and faculty representatives had informed him were some of its outstanding features: that 90 percent of the June, 1977, graduates had found employment, most of them in areas of their first choice, and that only 2 percent of the WVU graduates were unemployed. The fact that WVU graduates were faring well in the job market permitted Budig to emphasize that a WVU education is a good investment in the future. Other outstanding facts he carried to the state were that more than 82 percent of the graduates said they were pleased with their academic experience, a degree of approval Budig noted would gratify any business man surveying customers or any politician polling constituents.

The new president also filled his messages with citations of other WVU accomplishments: that one of every ten West Virginians had been treated at University Hospital since it opened in 1960; that WVU freshman students scored above the national mean in the American College Testing program; that WVU offered more than 160 fully accredited degree programs; that nearly two-thirds of the faculty possessed doctoral degrees; that WVU had sent 18 Rhodes Scholars to Oxford University (which was soon to increase to 19); that its students came from every West Virginia county; that tuition and fees charged resident students ranked WVU among institutions with the lowest student charges.

Budig also visited all units within the University where he announced another of his priorities particularly pleasing to faculty and staff: his dedication to raising the pay of WVU employees. On July 12, 1977, Budig described faculty salaries as "too low . . . by any reasonable competitive standard," and he also urged more and better housing for students as well as more and better parking.

In direct contrast to Harlow's style of administration, Budig directed the deans, excluding the health sciences, to report directly to Jay Barton, provost for instruction, and he advised the deans of the schools in the health sciences, the dean of the Charleston medical division, and the director of University Hospital to report directly to Charles Andrews, provost for health sciences. As Harry Ernst, director of University relations, described the break with the previous system to the *Dominion Post* on July 13, 1977, provosts had acted as advisers to President Harlow with no administrative power of their own; "under the new system, authority will be delegated by the president to provosts in certain areas."

Budig's concerns and involvements with teaching were underscored by the fact that during the previous decade of administrative duties he had taught a graduate course each semester, one in academic organization and another in academic budgeting. He said he would continue to do so at WVU. While at Nebraska and Illinois State, he also had supervised doctoral students. He said that he also would continue to pursue this role. Budig explained that he enjoyed teaching and he wanted to keep in close touch with students and the learning process.

He was asked early in his presidency if he felt there was too much emphasis on athletics in college. He told *The Charleston Gazette* on January 5, 1977, that the "commitment has already been made to the athletic program. Due to the fact that the commitment has been made, I want to win. With victories come added support to an institution."

The commitment to which he referred was obviously, in part, the building of the stadium and the shell building, which Budig said could be used not only for intercollegiate athletics but also to further the students' recreational programs. Governor Rockefeller, in turn, at the ground-breaking exercises for the new stadium, saw the new facilities extending beyond intercollegiate and intramural needs. For the Governor linked new construction with a quality academic program, for it "symbolizes the state's growing commitment to both academic excellence and excellence in the field of athletics." Believing that "what is good for West Virginia University is good for the State of West Virginia," and that the stadium would be good "for the WVU mystique," he further elucidated in the *Dominion Post* on May 4, 1979: "You can't separate what happens in the classroom from what happens in athletics. It's easier for the people of the state to relate to athletics than to the various research programs and what goes on in the classroom."

Budig went one step further in bolstering WVU's athletic image than had the preceding administration, not only by disposing of the head basketball and football coaches, but by requesting that the West Virginia University Foundation assist the University in circumventing the state law that forbade giving any University employee more than a one-year contract. Through money contributed to WVU's athletic department, the WVU Foundation set aside such funds for the purpose of providing multi-year contracts to head football and basketball coaches.

The rediscovery of coal as a key to solving the nation's energy problems appeared to give West Virginia University the opportunity to gain recognition as one of the nation's outstanding universities. The growth of the energy industry was expected to enable West Virginia to have a healthy economy over the next quarter century, an economy strong enough to build what Budig and others would consider a first-class public university.

The federal Strip Mine Reclamation Bill, passed in the summer of 1977, called for the designation of ten national centers for energy and coal research and further stipulated that one of the centers must be in the "coal provinces"

The new Mountaineer Field opened in 1980.

in which West Virginia was located. Governor Rockefeller, who had been appointed chairman of President Carter's Coal Industry Commission, asked the 63rd Legislature for $1 million to support a university coal and energy research center. Receiving it with little difficulty, he immediately designated WVU the state's mining and mineral research institute so that it might qualify for federal research funds under the new federal strip mine laws.

As West Virginia and West Virginia University faced the future, it appeared to administrators of each that federally sponsored energy legislation in the immediate years ahead might do for both what the Morrill Land-Grant College Act had done in 1862, or the Hatch Act had done in 1887, or the Second Morrill Act had accomplished in 1890. Ray Koppelman, vice-president for energy studies, graduate programs, and research, said to the *Dominion News* on August 27, 1978, that "West Virginia University and the state of West Virginia have a common vision of the future and I feel it's a very bright future."

In line with the growing emphasis upon energy, science, and technology, the Department of Chemical Engineering considered the time ripe to present to the University Senate on April 9, 1979, a new curriculum designed to correct deficiencies in its program as noted by two accrediting teams, the Engineering Council for Professional Development (ECPD) and the American Institute of Chemical Engineers (AIChE). The department proposed not only internal revision of existing engineering science courses, but also called for the addition of two chemistry courses. The latter change, the engineers believed, only could be incorporated if the number of hours required in both Core A (humanities) and Core B (social sciences) was reduced from 24 to 18 within the chemical engineering curriculum.

WVU administrators fashioned endorsements of the proposal they hoped would be palatable to the general faculties. In a memorandum to the Senate Executive Committee on February 22, 1979, Dean Bill L. Atchley of the College of Engineering and Dean William E. Collins of the College of Arts and Sciences, acknowledging that the new program was motivated by accreditation requirements, recommended the necessary changes in the engineering curriculum on a three-year trial basis beginning in August, 1979. The deans emphasized the program's experimental qualities with its "clusters of both new and existing courses dealing with specific themes appropriate to traditional Core A and B areas." To the deans, the novel undertaking ". . . should be viewed as an opportunity for the University to undertake development of, and test new models for, general education."

The opportunity as rendered by the deans was retranslated as a misfortune by the Senate Core Curriculum Committee. It saw this as a naked effort by one of the professional schools to make exception to the Core requirements, of which more demands from new sources would come in time. As the chairman of the committee viewed it, the change would open a "Pandora's box," and there would be no end to the irregularities. With great pessimism, he predicted to the *Daily Athenaeum* on April 10, 1979, "Technology will continue to expand greatly so that it will engulf all of our Core Curriculum." Looking upon the Core requirements as "the law" of the University, the committee backed their chairman by maintaining that the liberal arts were "the keystone to an abundant life," and that only liberal arts made a university a university.

In accord with the Core Curriculum Committee's advice, the University Senate voted down on April 24 the Chemical Engineering Department's proposed experimental core program, 51 to 31. To most of the voters, the cluster concept of new courses proved incomprehensible. According to Senate minutes, the vote was hailed as "the most important [Senate] decision in a decade," and was interpreted as a victory for the liberal arts. In the Core Curriculum chairman's opinion, the University had declared itself against cutting the proportion of time spent in the liberal arts.

The dean of the College of Arts and Sciences, called upon by his own faculty to explain his collaboration with the Engineering dean, doubted that the vote was necessarily "a resounding endorsement for the Core Curriculum and general education." Rather, he suggested on April 24, that he had participated in stopgap measures designed not to erode his college. He expressed new worries, which centered on counter proposals of Dean Bill Atchley of the College of Engineering and Dean Dale Zinn of the College of Agriculture and Forestry, permitting each college and school the privilege of setting its own general education requirements, with the only stipulation being that each baccalaureate curriculum require at least thirty general education hours. As the dean of the College of Arts and Sciences cautioned his faculty, "In all likelihood the net effect would be a reduction and redistribution of course selections in liberal studies subjects." To the dean of Arts and Sciences, the very concept of the university was in danger, with its organization becoming "more a loose confederation of colleges held together by the plumbing and the PRT."

While the future looked grim to one segment of West Virginia University, and indeed seemed remarkably similar to debates between the classicists and the professional colleges of an earlier era in WVU history, it did indeed look cheerful to the other university in the state. For WVU was not the only educational institution in the state whose policies were occasionally shaped by, and benefited from, the possibility of federal largesse. When Congress passed a law in 1973 providing that eight new medical schools could be established in conjunction with Veterans Administration hospitals, Governor Arch Moore, the Legislature, and the congressional delegation promoted a medical college for Marshall University in Huntington, where a VA hospital was located.

WVU never had responded favorably to the idea of another medical college. In an impassioned letter to Chancellor Ben Morton on October 10, 1974, President Harlow, in an effort to defend his own Medical Center budget request, had suggested a 55 percent increase in allocations for WVU medical needs to prevent further loss of programming and to meet the needs of ongoing programs. Trying to enlist the Chancellor's support, Harlow argued:

. . . in a general sense I think it likely that the Board will wind up with charges of having sandbagged the Medical Center, coming from both the Legislature and the Governor, unless all of the major problems of the Medical Center are displayed before the people. This is especially true given the controversy surrounding the Marshall proposal. For two or three years, there has been public argument concerning the impact of the Marshall proposal on the WVU effort. The closed operating rooms, two-man departments, and faculty facilities will show up someday; I should think the Regents would want to be on record concerning them. Not only do I not feel hesitant about presenting every single item requested to the Legislature, in many ways I feel duty bound to do so. West Virginia's elected officials deserve to know the magnitude of the problem: put bluntly, the people must now decide whether to start another medical school before they have completed the one they have. It is indeed a political and financial decision of considerable magnitude.

In January, 1975, the Board of Regents commissioned George T. Smith, dean of the School of Medical Sciences at the University of Nevada, to review medical education, both actual and potential, in West Virginia. Noting that the Legislature was considering the development of a new medical degree-granting school at Marshall and a request to fund the private Greenbrier School of Osteopathic Medicine at Lewisburg, Dr. Smith seriously questioned whether two new medical schools were needed in West Virginia. He saw that the real need was for adequate funding of the West Virginia University Medical Center, which he said was having difficulty recruiting and holding competent faculty members because the salary scale was below the national average.

Nonetheless, the Legislature and the Governor approved the two new schools, and the Liaison Committee on Medical Education of the American Medical Association gave the Marshall School of Medicine provisional accreditation in the summer of 1977. The VA then committed $15 million to the school over a seven-year development period, and the first class of Marshall medical students began work in January, 1978.

Two years later, the chancellor of the state Board of Regents, Ben Morton, told a legislative finance subcommittee that the three medical schools in West Virginia had produced a situation where it was now too easy to gain entrance. "There is no question that we have more places in our medical schools than anything like the number of qualified students we have in West Virginia," Morton testified. He charged that a number of students with academic averages "well below B" were being accepted just to fill the openings.

Governor Rockefeller seemed to be tackling the problem of the budget for three medical schools reaching $22.6 million costs in 1980 by recommending elimination of the third- and fourth-year programs at the osteopathic school. At the same time, State Finance Commissioner Miles Dean flatly stated that West Virginia could not afford three medical schools. Senator Mario Palumbo said that other state programs would suffer because of the costs of medical education. To the legislator, medical school expenditures were "absolute madness."

The financial needs of the medical schools were not the only problems for higher education in West Virginia.

The Budig emphases on coal research and athletic buildup via new facilities for the major sports encountered two obstacles, one external and the other internal, before his presidency ended. With Ronald Reagan's triumph over Jimmy Carter in the 1980 presidential election, national energy policy no longer seemed to focus on coal as the major oil substitute for the nation.

Not only did Reagan's stunning win (in which West Virginia was only one of four states to cast its vote for Carter) signal a diminution of federal funds for making state universities national energy centers, it also was followed by the administration's decision to cancel a U.S.-Japan-West German contract to construct a billion-dollar synthetic fuel plant near Morgantown, a facility believed of great import to the University, to Morgantown, and to West Virginia.

Budig's other major concern, athletics, was dealt a momentary setback with growing criticism of the athletic department's handling of its funds by the Morgantown *Dominion Post*, which was followed by a legislative investigation and audit, resulting in the resignation of Dick Martin, a Budig-appointed athletic director. However, the seventeenth president escaped living with these setbacks when the University of Kansas in mid-March, 1980, summoned Budig to become its chancellor. This was a challenge Budig felt compelled to accept because, as he explained in a farewell TV appearance before West Virginia audiences, the appointment offered a return to his Midwest homeland and a chance to be near an ailing parent. He was also of the opinion that a four-to-five-year presidency was now normal operating time for the modern college executive.

The University, as it had on two previous occasions, called Harry B. Heflin, who had retired, to assume the presidency for a short period. Being designated on July 1, 1981, the eighteenth president, rather than an acting president, Heflin was given full authority to administer the University. This he quickly did, soon filling the position of athletic director, which he considered the most immediate problem, with a former WVU athletic favorite, Fred Schaus. In his first year as athletic director, Schaus was treated to a very successful 8-3 football season by Coach Don Nehlen, a stunning WVU 26-6 victory over the University of Florida in the Peach Bowl, and a highly successful basketball season under Coach Gale Catlett.

In mid-November, 1981, with an assist from a seventeen-member search committee, the Board of Regents announced the selection of E. Gordon Gee as the nineteenth president of West Virginia University. A graduate of the University of Utah, with a major in history, Gee had added professional training with a doctorate in jurisprudence and a doctorate in education from Columbia University. Having served as an administrative assistant to Chief Justice Warren Burger of the United States Supreme Court and as an assistant law dean, Gee had become dean of West Virginia University's College of Law in 1978. When appointed WVU president, he was 37 years old, and, with an acknowledgment that the University was seeking stable leadership, he indicated his preference for an eight- to ten-year stint in the office.

But monetary needs had been, and undoubtedly were, the history of West Virginia University and her sister institutions in the thirty-fifth state.

E. Gordon Gee
November 16, 1981–

Whereas Charles Ambler concluded in his 1949 account of the state's educational history that there was general accord to the effect that West Virginia could and should support one university, there seemed to be consensus in the 1980s that West Virginia could and should support to a higher degree many institutions falling under the jurisdiction of a single, central Board of Regents.

Not alone, but at the head of the West Virginia educational system, West Virginia University, because of her land-grant and comprehensive character, was demanding her share in the state's bright future. For documentation, she was able to present a history of solid accomplishment in earlier eras that had afforded little historical optimism.

From its formal opening in September, 1868, when President Martin addressed 184 students in attendance (of which only six were enrolled at the college level) on the subject of the "Self-Evidencing Power of Revelation," to October 9, 1979, when President Budig addressed the Faculty Assembly on "WVU, the Energy Leader," West Virginia University had more than proved its survival abilities. The durability she had fostered had been accomplished, always with a proper nod to the political changes occurring within the state, sometimes delicately, and often indelicately, by balancing liberalism with conservatism throughout her more than century-old history.

From an original governing board believing in strong executive influence and preoccupied with the minutiae of discipline, University control had in an early era tipped to a Virginia faction not favoring strict regulation of either students or faculty, a preparatory department, or coeducation. In fact, the political pendulum in the state was so widely swinging after the Civil War and Reconstruction that educational authorities approved the abolition of both the presidency and vice-presidency and the ascendancy of a chairman of the faculty to guide the destiny of the institution. To add confusion to uncertainty, in defiance of the practical and vocational principles of the Morrill Act, the land-grant institution ostentatiously advertised itself as a complete product of the classical traditions, and with its flags hoisted on high, seemed momentarily not to care whether it lived or died, and much less whether or not it was then biting the only hand that cared to feed it.

However, total anarchy was narrowly averted in recognition of time-honored principles of institutional survival and stronger executives who devoted themselves to the establishment of rigid internal controls. There was quickly introduced a semblance of modernism more in tune with America's new industrial age. By the turn of the century, the disapproval of wholesale honorary degrees; the approval of new social science courses, the fine arts, coeducation; excursions into statewide service through correspondence courses and other types of extension work; and the buildup of the professional schools stemmed the design of making WVU too much of a local and almost private, undergraduate educational undertaking for the elite of northern West Virginia.

But the institution, true to form, vacillated again. The infusion of a more liberal, practical, twentieth-century model was dramatically scuttled by the firing of a dynamic, young president, Jerome Raymond. This traumatic event was followed by a conservative reaction in which little expenditures were made in behalf of an inadequate physical plant or in behalf of faculty expansion. As before, WVU became something of an isolated institution of higher learning on the northern perimeter of West Virginia in the period preceding the First World War, hardly a symbol of unity in a highly sectionalized state.

In a brief moment before World War I and up to the Depression, in the name of "new education," WVU came out of its shell. It upgraded its physical plant, almost trebled the staff, increased faculty salaries, and instituted more practical courses for the younger generation. But the seriousness of the Depression, deeply experienced in West Virginia, meant that the University in the Roosevelt era failed to realize a full-fledged graduate program and major library development, and fell irreparably behind in its commitment to faculty well-being, professional training, and an adequate physical plant. Between 1927 and 1947, for example, only one academic classroom building was added to WVU's holdings, and institutional salaries were never again equal to those in comparable institutions bordering the state as they once were in the 1920s, a period often recognized as a time of the greatest faculty talent.

After World War II, a twenty-year period stretching from 1945 to roughly 1965 saw the University for the first time freed by law from political domination, save only fiscal controls and limitations of the state budget.

Seizing the opportunity, the institution broke through most of its earlier barriers to forge a first-class school. Thus, it was able to service an ever-growing student body, made more cosmopolitan by a large infusion of veterans, women, and residents from outside the state and nation, and by the ending of segregated learning within the West Virginia educational system.

Using student fees for capital improvements, physical plant expansion became a planned event; soliciting private money for the WVU Foundation, Inc., intellectual and cultural achievements were no longer dependent on a restricted state budget; purchasing outlying acreage and setting up centers statewide, the University broke its physical confinements on the banks of the Monongahela and did indeed make the "entire state its campus"; establishing a Medical Center on the Morgantown campus, WVU ended, it thought, the seemingly perpetual question of dismemberment or relocation of the University proper. In fact, for one brief twenty-year period, the recognition of WVU as the state's one university was true both in fact and in deed. Complementing its new-found image were its successes in intercollegiate athletics.

With a larger thrust of the federal government into University affairs following the Korean conflict, new and debatable educational concepts ranging from the Appalachian Center to Personal Rapid Transit systems became the planning order of the day. In the more recent period, the allocation of construction monies favored athletic facilities, transportation systems, and the professional schools, over the more narrowly defined liberal arts needs. Internal academic reorganization was dedicated to recognizing the alliance between a state-supported institution and the national government as well as the growth of the student body. With improvements in the state's highway system, more students were in easier reach of West Virginia University than ever before in its history, and the argument that the University could service only a portion of the state's inhabitants became specious.

Major federal funding preceded more restrictive state involvement in WVU affairs when a new governing structure of higher education, a Board of Regents, embraced all institutions of higher learning in the state with the dawning of the 1970s. No longer the one state university, no longer the institution with the only medical college, no longer the University in charge of certain two-year colleges or graduate studies in the more industrial sectors of the state, WVU was expected to be more sharing with its sister institutions in its cut of the educational budget as well as in its academic programming. Its initial reaction after two decades of profiting from the direction and policies of its own governing board was one of shock and betrayal; its later reaction, as chancellors of the statewide system with an assist and a prod from the Legislature, allowed more self-government within the various colleges and universities, was one of growing cooperation.

And what of West Virginia University's future? In all likelihood, there will be in store, as frequently noted, smaller enrollments unless offset by adult and continuing education programs, regional dispersal of some of its functions, and perhaps an increase in graduate enrollments. Due to the demographic diminution of the number of college-age youths to the year 2000, and a growing trend for students to attend two-year colleges, a movement aided and abetted by central board policies, the geography of the state, and the rising costs and soaring inflation of the 1980s, the University cannot be expected to continue the dramatic growth in numbers it experienced after World War II. Its attention to the matter of student servicing may be expected to be of such a vital nature that it will emphasize the quality, rather than quantity, of the total educational package.

The authority of the University administration, conspicuously eroded in the presidency of James G. Harlow, will only be arrested by state educational authorities and boards of control if they see fit not to limit the power of chief executives merely to the operational aspects of WVU, or if the Legislature deems it proper to reduce and contain the power of the central governing boards. The Legislature is again wrestling with its age-old hierarchical problem of schooling: of whether to position WVU at the top of the state's educational pyramid, or to disperse leadership among a number and variety of institutions of higher learning beyond the state's financial abilities and capacities. Without recognizing the historic guidelines, limitations, and mandates of particular institutions, the latter path could well lead to mediocrity for all institutions rather than permitting the realization of the time-honored objectives of each.

At the same time, post-centennial presidents of WVU may be expected to become "managers," achieving a symmetry of supplies and services within the institution and devoting most of their attention to the most efficient utilization of the school's resources in the face of demands for educational services from competing groups. The pattern of centralizing power in the President's Office for operational aspects only, due to larger enrollments and diversified curricula, was demonstrated in the Harlow administration. The faculty, in turn, may well opt for organization and/or unionization in lieu of representative democary via a University Senate in their quest to participate in determining the interrelated policy and financial decisions of WVU.

The University's quest for federal support, to offset inadequate state support, will undoubtedly continue. Having recognized, particularly since the days of Roosevelt's New Deal, that government assistance can provide both employment and grants to students and faculty and that even long-needed repairs and improvements in the physical plant as well as outright grants to universities for new construction are available, the University will undoubtedly tilt its programming to accord with the most recent federal interests such as energy research.

Such opportunism, in turn, may well provide the definitive answer as to whether the University will become polytechnic or will realize its early history as the all-embracing institution planned by its founders. As an offset to materialistic-minded West Virginians, long motivated by their acquisitive interests in coal, oil, gas, limestone, and timber, and who may therefore be prone to accept the polytechnic model, more comprehensive planning and a broader conception of higher education on the part of the central administration and the faculty will become a necessary corrective within a state long dominated by its extractive industries and within a nation long dominated by its defense concerns if the comprehensive educational model becomes the University's preferred role.

As this history sometimes has shown, students usually see the answer of a balance in educational programming more clearly than their counterparts in the educational process, their teachers and administrators, and their patrons, the state and the federal governments. As a student wrote in the *Daily Athenaeum* on March 17, 1980, in a voice not too dissimilar from the clarion call sounded by the founders of the University:

The College of Arts and Sciences, more so than any other, should be kept under our constant highbrow scrutiny, for the liberal arts are the heart and soul of higher education. And, with the creation of such disciplines as the history of science and technology and the history of energy within the College, it's best we continue to keep our guard up. Yet further, with the English, Philosophy and Religious Studies departments exiled to an old gymnasium (however remodeled) on Beechurst, such a vigilance will let our banished friends know they have not been forgotten.

The themes of a University history will thus continue: the problem of attracting the necessary customers to its doors, the degree of political control exercised over the institution by boards of control and the state and national governments, the position of the University itself in the educational structure of the state, and the type of education and degree of organization found within. Its institutional history will of necessity repeat itself, but always with unique challenges, similar to, but not identical with, the earlier provocations.

Woodburn Circle, with the interiors of its three buildings renovated and their classic exteriors preserved, was rededicated on May 12, 1979, in a ceremony that included remarks by WVU's 17th president, Gene A. Budig.

Notes

Chapter 1

1. Earle D. Ross, *Democracy's College: The Land-Grant Movement in the Formative State* (Ames, Iowa: The Iowa State College Press, 1942), p. 79.

2. Festus Summers, manuscript, "History of WVU," p. 10.

3. Ross, *op. cit.*, p. 100.

4. *Ibid.*, p. 104.

5. Alexander Martin, *Inaugural Address*, June 27, 1867.

6. John Phillip Reid, *An American Judge: Marmaduke Dent of West Virginia* (New York: New York University Press, 1968), p. 47.

7. *Ibid.*, p. 7.

Chapter 2

1. M. H. Dent, "The First Experiment," *Monticola*, IX, pp. 76-77.

2. *Ibid.*

3. I. C. White, "The West Virginia University of Fifty or Fifty-Five Years Ago," *The West Virginia University Alumni Quarterly* (1923), p. 17.

4. Samuel Woods to George Sturgiss, January 20, 1876, President's Office Records.

5. As quoted in the *Morgantown Weekly Post*, September 11, 1875, from the *Grafton Sentinel* and September 4, 1875, from the *West Virginia Journal*.

6. As quoted in Charles H. Ambler, *Waitman Thomas Willey* (Huntington, West Virginia: Standard Printing and Publishing, 1954), pp. 184-85.

7. According to a letter to Lucas from T. C. Greene, August 14, 1878, which Lucas enclosed with his letter recommending Brooke to President Thompson in lieu of himself. Lucas to Thompson, September 2, 1878, President's Office Records.

8. *Morgantown Weekly Post*, January 31, 1880, from *Wheeling Register* correspondence signed "A.B.C." in an article entitled "Triumph of Law and Order: In the Contest with the Whiskey Dealers of Morgantown" dated December 29, 1879.

9. As quoted in James M. Callahan, manuscript, "History of WVU," p. 60.

10. Joseph Moreland to A. B. Fleming, May 27, 1881, and E. A. Bennett to J. B. Jackson, January 24, 1883, President's Office Records.

11. Festus P. Summers, *William L. Wilson*, Diary, p. 43.

12. See *New Dominion*, December 2, 1882; February 3, September 1, 1883.

Chapter 3

1. *West Virginia Journal of Education,* March 12, 1879.

2. *Morgantown Weekly Post,* October 15, 1892, quoting *Wheeling Intelligencer* correspondent's article on Campbell's speech of October 1, Mannington, West Virginia.

3. *Ibid.,* February 16, 1889.

4. Berkeley to Fleming, March 2, 1891, President's Office Records.

5. Goodknight to Elkins, February 3, 1897, President's Office Records.

6. *Morgantown Weekly Post,* October 5, 1895 and March 7, 1896.

7. *Morgantown Weekly Post,* May 2, 1896, quoting the *Wellsburg Herald.*

8. Flyer, *Prexy and His Efforts for Discipline* by "Truthful James," President's Office Records.

9. Flyer, *The Life of a Great (?) Man which will be Wisely Re(a)d for Everyone Nose Him,* abstract from the *Presbyterian Banner,* President's Office Records.

10. *Public Papers of Governor W. A. MacCorkle, March 4, 1893 to March 4, 1897* (Charleston, West Virginia: Moses W. Donnally, 1897), pp. 516-17.

Chapter 4

1. State press comment in *Fairmont Index* as quoted in *Morgantown Weekly Post,* July 1, 1897.

2. Frances E. Willard, "A Knight of the New Chivalry, or the Newsboy Who Became College President," *Success,* Volume I (December, 1897), n.p.

3. "Report of the Special Committee to Visit the University," *Journal of the House of Delegates of the State of West Virginia, 1899,* February 20, 1899, p. 587.

4. Letter, President Raymond to Harvey F. Smith, October 10, 1900, President's Office Records.

5. See Chapter 32, *Acts of the Legislature, 1901,* pp. 86-88 and letter, Alfred E. Thayer to President Raymond, March 23, 1900, President's Office Records.

6. Thomas C. Atkeson, *Pioneering in Agriculture,* p. 146.

7. Charles H. Ambler, *A History of Education in West Virginia* (Huntington: Standard Printing Company, 1951), pp. 337-38.

8. *Morgantown Evening Post,* May 11-12, 1900.

9. Letter, Frank P. Corbin, December 3, 1900; Mayor Posten, October 13, 1900; C. N. McWhorter, October 18, 1900 to Committee on Student Affairs.

10. John R. Wallace to Sub-Committee on Student Affairs, October 14, 1900.

11. Letters, E. T. Hartman to President Raymond, August 1, August 5, and November 21, 1898. President's Office Records.

12. See letter, Raymond to Professor H. N. Mateer, University of Wooster, June 23, 1898.

13. John Phillip Reid, *An American Judge: Marmaduke Dent of West Virginia* (New York: New York University Press, 1968), p. 103.

14. All of these negative criticisms can be found in committee report of a joint committee consisting of three Republicans and two Democrats to "Investigate the management and affairs of the . . . University," in *Journal of the Senate of the State of West Virginia, Twenty-fifth Regular Session* (Charleston: The Tribune Company, 1901), p. 345.

15. James M. Callahan, manuscript, "History of WVU," p. 295.

Chapter 5

1. J. B. Findley to George S. Laidley, May 29, 1910, President's Office Records.

2. Quoted in *Morgantown Post Chronicle*, December 29, 1911.

3. Charles C. Wise, Jr., "Development of Policy for Higher Education in West Virginia," August 9, 1977.

4. Charles H. Ambler, *A History of Education in West Virginia* (Huntington: Standard Printing Company, 1951), p. 506, quoting from the Glasscock papers.

5. Marshall Lee Buckalew, "The Life of Dr. Morris Purdy Shawkey," MA thesis, West Virginia University, pp. 125-27.

6. *Athenaeum*, October 31, 1910.

Chapter 6

1. James M. Callahan, "Presidents of WVU: Sketches of their Educational Service," (1944), p. 93.

2. James M. Callahan, "Frank Butler Trotter," *WVU Alumni Magazine*, Vol. V, No. 4 (Spring, 1940), p. 6.

3. Charles H. Ambler, *A History of Education in West Virginia* (Huntington: Standard Printing Company, 1951), pp. 511-13.

4. O. P. Chitwood, "West Virginia and the World War," Chapter 38 in James M. Callahan, *History of West Virginia, Old and New* (Vol. I) (Chicago: American Historical Society, 1923), pp. 697-710.

5. H. A. Stansbury, "The University Athletic Problem," *WVU Alumni Magazine*, Vol. I, No. 2 (January, 1936), p. 6.

6. George Trevor, "West Virginia's All-Time Eleven," *WVU Alumni Magazine*, Vol. I, No. 1 (October, 1926), p. 9.

7. Jane Holt to Rush Holt, April 6, 1933, Rush D. Holt Papers.

Chapter 7

1. John Roscoe Turner, *Inaugural Address*, November 28, 1928.

2. *Morgantown Post*, December 5, 1927.

3. John Roscoe Turner, "Reasons Why West Virginia Veterans Hospital Should Be Located at West Virginia University," pamphlet, n.d.

4. See General Education Board inter-office memorandum, "Re: appropriation GI 2120 to West Virginia University," Rockefeller Archive Center, North Tarrytown, N.Y.

5. West Virginia University Bulletin, Series 32, No. 13, *Announcements, Graduate Courses and Degrees*, 1932-33.

6. C. R. Jones to George Wallace, Huntington, West Virginia, February 15, 1932.

7. *Morgantown Post*, September 25, 1930.

8. W. P. Shortridge to President Turner, June 20 and June 27, 1933.

9. Leo M. Farrot, memo to Rockefeller officials, January 2, 1932. Also see Earl Hudelson to Leo M. Farrot, November 24, 1933. Rockefeller Archive Center, North Tarrytown, N.Y.

10. Governor H. G. Kump to E. G. Smith, August 6, 1934 and E. G. Smith to H. G. Kump, August 16, 1934.

Chapter 8

1. Thurman Arnold to O. P. Chitwood, February 18, 1931, Oliver P. Chitwood papers, West Virginia Collection.

2. Committee reports to Dr. John Sly, 1935, President's Office Records.

3. Minutes of the Board of Governors, July 29, 1935.

4. Minutes of the Board of Governors, August 29, 1936.

5. "Cooperative Administration," *WVU Alumni Magazine*, Vol. I, No. 2 (January, 1936), p. 3.

6. Minutes of the Board of Governors, November 1, 1935.

7. Minutes of the Board of Governors, December 7, 1935.

8. "President's Message," *WVU Alumni Magazine*, Vol. V, No. 2 (Fall, 1939).

9. Bulletin of the American Association of University Professors, Vol. XXVI, No. 3 (June, 1940), pp. 315-34.

10. Minutes of the Board of Governors, June 16, 1944.

11. "Program for WVU Development," adopted by the Faculty, July 13, 1944.

12. Charles C. Wise, Jr., "Development of Policy for Higher Education in West Virginia," August 9, 1977.

13. *AAUP Newsletter*, No. 2, January, 1945.

Chapter 9

1. See *Press Guides*, 1956-58, edited by Edgar O. Barrett, WVU Athletic Publicity Director.

2. *West Virginia University Bulletin*, Series 58, No. 12-2, June 1958, p. 35.

3. *Charleston Gazette*, July 29, 1956 and *Wheeling Intelligencer*, July 6, 1956.

4. Board of Governors Minutes, January 27, 1951, and Resolution No. 678, June 2, 1951.

5. Board of Governors Resolution 787 in Board of Governors minutes of April 28, 1956.

6. Irvin Stewart to Edward L. Blake, Ranson, West Virginia, January 12, 1948.

7. Rush Holt to Irvin Stewart, May 22, 1951, and Irvin Stewart to Board of Governors, May 23, 1951.

8. William R. Ross to Irvin Stewart, January 28, 1952, and Irvin Stewart to William R. Ross, January 30, 1952.

9. Irvin Stewart to Board of Governors, July 2, 1958; Robert Donley to Irvin Stewart, July 3, 1958.

Chapter 10

1. See Article 19, Section 999, "Soft Drinks Tax," *Taxation*, pp. 526-28.

2. Irvin Stewart, Memorandum to members of the West Virginia Legislature, February 6, 1957.

3. "Dr. Gregg comments on Dean Davison's Report," *The Case for Keeping School of Medicine on University Campus* (Morgantown, West Virginia: Morgantown Printing and Binding Company, n.d.), p. 6.

4. Kenneth A. Penrod, "A Modern Medical Center is Born," *Journal of Medical Education*, Vol. 36, No. 5, May, 1961, pp. 393-397.

Chapter 11

1. Report of the Comptroller to the President of West Virginia University, 1958-59; 1959-60; 1960-61; 1961-62.

2. Report of the President of West Virginia University, July 1, 1960, to June 30, 1961, to Members of the Board of Governors.

3. UPI dispatch, March 2, 1961, Huntington, West Virginia.

Chapter 12

1. Paul Miller to Irvin Stewart, August 3, 1966.

2. Paul Miller to Professor John S. Zawacki, May 12, 1964.

3. Board of Governors Minutes, July 7-9, 1966.

4. Stanley Lawson, Superior Court of the State of California, to the Board of Governors, August 16, 1966.

5. James H. Brewster, Jr., Weston, West Virginia, to Harry B. Heflin, June 21, 1967.

Chapter 13

1. John Douglas Machesney, "The Development of Higher Education Governance and Coordination in West Virginia," Ph. D. dissertation, West Virginia University, 1971, p. 112.

2. Memorandum to Ed Smith from Mary Ann McWhorter, March 15, 1978, on the subject of: "the percentage of the state's budget allocated to higher education since 1965."

3. Jay Barton to Professor I. D. Peters re: "July 18 Draft on Academic Freedom and Responsibility, Appointment, Promotion, Tenure and Termination of Employment of Professional Personnel," August 9, 1973.

4. *Railway Age*, September 8, 1975 and *Aviation Week and Space Technology*, November 8, 1971.

5. See *Congressional Record — House*, June 14, 1974, p. H 5283; *Washington Post*, June 2, 1974; *U. S. News and World Report*, April 29, 1974; *The New York Times*, April 13, 1974.

Chapter 14

1. Board of Governors Minutes, June 21, 1969.

2. *West Virginia University Magazine*, Vol. 7, No. 2, Summer, 1975, p. 8.

3. Memorandum from Jay Barton to Harry Heflin re: telephone call from Chancellor Woodard, 4:15 p.m., September 17, 1971.

4. Nicholas Von Hoffman, "Protest on the March," *Washington Post*, October 17, 1969.

5. Request for Intra-Fund Transfer for Fiscal Year, 1969-70, IM No. 00945, March, 1970.

6. *Daily Athenaeum* (special edition), May 7, 1970.

7. *Loc cit.*

8. *Daily Athenaeum*, June 25, 1970.

9. *Dominion News*, June 25, 1970.

10. *Ibid.*, July 6, 1970.

11. Harold Shamberger to Londo Brown, June 5, 1975.

12. "Report on the State of the Campus," WVU, February 2, 1967.

Chapter 15

1. *Charleston Gazette*, March 11, 1978.

Selected Bibliography

Chapter 1

GENERAL: Henry Steele Commager, *Documents of American History;* James D. Richardson, ed., *A Compilation of the Messages and Papers of the Presidents;* Earl D. Ross, *Democracy's College: The Land-Grant Movement in the Formative State;* Festus P. Summers, *The Baltimore and Ohio in the Civil War; U.S. Statutes at Large,* XII; *Congressional Globe,* 37th Congress, 2nd Session; *Lincoln Papers.*

WEST VIRGINIA: Charles Ambler, *A History of Education in West Virginia from Early Colonial Times to 1949;* Charles Ambler, Frances Atwood, and W. B. Matthews, eds., *Debates and Proceedings of the First Constitutional Convention of West Virginia, 1861-63;* Charles Ambler and Festus Summers, *West Virginia: The Mountain State;* James M. Callahan, *History of West Virginia Old and New;* Elizabeth Cometti and Festus P. Summers, *The Thirty-Fifth State: A Documentary History of West Virginia;* John Philip Reid, *An American Judge: Marmaduke Dent of West Virginia;* Samuel T. Wiley, *History of Monongalia County, West Virginia.*

STATE DOCUMENTS: *Acts of the Legislature of West Virginia,* 1867; *Journal of the House of Delegates of the State of West Virginia,* 1866-69; *Journal of the Senate of the State of West Virginia,* 1866-69.

WEST VIRGINIA UNIVERSITY: *Annual Reports of the Board of Regents of West Virginia University,* First, 1868; Second, 1869; Third, 1870; Fourth, 1871; *Biennial Report of the Board of Regents of West Virginia University for the years 1873 and 1874; Catalogs of West Virginia University,* 1869-70; West Virginia University Board of Regents Minutes, 1869-73; Alexander Martin, "Inaugural Address," June 27, 1867; Harry W. Ernst, ed., *West Virginia University, A Pictorial History, 1867-1979.*

NEWSPAPERS: *Preston County Journal; Morgantown Weekly Post; Wheeling Intelligencer.*

MANUSCRIPTS, DISSERTATIONS, AND PAPERS RELATING TO WEST VIRGINIA UNIVERSITY: James Morton Callahan, "History of WVU"; Robert Munn, "West Virginia University Library, 1867-1917"; Festus P. Summers, "History of WVU"; President's Office Records, 1867-69.

Chapter 2

GENERAL: Frederick Rudolph, *The American College and University;* William Warren Sweet, *Indiana Asbury-Depauw University 1837-1937: A Hundred Years of Higher Education in the Middle West;* Francis Butler Simkins, *A*

History of the South; Festus P. Summers, *William L. Wilson and Tariff Reform;* Festus P. Summers, ed., *The Cabinet Diary of William L. Wilson, 1896-1897.*

WEST VIRGINIA: Charles Ambler, *A History of Education in West Virginia from Early Colonial Times to 1949;* Charles Ambler, *Waitman Thomas Willey;* Charles Ambler and Festus P. Summers, *West Virginia: The Mountain State;* Millard K. Bushong, *Historic Jefferson County;* William T. Doherty, *Berkeley County, U.S.A.;* Minutes of the West Virginia Annual Conference of the Methodist Episcopal Church, 1877 and 1878; *West Virginia Educational Monthly,* April, 1876; *West Virginia Journal of Education,* 1878 and 1879; *West Virginia School Journal,* 1884.

STATE DOCUMENTS: *Acts of the Legislature of West Virginia,* 1867-1882; *Constitution of the State of West Virginia,* 1872; *Journal of the House of Delegates of the State of West Virginia,* 1872-1885; *Journal of the Senate of the State of West Virginia,* 1885; *West Virginia Public Documents,* 1871.

WEST VIRGINIA UNIVERSITY: *Annual Reports of the Board of Regents of West Virginia University,* First, 1868; Second, 1869; Third, 1870; Fourth, 1871; Fifth, 1872; *Biennial Report of the Board of Regents of West Virginia University,* 1877-78; 1883-84; 1885-86; *Special Message and Report of the Board of Visitors of West Virginia Agricultural College,* 1868; Faculty Minutes, 1873-84; *Catalogs of West Virginia University,* 1867-85; *The Monticola of West Virginia University,* 1901; Harry W. Ernst, ed., *West Virginia University, A Pictorial History,* 1867-1979.

NEWSPAPERS: *Charleston Courier; Grafton Sentinel; Martinsburg Statesman; Morgantown Weekly Post; New Dominion; Parkersburg State Journal; Shepherdstown Register; Weston Democrat; Wheeling Daily Register; Wheeling Intelligencer; Wheeling Standard.*

MANUSCRIPTS, DISSERTATIONS, AND PAPERS RELATING TO WEST VIRGINIA UNIVERSITY: James Morton Callahan, "History of WVU"; James Morton Callahan Papers; Festus P. Summers, "History of WVU"; President's Office Records, 1867-1885.

Chapter 3

GENERAL: Thomas Clark and Mary Meek Atkeson, *Pioneering in Agriculture, One Hundred Years of American Farming, and Farm Leadership; Dictionary of American Biography; The Statutes at Large of the United States of America from December 1885 to March 1887 and Recent Treaties, Postal Conventions and Executive Proclamations.*

WEST VIRGINIA: Charles Ambler, *A History of Education in West Virginia from Early Colonial Times to 1949;* Charles Ambler and Festus Summers, *West Virginia: The Mountain State;* George W. Atkinson and Alvaro F. Gibbons, *Men of West Virginia;* James M. Callahan, *History of the Making of Morgan-*

town, West Virginia; Tony Constantine, *Mountaineer Football, 1891-1969; West Virginia School Journal.*

STATE DOCUMENTS: *Acts of the West Virginia Legislature,* 1887, 1891, 1895, 1897; *Journal and Bills of the Senate of the State of West Virginia,* 1897; *Journal of the House of Delegates of the State of West Virginia,* 1889-1892; *Journal of the Senate of the State of West Virginia,* 1889; *Public Papers of Governor W. A. MacCorkle, March 4, 1893 to March 4, 1897; West Virginia Blue Books,* 1893-1901; *West Virginia Constitution,* 1872.

WEST VIRGINIA UNIVERSITY: West Virginia Agricultural Experiment Station, Bulletin No. 1, July 1888; *West Virginia University Alumni Magazine,* 1938; *Biennial Reports of the Board of Regents of West Virginia University,* 1885-86; 1887-88; 1889-90; 1891-92; 1895-96; West Virginia Board of Regents Minutes, 1884-97; *Catalogs of West Virginia University,* 1883-84; Faculty Minutes, 1896; *The Monticola of West Virginia University,* 1896; Harry W. Ernst, ed., *West Virginia University, A Pictorial History, 1867-1979.*

NEWSPAPERS: *Charleston Evening Mail; Clarksburg News; Daily Athenaeum; Fairmont Index; Fairmont West Virginian; Grafton Leader; Kingwood Argus; Morgantown Weekly Post; New Dominion; Parkersburg State Journal; Wellsburg Herald; Wetzel Democrat; Wheeling Intelligencer; Wheeling News; Wheeling Register; Uniontown (Pa) Standard.*

MANUSCRIPTS, DISSERTATIONS, AND PAPERS RELATING TO WEST VIRGINIA UNIVERSITY: James Morton Callahan, "History of WVU"; James Morton Callahan, "Presidents of WVU: Sketches of Their Educational Services"; A.B. Fleming papers; Robert F. Munn, "West Virginia University Library, 1867-1917"; Festus P. Summers, "History of WVU"; President's Office Records, 1885-97.

Chapter 4

GENERAL: Thomas Clark and Mary Meek Atkeson, *Pioneering in Agriculture, One Hundred Years of American Farming, and Farm Leadership;* H. S. Commager review, "Lester Ward and the Welfare State," *Washington Post,* November 2, 1967; Lester F. Ward, *Outlines of Sociology, Dynamic Sociology,* and *Psychic Factors of Civilization; Journal of Education,* 1899; *Review of Reviews,* 1897; *Success,* 1897; *Who Was Who in America.*

WEST VIRGINIA: Charles Ambler, *A History of Education in West Virginia from Early Colonial Times to 1949;* Charles Ambler and Festus Summers, *West Virginia: The Mountain State;* John Phillip Reid, *An American Judge: Marmaduke Dent of West Virginia;* Edward J. Van Liere and Gideon S. Dodds, *History of Medical Education in West Virginia;* John Alexander Williams, *West Virginia and the Captains of Industry; The West Virginia School Journal,* 1899.

STATE DOCUMENTS: *Acts of the Legislature of West Virginia,* 1895, 1897, 1899, 1901, 1903; *Journal of the House of Delegates of the State of West Virginia,*

1899; *Journal of the Senate of the State of West Virginia,* 1901; *West Virginia Reports,* 1902.

WEST VIRGINIA UNIVERSITY: *Announcements for the Summer Quarter,* 1898; *Athenaeum; Aurora; Biennial Report of the Board of Regents and the President of West Virginia University,* 1898, 1900; *Biennial Report of the President of the University to the Board of Regents,* 1902; Board of Regents Minutes, 1897-1900; Bulletins from the Committee on Student Affairs, 1900; *Catalogs of West Virginia University,* 1897-1900; Executive Committee Minutes, 1897-1900; Faculty Minutes, 1897; Mary Ann McWhorter, ed., *West Virginia University Statistical Profiles,* 1977-78; *Monticola,* 1901; Report of the President of West Virginia University to the Board of Regents, 1898, 1900; Harry W. Ernst, ed., *West Virginia University, A Pictorial History, 1867-1979.*

NEWSPAPERS: *Fairmont Index; Madison* (Wisc) *Democrat; Morgantown Evening Post; Morgantown Weekly Post; New Dominion.*

MANUSCRIPTS, DISSERTATIONS, AND PAPERS RELATING TO WEST VIRGINIA UNIVERSITY: James Morton Callahan, "History of WVU"; Robert Munn, "West Virginia University Library, 1867-1917"; Festus P. Summers, "History of WVU"; President's Office Records, 1897-1901.

Chapter 5

GENERAL: Merle Curti, *Social Ideas of American Educators;* Merle Curti, *The Growth of American Thought;* Walter Lynwood Fleming, ed., *Documentary History of Reconstruction;* Walter Lynwood Fleming, *Reconstruction of the Seceded States;* Walter Lynwood Fleming, *Civil War and Reconstruction in Alabama;* Eric Goldman, *Rendezvous with Destiny: A History of Modern American Reform;* Richard Hofstadter, *The Age of Reform; Who Was Who in America.*

WEST VIRGINIA: Charles Ambler, *A History of Education in West Virginia from Early Colonial Times to 1949;* Charles Ambler and Festus Summers, *West Virginia: The Mountain State;* Phil Conley and William T. Doherty, *West Virginia History;* Tony Constantine, *Mountaineer Football, 1891-1969; West Virginia School Journal.*

STATE DOCUMENTS: *Acts of the West Virginia Legislature,* 1907, 1909, 1919; 1927; *Journal of the West Virginia House of Delegates,* 1907; *Public Documents of West Virginia,* 1913-14; *Report of Committee Appointed under House Substitute for Senate Joint Resolution No. 21,* 1907; *Third Biennial Report of the State Board of Control,* 1914.

WEST VIRGINIA UNIVERSITY: *Athenaeum;* Board of Regents Minutes, 1909; *West Virginia University Alumni Magazine,* 1936, 1937; *The Campus Scene,* 1978; Harry W. Ernst, *West Virginia University, A Pictorial History, 1867-1979; Catalogs of West Virginia University,* 1901-1914.

NEWSPAPERS: *Charleston Mail; Clarksburg Telegraph; Huntington Advertiser; Morgantown Post Chronicle; New Dominion; Parkersburg State Journal; Wheeling News; Wheeling Register; Wisconsin State Journal.*

MANUSCRIPTS, DISSERTATIONS, AND PAPERS RELATING TO WEST VIRGINIA UNIVERSITY: Marshall Lee Buckalew, "The Life of Dr. Morris Purdy Shawkey"; James Morton Callahan, "Presidents of West Virginia University: Sketches of Their Educational Service"; James Morton Callahan, "History of WVU"; Walter Lynwood Fleming Papers, Auburn University; W. E. Glasscock Papers; John Douglas Machesney, "The Development of Higher Education Governance and Coordination in West Virginia"; Festus P. Summers, "History of WVU"; Gary Tucker, "William E. Glasscock Thirteenth Governor of West Virginia"; Charles C. Wise, Jr., "Development of Policy for Higher Education in West Virginia."

Chapter 6

GENERAL: Paolo E. Coletta, *William Jennings Bryan;* Everett B. Sakett, *New Hampshire's University: The Story of a New England Land-Grant College; Who Was Who in America.*

WEST VIRGINIA: Charles Ambler, *A History of Education in West Virginia from Early Colonial Times to 1949;* Charles Ambler and Festus Summers, *West Virginia: The Mountain State;* James M. Callahan, *History of the Making of Morgantown, West Virginia;* James M. Callahan, *History of West Virginia Old and New;* Tony Constantine, *Mountaineer Football, 1891-1969;* Earl Core, *The Monongalia Story;* William T. Doherty, *Berkeley County, U.S.A.; History of the Sesqui-Centennial of Monongalia County, West Virginia, 1926.*

STATE DOCUMENTS: *Acts of the West Virginia Legislature, 1927; Public Documents of West Virginia, 1913-14; West Virginia Blue Books, 1914-1928.*

WEST VIRGINIA UNIVERSITY: *Athenaeum;* Board of Regents Minutes, 1916; Harry W. Ernst, ed., *West Virginia University, A Pictorial History, 1867-1979; West Virginia University Alumni Magazine,* 1926, 1936, 1940; *West Virginia University Handbook, 1978-79; Catalogs of West Virginia University,* 1914-1928.

NEWSPAPERS: *Charleston Gazette; Charleston Mail; Dominion News; Huntington Herald Dispatch; Morgantown Post; Morgantown Post Chronicle; Parkersburg Sentinel; State Journal; Wheeling Intelligencer; Wheeling News.*

MANUSCRIPTS, DISSERTATIONS, AND PAPERS RELATING TO WEST VIRGINIA UNIVERSITY: James Morton Callahan, "History of WVU"; James Morton Callahan, "Presidents of WVU: Sketches of Their Education Service"; James Morton Callahan, Jr., "Morgantown, 1925-50, An Economic and Social Study"; Rush D. Holt Papers; John Douglas Machesney, "The Development of Higher Education Governance and Coordination in West Virginia."

Chapter 7

GENERAL: John Roscoe Turner, *Introduction to Economics; The Ricardo Rent Theory in Early American Economics.*

WEST VIRGINIA: Charles Ambler, *A History of Education in West Virginia from Early Colonial Times to 1949;* Phil Conley and William T. Doherty, *West Virginia History;* Earl Core, *The Monongalia Story;* Tony Constantine, *Mountaineer Football, 1891-1969.*

STATE DOCUMENTS: *Acts of the West Virginia Legislature,* 1927; "John Roscoe Turner's report to the House Committee on the Investigation of the University, West Virginia Legislature, December 27, 1933"; *Morgantown Municipal Financial Picture,* 1939; *West Virginia Blue Books,* 1928-46.

WEST VIRGINIA UNIVERSITY: *Athenaeum;* "First Annual Report of the Board of Governors of West Virginia University from July 1, 1927 to October 1, 1932"; *Program, Inauguration of John Roscoe Turner, November 27 and 28, 1928;* John Roscoe Turner, *Inaugural Address, 1928;* John Roscoe Turner, "Reasons Why West Virginia Veterans Hospital Should Be Located at West Virginia University," *West Virginia University Bulletin Series 32, No. 13, 1932-33";* "Report of the College of Arts and Sciences, West Virginia University, October 1, 1933 to September 30, 1934"; *Catalogs of West Virginia University,* 1928-35.

NEWSPAPERS: *Charleston Daily Mail; Charleston Gazette; Dominion News; Huntington Advertiser; Morgantown Post; New Dominion; West Union Record; Wheeling News.*

MANUSCRIPTS, DISSERTATIONS, AND PAPERS RELATING TO WEST VIRGINIA UNIVERSITY: James Morton Callahan, "History of WVU"; James Morton Callahan, "Presidents of WVU: Sketches of Their Education Services"; General Education Board's inter-office memoranda re appropriation to WVU, and correspondence on University Demonstration High School between Earl Hudelson and Leo M. Farrot, Rockefeller Archive Center; H. G. Kump papers; John F. Sly correspondence.

Chapter 8

GENERAL: Chauncey S. Boucher, *The Nullification Controversy in South Carolina; The Ante-Bellum Attitude of South Carolina towards Manufacturing and Agriculture; The Secession and Cooperation Movements in South Carolina; South Carolina and the South on the Eve of Secession, 1852 to 1860; The Annexation of Texas and the Bluffton Movement in South Carolina; Correspondence addressed to John C. Calhoun, 1836-1949; The Chicago Plan.*

WEST VIRGINIA: Charles Ambler, *A History of Education in West Virginia from Early Colonial Times to 1949;* Earl Core, *The Monongalia Story;* Tony Constantine, *Mountaineer Football, 1891-1969.*

STATE DOCUMENTS: *Acts of the West Virginia Legislature*, 1921, 1947; Matthew
M. Neely, *State Papers and Public Addresses*, 1945; George D. Strayer, *A Report of a Survey of Public Education in the State of West Virginia.*

WEST VIRGINIA UNIVERSITY: *Athenaeum; Bulletin of the American Association of University Professors*, XXVI, Number 3 (June 1940); Minutes of the Board of Governors, 1935, 1936, 1944; Faculty Bulletin, "Program for West Virginia University Development," 1944; John Roscoe Turner, *Inaugural Address, 1928;* The American Association of University Professors Newsletter, West Virginia University, 1945; "The West Virginia University," broadcast by Matthew M. Neely, 1945; *West Virginia University Alumni Magazine*, 1936, 1938, 1939; Harry W. Ernst, ed., *West Virginia University, A Pictorial History, 1867-1979; Catalogs of West Virginia University, 1932-45.*

NEWSPAPERS: *Charleston Gazette; Morgantown Post; Morgantown Sunday Dominion News; PM* (New York); *Raleigh Register; Wheeling Intelligencer.*

MANUSCRIPTS, DISSERTATIONS AND PAPERS RELATING TO WEST VIRGINIA UNIVERSITY: S. P. Burke correspondence; James Morton Callahan, "Presidents of WVU: Sketches of Their Education Service"; Oliver P. Chitwood papers; H. G. Kump papers; Albert Steven Gatrell, "Herman Guy Kump: A Political Profile"; John Douglas Machesney, "The Development of Higher Education Governance and Coordination in West Virginia"; President's Office Records; Charles C. Wise, Jr., "Development of Policy for Higher Education in West Virginia."

Chapter 9

GENERAL: Irvin Stewart, *Organizing Scientfic Research for War.*

WEST VIRGINIA: Charles Ambler, *A History of Education in West Virginia from Early Colonial Times to 1949;* John E. Brewton, *Public Higher Education in West Virginia;* George D. Strayer, *A Report of a Survey of Public Education in the State of West Virginia;* Irvin Stewart, "West Virginia University and Medical Education in West Virginia," *West Virginia Medical Journal,* 1948; Tony Constantine, *Mountaineer Football, 1891-1969.*

STATE DOCUMENTS: *Glover* vs. *Sims,* State Supreme Court, June, 1939; Senate Concurrent Resolution No. 6, February 26, 1945.

WEST VIRGINIA UNIVERSITY: *Athenaeum; Bulletin of the Bureau for Government Research,* 1967; *Catalogs of West Virginia University,* 1946-58; Harry W. Ernst, ed., *West Virginia University, A Pictorial History,* 1867-1979; West Virginia University Board of Governors Minutes, 1946-58; West Virginia University Loyalty Oath; West Virginia University Comptroller's Report to the President of West Virginia University, 1946-58; *West Virginia University Bulletin,* 1958; *West Virginia University Magazine,* 1975; Edgar O. Barrett, *Press Guides, 1956-58.*

NEWSPAPERS: *Bluefield Telegraph; Charleston Gazette; Dominion News; Huntington Herald Advertiser; Jefferson Republican; Morgantown Post; Parkersburg News; Sunday Exponent Telegram; Wheeling Intelligencer.*

MANUSCRIPTS, DISSERTATIONS, AND PAPERS RELATING TO WEST VIRGINIA UNIVERSITY: President's Office Files, 1948-58; President's speeches; President's memoranda to the President and Members of the Board of Governors, 1946-58.

Chapter 10

GENERAL: *The Board of Curators Report on the University of Missouri Survey of Medical Education,* 1945; Kenneth E. Penrod, "A Modern Medical Center Is Born," *Journal of Medical Education,* 1961; Vernon W. Leopard, *Report of the Director of the Survey and Advisory Committee to the Committee on the Medical Survey of Florida,* 1949; William T. Sanger, *Final Report on the North Carolina Medical Care Commission, National Committee for Medical School Survey,* 1946.

WEST VIRGINIA: Charles Ambler, *A History of Education in West Virginia from Early Colonial Times to 1949;* Pamphlet, "The Case for Keeping the School of Medicine on the University Campus," 1950; Resolution, West Virginia State Medical Association, November 21, 1950; Irvin Stewart, "West Virginia University and Medical Education in West Virginia," *West Virginia Medical Journal,* 1948; *West Virginia Medical Journal,* 1945-51.

STATE DOCUMENTS: *Report by Governor Okey L. Patteson concerning the location of the Medical School for Doctors, Dentists and Nurses in the State of West Virginia,* June 30, 1951; *Report of the Legislative Interim Committee on Medical Education in West Virginia,* 1951; Senate Concurrent Resolution Number 9, West Virginia Legislature, 1949; Article 19, Section 999, Soft Drink Tax, *Taxation,* West Virginia Legislature, 1951.

WEST VIRGINIA UNIVERSITY: Annual Report of the President of the University to the Board of Governors, July 1, 1950 to June 30, 1951; Resolution on Medical Education by the Board of Governors of West Virginia University, October 27, 1950; *West Virginia University Alumni Magazine,* 1952; West Virginia University Board of Governors Minutes, 1946-58; West Virginia University Board of Governors Press Releases, 1948, 1959; Harry W. Ernst, ed., *West Virginia University, A Pictorial History, 1867-1979.*

NEWSPAPERS: *Bluefield Daily Telegraph; Charleston Daily Mail; Charleston Gazette; Fairmont Times; Huntington Herald Dispatch; Morgantown Post; Parkersburg News; Wheeling Intelligencer.*

MANUSCRIPTS, DISSERTATIONS, AND PAPERS RELATING TO WEST VIRGINIA UNIVERSITY: Charles E. Hodges correspondence, 1952; President's Office Files, 1946-58; President's speeches; President's memoranda to the President and members of the Board of Governors, 1946-58.

Chapter 11

GENERAL: Congressional Quarterly Service, *Congress and the Nation, 1945-64.*

WEST VIRGINIA: Tony Constantine, *Mountaineer Football, 1891-1969*; Roul Tunley, "The Strange Case of West Virginia," *Saturday Evening Post,* February 6, 1960.

STATE DOCUMENTS: *Acts of the West Virginia Legislature,* 1961.

WEST VIRGINIA UNIVERSITY: *Athenaeum; Catalogs of West Virginia University,* 1958-61; Harry W. Ernst, ed., *West Virginia University, A Pictorial History, 1867-1979;* Minutes of the Council of Administration, 1961; Report of the Comptroller to the President of West Virginia University, 1958-61; Report of the President of West Virginia University, July 1, 1960 to June 30, 1961; Elvis Stahr's address, 1959, before Governor Underwood, Members of the Board of Public Works, and Members of the Council of Finance and Administration; *West Virginia University Alumni Magazine,* 1958-61; West Virginia University Board of Governors Minutes, 1958-61; *West Virginia University Bulletin,* Series 58, No. 12-2, 1958; *West Virginia University Statistical Profiles, 1977-78.*

NEWSPAPERS: *Charleston Gazette; Dominion News; Fairmont Times; Hinton Leader; Morgantown Post; Point Pleasant Register; Wheeling Intelligencer.*

MANUSCRIPTS, DISSERTATIONS, AND PAPERS RELATING TO WEST VIRGINIA UNIVERSITY: President's Office Records, 1958-61; President's speeches; President's memoranda to the President and members of the Board of Governors, 1958-61; President's telegrams to the Committee of 55.

Chapter 12

GENERAL: Congressional Quarterly Service, *Congress and the Nation, 1945-64.*

WEST VIRGINIA: Donovan Bond, *The 100th Anniversary Observance of West Virginia University: Through Changing Knowledge to Enduring Wisdom,* October 15, 1968; Tony Constantine, *Mountaineer Football, 1891-1969.*

STATE DOCUMENTS: House Bill 231, *West Virginia Legislature,* 1963.

WEST VIRGINIA UNIVERSITY: *Athenaeum;* AWS Executive Council Minutes, 1962; *Bulletin of the Bureau for Government Research,* 1967; *Catalogs of West Virginia University,* 1962-67; Comptroller's Report to the President of West Virginia University, 1962-67; Harry W. Ernst, ed., *West Virginia University, A Pictorial History, 1867-1979; Growth* (WVU publication); Panhellenic Council Minutes, 1962; Report of the Acting President of West Virginia University, July 1, 1966 to June 30, 1967, to the Members of the Board of Governors of West Virginia University; Report of the Provost, July 1, 1966 to June 30, 1967, to the President of West Virginia University; Reports of West Virginia University, 1962-63 to 1966-67 in *West Virginia Bulletin* Series

64, 65, 66, 67, 1962-67; West Virginia University Board of Governors Minutes, 1962-67; West Virginia University Senate Minutes, 1962-67.

NEWSPAPERS: *Charleston Daily Mail; Charleston Gazette; Dominion News; Fairmont Times; Morgantown Post; Sunday Gazette Mail; Wheeling Intelligencer; West Virginia Hillbilly.*

MANUSCRIPTS, DISSERTATIONS, AND PAPERS RELATING TO WEST VIRGINIA UNIVERSITY: President's Office Records, 1962-67; President's speeches; President's memoranda to the President and members of the Board of Governors, 1962-67.

Chapter 13

GENERAL: *Aviation Week and Space Technology*, 1971 and 1974; *Chicago Tribune*, 1974; Congressional Quarterly Service, *Congress and the Nation, 1945-64; Congressional Record*, House, 1974; *Engineering News Record*, 1973 and 1974; *Modern Railroads*, 1975; *The New York Times*, 1971 and 1974; *Railway Age*, 1975; *Readers Digest*, 1977; *U.S. News and World Report*, 1974; *Washington Post*, 1974.

WEST VIRGINIA: John E. Brewton, *Public Higher Education in West Virginia, A Survey, 1956.*

STATE DOCUMENTS: *Acts of the West Virginia Legislature*, 1961, 1965, 1966, 1969; "Joint Committee of the West Virginia University Board of Governors and the West Virginia Board of Education — An Historical Summary and Review," 1961; *Journal of the West Virginia House of Delegates*, 1957, 1968, 1969; *Journal of the West Virginia Senate*, 1967; West Virginia Committee on Higher Education, Report to the Honorable Hulett C. Smith, Governor of West Virginia, and the Legislature of the State of West Virginia, 1965.

WEST VIRGINIA UNIVERSITY: *Athenaeum; Catalogs of West Virginia University*, 1967-1977; Harry W. Ernst, ed., *West Virginia University, A Pictorial History, 1867-1979*; North Central Association of Colleges and Secondary Schools Visitation Report, 1974; West Virginia Board of Regents Enrollment Reports, 1973-77; West Virginia University Annual Report, 1967-1977; *West Virginia University Magazine*; West Virginia University Senate Minutes, 1967-1977.

NEWSPAPERS: *Charleston Daily Mail; Charleston Gazette; Dominion News; Fairmont Times; Martinsburg Journal; Morgantown Post; Sunday Gazette Mail.*

MANUSCRIPTS, DISSERTATIONS, AND PAPERS RELATING TO WEST VIRGINIA UNIVERSITY: President's Office Records, 1967-77; President's speeches; President's memoranda to the President and members of the Board of Governors, 1967-69; John Douglas Machesney, "The Development of Higher Education Governance and Coordination in West Virginia."

Chapter 14

GENERAL: Richard N. Current, T. Harry Williams, Frank Freidel, *American History: A Survey;* John A. Garraty, *The American Nation: A History of the United States Since 1865;* Irvin Kristol's review of William O'Neill's *Coming Apart: An Informal History of America in the 1960's;* Nicholas Von Hoffman, "Protest on the March," *Washington Post,* October 17, 1969; *Time Magazine; The Chronicle of Higher Education,* 1975.

WEST VIRGINIA: Tony Constantine, *Mountaineer Football, 1891-1969;* John Alexander Williams, *West Virginia: A Bicentennial History.*

WEST VIRGINIA UNIVERSITY: *Athenaeum;* Harry W. Ernst, ed., *West Virginia University, A Pictorial History, 1967-1979; Catalogs of West Virginia University,* 1967-77; West Virginia Board of Governors Minutes, 1967-69; West Virginia Board of Regents Minutes, 1971; West Virginia University Senate Minutes, 1979.

NEWSPAPERS: *Charleston Daily Mail; Dominion News; Fairmont West Virginian; Morgantown Post.*

MANUSCRIPTS, DISSERTATIONS, AND PAPERS RELATING TO WEST VIRGINIA UNIVERSITY: President's Office Records, 1962-67; President's speeches; President's memoranda to the President and members of the Board of Governors, 1967-69; Harlow's statement of January 26, 1970 re conditions at West Virginia University.

Chapter 15

GENERAL: *Chronicle of Higher Education,* 1978.

WEST VIRGINIA: Charles Ambler, *A History of Education in West Virginia from Early Colonial Times to 1949;* Elizabeth Cometti and Festus P. Summers, *The Thirty-fifth State: A Documentary History of West Virginia;* John Alexander Williams, *West Virginia: A Bicentennial History.*

STATE DOCUMENTS: *West Virginia Board of Regents Messenger,* 1977 and 1979.

WEST VIRGINIA UNIVERSITY: *Athenaeum; Catalogs of West Virginia University,* 1977-80; Harry W. Ernst, ed., *West Virginia University, A Pictorial History, 1867-1979;* Highlights of the WVU Annual Plan and Operating Budget Request, 1979-80; Report of the Survey of the West Virginia University School of Medicine, November 1-4, 1976, Liaison Committee on Medical Education's ad hoc survey team of the American Medical Association and the Association of American Medical Colleges; *Viewer-WWVU-TV; West Virginia University Magazine;* West Virginia University Senate Minutes, 1977-80.

NEWSPAPERS: *Charleston Daily Mail; Charleston Gazette; Dominion News; Martinsburg Journal; Morgantown Post; Morning Reporter; Pittsburgh Post Gazette; Pittsburgh Press.*

Index

About the Authors

WILLIAM T. DOHERTY, JR., professor of history and University historian at West Virginia University, wrote *Louis Houck: Missouri Historian and Entrepreneur; Minerals,* Volume IV of *Conservation in the United States: A Documentary History; Berkeley County, U.S.A., A Bicentennial History of a Virginia and a West Virginia County, 1772-1972;* and he coauthored *West Virginia History.* He also is editor of *West Virginia History,* a quarterly published by the State Department of Culture and History. Dr. Doherty, who received his doctoral degree in history from the University of Missouri, was chairperson of the WVU Department of History from 1963 to 1979.

FESTUS P. SUMMERS, who died in 1971 at the age of 76, began the work on this first comprehensive history of West Virginia University where he was the first University historian and chairperson of the Department of History from 1946 to 1962. He was the author of biographies of Johnson N. Camden and William L. Wilson, *The Baltimore and Ohio in the Civil War, A Borderland Confederate,* co-author of *West Virginia: The Mountain State,* co-editor of *The Thirty-Fifth State,* and editor of *The Cabinet Diary of William L. Wilson, 1896-1897.* He received his bachelor's and doctoral degrees from WVU and his master's degree from the University of Chicago.